"Very readable, easy to dip into for spec[...] particular issues. A reference book that [...]

Bruce Carnegie-Brown, Chair of Lloyds of London

"This is a rich, fresh resource for both directors in any sector on boards of all kinds and those working with them or otherwise advising them, including CEOs and other senior leaders. The key themes Purpose, People and Process would also be a good frame for approaches to wider leadership development. Patrick Dunne rightly focuses on 'how' to do it well and resolve challenges rather than on 'what' to do. This is the guide to EQ in Governance which is vital, especially for all Chairs, established, new in post and aspiring, which is generously shared from the wise experience of the author."

Dame Mary Marsh, Chair of Royal College of Paediatrics and Child Health

"Patrick has covered all of the bases in boards from the how and why to very practical areas that aren't usually examined in such depth in the 'People' and 'Dilemmas' sections. It's a fascinating read and an invaluable reference for anyone involved in working with boards. It's the best book on boards I've ever read."

Brenda Trenowden CBE, Global co-Chair 30% Club, PwC Partner

"Hugely readable and full of wise counsel. Patrick Dunne brings to life an important topic for all who serve on boards, from the smallest charity to the biggest corporate titan. A vital read for anyone starting a career in the boardroom."

Martin Webster, Partner, Pinsent Masons

"I would commend this book to all entrepreneurs, directors and anyone who wants to one day help lead an organisation. If you don't understand how governance and boards work you will never be effective. This immensely practical guide, explains how it all works, is littered with great guidance and will enable you to be a wiser and better director. A must read, one to put on the top of your reading list."

John Jeffcock, CEO Winmark

"Patrick wears his learning lightly, drawing on his experience across different sectors and continents to provide some great practical insights into the job of a director."

Chris Hodge, Director, Governance Perspectives

"Possibly the most practical guide around. So easy to read because it is written by a Board Director and Chairman who has operated in nearly every type of board; from Private Equity to Social Enterprise, and Business Advisory to University."

Paul Drechsler, Chair of Bibby Line Group, London First, Teach First, Chancellor Teesside University, Former President CBI, Chair of Non-Executive Director Awards (Sunday Times/Peel Hunt)

Boards
A PRACTICAL PERSPECTIVE

Patrick Dunne

GOVERNANCE

The Author

Patrick has extensive experience of working with boards around the world in the business, public body, education and social sectors. He Chairs board consultancy Boardelta and the charities EY Foundation and ESSA - Education Sub Saharan Africa. He is a Trustee of the Chartered Management Institute, a Visiting Professor at Cranfield and the Founder of Warwick in Africa.

The author of three other books on the subject, he was a member of the Higgs Review and is a regular contributor to board skills programmes, including the Financial Times Board Director Programme.

His executive career was with Air Products and FTSE100 3i Group plc where he was a member of its operating committee. He has a degree in Mathematics and Statistics from Warwick and an MBA from Cranfield.

© 2021 Boardelta

This book is sold subject to the condition that it shall not, by way of trade or otherwise, be lent, resold, hired out, or otherwise circulated without the publisher's prior consent in any form of binding or cover other than that in which it is published and without a similar condition including this condition being imposed on the subsequent publisher.

The moral right of Patrick Dunne has been asserted

First published in Great Britain in 2019 by Governance Publishing and Information Services Ltd

ISBN 978-1-9162569-2-7

Designed and typeset in 11pt Times New Roman by Geoff Fisher
geoff.fisher@yahoo.co.uk

Printed by CPI Group (UK) CR0 4YY

Dedication

To my Mother Margaret Dunne

Her resilience, thoughtfulness and passion for education have always inspired.

Acknowledgements

Writing the acknowledgements section is always tough. Especially so in this case, as much of the content is derived from the wisdom of so many people who have generously shared their experiences and helped me over the years. Listing them all would be a book in itself.

Since a child I have believed fervently that you can learn almost as much from observing those who do something badly as you might from the exemplars. However, it seems a little unfair and unnecessary to acknowledge anyone whose bad day convinced me that there must be a better way, or that I would never do it like that if I ever got to be a director or Chair. Better I think to anonymise them in the dilemmas!

There's very little original thinking on my part in here and, I suspect, even where I think there might be, it is probably down to my ignorance.

I have therefore taken a simple approach by name checking relative to specific points throughout the book, providing an extensive bibliog- raphy and useful links section and focussing here on those who have helped me to get the book done.

My good friend, Lesley Stephenson of *Governance* and *FT Board Director Programme* fame, not only charmingly persuaded me that it was about time that I got back to writing again but also agreed to publish it and has provided a huge amount of practical support. Her band of helpers including Katharine Jackson, Geoff Fisher and Zea Lindstrom have also been excellent in sense checking, correcting my spelling and grammar and crafting illustrations far more elegantly than I am capable of.

Fellow tutors at the *FT Board Director Programme*, Ali Gill, Murray Steele and Sarah Boulton also provided considerable encouragement throughout. As did Professor Ruth Bender at Cranfield. I am also very grateful to those who very kindly ploughed through review copies and provided incisive comment.

The directors and trustees of the various boards on which I serve and have served have also been a great source of knowledge and wisdom.

Finally, my wife Rebecca and sons Patrick, Nick and Rory deserve acknowledgement for their unerring support and tolerance.

Contents

Acknowledgements viii
List of illustrations xiii
Introduction xv

Section 1: Purpose

Introduction 1
Role of the board 6
Role of the executive 10
Alignment of board and executive 12
Role of sub-committees (audit and risk, nominations,
  remuneration) 15
    ○ Terms of reference 17
    ○ Focus or objectives 17
    ○ Composition 18
Role of advisory groups or boards 19
Roles of key participants 22
    ○ The Chair 22
    ○ Independent director, non-exec or outside director 31
    ○ Senior independent director (SID) 33
    ○ Trustee 36
    ○ Patrons 38
    ○ Chief executive officer (CEO) 39
    ○ Chief financial officer (CFO) 41
    ○ Company secretary and chief legal officer 44

o Communications director	46
Different contexts and influences	48
o Business	49
o Charities and social enterprises	58
o Professional services firms	62
o Public bodies	63
o Universities	65
o Media and social media	66
o Governance advisory services	68
Directors' duties	69
o Statutory duties and obligations	70
o Common law and fiduciary duties	74
Company's constitutional documents	75
Codes of best practice	76

Section 2: People

Introduction	85
Self-awareness, feedback, feelings and respect	90
Composition and board building	106
Aligning people	117
Power and influence	120
Common causes of dysfunction	128
Managing diversity, difference and inclusion	131
Managing conflict	137
Removing directors	146
Training and development	148

Section 3: Process

Introduction	153
Board review	156

Agreeing the vision, mission, purpose, strategy, brand, values, culture and approach to stakeholders	164
Terms of reference for sub-committees	173
○ Audit and risk committee	175
○ Remuneration committee	178
○ Nominations committee	188
Board composition, recruitment and managing succession	192
Diversity and inclusion	197
Board awaydays	199
Agendas and board papers	202
Convening and managing meetings	213
Board minutes	217
Decisions and approvals relating to other matters reserved for the board	219
○ Nature of decisions	222
○ Dilemmas	226
○ Who should be involved in decisions	228
○ When to decide	230
○ Financial implications	232
○ Making decisions	234
○ Recognising bias and managing our instincts	236
○ Communicating and implementing what has been decided	254
○ Reviewing decisions	256
Board communications	259
Use of technology to increase board efficiency and effectiveness	262

Section 4: Dilemmas

Introduction	269
The nature of dilemmas	269

Dealing with dilemmas	271

The dilemmas:

1. Dave's dreaming is disturbed – *How involved do you want to get?*	274
2. The departing director – *Going with dignity*	281
3. Boiling point with too many cooks – *A charity forgets its purpose*	287
4. The radio-controlled accountant - *Goes for a spin and has a little bump*	299
5. Convo – *The star falls to earth*	304
6. Reserves – *The long and the short of it*	316
7. Money, money, money - *Six short remuneration dilemmas*	329
8. RemCoCoCo – *"But it's my company!"*	357
9. Journalistic licence - *"They're all out to get me"*	370
10. The revolution – *A palace coup*	375
11. I wish we'd told them earlier - *What to tell my analyst*	382
12. Bone & Sons – *A family at war*	388
13. Falling in the Strid - *An entrepreneur gets confused about money*	399

Appendices

Appendix 1 – Bibliography	407
Appendix 2 – Useful links	411

List of illustrations

Figure 1:1	Role of the board	6
Figure 1:2	Executive team	11
Figure 1:3	Alignment of board and management team	12
Figure 1:4	Alignment	13
Figure 1:5	Sub-committees	15
Figure 1:6	Advisory groups	19
Figure 1:7	Deloitte four faces of the CFO	42
Figure 1:8	Directors' duties	71
Figure 2:1	Self-awareness	92
Figure 2:2	Effectiveness and pressure curve	94
Figure 2:3	Assessing team	107
Figure 2:4	Hierarchy of needs for board development and succession	110
Figure 2:5	Universal characteristics	111
Figure 2:6	CFOs – a hierarchy of needs	115
Figure 2:7	Sources of power	121
Figure 2:8	Hill of influence	123
Figure 2:9	Psychoses and neuroses	131
Figure 2:10	Cultural differences	136
Figure 2:11	Managing conflict	140
Figure 2:12	Catastrophe theory	144
Figure 3:1	Seven phases of agreeing a clear and full aligned vision, mission, purpose, strategy, brand, values and culture and approach	167
Figure 3:2	Where are we and where do we want to be on the spectrum (in relation to stakeholder engagement)	172
Figure 3.3	The Performance Prism	173
Figure 3.4	Managing the 'agenda challenge'	204
Figure 3.5	Board papers	211

Figure 3:6   Maslow Hierarchy of needs   223
Figure 3:7   Stages of types of decisions taken on boards   224
Figure 3:8   Bain RAPID® approach to decision making   229
Figure 3:9   Pressure in decisions   232
Figure 3:10 Types of bias   236
Figure 3:11 Abraham Wald: selection bias   250

Introduction

"*Boards*", only a six letter word but a massive subject and one on which much has been written. So, why bother producing something else? After all few directors are short of reading material.

The reason was quite simple and happily it led to an obvious title. A lot of people had been asking me if I could recommend an accessible book on *boards* which covered more than the basics and formalities. Although they came from organisations of all sorts of sizes and stages of development and spanned business, charity and public bodies, as well as a whole myriad of other types of organisation, what they wanted sounded similar. As they described it in greater detail it seemed to be as much about behaviours, making decisions and managing conflict or tricky situations as it was about best practice in terms of compliance, composition or structure.

After failing to find something that quite fitted this brief, I decided to end a long break from writing and have a go myself. The three books I wrote a while back, "*Running Board Meetings*", "*Directors Dilemmas*" and the "*Non-executive Directors Handbook*" were fun to do and seemed to strike a chord. So, why not?

An executive career in private equity, combined with a passion for social enterprise and education, as well as a bit of good luck has meant that I have had the privilege of being on a variety of boards over the years, including chairing a few. This has led to learning from masters of the art as well as those who are somewhat at the other end of the effectiveness spectrum.

The best, as in many other walks of life, seem to be endlessly restless about their performance. They are constantly thoughtful about what goes on in the boardroom as well outside. Their ability to use their highly-tuned antennae and combine this with great judgement and superb interpersonal skills helps them make the right point in the right way at exactly the right time.

It can also be the case that a reaction to the negative might provide just as powerful a boost as that gained from seeing a great role model in action. Seeing the consequences or feeling the direct pain that a more challenged board or director might create, not just for those in the organisation but for all those affected by the quality of its decisions, can be deeply instructive.

Occasionally people appear to have had the *"responsibility by-pass"* operation or worse didn't need it. However, in my experience the overwhelming majority of directors and boards want to do a good job and want their organisations to be successful. Yet it is not easy to achieve the ever-increasing level and near omnipotent knowledge that those who don't practise the art themselves expect of you. Tricky situations are also critical in forging views on how to deal with the stuff that comes along to test you. These situations are also easier if you have a little practice in the boardroom simulator.

Through Boardelta, the consultancy business I set up when I retired from 3i, and 3i itself, I have had the opportunity to have worked with a wide range of boards across the world in business, government and the social sector. This work has mostly been about helping them to refresh or press the reset button at a major point of change, but it has also involved setting up and delivering training on board skills. Indeed, it was Lesley Stephenson from the FT Board Director Programme who gave me the most encouragement to get this book done.

Like most Chairs I am always learning, never getting everything as spot on as I would like it to be and very aware that good process is never enough. The aim in writing this book was not to produce another weighty guide to governance or post rationalised tale of how I, or others, have won or lost the west in the boardroom. It is simply to produce something practical, realistic, thought-provoking and useful on life both in and outside the boardroom.

One of my favorite triangles *"Purpose, People and Process"* has been used to provide some structure and each of these Sections has its own more detailed introduction. As you will see I have tried also to recognise that the board doesn't operate in isolation and so in considering the role of the board we also need to consider the role of the management, investors, members of a charity and other key groups.

As a board often makes its biggest contribution when the choice isn't always clear, this has been supplemented with a reprise and refresh of some of the most popular situations from an earlier work, *"Directors Dilemmas"*, as well as some new ones. There are few *"no-brainer"* choices for boards and those that look like they are prove often to be illusory.

All of these *"Dilemmas"* are real but sufficiently disguised to protect confidentiality. After a description of the situation, each has a short summary of the issues, the choices that you may have and then a description of what actually happened. The outcome may, of course, not always be the best.

The first edition of this book was published just prior to the covid-19 pandemic. This second edition takes account of the impact of the pandemic on boards and on board practice. The crisis has been a monumental stress test for boards. Resilience, capabilities, culture, judgement, relationships, values and the ability to manage complex and often competing stakeholder needs have all been put to the test.

The good news is that despite the challenges, the majority of boards have been able to navigate through the storm, providing the level of oversight and support to help their executives and their teams to protect lives and livelihoods as well as their organisations. Yet even the best have made mistakes and learnt a huge deal in the process.

Like all major crises the ensuing pressures have the power to strengthen bonds between us and to enable us to see the strengths of others more clearly. The urgent need for creativity has also led to a surge of innovation which in turn has driven successful regeneration and reinvention.

Sadly, this hasn't been the case for all. The impact of the crisis for some has been to expose latent weakness and tensions and result in failure. It has also overwhelmed many fine organisations and boards not just those who have been found wanting.

A number of trends already underway have been accelerated by the pandemic crisis in terms of the way we work, make decisions, view risk, communicate and manage uncertainty.

In some countries a timely revaluation of the nature of the fundamental contract and relationship between employers and those they employ and a greater recognition of those less in the spotlight who really make organisations work is also taking place.

The shift from *"just in time"* to *"just in case"* risk mindsets and a greater focus on the consequences of events rather than the events themselves is understandable given the scale of the disruption. The increasing use of dynamic budgeting and strategic frameworks as opposed to annual budgets and strategy bible documents likewise.

Much of this has been as liberating and energising as it has been challenging. It is hard to say at this stage how much of what has changed will stick and how much we will revert to old ways when we can but it seems clear that for most of us it won't revert to *"old normal"*. Rather than have a section on the pandemic I have chosen to refer to it throughout where relevant.

Enormous though its impact has been, the pandemic is not the only thing of significance to influence the context in which boards operate. Political flux across the world, the much needed increased focus on diversity triggered by the killing of George Floyd in the US, BREXIT and major climate and human rights related events have all produced an opportunity for boards to step up and lead by example on values based issues. These tragic events and the campaigns arising from them have given fresh impetus to tackling deep and poorly addressed issues relating to Diversity and Inclusion across the world.

This edition also includes additional content in a number of areas including culture, stakeholder management, board reviews and the use of technology.

What's not in the book? A lot of legal and regulatory stuff. There are plenty of places that you can get that and in my view it's best to get this online as well as from the many excellent briefing sessions that professional advisers provide. However, Appendix 2 contains a list of useful links where you currently might find things and the *"Purpose"* Section contains some high-level comments on some of the codes and legal duties you may need to be aware of.

I do hope that you enjoy the book and find it useful. Please do get in touch if you have a different view on something or another handy tip. Please send any comments to info@governance.co.uk.

Section One

Purpose

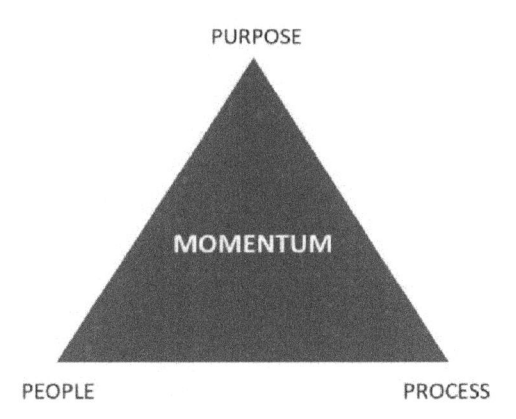

```
        PURPOSE
          /\
         /  \
        /    \
       / MOMENTUM \
      /          \
     /_____\
   PEOPLE      PROCESS
```

Introduction

The basic premise of this first section of the book is that clarity of purpose for the organisation and for each individual as well as the board as a whole, combined with getting the right people involved, ought to maximise the chances of success and minimise the risks of failure. It absolutely doesn't mean that success is guaranteed or that risks will be obliterated. You still have to execute successfully, but it ought to mean you stand a better chance.

First, we will look at the role of the board itself, then at the role of the executive and how they interact and align with the board. We will follow that up by exploring the role of subcommittees and advisory boards as well as the key board participants. Then, after looking at the influence of differing contexts for boards, eg those in business, public bodies, charities and professional service firms, we will conclude with a high-level summary of directors' duties and a tour of some of the relevant governance codes.

I am conscious that this and the *"Process"* section hardly sound like ripping yarns and that you may be tempted to leap straight to the *"People"* and *"Dilemmas"* sections as they might sound a lot more fun. However, without the base of what lies within here and the plumbing in *"Process"* being right, the rest won't be half as useful.

When I first wrote about the *"Purpose"* of a board and the key participants in *"Running Board Meetings"* in the late 1990s the *"Purpose"* word was nowhere near what it is today. These days it seems that the word has become very fashionable in a range of contexts. In an organisational sense this is probably being driven by the combination of societal questioning of the role of businesses, charities and the State; by the breakdown in trust in institutions; by the digital, data and communications revolution that is disrupting business models; by the emergence of *"Social Enterprise"* and a whole host of other factors, including political flux.

The consequence is that boards of all sorts of organisations across the world are being prompted and challenged to answer that most basic of existential questions "What's the point of the organisation?" as well as the consequential one: "What's the point of the board?" The pandemic provided fresh impetus for boards to address these questions no matter how successful their organisations had been before.

How a board might review the core purpose of the organisation, or perhaps re-purpose it, is covered on page 164 in the *"Process"* section. In this section we will make the simplifying assumption that the organisation has a valid purpose and focus our attention on what might be the purpose of the board, its sub-committees and advisory groups as well as that of the key participants involved including executives and advisers.

In summary, I think that the purpose and role of the board is to ensure that there is the right vision, purpose and strategy as well as the right resources and right governance to achieve them.

From a legal and regulatory perspective, we also need to ensure that in fulfilling our purpose we comply with, or take into account as relevant, our directors' or trustees' statutory duties and obligations, common law and fiduciary duties, the company's constitutional documents and any relevant codes of best practice. There are of course differences from country to country in the legal and regulatory frameworks, such as the preference for unitary or two-tier boards, and we will cover some of these. As mentioned in the general introduction on page xviii, this book is intentionally light on the legal and regulatory aspects, but this section does contain a high-level summary of the key points and signposts to where to find more.

The context of the organisation and the nature of its stakeholders will also have an important influence on its purpose and ability to achieve it. Investors and investor relations influence an organisation's purpose as well as its ability to align with other stakeholders and secure the support and resources to achieve that purpose.

Investors are far from homogeneous in their nature, preferences, time horizon or behaviour and there is inevitably a *"chicken and egg"* like quality to these relationships in terms of who comes first. As a private business you can choose who your investors are but not so for public companies. Yet, even in a private company your investors' objectives may diverge from their original ones with time and produce conflicts over organisational purpose and strategy.

For charities, the role of members and funders in terms of influencing purpose is analogous. Examples of charities who suffer mission drift because funding isn't available for their real mission but is for something adjacent to it are as common as businesses adapting their aims to get funding. The range in nature of charity funders is probably as broad as those for business and the debate around how performance should be measured as lively. Competition for funding is also stimulating the adoption of Key Performance Indicators more closely associated with business. The rise of *"social enterprise"* and *"impact investing"* and the morphing of many traditional foundations away from classic grant makers as well as the debate over *"Purpose"* for business is causing the line between charity and business to become a better understood spectrum.

Professional service firms are also becoming a fascinating area in governance globally. Their complex structures combined with ever more challenging regulatory environments and demands for greater transparency are just some of the pressures forcing change. Add to this the challenges of achieving partner buy-in, containing risk, making timely decisions in the interests of the firm as a whole and ever broadening portfolio of services and it looks like a challenging time ahead for those responsible for their governance.

Public body boards are another area where the landscape for boards is changing globally. Quite rightly governments have a need to show taxpayers and users of services provided by such bodies that they are well governed in every respect. Those interested in serving on such boards are generally public spirited, expect to, and are prepared to, provide their skills and experiences for well below their market rate. However, in recent years in some countries, the UK being one of them, the growing asymmetry between fulfilment and the amount of work, risk and pure hassle has led to many people who would be able to add a great deal to such boards to find other ways to contribute to society.

In many countries government departments have also been appointing independent non-executives and, although best practice is still developing in this space, there are many examples of this adding considerable value. The wise on such department boards will be well aware of where the power really lies and alert to the *"majority of one"* power of a minister whether they are formally a member of the board or not. Most government departments are of the scale of large corporates and have many common challenges in terms of retaining clarity of purpose, attracting and developing talent and dealing with rapid changes in technology, communications and expectations.

However, the annual budget mindset and the short tenure of ministers can often bring an overweight focus on the short-term at the expense of the future.

University boards can also make for fascinating appointments. These are complex organisations with demanding stakeholders and a heavy regulatory influence in most countries. They are legitimately polymath in purpose, subject to a wide range of external influences and have an interesting mix of short- and very long-term decisions to make. My time on the University of Warwick board was endlessly interesting and challenging. Not least because of the colourful cocktail of board members including faculty, students and people from a wide cross-section of society. In order to sustain academic excellence and meet ever rising expectations in terms of student experience, universities are increasingly investing in commercial activities to generate sustainable income. Warwick was a pioneer in this right from its inception in 1965 so this all felt natural.

A frequent challenge for university boards is often their size. In an attempt to achieve diversity and satisfy the needs of a wide range of stakeholders they can often end up being too big. The common way to address the challenge is to use some of the sub-committees effectively as the real decision-making bodies, with the board as a whole then effectively endorsing their decisions. In the UK the Finance and General Purposes Committee tends to be the powerhouse in this context.

Much has been written recently about the importance of organisational culture and values. It is good to see this as it is implicit to having the right vision and resources. We will cover the board's role in defining and shaping culture and values in the *"Process"* section on page 164. An important element of an organisation's culture and values is its approach to Diversity and Inclusion and so this will also be covered there.

In clearing out some old papers the other day I came across notes from our work on the 2003 Higgs Review. It was striking how important we all felt it was to change the game on gender diversity, as well as to find a mechanism to enable swifter change of *"mouldy"* Chairs. At the time only 4 per cent of executive directors and only 6 per cent of non-executives in UK listed companies were women and there were only two female Chairs in the FTSE 350 (one at 3i by the way). The formalisation of the role of the senior independent director (SID) has led to shorter sell-by dates for Chairs. Yet almost two decades later according to the 2021 Hampton-Alexander report we have only just passed the 34 per cent point for women and according to the 2020 UK Spencer Stuart Board Index only 5% of the FTSE150 have female Chairs. This feels like very slow progress and with regard to ethnic and social diversity or disability it feels like there is still an enormous amount to do.

The role of the sub-committees is to undertake work delegated by the board, make recommendations to the board and to enhance board productivity. We'll consider some general points about sub-committees and how they interact with the board and executive. We'll go into more detail on the most popular ones namely audit and risk, remuneration and nominations committees as well as look at some of the issues around having committees for other organisational or sectoral aspects, eg regulatory committees, in the "*Process*" section on page 173. In doing all of the above we will also consider how their role changes in different operating environments, eg the nature of a remuneration committee changes significantly when a company goes public.

The role of the senior executive group is to develop and deliver the strategy and business plan, with input from others including the board, and to maintain financial and operational integrity.

For the key participants we will focus on the Chair, chief executive officer, chief financial officer, SID, independent director, company secretary and communications director. First looking at their roles and then looking at how they interact and are aligned with the board in this section. Then looking in more detail at selection processes and the characteristics required to fulfil these roles as well as the behavioural dynamics of the board in the "*People*" and "*Process*" sections. The dilemmas (page 269) will also dive deep into the practical challenges of these roles.

As a boy I was mesmerised by the brilliance of the Venn diagram and how such a simple thing could be used in so many ways. I was also struck by the power of the idea that we can be ourselves and do our own thing, but we can also be part of a group where we have a common purpose or common characteristics. I think this concept has a lot of relevance in the boardroom in the context of the alignment between the board and the executive and for the independent directors or trustees who have to be their own person but also part of a group.

John Venn, born in 1834, was not only a brilliant mathematician, philosopher and logician but also belonged to the "*Clapham set*" of pioneering social entrepreneurs and was a strong advocate of votes for women. I would imagine that he saw himself as being multi-purpose and that he was someone who was adept at modifying his purpose, or of those he was helping, to adapt to circumstances either present or anticipated. This I think is fundamental to success as a board and as a board member. We have to have both the conviction to stick to our purpose and the antennae and good sense of judgement to know when to adapt it to ensure that we survive, to sustain success or to fulfil our organisation's and our own potential.

To conclude, it's hard to have a board that is fit for purpose if you don't know what the purpose is. It's dangerous to assume that everyone arrives with the same idea about what the purpose of the board, the executive, the sub-committees and individual roles is. A good Chair will ensure that there is a discussion as well as a common agreement and understanding of what it is and that the board and the executive use this as a touchstone for all that they do.

Role of the board

Assuming that the purpose of the organisation is clear, then the role of the board ought to be to ensure that the organisation has the right strategy, resources and governance to achieve this purpose in the context that it operates in. It fulfills this role by providing the right balance of oversight and support.

If the purpose of the organisation is unclear or needs adapting, then it is the board's responsibility to clarify or reset it with the agreement of shareholders or members and other relevant stakeholders. This is covered in the "*Process*" section on page 164. Here we will make the simplifying assumption that the organisation's purpose is clear and agreed.

Figure 1:1 Role of the board

- Right strategy
- Right resources
- Right governance

For any new board coming together or for any new member joining a board it is vital that there is a discussion about what the role of the board is and how it relates to other key groups including shareholders in a business or members in a charity, to the executive and to employees, the sub-committees and, if relevant, advisory groups and so on. There will be some things each of these groups does alone but also a fair bit that they do together, eg the board and the executive interacting around strategy.

So, let's take each of these three core aspects of a board's role and look at what they mean in practice.

In terms of *"Right strategy"* this is to ensure that:

- there is the right strategy for the ownership of the organisation, where relevant, as well as the organisation itself to achieve its stated purpose:
- there is a good process for formulating and adapting strategy that takes into account both ambition and risk and that;
- the agreed strategy is being implemented and monitored and if there is a divergence from it then appropriate and timely action is taken.

How boards do strategy is covered in *"Process"* (page 164).

In terms of *"Right resources"* this is simply to ensure that the organisation has the right resources in place to meet the agreed strategy. The most obvious resources relate to people, culture and money but there are usually other critical resources such as brand, physical assets, intellectual property, regulatory approvals, key relationships and others which are critical for the board to ensure are being nurtured and protected to achieve success.

In terms of *"Right governance"* there are many views on what constitutes good governance and there have been numerous codes and consultancy services set up to help us. Appendix 2 contains links to the formative codes for a wide range of countries for business and charities. Many of these are based upon the seminal work of the late Sir Adrian Cadbury, whose straightforward definition of corporate governance in his 1992 *"Financial Aspects of Corporate Governance"* report was:

"The system by which companies are directed and controlled".

His approach to regulation was similarly clear in that he believed that there was the law by which all organisations must adhere and that this should be supplemented by a *"code of best practice"* which should be followed on a *"comply or explain"* basis.

It is interesting that such codes now are no longer restricted to large stock market listed companies but also exist in many countries for large private companies, smaller listed companies and private equity-backed businesses, the charity sector as well as government departments and agencies.

Another view, which has always resonated very strongly with me, is that of Jonathan Charkham, the late governance guru and collaborator with Sir Adrian. I was reminded of this in researching for this book when I came across Sir Christopher Hogg's memorial lecture for Jonathan. Sir Chris, a former Chairman of Reuters and of GSK, reminded us that Jonathan concluded his very practical and thought- provoking 2005 book, *"Keeping Good Company"*, with the following words:

> *"Corporate governance must not become a religion or cult, complete with high priests and compelling sects, nor must it become a honey-pot for consultants. When the last principle has been pronounced, when the last code promulgated, when the last sanction has been sanctified, it will be seen for what it is – the proposition that the business of the world will be better run if:*
>
> - *the men and women who drive it forward enjoy power without abusing it, and are competent to exercise it;*
> - *they act with integrity and do not just pontificate about the morals they have no intention of following if they do not suit this quarter's results;*
> - *they describe clearly, succinctly, promptly, and honestly how matters stand;*
> - *they have the wit and skill to balance the economic imperatives of the company with the need to tend the fabric of society;*
> - *accountability is real and produces the appropriate responses from directors and shareholders."*

PURPOSE

This sums up *"Right governance"* rather well for me in that it is a lot more about behaviours than process, even though good process tends to reinforce good behaviours.

Of course, the art and the science of governance are ever evolving. For example, notable recent contributions in the UK have been from the Financial Reporting Council (FRC) on *"Values and Culture"* (page 413) and on *"Corporate Governance Principles for Large Private companies"* (page 412), the Quoted Companies Alliance Governance code (page 412) for smaller listed companies and from the National Council for Voluntary Organisations (NCVO) on *"Ethical principles for charities"* (page 415) in the wake of a number of high-profile issues in the sector.

To quote the leaders of each of these publications:

"The strategy to achieve a company's purpose should reflect the values and culture of the company and should not be developed in isolation. Boards should oversee both."

Sir Win Bischoff, Chairman FRC

"The QCA code is a practical outcome-oriented approach to corporate governance tailored for small and mid-sized quoted companies in the UK."

The Quoted Companies Alliance

"These principles provide an overarching framework to guide decision-making, good judgement and conduct. They do not provide a set of rules that prescribe how one should act in all situations."

Dame Mary Marsh, Chair of Charity Ethical Principles Review for NCVO.

"These principles provide a tool to help large private companies look at themselves in the mirror, to see where they have done well and where they can raise their corporate governance standards to a higher level."

Sir James Wates, CBE Chairman Coalition Group for the FRC.

I like the fact that, although setting expectations, each of these has avoided being overly prescriptive. It reflects the real world for boards and affords them the flexibility to make what they think are the right judgements given the issues that they are presented with.

I also like the emphasis on culture and see it very much as the board's job to decide what culture you want and to ensure that you get it. A simple rule that I have is that everyone we add to the board must be additive to the culture we want. This doesn't mean cloning, as the culture you want should be diverse. It can, however, make recruitment processes challenging from time to time.

On the subject of culture and the culture of regulation and Codes in particular there is a very important debate raging in some countries in relation to directors' responsibilities and accountability (page 69). It is driven by a well-intentioned push for greater accountability it will be important for regulators and politicians to strike the right balance on this for non-executives in particular. Failure to do so risks inhibiting progress on diversity and deterring many good potential non-executives who may consider the risks too great.

The core processes and some of the detailed issues with respect to "*strategy*", "*resources*" and "*governance*", are included in the "*People*" and "*Process*" sections.

We will look in more depth at the roles of the Chair, senior or lead, independent, non-executive or outside director as well as trustee, the term most used for Charity board members, in the "*Role of key participants*" section (page 22).

Role of the executive

A deep concern of mine from first getting involved in the world of boards was that so much of the general discussion seemed to ignore the role of the executive (exec) management. I couldn't see how you could discuss or hope to define the role of the board without being clear what you thought the role of the exec was and how they interacted with the board. The following description is one I think works for a wide variety of organisations:

In developing the business plan the exec should involve a variety of other people, including the board, to gain input and to sense check ideas before putting a formal proposal to the board. This needs to be realistic about the risks as well as the opportunities and take account of the resources that will be required.

Figure 1:2 The executive team

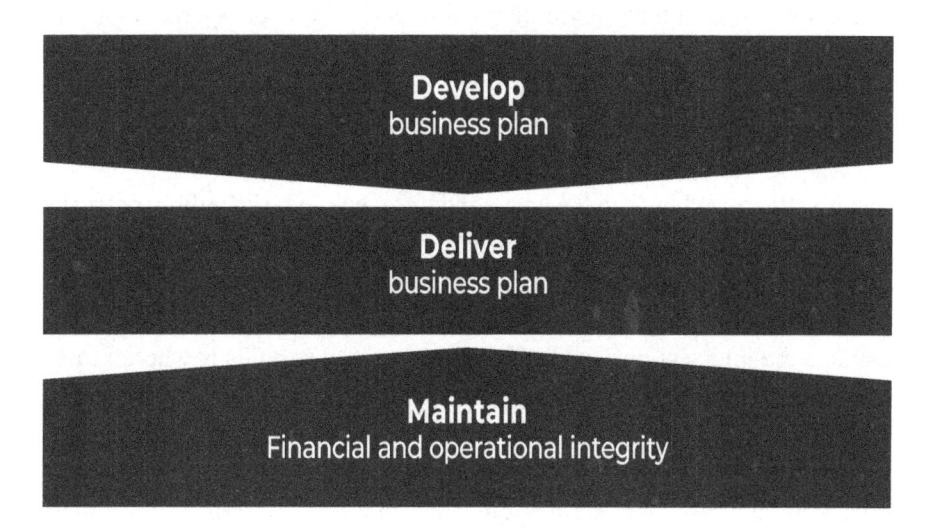

Develop
business plan

Deliver
business plan

Maintain
Financial and operational integrity

Perhaps the most obvious element of the exec's role is in executing the strategy and delivering the business plan for the period that it relates to. Less discussed is their fundamental role in maintaining financial and operational integrity. Without this, the most brilliantly conceived, articulated and galvanising strategies turn to dust.

We also must be clear what we mean by the *"executive"*. In a board context it will normally refer to that small nucleus of execs, usually less than ten, who form the organisation's key exec decision-making body. They are typically described as the *"executive group"*, *"executive committee"* or similar and are made up of the chief executive officer (CEO), chief financial officer (CFO), chief operating officer (COO), company secretary, heads of major business units and the communications and human resources (HR) directors.

An important element of the exec's role, and the CEO's in particular, is to ensure that the broader leadership in the organisation is connected appropriately to the board and understands what decisions go where. The board's visibility of this broader leadership group is important and the Chair will need to ensure that there are the right mechanisms for sufficient and relevant interaction beyond seeing them in action presenting proposals to the board.

We will look in more depth at the roles of the CEO, CFO as well as the pivotal supporting roles of the company secretary and communications director in terms of their board interaction in the *"Role of key participants"* section (page 22).

Alignment of board and executive

Superb alignment between the board and the exec can be incredibly powerful just as the opposite can be an organisation destroyer as well as an obliterator of value for others. There is more to this than simply having clear and complementary roles, important though that is. In my experience, how you manage the intersections successfully is as crucial and this is where I think John Venn's brilliant concept comes in handy.

You may, like me, have seen a board and an exec operating in parallel universes. Here, the exec see the board as something to get through, give their presentation, tolerate a few questions and then head off to do exactly what they were going to do anyway. Or perhaps, the non-execs or trustees see their role as simply *"police men and women"* at board meetings providing oversight and ensuring that they keep a distance. Either way it all feels very *"us"* and *"them"*. You can get a strong sense of this when you do your first interviews with either the Chair and CEO and others when the *"they"* count is so much higher than the *"we"* count, or if the exec get into victim language.

At the other end of the spectrum, despite what may be written down in well-crafted terms of reference, the reality is that the roles of the board and

Figure 1:3 Alignment of board and management team

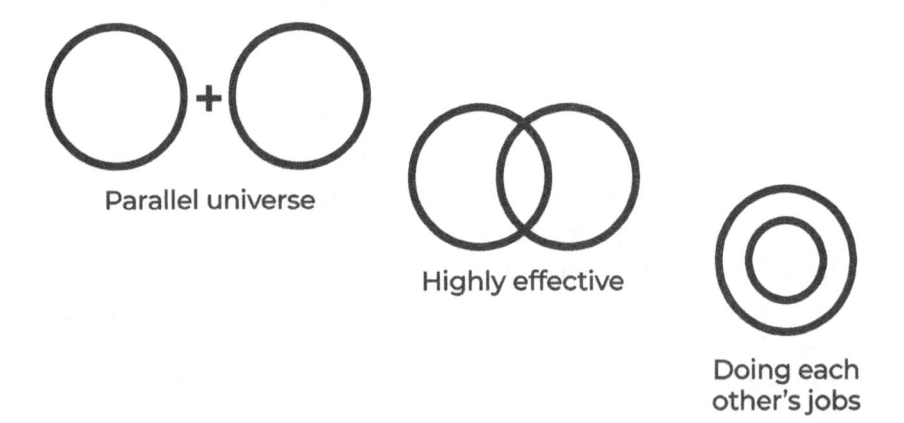

Parallel universe

Highly effective

Doing each other's jobs

the exec are so intertwined that they are effectively doing each-other's jobs. I remember one board meeting, where I was observing for the first time and found it hard to work out who was a non-executive (non-exec) and who was an exec given the way they were behaving.

However, highly effective boards seem to be able to achieve great clarity. They use it when it comes to their specific roles as an exec or board member and equally have a very constructive time when they come together for what are usually the most important decisions they are likely to take. Strategy is the obvious one for this. Deciding what culture you want and ensuring that you get it is one of the most important things to have in the intersection.

The reality is these are not entirely discrete states, we tend to operate across the spectrum and even the very good have occasional lapses into marginal dysfunction. The key is to talk about it and to work at it and this is exactly what good boards did during the pandemic.

It was clear at the beginning that the intersection would grow. The level of oversight and support required to ensure organisations could fulfill their responsibilities, survive and manage competing stakeholder needs as well as adjust to new ways of working during lockdowns and travel restrictions created considerable pressure. Good Chairs ensured that in agreeing who was going to do what and supporting, rather than overwhelming their executive teams that it was a conversation, that they also reflected together and constantly adapted. It will be fascinating to see where the intersection settles.

Another mathematically-orientated graphic is helpful here:

Figure 1:4 Alignment

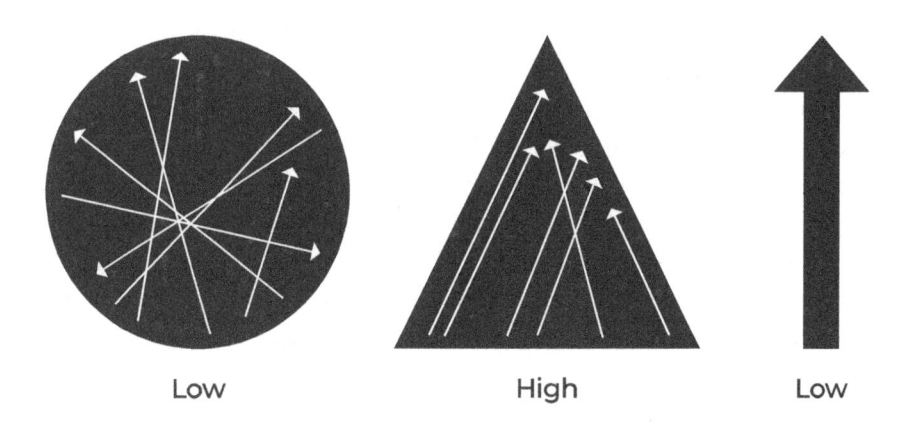

| Low | High | Low |

This can be useful when trying to get a feel for how aligned a board are. From individual conversations with directors or from observing first meetings you can generally tell where the board might be on this spectrum: from disorganised rabble to monarchist state or happily being in the centre where they are all pointing in the same direction but have enough creative tension and challenge to avoid complacency and groupthink. The paragons in the middle are rarely satisfied, value diversity and different perspectives and have a healthy and robust way of challenging themselves.

The questions to ask each director which can help you decide where they might be before you take an appointment are surprisingly straightforward:

- What do you think the point of the organisation is?
- How would you describe the strategic priorities?
- How do you feel about the strategy overall?
- How would you describe the relationship between the board and the exec, the Chair and the CEO, the CEO and the non-execs, the CEO and the CFO?
- What do you think are the top 3 opportunities and challenges that the organisation has over the next few years and in the longer term?
- What are the most important decisions the board will have to make in the coming year?

My favourite response to the *"What do you think are the top three opportunities and challenges?"* question was from a board of 8 who gave me 27 different challenges.

We should naturally expect shades of difference and a healthy variety of opinion but it is surprising how often these simple questions shine a light on either fundamental disagreement or simply a lack of communication or discussion on what matters most.

We'll cover *"Dealing with conflict"* on page 137 and *"Agenda setting"* on page 202, both of which are central to supporting alignment or at least bringing differences to a head in time. The *"Convo"* dilemma on page 304 is a good example of where lack of alignment on the board between an executive group, a trade investor representative and private equity investor representatives has a devastating effect on performance and success.

Role of sub-committees

In general, the objective of board sub-committees is to enhance board effectiveness and it does this through undertaking work delegated by the board, making recommendations to the board and enhancing board productivity through undertaking preparatory work to help the board make informed decisions.

The classic and most common sub-committees whether you are a business, charity or public body are audit and risk, nominations and remuneration. Organisations then may have additional sub-committees to serve a purpose specific to their sector, form of ownership or nature of business, eg regulatory, health and safety or treasury sub-committee.

Here we will look at the headline aspects of the role of the audit and risk, remuneration and nominations sub-committees and cover more of the detail in the "*Process*" section (page 173).

Figure 1:5 Sub-committees

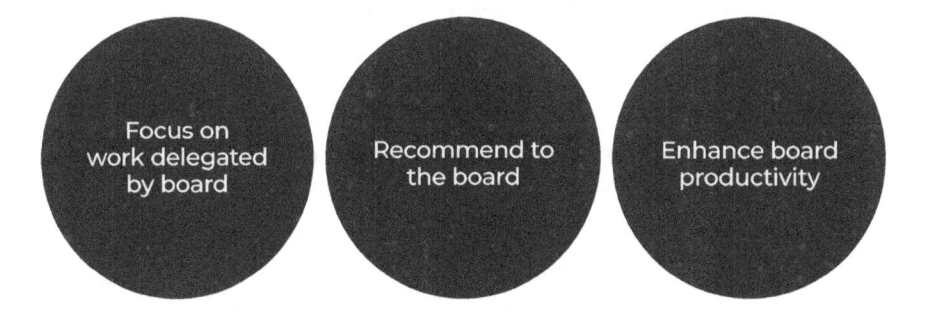

- Focus on work delegated by board
- Recommend to the board
- Enhance board productivity

The typical role of an audit and risk committee is to:

- Monitor the integrity of the organisation's financial statements and review significant financial judgements.
- Review the internal financial control and risk management systems and satisfy themselves that they are robust and defensible.
- Monitor and review the effectiveness of internal audit.
- Oversee the relationship with the external auditor including recommending their appointment, and remuneration as well as reviewing their independence and non-audit service policy.

- Ensure that the organisation has a robust and effective system of identifying, communicating and managing risk and has the relevant reporting mechanisms in place to meet the organisa- tion's compliance requirements.
- Report any significant issues to the board in a timely and accurate fashion.

The trend towards combining audit and risk in one sub-committee has been driven by the overlap in work, the need for a joined-up approach to both topics and for many boards the practical reality of having enough independent directors to staff sub-committees.

The role of the remuneration committee depends much on the nature of the organisation and this, along with other practical issues relating to remuneration committees, is discussed in more detail on page 178. However, essentially the core role is to be responsible for recommending to the board the:

- policy for exec remuneration;
- remuneration for the Chair, execs and senior managers;
- overall policy for remuneration in the organisation; and
- disclosure to be made with regard to remuneration.

Remuneration is inevitably a complex and emotive topic and the "*Money, Money, Money*" and "*RemCoCoCo*" dilemmas on pages 329 and 357 respectively illustrate just some of the issues that may emerge.

The nominations committee may be a standing committee for larger organisations or an ad-hoc one, put together for specific situations, for smaller ones. The role of this sub-committee is generally to be responsible for:

- managing the recruitment and selection process for board positions and recommending suitable candidates to the board for appointment;
- ensuring that there is a robust succession plan in place for both board and key exec positions and, more recently; and
- having oversight of the organisation's diversity and inclusion policy and practice.

In some cases they may also be delegated by the board to review the strategy and practice for senior management positions more broadly.

For the UK, the FRC, the Chartered Governance Institute and Charity Commission websites have helpful guides to sub-committees and include the latest best-practice thinking in terms of reference and composition. The equivalent bodies in other countries do the same (*see* Useful links).

The typical problems relating to sub-committees tend to revolve around the following:

- fuzzy or too broad terms of reference;
- lack of focus or objectives for the year;
- poor composition or inappropriate Chair;
- duplication of effort with other committees; and
- poor communication/interaction with other committees, the exec or the board itself

all of which can lead to the sub-committee reducing rather than enhancing board effectiveness. Let's look at each of these in turn.

Terms of reference

When it comes to fuzzy or too broad terms of reference, the fundamental issue lies in leadership from the board Chair and the CEO combined and it is a good signal that interaction between the board and the executive may not be as good as it could be. Why? Because both are tolerating or ignoring under-performance and either not acting to address it or not persuading the other that it matters to sort it out. Sometimes it is because the sub-committee Chair likes it fuzzy as it allows them to expand the envelope of their influence and power.

Whatever the cause, the solution is straightforward and simply a matter of the board agreeing to refresh the terms of reference for its sub-committees on a regular basis. Good practice tends to be a short review on an annual basis, with confirmation by the board of the terms of reference and the priorities or objectives for the sub-committee for the year ahead.

Focus or objectives

If there aren't clear objectives for the sub-committee for the year ahead then this again is a straightforward matter. My preference is for each sub-committee, led by the Chair, to discuss with the relevant exec lead, eg CFO for audit and risk, what it would like to recommend to the board as a whole. This then should ensure that there is a focus for the sub-committee's work and objectives for the year ahead which the board, the exec and the committee itself all agree upon.

In addition to communicating well with the board and the sub- committees, it should also sort out any duplication of effort by different committees. One of the contributory factors behind the rise in popularity of a combined audit and risk committee has been historic duplication of work when they have been separate bodies as well as increased focus and accountability for risk.

Composition

The most important aspect to get right in terms of the composition of sub-committees is to select the right Chairs. If you get this right the rest tends to sort itself out as people will be keen to work with effective chairs. The Chairs need to have a collaborative approach to chairing to be able to bring out the best in those with specialist expertise, to be motivated by the work of the committee and be clear what the sub-committee's contribution to the board is. They will also use this collaborative expertise alongside that of other sub-committee Chairs to ensure a joined-up approach.

If you are a small board it can be hard to have the right mix on the board to staff the sub-committees that you need. In this case there seem to be two obvious ways to go: either grow the board a little to recruit what you need or have a small number of people with specialist knowledge or expertise on the sub-committee who are not members of the board. Some organisations use this approach to get to know people before they join the board. If you are going to do this non-board members should be a minority of the sub-committee membership.

The synchronisation of sub-committee meetings with board meetings is one way of ensuring good communication and interaction with other committees, the exec and the board itself. The entire board being aware and agreeing what each sub-committee's objectives for the year ahead and what they are focused on is another. Yet the main way I think that communications are strong is when the Chair and the CEO make it more than process, emphasise that it matters, help in a way that's relevant for them and lead by example.

Role of advisory groups or boards

Figure 1:6 Advisory groups

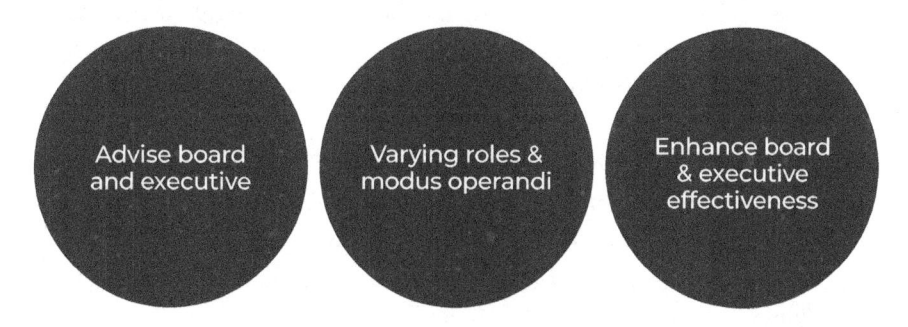

- Advise board and executive
- Varying roles & modus operandi
- Enhance board & executive effectiveness

The best advisory boards or groups are those which are set up for a specific topic, theme or issue and time. They have clear individual and collective goals and provide insights, credibility and relationships beyond the board's and the executive's own experience. The worst, despite perhaps the best of intentions at the start, become expensive talking shops that consume considerable amounts of management effort and cost, produce little useful insight and then cause embarrassment when everyone eventually recognises that it isn't working.

The most important word in all of this is *"advisory"* in that whether they are called a board or a group their role is to advise the board and the exec and to enhance their effectiveness, not to get involved in the governance. Advisory boards are not legally constituted and have no decision-making powers unless specifically delegated by the board. Moreover, the board or executive are under no obligation to follow their advice. Those with experience will know that to stray down the decision-making path risks becoming a shadow director.

An *"advisory board"* will sound more impressive and important and may make it easier to recruit people but it also, because of the word board, has connotations of decision-making and governance and creates the potential for confusion with sub-committees. Naming it an *"advisory group"* has the benefit of accurately reflecting what it is as well as reducing the risk of governance confusion but it sounds less grand and attractive to join.

Following our *"Purpose, People and Process"* approach, the first thing to think hard about is what you want an advisory board or group for and why you want a formal group rather than to work with a number of advisers independently. Common drivers tend to include the following:

- The need to gain additional insights on a strategic theme, eg international strategy, regulatory, mergers and acquisitions, research, scientific or technical, country, diversity and inclusion and so on.
- The desire to enhance the credibility of the organisation, its strategy and decisions in a certain area.
- For young or small organisations to gain access to expertise that it couldn't afford to have on the board or through consultancy.
- To gain access to people who have much to offer and would like to help but don't want to be involved in, or responsible for, the governance of the organisation.
- For the reassurance that a trusted knowledgeable and objective group might bring.
- To recognise that human interaction can spark creativity and produce results which are "greater than the sum of the parts".
- A high performing advisory board may also be a good mechanism for engaging and developing potential board members.
- In smaller organisations, because an investor or funder tells you that you need one.

Gaining that clarity over the need and then being specific and realistic about objectives makes it easier to decide on the form, composition and way in which you want it to operate, as well as how much to invest in terms of time and money. Another important decision to take is who from the executive will be the focal point for the advisory board or group and to ensure that they have a specific objective relating to it.

Views differ as to whether appointing a Chair is advisable. On the one hand it enables the board or executive to focus on the advice rather than managing the meeting and on the other it increases the independence of the group and places an extra burden on one of the members. Either works and a good board chair will be able to judge what's right for the circumstances.

In terms of size, I've seen groups as small as three and as big as eleven do a good job but somewhere in between seems to be the norm. The smaller ones tend to work well for a specific issue or project: the larger ones for more general consultative or sense-checking purposes.

It can be tempting to go for the biggest names in your sector and for start-ups and early-stage situations this can prove powerful but it doesn't always work due to some common challenges including that:

- It can sometimes be hard for highly-driven successful people who are action-orientated to remember that it is an advisory board. Not all highly successful CEOs make good advisers.
- The experience of the advisers may be glittering but not relevant to what the organisation needs.
- The original purpose or need may pass and neither the company nor the advisers recognise it or are prepared to deal with it.
- We're sometimes disappointed by our idols when we meet them in practice.

It is always advisable to agree clear terms of reference which have been approved by the governing board including individual objectives, term of the appointment, review process, frequency and location of meetings, fees and expenses as well as to how the adviser will be kept informed of the progress of the organisation. My preference is to set the tone by having something in the *"Context to the appointment"* or *"Background"* to the effect that the appointment is for a specific phase of the organisation's development and is envisaged to last for the period you have in mind.

On fees and expenses, for well-established and funded organisations then it is generally a straightforward daily rate plus reasonable expenses. As with all professional relationships it is critical to agree what *"reasonable"* means up front and to have a clause to say that such expenses should be approved in advance. For most of us, arriving by private jet and charging the organisation isn't reasonable but that may be the way of life of the adviser.

In some circumstances, typically the US Tech sector, advisers might waive fees and take a tiny equity incentive in lieu but this can turn out to add too much complexity and cost unless the investment agreements already have a provision in them relating to this.

Another aspect well worth setting out in the appointment letter is confidentiality and the process for recording and managing conflicts of interest. It is likely that a big hitter in your sector will be involved in other organisations in your space, so there is a good possibility that conflicts of interest may emerge. It is usually fairly straightforward to adapt the process you have for board members and trustees.

As you can probably sense, my overall feeling is that a small group of advisers focused on addressing specific issues and working individually with the company is often more effective and more efficient than an advisory board or group.

Roles of key participants

The nucleus of a board tends to be the Chair, SID, CEO and CFO. If you have the right people in those roles and they have good working relationships with each other, then the rest tends to sort itself out. Good Chairs and CEOs are magnets for talent and almost by definition also good at dealing with underperformers or those that may have been appointed for all the right reasons but just don't work out in practice. They also recognise the value of diversity and are skilled at bringing out the best in a diverse group.

Three other executive roles, especially in public companies or public bodies, play a key role in boosting board performance and these are the company secretary, the chief legal officer and the communications director. In many organisations the former two are combined.

In this section, we'll look at the roles of those in the nucleus, these other executive roles, from a board perspective, as well as the obviously important roles of independent directors or trustees. We will also briefly discuss the role of patrons in a charity. The characteristics required for all of these roles are covered in the "*People*" section. As you will see, to avoid repetition between the roles in different sectors, I have started with the role in a public company and then looked at some of the differences in other settings.

The Chair

If the board's role is to ensure that there is the "*Right strategy, Right resources and Right governance*" then as leader of the board team, the Chair's primary role, and ultimate responsibility, is to make that so. To achieve it they need to ensure that they have the right board and that they are working together in the right way and that collectively they have the right interactions with other key groups including the executive, key stakeholders, regulators and so on. I think this holds across the spectrum from fledgling charity to major global corporate and all points in between.

Defining the specific role of the Chair for a particular organisation needs care. The job changes subtly from organisation to organisation, depending upon its situation and context as well as the strength of the board and executive at the point of entry. It's pretty obvious that chairing a start-up is a very different job to chairing a FTSE 100 but any category is not homogeneous and the exact role varies a lot depending upon its situation, especially its performance and how well its executive are doing. Yet there are certain core elements of the role, those described at the start of the previous paragraph, which are fundamental and don't change.

According to the Oxford English Dictionary, in our context, a *"Chair"* can be a noun or a verb. The definitions are:

Noun: *"The person in charge of a meeting or of an organisation (used as a neutral alternative to chairman or chairwoman)."*

Verb: *"Act as chairperson of or preside over (an organisation, meeting, or public event)."*

These appeal to me as it suggests that the job is more than a title and indicates the possibility that it is an active role.

Most Chairs today would say that expectations and practice have moved considerably along the noun to verb spectrum and that there has even been a noticeable shift in the last few years, especially in large financial institutions and public bodies. Yet, at the same time, people in the organisations some Chairs lead might feel that things haven't changed much and see their Chair as little more than a weighty adornment. The pandemic certainly provided the opportunity for Chairs to demonstrate their value and I know many who have more than risen to the occasion.

There are several versions as to the origin of the word *"Chair"* one of which, from the middle English period (from 1066 to the 15th century), is certainly more noun than verb like.

"To carry (someone) aloft in a chair or in a sitting position to celebrate a victory."

"no one seemed anxious to chair him round the hall."

Dealing with the gender point I much prefer *"Chair"* to *"Chairman"* or *"Chairperson"*. For one thing it describes the position rather than the person; for another, you don't need to change the title if the gender of the holder changes and finally it is also has the benefit of brevity.

The other issue around the title is whether it carries the pre-descriptor of *"non-executive"* or *"executive"*. To me a Chair is a Chair and I don't think it needs either descriptor attached to it. Of course, there are situations in early stage, transition or crisis where the Chair needs to assume a more exec position for a brief period but, in general, I see the role as being distinct from the *"non-executives"* and the *"executives"*.

A lot has been written on the role of the Chair in many different contexts. Sir Adrian Cadbury's two books *"The Company Chairman"* and *"Corporate Governance and Chairmanship"* may have been published long ago (1995 and 2002 respectively), but much of their wisdom remains relevant to today. For example, his emphasis on the Chair's role in *"board leadership"* and that the board should be the *"driving force"* and not simply a *"monitoring or rubber-stamping body"* nails it for me.

Leadership and momentum matter. If the board have them then the Chair needs to maintain and develop them but if it doesn't then the Chair needs to inject that leadership and drive the process of creating momentum through *"Purpose, People and Process"* (the 3Ps). The Chair's role in the various aspects of the 3Ps is described in each section.

In practice Sir Adrian also believed strongly that the Chair's role *"cannot be defined in isolation from the other members of the (Board) team."* He also saw that the context was critical. I would go further and say that it also cannot be defined in isolation from the executive team and the CEO in particular.

The various regulatory bodies also have a view on the role of the Chair.

For public companies, according to the FRC's *"Guidance on Board Effectiveness"*
(*See* Useful links, page 414.)

"The chair is pivotal in creating the conditions for overall board and individual director effectiveness, setting clear expectations concerning the style and tone of board discussions, ensuring the board has effective decision-making processes and applies sufficient challenge to major proposals. It is up to the chair to make certain that all directors are aware of their responsibilities and to hold meetings with the non-executive directors without the executives present in order to facilitate a full and frank airing of views.

The chair's role includes:

- setting a board agenda primarily focused on strategy, performance, value creation, culture, stakeholders and account- ability, and ensuring that issues relevant to these areas are reserved for board decision;
- shaping the culture in the boardroom;
- encouraging all board members to engage in board and committee meetings by drawing on their skills, experience and knowledge; fostering relationships based on trust, mutual respect and open communication – both in and outside the boardroom – between non-executive directors and the executive team;
- developing a productive working relationship with the chief executive, providing support and advice, while respecting executive responsibility;
- providing guidance and mentoring to new directors as appropriate;
- leading the annual board evaluation, with support from the senior indepent director as appropriate, and acting on the results;
- considering having regular externally facilitated board evaluations."

It is worth noting the range of the role as well as that each of their bullet points starts with an active word.

For charities, the NCVO Guidance is as follows with regard to the role of the Chair on a trustee board:

> The chair is a trustee with a specific role on the board. The chair is elected or appointed to this role as set out in the charity's governing document. The role of the chair is to chair meetings of the trustee board.
>
> Some chairs take on a number of additional roles. The chair can only take on these additional roles if they have been authorised to do so. This authorisation might be set out in the governing document or related procedure, or agreed by the other trustees in a role description or some other document.
>
> Additional roles of the chair sometimes include:
>
> - supporting and supervising the head of staff or chief executive and acting as a channel of communication between board and staff;
> - acting as a Figurehead for the charity (for example, representing it at functions, meetings or in the press);
> - leading on the development of the board and ensuring its decisions are implemented; and
> - taking urgent action (but not decision-making unless authorised) between board meetings when it isn't possible or practical to hold a meeting.
> - The roles above are not exclusively roles of the chair. For example, in some charities the development of the board might be led by another trustee; in others, the charity's press spokesperson might be a member of staff."

Accurate and helpful though the FRC and NVCO Guidance are, they feel a bit *"processy"* to me. Before you email to correct my use of English, I know that isn't really a word, but I think you know what I mean.

At 3i, where we were investing in growth businesses across a broad range of sectors and countries, I came up with the following shorter description for what we expected the Chair's in our portfolio companies to do. They were almost always independent Chairs, not employees of 3i, and the majority were experienced CEOs in private equity (PE) situations.

The Chair

- leads the board in the determination of the organisation's vision, purpose and strategy;
- ensures that the board has clear visibility of results;
- ensures that effective relationships are maintained with all stakeholders;
- runs the board and allows CEO to run the company;
- implements investment strategy/exit;
- judges the executive team on operational/financial performance and finally;
- is responsible for management change.

This, I think, is a more strategic take on what a Chair's role is and I think has application for a wider range of contexts than just PE. In trying to practice what I preach I have found it helpful, especially in chairing social enterprises. When reflecting on my own performance I often get this list out and think about what I have done on each of the points in the last quarter and where I need to increase the emphasis in the quarter ahead.

Leading the board in the determination of its vision, purpose and strategy means being the guardian of the process not doing it. This is definitely an issue which falls in the intersection of the Venn diagram (page 12) for the board and exec. Clearly the exec do the bulk of the work, are normally driving the creation of strategic options and must own the strategy that they will be responsible for executing. Yet, the Chair must ensure that it means that there is a proper and engaging process that ends up with the right level of alignment from other stakeholders and the conviction from all of those needed to carry it out and enable it to happen. Many of us have seen situations where management *"over-own"* the strategy and process, excluding others, only to fail because key enablers don't provide the help required.

One thing that PE firms are good at is ensuring that there is a strategy for the ownership as well as the business or organisation. It is vital that a Chair, especially in a family company ensures that "*Ownership*" strategy is considered on as regular a basis as business strategy: the "*Bones & Son*" dilemma on page 388 is a good example of what might happen if they don't. In a PE context the "*Ownership*" strategy is an important element of the investment strategy and the Chair is ultimately responsible for ensuring that the investment strategy is implemented and that the exit happens in line with plan.

Ensuring that the board has clear visibility of results might seem like a statement of the blinding obvious, but in practice people often confuse volume with visibility and charm with clarity. One advantage the PE sector has is the general practice of having an agreed value creation plan which contains the many actions which need to be taken to deliver value growth. The financial results and achievement of other actions and outcomes, such as key appointments or market objectives, are way points to achieving the ultimate goal and there is regular attention given to achieving all of these way points, not just the financial ones. A lot of effort is taken up front to get the reporting in a form so that it will be easy to chart progress against that value creation plan.

Good Chairs know that you absolutely have to deliver the numbers today but that the secret to sustaining performance and to creating real long-term value growth or impact is about a lot more than today's performance and that you need clarity and visibility of all of the other value or impact drivers as well as to have good forecast analysis. Fundamentally, if the executive can't produce what a good Chair thinks is needed to know what the current position is and what the likely forecast performance is then that Chair will want changes either to process or people and mindset.

I have adopted such thinking in the social enterprises that I have been involved in and there is no doubt in my mind that the clarity and visibility of results on the non-financial progress has been as important as that on the numbers. During my time on the advisory board of Bridges Social entrepreneurs fund I especially appreciated the format of portfolio performance reports which placed equal emphasis on social impact and commercial performance. Without the former what's the point and without the latter it isn't sustainable.

In order to ensure that there are effective relationships with stake-holders you first of all need to be clear what you mean by a stakeholder, to know who they are and to understand their motivations and culture.

As far as I can tell the term *"Stakeholder"* was first coined by R Edward Freeman in 1984 and defined as *"Anyone who affects or is affected by your organisation"*. I really like the definition and that the word is similar to shareholder but much broader but for some reason it never feels like a natural word.

There is much more on the Board's role in developing and supporting a stakeholder strategy on page 171. The key point being that this is something a board needs to own and ensure that it is deliberate and proactive rather than un-coordinated and reactive.

Gaining an understanding of the power dynamic is one of the most important items of due diligence a Chair will undertake. It covers everything from who really owns the company or who are the key funders, to the people in the business, customers or beneficiaries, suppliers and partners, regulators and other groups.

Once you know who they are and, as importantly, what their current view and capability to help or hinder you in meeting what you feel are the best interests of the organisation, it is then much easier to come up with a stakeholder strategy and plan (Page 171). Being armed with the best intelligence, strategy and plan, still requires the Chair to be good at this and to have the judgement and interpersonal skills to interact with a wide range of people who may want and value different things and approaches.

In doing this, smart Chairs use their advisers intelligently and, although in fact they are essentially suppliers of services, manage the relationship with them on more of a partnership basis. For any Chair having a good set of relationships with a range of professional advisers is essential and is usually one of the values that you bring.

It is worth pointing out that there are significant cultural differences in the role of the Chair around the world and between sectors. In part this is driven by whether the prevailing culture is to split or combine the roles of Chair and CEO. In the UK and Commonwealth countries the roles tend to be split whereas in the US they tend to be combined. I prefer the split approach for the following reasons:

- An important element of the Chair's role is to judge the CEO's performance and to recommend to the board if change is required.
- The combined role places too great a concentration of power in one person.

- Running the board and running the company are connected but distinct and significant challenges in their own right and;
- It can be helpful for the CEO to have the shield of the Chair.

The CEO is there to run the company and the Chair's there to make sure that the company is well run. It can be really hard to do in practice due to a number of factors including personality. We'll cover that aspect in the *"People"* section on page 85. Other factors might include a genuine desire to support an under-pressure CEO or in the early stages of an organisation where there simply isn't sufficient resource. Here the Chair may find themselves sliding down the slippery slope of helpfulness and ending up with an embarrassing playground battle for their good intentions. More typically it can be a Chair finding it hard to transition from an executive role into the quite different role of a Chair.

The best way to ensure that there isn't a problem is to agree up front when the appointment of a new Chair or CEO is made, who does what and what goes in the Venn intersection (page 12). There is usually considerable flexibility and the opportunity to play to strengths whilst preserving the fundamental duties of a Chair and CEO.

In PE land we would expect the Chair of a portfolio company to be spotting the under-performance of an exec or non-exec before we do, to have a plan in place to deal with it, to be letting us know what they and/or the CEO would like to do, gaining whatever board approval is required and then dealing with it. We would be disappointed if it is us who had to alert, nudge or prod a Chair into realising that there was a management issue and into doing something about it. Obviously, the Chair's role in CEO succession is pivotal and this is covered in the *"Process"* section on page 192.

More positively, the Chair has an important role to play in the development of the CEO and I have seen some wonderful examples of this in practice, especially with first time CEOs. The best Chairs are also good at developing independent directors and put the effort in to doing so. It makes sense, as the more effective the independent directors are the better the performance of the board is likely to be. We will look in more detail at the characteristics required to be a good Chair in the *"People"* section (page 85) and there are plenty of practical challenges for Chairs in the *"Dilemmas"* section (page 269).

In summary, the Chair's role is multi-faceted, is hugely demanding and requires a broad range of skills. Holding the ultimate responsibility and accountability for an organisation can occasionally be anxiety inducing. Yet, the professional challenge and the satisfaction of moving an organisation forward during your tenure can more than compensate for that.

Independent director, non-exec or outside director

These days, the terms independent director (ID) and non-exec are used interchangeably. I have always preferred the former for a variety of reasons, even though I know full well that it isn't always a perfect descriptor. First, describing a role by what it is not doesn't seem to me to be that helpful. Second, describing it as *"Outside"* seems a bit odd when they are inside, arguably, what should be the most influential room in the organisation. Finally, although those who argue against ID point out quite rightly that very few people are genuinely independent in every relevant sense, I believe that it is possible to be objective and independent of mind even if you have an interest in the outcome.

Novelist F. Scott Fitzgerald's wonderful quote seems apposite in this context:

> *"The test of a first-rate intelligence is the ability to hold two opposed ideas in mind at the same time and still retain the ability to function."*

It is also worth thinking about what independence means. It feels to me like a multi-dimensional set of spectrums. We have investments in more than simply a financial context. Frequently it is our investments in relationships that will blur thinking and prevent us from doing what we know is the best thing to do. The classic example being the reluctance of a Chair who hired an underperforming CEO to deal with it. We also have investments in our reputations which lead us sometimes to make decisions which defer potential embarrassment in the hope, despite the evidence to the contrary, that something will emerge to avoid that risk materialising.

As I have observed, humans don't always make decisions based on one criteria or even what might be in their best interests. If you don't believe me read *"Thinking, Fast and Slow"* by Nobel prize winner Daniel Kahneman. I've seen *"angel"* investors who have invested a tiny proportion of their net worth into a company, sit on the board, act like they own it and block future funding because they don't have the funds to follow even if it means wiping out their initial investment. I've also seen other board members who have invested significantly greater proportions of their wealth do the right thing even when it means they are going to lose all of their money. Maybe I have been lucky but, in my experience, people generally tend to do what they believe is the right thing even if it may not be the best for them individually, especially if they are surrounded by others who act in that way.

It seems that the FRC in the UK is sticking with the *"non-executive"* director but content to have one of them called the *"senior independent director"*. In the US (on NYSE and NASDAQ) the term *"independent"* director seems to be replacing *"outside"* director, largely because they ideally want their *"outside"* directors to be independent. So, and somewhat amusingly, there's a sense that we might get there on having one descriptor in the end and that it's *"independent"*.

Each stock exchange and regulator will have either legal or *"in principle"* descriptions of what independence means. By way of example, for NASDAQ in its *"Market Place Rules"* (*see* Useful links, page 415) the definition of an "*independent director*" is as follows:

> *"A person other than an executive officer or employee of the company or any other individual having a relationship which, in the opinion of the issuer's board of directors, would interfere with the exercise of independent judgement in carrying out the responsibilities of a director."*

They then go on to list obvious situations where a person cannot be deemed to be independent, such as a family member and so on.

I quite like this definition as it places the onus and the judgement on the directors and good boards will take that responsibility seriously. But I guess therein also lies its weakness as weak boards won't. In that case the media and shareholders will have to provide that control mechanism.

Having dealt with the title, what do non-execs, IDs and outside directors do?

As with the other *"Key participant"* roles, regulators have a view as to what the role entails in order to meet regulatory and best practice requirements but, as you might by now expect me to say, there is more to the job than that. So, this time let's start with the broader role then look at it from the regulator's perspective.

The starting point is their general role as a board member in contributing to ensuring that the organisation has the right vision, purpose, strategy, resources and governance. They also support the Chair in delivering the value or impact creation strategy without getting involved in the management. In doing this, if their contribution has the feel of helping the management to achieve their plans they will tend to have greater influence. The ID may also have a role to play in ensuring that there are effective relationships with stakeholders.

Some roles can be tightly defined and leave little wriggle room. This, however, is far from the case with the ID role both in terms of what they specifically do and, as importantly, how they do it. The 1939 hit written by Oliver and Young *"Tain't what you do it's the way that you do it and that's what gets results."* seems very relevant. What IDs do will also depend greatly on what needs doing. For example, the ID has a key role to play if others are too focused on the short term at the expense of long-term sustainability.

They may become an interlocutor and peacemaker when relationships become strained and from time to time they may have to fulfil the shock absorber role when others are crashing about or are overwhelmed by a crisis. Again the pandemic has enabled many IDs to step up and provide this vital service at a time of crisis.

Another important part of the role is to allow others to take the credit for your input. The *"praise and blame"* game is acutely asymmetric for the ID: if all goes brilliantly it is the CEO and execs who will be applauded; however, if it all goes wrong the cry goes out pretty swiftly *"What were the IDs doing?"*

When it comes to power and influence (*see* page 120) the ID generally has to depend more on *"personal"* power than *"positional"* power. Their expertise, track record, attractiveness and visibility tend to be greater sources of power than their formal authority.

All of the situations in the *"Dilemmas"* section involve an ID and there is more in both the *"People"* and the *"Process"* sections so we'll leave it there for now.

Senior independent director (SID)

Given the publicity when the role of the SID was established in 2003, as a result of the Higgs Review (*see* page 412), it has proved to be a remarkably resilient feature of UK public company life and has spread to many other countries and contexts. Indeed, as Sacha Sadan, Director of Corporate Governance at Legal and General Investment Management said in a 2017 report on *"The Role of the Senior Independent Director"* with Zygos:

> *"The role and importance of the Senior Independent Director has grown enormously. Shareholders really value this safety valve and not just in extreme situations."*

The FRC at time of writing describes the role almost identically to that set out in Sir Derek's 2003 report, as shown in the box overleaf.

The germ of the idea for the role was a discussion about a number of things. Firstly, there were a few *"mouldy"* Chairs about despite the fact that institutions had thought they had given strong signals that the Chair needed to move on. The problem being that those signals were given to the Chair themselves and not all had relayed this to their boards. Secondly there was a feeling that the role of the Chair was becoming increasingly demanding especially in some sectors and that although the deputy Chair role existed in many companies it would be helpful to have both a more formal sounding board as well as someone to delegate ambassadorial or other duties to. Thirdly, in an atmosphere of belief in the view that there should be performance reviews for all, the question was asked who was going to lead the Chair's review? Additionally, there was a general feeling that in many cases where there had been significant issues between a Chair and a CEO, having a pre-determined interlocutor and arbiter within the board may have avoided situations getting out of hand and resulting in a public bust-up which was damaging to the company.

When Sir Derek Higgs mooted the idea in the consultation process preceding the finalisation of his report, the inevitable happened.

> "The senior independent director should act as a sounding board for the chair, providing them with support in the delivery of their objectives and leading the evaluation of the chair on behalf of the other directors. The senior independent director might also take responsibility for an orderly succession process for the chair, working closely with the nomination committee. It is a good idea for the

> senior independent director to serve on committees of the board to improve their knowledge of company governance. The senior independent director should also be available to shareholders if they have concerns that contact through the normal channels of chair, chief executive or other executive directors has failed to resolve or for which such contact is inappropriate.
>
> When the board or company is undergoing a period of stress, the senior independent director's role becomes critically important. They are expected to work with the chair and other directors, and/or shareholders, to resolve significant issues. Boards should ensure they have a clear understanding of when the senior independent director might intervene in order to maintain board and company stability. Examples might include where:
>
> - there is a dispute between the chair and chief executive;
> - shareholders or non-executive directors have expressed concerns that are not being addressed by the chair or chief executive;
> - the strategy is not supported by the entire board;
> - the relationship between the chair and chief executive is particularly close;
> - decisions are being made without the approval of the full board; or

A number of the establishment saw this as an affront as well as a serious threat and got busy on the phone to journalists. Their arguments were simple, that it would make governance even more cumbersome, unnecessarily weaken the role of the Chair and, with a somewhat misogynist tone, make it hard to attract "*good men into the role*". Sir Derek had anticipated this as well as the risk of overloading investors with too many meetings. He had already suggested the SID should not be someone who would be considered as a candidate to succeed the Chair. Nevertheless, there were a bumpy few months.

Despite all the huffing and puffing the role was introduced into a refreshed Combined Code in 2003 and is now a well-established feature of the governance landscape in the UK and elsewhere. It hasn't eradicated Chair and CEO bust-ups, yet I know, without revealing secrets, that it has provided a way of managing a fair few much more effectively. It has also led, in my view, to greater diversity on boards through better succession processes and actually protected the odd Chair from losing their job through personal friction with an investor. Strong SIDs are just as capable of changing an investor's perspective on a Chair or CEO as they are in reinforcing one.

Today, there still remain cases where the role isn't as well defined or understood as it might be but in the main I think the creation of the SID role has been a success. To do it successfully, especially to fulfil the "*safety valve*" aspect, also means that you need to invest the time in building the relevant relationships before you need them. In the Legal and General and Zygos report there are a couple of lovely lines emphasising this aspect:

"Cometh the hour cometh the SID."

"To fulfil the roles highlighted above effectively, however, the SID requires healthy and actively-maintained relationships with both fellow directors and investors. The effective SID's role is one of continuous diplomacy, rather than sporadic action."

As a footnote, ironically the self-identification of the "*huffers and puffers*" probably sped up their succession.

Trustee

The role of the trustee in a charity is analogous to the role of the ID or non-exec in a business.

The headline description of the role in the UKCC Guidance "*The Essential Trustee: what you need to know, what you need to do*" (*see* Useful links) sums the governance role up well and aims to balance "*What you must do*" with "*What you should do*". "*Must*" being things which are legal or regulatory requirements that trustees must comply with and "*should*" meaning things which are in line with best practice and that the Commission expects you to do. The various other "*duties of trustees*" around the world follow similar patterns with some more detailed than others and some focusing more on the legal duties and obligations rather than best practice.

The main headings in the UKCC are as follows with the first one setting the tone of their Guidance in terms of its practicality and accessible language:

- Before you start - make sure that you are eligible to be a charity trustee.
- Ensure your charity is carrying out its purposes for public benefit.
- Comply with your charity's governing document and the law.
- Act in your charity's best interests.
- Manage your charity's resources responsibly.
- Act with reasonable care and skill.
- Ensure your charity is accountable.

It also sets out who can and cannot be a trustee and contains the wonderfully English statement, oozing support with a hint of menace, that:

"The Commission recognises that most trustees are volunteers who sometimes make honest mistakes. Trustees are not expected to be perfect – they are expected to do their best to comply with their duties. Charity law generally protects trustees who have acted honestly and reasonably."

By "*volunteers*" they mean unpaid and perhaps to cover the situation as exists in many smaller charities that trustees may also be undertaking some element of what might be perceived as operational activity.

Anyone taking on a trustee role is clearly not doing it for the money and accepts that there is financial risk if things go wrong even if it is simply meeting legal fees. Consequently, as with businesses the charity, if it has the appropriate legal structure, will look to take out Directors and Officers Liability insurance.

In terms of a Maslow's hierarchy of needs (*see* page 223) the UKCC Guidance on the role of a trustee is fine in meeting the basic needs and ensuring that a charity is well governed and risks are managed. Yet, a trustee is required to do a lot more than that if they are to contribute to the success of the organisation and to help it fulfil its social purpose.

In order to do more than simply fulfil their oversight role they need to contribute to those three key elements of the role of the board "*Right strategy, Right resources and Right governance*" and not just the latter. Also, in smaller charities, which represent the vast majority as noted above, they may also be operational undertaking tasks. In doing so they need to be strong minded enough to be clear when they are operating as a board member and trustee and be able to retain their objectivity when it comes to decision-making. Many a trustee has also slipped down the slippery slope of helpfulness.

A good example of how to avoid this is where a financially-orientated trustee steps in when a finance director leaves and there isn't a suitable resource internally. The smart trustee will make it clear that this is for a limited period only and will ensure that the process of finding the replacement gets underway as soon as possible. The weaker trustee will enjoy getting their hands dirty again, not get on with helping the Chair and CEO to recruit a successor and then find it hard to be objective at the board.

As with independents or non-execs the trustee will generally rely more upon "*personal*" powers than "*positional*" ones (*see* page 121) to achieve their influence. They will also need to deploy a balance of "*cuddle and kick*" and avoid falling into the trap of being mono-modal in either "*policeman or woman*" mode or "*going native.*"

Patrons

Many charities have access to high-calibre and high-profile people who don't have either the time, skills or desire to become a member of the board but would like to be able to contribute in a significant way. A diverse group of engaged patrons can provide a powerful boost to a charity's profile, network and fundraising efforts as well as provide useful insights to its board and executive. However, in some cases patrons groups add little value, are a big burden for the executive to manage and prove to be little more than a costly adornment.

I have been fortunate in having good experiences at EY Foundation and ESSA- Education Sub-Saharan Africa and in being a patron myself at youth and conflict charity Leap Confronting Conflict. The things that have made it work in these situations have been having:

- clear and explicit roles and objectives for the patrons group as well as the individual patrons themselves;

- a diverse group of patrons in terms of age, sector of focus, style and network;
- a specific focus in terms of bringing benefit to the charity for each patron, eg bringing advice and representing the charity in a specific community, corporate fund-raising or using their profile to enhance awareness of the charity;
- an executive to be the focal point/buddy for each patron and have a specific item relating to maximising the relationship with the patron in their objectives;
- that executive manage a thorough on-boarding process for the patron;
- a proper annual review process for the group as well as individuals as to how it is working;
- really good communication on a one-to-one basis with patrons so that they are well informed as to the charity's progress, opportunities, challenges and needs; and
- few big meetings – it is much better to involve patrons in the regular flow of events and activities. If you do this well then you will probably only need one meeting of the group each year and this is generally a combination of thank you and look ahead.

Chief Executive Officer (CEO)

If the role of the executive is to develop the business plan, deliver the business plan and to maintain financial and operational integrity then the role of the CEO essentially is to lead the executive in delivering all of that. This is so simply put but so challenging to do, whatever the size of the organisation.

In a large listed organisation, a public body or a big charity, you may have considerable resource at your disposal but you also have the complexity that goes with it, combined with the increased personal pressures from being in the spotlight. In a smaller organisation, you might not have all of those challenges but with thinner resources there is likely to be a much higher operational workload and the differential power balance between you and your customers and suppliers can make it harder to achieve what you would like.

From a regulator's perspective the CEO role looks fairly straightforward.

According to the UK's FRC "*Guidance on board effectiveness*" it is as set out in the box below.

> "As the most senior executive director, the chief executive is responsible for proposing company strategy and for delivering the strategy as agreed by the board. The chief executive's relationship with the chair is a key influence on board effectiveness.
>
> When deciding the differing responsibilities of the chair and the chief executive, particular attention should be paid to areas of potential overlap.
>
> The chief executive has primary responsibility for setting an example to the company's workforce, for communicating to them the expectations in respect of the company's culture, and for ensuring that operational policies and practices drive appropriate behaviour. They are responsible for supporting the chair to make certain that appropriate standards of governance permeate through all parts of the organisation. They will ensure the board is made aware of views gathered via engagement between management and the workforce.
>
> It is the responsibility of the chief executive to ensure the board knows the views of the senior management on business issues in order to improve the standard of discussion in the boardroom and, prior to a final decision on an issue, explain in a balanced way any divergence of view.
>
> The chief executive is also responsible for ensuring that management fulfils its obligation to provide board directors with:
>
> o accurate, timely and clear information in a form and of a quality and comprehensiveness that will enable it to dis- charge its duties;
>
> o the necessary resources for developing and updating their knowledge and capabilities; and
>
> o appropriate knowledge of the company, including access to company operations and members of the workforce."

Understandably this description of the role is through the prism of governance and therefore narrower than the true wider role of a CEO. For example, as we have said above, it is the primary responsibility of the CEO to develop and deliver the business plan and ensure financial and operational integrity, which the FRC code, I suppose, implicitly means as part of "*delivering the strategy*". The Guidance however does cover a lot of the ground and is helpful in defining important topics that go in the Venn diagram like intersection between board and management, as discussed on page 12.

The FRC description of the role also highlights the importance of the relationship between the Chair and CEO and it is most welcome that this isn't prescriptive and allows the flexibility that is required. Ideally it might have gone a little further and talked about developing high quality relationships with all of the board and effective relationship between the executive as a group and the board.

Ensuring that there is a high performing executive team and that there is a good succession plan in place, including for themselves, is another important part of the CEO's role. As a Chair I think it is healthy to talk about this with the CEO and to gain their input rather than for the board to have a secret plan. This doesn't mean that you will always agree with their views on what is required but it can be very useful input as well as helpful to the relationship. We'll cover CEO succession more fully in the "*Process*" section on page 192.

As a board it is important that the CEO accepts that it is the board that appoints the CEO and not the other way around. As we will discover in a number of the dilemmas (*see* page 269) the board must be in control and not be manipulated. I think it makes sense, just as it does when appointing a Chair or ID, that the CEO understands that they are being recruited for the next phase of development and not for life.

It is good also that the CEO's role in building the culture and setting an example are highlighted by the FRC, even if with a slightly old-fashioned air. I've never liked the word "*workforce*". It always seems somewhat divisive, a bit 1970s and increasingly outdated given modern organisational realities.

Chief Financial Officer (CFO)

Whether the CFO is on the board or not, they are critical to its success. Fundamentally this is through their role in maintaining financial and operational integrity but also because the CFO is the chief provider of information for decision-making. Good CFOs, who are partners to the CEO, also boost the power and capacity of the CEO.

One useful description of the role of the CFO is contained in the Deloitte report "*Four Faces of the CFO*" (*see* Useful links and Fig. 1.7 below).

I like it because it goes well beyond seeing the CFO as simply "*the numbers*" person or a functionary and has a more strategic, proactive and forward-looking feel to the role. At the same time, it doesn't forget that the basics matter and that without them the important financial and operational integrity I was talking about earlier collapses.

The CFO's role in leading the finance function, ensuring control and efficiency, that performance and execution are not just tracked and watched but are driven, is the bedrock of success in the role and places the CFO naturally as both "*steward*" and "*operator*". Successfully achieving those things then gives the CFO the right to take that more strategic role as a "*catalyst*" and "*strategist*", assuming that they have the capabilities. Failing to do so takes that right away.

According to the Deloitte report they become a "*catalyst*" by "*using the power of their purse strings*" to "*selectively drive business improvement initiatives such as improved enterprise cost reduction, procurement, pricing execution, and other process improvements and innovations that add value to the company.*" That's right but I think to be a truly powerful catalyst they need more than just control of the cheque book. Character and relationships matter as much.

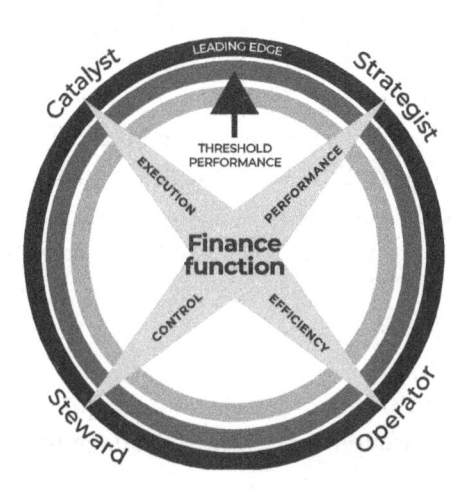

Figure 1:7 Deloitte four faces of the CFO

With reference to strategy the Deloitte report states that CFOs are vital in providing financial leadership and aligning business and finance strategy to grow the business. In addition to M&A and capital market financing strategies, they can play an integral role in supporting other long-term investments of the company. I would go further and say that for a CFO to be strategic they need to be able to contribute from more than a financial perspective.

Fulfilling the *"catalyst"* and *"strategist"* role depends much on the CFO having the right relationship with the Chair and the CEO. If either see the CFO as simply the numbers person and a functionary, then it isn't likely to happen. However, if they see their CFO as a true partner in driving the success of the organisation then the chances are far higher. It is absolutely critical before you take a role on a board that you know which of these it is and the best way to find out is through your individual conversations with the Chair, CEO and CFO. We cover this in more detail in the *"Process"* section (*see* pages 114 and 192) and in particular where we explore both the *"Hierarchy of needs"* for a CFO and some useful things to go through with the CFO before you take a board position.

Whether the CFO is on the board or not will give you a clue as to how they are viewed. After all, if you want your CFO to be more strategic and to take this broader role then it is easier for them to do this if they are also on the board. I find CFOs on boards generally also feel a greater sense of ownership with decisions, find it harder to slip into a board adviser mindset and have strengthened authority with other executives. Additionally, when recruiting you may find it easier to attract higher calibre candidates for a board position. Finally, on this point I quite like the CFO to share exactly the same sense of legal risk as the rest of us.

If your CFO is on the board then it is reasonable to expect that not only will they have the capabilities of a board member but also the mindset. Putting a CFO on the board to make them happy if they haven't got the right capabilities or mindset usually ends badly.

We will cover the characteristics of successful CFOS and these relationships in more depth in *"Composition and board building"* on pages 114 and 192.

It is vital for independent directors or trustees to have a strong connection with the CFO and to achieve this without the CEO feeling sidelined. This is easily done if the CEO and CFO have the right relationship, where they respect each-other's complementary expertise and knowledge and have a high level of trust and respect. Where this isn't the case you need to tread very carefully.

Company secretary and chief legal officer

Please don't skip this if you think your organisation is too small to have a full-time company secretary or chief legal officer. Whatever your size you will need someone to carry out aspects of these roles. In smaller organisations it is normal for them to be part conducted by an administrator, often within the finance team, and part by an adviser or consultant contracted by the organisation to provide the service.

Every potential board member should ask, before they join a board, how the company secretarial and legal functions are carried out and satisfy themselves that, however it is done, it is sufficient for compliance and for the board member to be able to meet their responsibilities. I like to have an annual compliance statement which not only sets out the key things that we need to be compliant with but also the confirmation that we are.

Practice varies in other countries but in the UK, it hasn't been a legal requirement for a private company to have a company secretary since 2008 unless the company's articles of association require it to do so. If they don't then the responsibilities for undertaking such duties fall on the directors. As many charities in the UK are companies limited by guarantee, trustees are in a similar position in such situations.

Public companies in most countries that I have been able to check, including the UK, do need to have a formally-appointed company secretary and this is, generally, at least a full-time role. In most countries there are also well-developed associations or Institutes of Company Secretaries. These organisations generally provide a range of resources including guidance and best practice notes, as well as template documents for most of the things that you might need, in addition to good networking opportunities. Another good due diligence question is how well connected and up to date the company secretary is with their local body and best practice.

It might be natural to think that it is smaller organisations that have a combined company secretary and chief legal officer roles, but in practice it actually tends to be the larger ones. This is because in very small organisations both roles tend to be contracted out and in small and mid-size they will tend to have the company secretary inside and the legal advice out. For larger corporates the arguments for combining the roles are similar to those for having one communications leader (*see* page 46).

The specific responsibilities and tasks of a company secretary naturally vary depending upon the nature and scale of the organisation as well as the relevant regulations and how well developed the finance function is. They will also include servicing the board and sub-committees and typically include:

- Ensuring compliance with legal and regulatory obligations.
- Maintaining the company's statutory registers.
- Updating the records held by the relevant companies or charities register.
- Managing and storing the company's records, eg re-investments, property, payroll, insurance, accounting, taxation, register of interests and conflicts of interest etc.
- Maintaining the registered office.
- Organising meetings (board, sub-committee, extraordinary, special, AGM etc).
- Drafting agendas, resolutions and other required documents for such meetings.
- Recording and communicating the minutes of such meetings as well as tracking and reporting actions emanating from them.
- Overseeing policies, making sure they are kept up to date and referred to the appropriate committee for approval.
- Monitoring changes in relevant legislation and the regulatory environment and taking appropriate action.
- Developing and overseeing the systems that ensure the company complies with all applicable codes, in addition to its legal and statutory requirements.
- Liaising with external regulators and advisers, such as lawyers and auditors.
- Taking responsibility for the health and safety of employees and managing matters related to insurance and property.
- Advising the board of directors on their legal and corporate responsibilities and in matters of corporate governance.
- Liaising between the company and its stakeholders and shareholders directly or through its registrars.

- Ensuring, in collaboration with the CFO, that the board and the organisation has appropriate insurance in place and that premiums are paid.

It's a long list and one which all of the directors or trustees need to know is being done to the right standard. Yet this isn't all that a good company secretary and chief legal officer will do. The best act as the board's extra conscience and confidant to every member. They will also play a central role in ensuring that relations between the board and executive are effective and that the "*Venn Intersection*" between these two groups, as described on page 12, is effective. In the process they play a pivotal role in ensuring board and executive are aligned.

The company secretary is generally not on the board but is usually a member of the executive group, especially in larger listed or heavily-regulated organisations. It is tremendously comforting for any board member to know that the executive quartet of CEO, CFO, communications director and company secretary is highly competent and working well together.

Communications director

The Chair and the CEO together should have a clear view about what sort of communications they want for the organisation and how they should be directed and managed. Reputations, theirs, the rest of the board and, most importantly, the organisation's reputation depend upon their judgement of this. Again, it is back to "*Purpose, People and Process*" clarity is required over the purpose of communications, you need the right person leading it and no matter whether you are in the public eye or not, the right processes in place both to position the company and to manage reputational risk.

It is fairly easy to tell in your due diligence whether the company has the right communications capability and it is worth spending time with the communications director beforehand. After all they should be the person who can tell you as clearly and succinctly as anyone what the company does, how it does it, what the key messages are, who the stakeholders are and how the company is viewed by them. They should also have their finger on the pulse of the organisation and be as good at listening and picking up signals as crafting messages and statements.

Given the radical changes in the nature of communications, in every sort of organisation, the communications function has become even more central and critical to success. Historically, compartmentalised leadership and management, with the role spread between marketing, investor relations, internal communications, operations and other functions, are becoming outdated models. The mechanisms and economics of communication have changed. The need for clarity, consist- ency, simplicity, transparency and especially speed has never been greater. As a consequence, the opportunities and risks associated with how you manage and govern the organisation's communications have never been higher.

Many organisations now have a fully-integrated model where the communications director is a member of the executive group but is not on the board. Others prefer to divide the role and have specialists heading each function and reporting to different members of the executive (eg investor relations to the CFO, internal communications to the HR director). My preference, biased by my own experience at 3i Group plc, and the organisations that I have chaired, is for the fully-integrated model. The benefits include more consistent and joined up communications, better-informed communications which consider all stakeholders, as well as speed.

It's a challenging role especially within a global organisation but a hugely fulfilling one which places you at the centre of things. As with the CFO role, to do the job successfully you need to see yourself working for the organisation not a particular person or function. This is especially true in large listed businesses where in those most tricky of situations, a change of CEO or Chair, you are likely to be working for the Chair or SID directly.

Communications are often considered to be *"One-Way"*, ie from the board or organisation out or to staff. It is just as important for a board to know how the organisation is really perceived by key stakeholders as to know what it wants people to know. I always saw it important to ensure that the board was fully informed as to what people thought even though this might be deeply uncomfortable from time to time.

As it is far easier to blame the communications than accept the facts, the role is a vulnerable one. I was hugely privileged at 3i to work for four different CEOs and 3 different Chairs. They were all very different but every one of them recognised the importance of communications and the need for it to have a very close connection to the board. There were many times when I had uncomfortable things to report or views to state but I never felt inhibited providing them.

The communications director and their teams are frequently a shock absorber for the board and the executive absorbing the ire of press, analysts, shareholders, staff and others when there is bad news. When you are the one thrust in front of the cameras to shield the CEO or Chair it is always important to remember the old saying to *"never allow yourself to become the news"*.

It can also be hard to shake off some of the negative stereotypes that have emerged from the political world. Of course, the communications director will always want to portray the organisation in the best light and limit the damage of a negative story but to *"spin"* or to *"bully"* will only buy temporary success. If you really want to be effective in the long run you need to have a reputation for integrity and to treat people fairly especially if they don't reciprocate.

Finally, the communications director will also provide the main linkage to the organisation's PR advisers. In larger listed companies these advisers, as well as investment banks and brokers, play a key role at the time of results or major announcements, events or when they are in a crisis. Although some sadly create an unhealthy co-dependent relationship with the CEO feeding on their insecurity, narcissism and paranoia, most add considerable value in sense checking or in giving a board a harsh dose of reality from time to time as well as more creative ways to use words.

Different contexts and influences

Context matters and different organisational purposes and constructs are subject to varying influences depending upon the nature and relative powers of their stakeholders.

For businesses the type of ownership is a key determinant of how the board might fulfil its' purpose in practice as well as what is expected of it. To cover this we will look at the influence investors play starting with public companies, then private equity, venture capital and angel-backed businesses followed by independent founder-owned and family businesses.

We will then look at some of the issues for charities and social enterprises and consider public bodies including NHS Trust boards as well as professional service firms and universities. I know that this is not comprehensive and that it is with a UK focus, but the issues should resonate in other places and types of organisation.

Finally, we will look at the influence of the media and social media as well as that of governance advisory services.

Business

Investors come in many forms and it is critical for any director to understand their motivation and objectives as well as their modus operandi.

Most organisations have a blend of investors to suit different needs and timescales. What all investors have in common is the objective to make a return commensurate with the risk they are taking. What all investors would like though is to do better than that and to have minimal hassle doing it. Those managing funds for others also want to have an investment which strengthens their case for getting more funds to manage.

The long-running debate about the role that institutional shareholders should play in the governance of listed companies has moved forward significantly in recent years. Yet there remains a spectrum of views and practice across the investment community. At one end, you have essentially what might be best described as those with "*trader*" mindsets and behaviours and at the other those who think and act like "*owners*". Both have a place and serve a purpose in the financial markets and many of the "*owner*" orientated firms will also manage "*trader*" mindset funds as well. It is therefore critical, when looking at who owns the business before you decide to join the board, that you know which funds are the main holders, not just which institutions hold the stock. The finance director (FD) should be able to tell you what the make-up of the share register is and if they can't, well that's a different issue.

For "*traders*", especially those who are event driven and where there is not much intention of holding the stock for long, the view typically is that if they don't like the way it is run they'll just sell. Occasionally weaknesses in governance can be used by "*traders*" to engineer what they describe as catalytic events such as change of Chair, CEO or FD. So, they may appear to be more concerned about governance than they really are.

At the other end of the spectrum you have some of the largest fund managers who have an "*owner*" mindset. As they are likely to hold a large number of stocks for lengthy periods these institutions are more likely to invest the time and resources to influence governance in their portfolios, driven by the belief that in the long run they will achieve a higher return across their portfolios through doing so. An element of their motivation to take this approach is the encouragement for them to do so from the sources of their funds, typically pension funds, who are more interested in more predictable and sustainable returns. These institutions usually have governance officers who both work alongside the fund managers to provide input and also develop and monitor the institutions overall governance policies. Ironically not all of these institutions practice what they preach in the way that their own institutions are governed.

There are many good examples of an *"owner"* mindset in practice, one being Larry Fink's 2019 letter to CEOs. Larry Fink is the Chair and CEO of global investor Blackrock which had over $5 Trillion under management at the beginning of 2019. Each year he writes to the CEOs of their portfolio companies and his 2019 theme was *"Purpose and Profit"*. His core message is below:

Purpose and Profit: An Inextricable Link

"I wrote last year that every company needs a framework to navigate this difficult landscape, and that it must begin with a clear embodiment of your company's purpose in your business model and corporate strategy. Purpose is not a mere tagline or marketing campaign; it is a company's fundamental reason for being – what it does every day to create value for its stakeholders. Purpose is not the sole pursuit of profits but the animating force for achieving them. Profits are in no way inconsistent with purpose – in fact, profits and purpose are inextricably linked.

Profits are essential if a company is to effectively serve all of its stakeholders over time – not only shareholders, but also employees, customers, and communities. Similarly, when a company truly understands and expresses its purpose, it functions with the focus and strategic discipline that drive long-term profitability. Purpose unifies management, employees, and communities. It drives ethical behaviour and creates an essential check on actions that go against the best interests of stakeholders. Purpose guides culture, provides a framework for consistent decision-making, and, ultimately, helps sustain long-term financial returns for the shareholders of your company."

Larry Fink, Chairman and CEO BlackRock 2019

I liked this because it is straightforward, pragmatic and well balanced as well as clearly communicated. Interestingly Blackrock's own corporate governance guidelines at time of writing (*see* Useful links) are a very good example of them trying to practice what they preach. Amusingly though, they neatly side-step the issue of having a combined Chair and CEO themselves, admittedly more common in the US, by emphasising the role of the lead independent director.

What about smaller listed companies? According to QCA who champion the interests of the small to mid-size quoted companies in the UK there are 1,250 of them making up 93% of the total number of listed companies. They also employ over 3 million people so are a significant part of the economy.

The latest QCA Corporate Code on Governance, (*see* page 412) at the time of writing, was published in 2018 and is consistent with the Combined Code in many ways including the embodiment of the principle of comply or explain which applies to larger quoted businesses.

The framing of the Code is noticeably different in style and emphasis though with an emphasis on ten principles under the three headings of *"Deliver Growth", "Maintain a Dynamic Management Framework"* and *"Build Trust"*. The inclusion of the words *"Growth", "Dynamic"* and *"Build"* will obviously have resonance with the market that QCA serves, the smaller listed growth companies and their investors. I really like the fact that the first principles are about delivering growth in value because this is the fundamental purpose of these companies. As it should be for larger businesses.

The ten QCA principles are to:

Deliver Growth

1. Establish a strategy and business model which promote long-term value for shareholders.
2. Seek to understand and meet shareholder needs and expectations.
3. Take into account wider stakeholder and social responsibilities and their implications for long-term success.

> 4. Embed effective risk management, considering both opportunities and threats, throughout the organisation.
>
> **Maintain a dynamic management framework**
>
> 5. Maintain the board as a well-functioning, balanced team led by the Chair.
> 6. Ensure that between them the directors have the necessary up-to-date experience, skills and capabilities.
> 7. Evaluate board performance based on clear and relevant objectives, seeking continuous improvement.
> 8. Promote a corporate culture that is based on ethical values and behaviours.
> 9. Maintain governance structures and processes that are fit for purpose and support good decision-making by the Board.
>
> **Build trust**
>
> 10. Communicate how the company is governed and is performing by maintaining a dialogue with shareholders and other relevant stakeholders.

Each of these ten principles is accompanied by an explanation of what the principle is intended to achieve plus a suggested disclosure which companies are expected to tailor (either in the annual report or on the company website).

The Code requires a company to apply the ten principles and also to publish related disclosures. The emphasis is very much on the Chair being accountable for this and for them to set out and demonstrate what they have done to meet the principles, why and how this supports the company's medium to long term success. It definitely feels *"Compliance plus"* and conveys that accountability matters.

In many countries PE and Venture Capital (VC) funds represent a significant proportion of the ownership of companies and are represented on boards, typically by the investor who did the deal but also with non-exec or outside directors who are strongly connected with the investing firm. In these situations, it is common for the investor to appoint an observer to the board whose job is principally to leverage the *"investor director"*.

Whether it is a majority or minority control situation and whether there is a sole PE or VC investor or a syndicate there is generally an investment agreement between the investor or investors and the company. It is wise if you are invited to join the board of such a company that you obtain a copy of the investment agreement and understand what the board has signed up to. While you are at it, it is also worth checking out what banking covenants are in place.

There should be an aligned interest between investor and company and how this is planned to be achieved is usually set out in a *"Value Creation Plan"*. This plan will describe the nature and time horizon of a partial or complete exit, perhaps through a listing of the business on a stock exchange or sale of the company as well as the detailed steps to be taken to grow value in the meantime. This focus on value creation and having a clear plan to support it is one of the drivers of the industry's performance but you don't need to be PE backed to take this approach. There are surprising numbers of private and quoted businesses who don't have such objectives or plans. Going through the process of coming up with one helps to sort out alignment issues and provides a good framework for decision-making.

In 2007 when the PE industry in the UK was under pressure from unions and politicians I conducted an analysis which showed for 3i where the value had been created in over 100 realised mid-market growth and buyout investments over a ten-year period. The value created was defined simply as the difference between the valuation that the original investment was made upon and that which it was sold at. This analysis showed that approximately 60 per cent of the value growth in these companies came from the growth in their earnings during the period the investment was held. A further 30 per cent came from what is known in the trade as *"multiple enhancement"*, ie the difference in the multiple of earnings that the business was sold on compared to that it was invested upon. Only approximately 10 per cent could be attributed to what might be described as financial engineering, eg having a more efficient balance sheet.

When other investors in the mid-market did the same analysis with their portfolios they found broadly the same in that the largest gains came from growing earnings and then multiple enhancement. For the large leveraged buyout houses the pattern was again broadly the same although, as one might expect, the contribution from financial engineering was higher but rarely above 20-25 per cent.

The charge against the industry was that all their profits came from job cutting and leveraging up companies, whereas the facts demon- strated that this wasn't the case and not just because earnings growth was the highest contributor. The contribution of *"multiple enhancement"* was no surprise to me as I remembered countless occasions in discussions with boards on corporate responsibility, the importance of staff engagement, good environ- mental practice and governance and so on, that these mattered not just because they were the right thing to do but also that the business would be a lot easier to sell. *"Try selling a business with a grumpy workforce, disenchanted suppliers, environmental, legal or tax issues."* was my line with the occasional rampant entrepreneur who didn't get it immediately.

There is no doubt that having PE or VC investment changes the board dynamic and the power dynamics within it. If it is a majority control investment then the PE house will usually appoint an independent Chair, put one or two of their own people on the board and have an observer attend meetings as well. The observer will usually be the person managing the investment for the PE House and will be providing the briefs and undertaking the follow-up actions on behalf of the more senior colleague on the board.

Issues can arise when the investor director, who can't get out of a representative mindset or is overly confident, doesn't feel the need to ensure others are bought into decisions and acts like they own 100 per cent. At the same time, in my career in PE I came across several business-owners who forgot when they sold a big stake in their business that they lost the right to do whatever they liked, the *"Falling in the Strid"* dilemma on page 399 being a good example. When equity changes hands so does power, even if you still have a majority. One of my favourite cartoons is *"majority of one"* by Charlie Barsotti which shows a gruff Chair-looking type peering imperiously from his desk. I have always felt that even if you do have a majority and know that the power is there if you need it, it is way more effective to put your case as if you haven't and to work hard to maximise buy in.

One of the most powerful attributes of the PE and VC model is the alignment of objectives agreed at the outset with everyone signing up to an agreed value creation plan and responsibilities and timetable for achieving it. Yet objectives can diverge over time if more money is required, if an early offer is received or if management under performs. Equity ratchets, where the management's share of the equity rises on over-performance or earlier exit, can also sometimes ironically defeat their intended purpose because of poor structuring or drafting or both. *"Liquidation preferences"* can be another source of considerable tension especially when a company is in difficulty, when further funding is required or when it is being sold for less than the total capital invested. For those unfamiliar with this term it simply describes the ranking in which people get their money back when their shares are sold. It is normal for PE and VC investors to rank ahead of management and for banks providing senior or mezzanine or secondary debt to rank ahead of the PE and VC investors.

Another aspect that can be challenging if you have a syndicate of VC investors is getting the balance right on the board between investor directors and others and managing the differing styles, experiences and preferences of the different investor directors. Typically, there will be a lead investor who will see it as their role to support the Chair by co-ordinating investor views and positions on matters. However, with humans involved and the objectives and capabilities of funds not always the same, there is the potential for the occasional challenge. Having a Chair who has experience of working with a range of VCs will help considerably.

Finally, if you are joining the board with a PE or VC firm invested, find out the life of the specific fund that is invested in the company as well as the *"follow on"* capacity. Even if all you discover is that you are one of the final investments from the fund, so patience over exit timing may not be as high and that the likelihood of further finance if you need it is low, at least you will know.

"Angel" investors can be a good source of early finance for a business but they come in many shapes and sizes from the benign family member doing you a favour with low expectations of getting their money back to the professional *"angel"* investor who has a sizeable portfolio, plays an active role and can add a lot more than money. Sadly, there are also rapacious *"devil"* investors about who love nothing more than taking advantage of the naïve. It is obvious to put the effort into knowing who is going to invest and into agreeing how the relationship is going to work in practice as well as what will happen if further funding is required.

Experienced and successful *"angel"* investors know that they will invariably end up investing more money to avoid their value being diluted by subsequent investors. They will hope that each round of funding is at a higher capitalisation than the preceding one and therefore that their initial investment grows in value. Yet early-stage businesses rarely follow a linear progression in creating value. Setbacks along the way are normal and frequently require further funding. Again, if joining a board of a small business it is important read the articles of association, understand the rights of any *"angel"* investors and look at any written agreements that might be in place.

My experience with *"angel"* investors is highly variable with some being absolutely outstanding during the early phases and providing a powerful way to boost a business to the point where it can then raise significant further investment. Others, however, can be a complete nightmare and unwittingly destroy value for themselves and others through their behaviour. As ever it comes back to judgement and doing your homework before you commit.

Family companies span the range from small- or medium-sized enterprises to some of the largest global businesses, eg US-based Walmart or German-based Robert Bosch. EY's *Global Family Business Index* (*see* Useful links, page 414) contains a fascinating analysis of the largest family companies from across the world from which it is clear that the family company model can be highly successful over long periods of time.

However, we also know, if only from legendary case studies, numerous films and TV series that the family company model also has its challenges. The *Bones & Son* case study in the *"Dilemmas"* section on page 388 gives you a good feel for some of these challenges. They typically relate to succession, decision-making, emotions clouding judgements, the negative influence of nepotism and so on, though it is worth noting that most of these challenges are not confined to family companies. Founder-led businesses, especially those with a number of founders, are equally susceptible.

It is a good idea therefore for a family business to have a *"family business constitution"*. These essentially provide an agreed framework for taking decisions, dealing with conflicts, succession and other matters. There are many professional service firms (lawyers and accountants) who have specialist units which focus on family companies and they have produced some excellent guides as to what might go in a family constitution. One I particularly like is the *"Taylor Wessing Guide"* (*see* Useful links). It is very accessible and pragmatic, written from an international perspective and contains a list of useful questions that the constitution needs to address. It's a long list which essentially covers:

- What the strategy for the ownership should be and what mechanisms there will be for agreeing, monitoring and adapting it.
- How family members can realise their investment in the company if they should choose or need to. Alongside that, what conditions or restrictions might be imposed on those wishing to sell.
- The criteria and processes for employing family members.
- The processes for resolving conflicts or disputes.
- How future generations might engage with the family business and the distribution of its wealth.
- The governance of the company and the governance of family decisions relating to the company. This includes family representation on the board.
- Leadership, when should it change, the criteria and process for succession.
- The involvement of non-family members, or trusted advisers including whether family members have the right to involve their own trusted advisers on specific issues.

Being a non-family member of a family company board can be both fascinating and frustrating. You ought to have the increased power of independence, objectivity and being different. At the same time you may feel an outsider and not part of the inner sanctum where the big decisions get made. Having worked with many family companies across the world at 3i, large and small, successful and otherwise, the balance for me was hugely positive. Of course there were many dramatic occasions where family feelings got in the way of good business sense and you needed all of your conflict management skills, but most times common sense and common interest prevailed and long-term, stewardship mind-set won through.

Independent growth business boards can be tremendously enjoyable to be part of and they are rich in issues to deal with. If not PE- or VC-backed they are usually owned by the founders or entrepreneurs who have bought them. Here, other than the usual issues relating to growth and scale, the challenges for independent directors often relate to dealing with dominant individuals or the diverging objectives and capabilities of the founders. These are dealt with in the "*People*" section as well as in the "*Dilemmas*" section. "*The Departing Director*" on page 281 deals with diverging capabilities and interests as well as a breakdown in relationships between founders and *"The radio-controlled accountant"* on page 299 covers the challenges of dependence on key people and attracting talent to smaller companies.

Another challenge for independent directors in such companies might simply be your fit with them. If you aren't used to thinly-resourced environments where the power balance between the company and its customers and suppliers is different, where you have to influence rather than instruct, it can be disorientating.

Charities and social enterprises

Most countries will have a regulatory body which oversees the charities registered in its country, eg the *"Charity Commission"* in the UK or the *"NGOs Co-ordination Board"* in Kenya.

In the US they tend to be regulated both at a Federal and State level. At the Federal level, the Internal Revenue Service (US Tax Authority) grants tax-exempt status to eligible charities and regulates their activities to ensure that they serve the public good. At the State level it is all about oversight of fund-raising and other activities carried out within the State and the Attorney General of the State also has certain other powers such as approving asset transfers.

The description of the mandate for the NGOs Co-ordination Board in Kenya which is to:

- maintain the register of National and International NGOs operating in Kenya, with the precise sectors, affiliations and locations of their activities,
- receive and discuss the annual reports of NGOs, and
- advise the government on the activities of the NGOs and their role in national development within Kenya;

is fairly typical of the approach taken, but many countries also see the role of the regulator as one of promulgating best practice as well as providing oversight.

For charities and social enterprises the beneficiaries assume primacy in thinking and decision-making and it is common to have beneficiaries or former beneficiaries on the board.

At both Leap Confronting Conflict and the EY Foundation, which I have chaired and Chair now, this has worked well. Leap and EYF both support young people, one in helping them manage conflict more effectively and the other in helping young people facing barriers in getting from school to work. Having alumni from our programmes on the board has been fundamental to our success. Placing them at the *"Head and Heart"*, as we say, has led to better decisions, greater legitimacy and helped to make it absolutely clear what our impact can be.

However, not everyone has had the same experience and things sometimes don't work out either for board or beneficiary. The worst examples are where the trustee with beneficiary experience is a token, lonely and not given the support. Sometimes it is because the trustee can't get out of representative mode or feels that because they are a beneficiary their views must always be right. Not much different to some other sorts of representative directors then I hear you say.

To make it work requires a lot of forethought, commitment and increased work. From experience, you can increase your chances of success through the following:

- Having more than one. I've found it has always been helpful to have two. Having a kindred spirit around the board table, them not feeling quite so different at the start helps as well as gaining a broader range of beneficiary input.
- Considering them as *"trustee with beneficiary experience"* rather than a *"beneficiary trustee"*. After all a trustee is a trustee and you don't label other trustees like that or confine their contributions to their area of expertise.
- Never assume that the trustee with beneficiary experience is speaking for all beneficiaries.
- Invest in the additional support required to induct and support them thereafter.
- Have an executive and trustee buddy system where each trustee with beneficiary experience has a trustee and an executive buddy to speak to between boards.
- Involve them in a sub-committee and again support them to help them up the knowledge curve in that area.
- Finally, remember that it may of course be the case that the

beneficiary trustee may have a lot more relevant experience than others around the table.

The stand out example for me of a trustee with beneficiary experience making a contribution, well in advance of what one might normally expect, was Peter Olawaye, a young trustee at Leap. Shortly after being appointed I asked him if he was up for conducting the board review for that year. It seemed a good way of helping him get up the learning curve on what a board was for and what might be best practice as well as engage with all of the board members and executive on something that really mattered. After some understandable initial anxiety Peter did a tremendous job and managed to gain insights from the trustees and team that I really don't think we would have got from more conventional approaches. His recommendations were spot on, grounded, practical and, most importantly, implemented.

Increasingly, charities have used a broader range of types of finance to fund their development from traditional pure unrestricted grant finance, through various forms of debt to very specific "*stapled to impact*" finance where the amount of funds is tied to specific deliverables. The growth of "*social*" finance and "*venture philanthropy*" has in some ways mirrored that of VC. An industry has grown both to provide the funds and to advise both charities and funders on raising finance, investing in the sector and other specific forms of advice, including impact assessment.

Grant funders cover a broad spectrum from the world's major foundations to small individual charities. Practices vary considerably but they will tend not to take board seats preferring to govern their investment through a funding agreement which sets out reporting requirements and adherence to certain practices and standards.

Their investments will essentially be either "*project*" or "*core*" funding, with "*core*" being for building core capabilities, eg an IT system or key leadership roles. An important distinction is whether the funding is provided on a "*restricted*" or "*unrestricted*" basis and, if all of the money granted is not used for the purpose originally intended, whether the remaining amount needs to be returned to the funder.

The debate around the level of unrestricted reserves that a charity should hold revolves around the balance between maximising today's impact with the funds that you have at your disposal at the same time as ensuring sustainability so that you can continue to support beneficiaries. Ideally the board will develop a mix of income streams that satisfy both and the reserves policy will reflect that as well as the nature of the organisation.

Before joining the board of any charity it is important to get the FD to go through the profile of current funding and to understand the charity's reserves position in terms of restricted and unrestricted reserves.

Two of the first organisations in the "*social finance*" space in the UK were Bridges Fund Management (originally Bridges Ventures) and Impetus Trust, both founded by successful PE leaders, Sir Ronald Cohen and Stephen Dawson OBE, respectively. When it was founded in 2002 Bridges had £10 million as its first fund and 3i was one of the investors. It was an investment that raised a few eyebrows at the time. Since then Bridges has raised over £900m across its platform of funds, pioneered many of the techniques used in social impact investing and, much more importantly, has fuelled the growth of some of the country's most successful social enterprises. As a former member of the advisory board for the Social Entrepreneurs Fund I have seen first-hand the power of the model and the focus on a balance of social and commercial key performance indicators with the social coming first.

Impetus Trust (now Impetus PEF) was founded at about the same time. One of its first investments was £100k in Leap Confronting Conflict, the youth and conflict charity where I was on the board and became Chair. For Leap at the time this funding was catalytic as it was for investment in our capabilities, both management and facilities. Yet the biggest value was the due diligence process which, despite almost overwhelming our thin resource at the time, forced us to focus on where we could have the greatest impact in the most effective way.

A very positive development in some countries over the last few years has been the rise of the "*young*" trustee. Historically many people left it until their executive careers were coming to an end before they joined charity boards. More recently, as in other sectors, Chairs have seen the great benefits of having a broader range of ages on their boards and at the same time a growing "*social conscience*" has led younger people to want to become engaged throughout their careers. My experience at Leap Confronting Conflict and at the EY Foundation was that our younger board members add a huge amount of value to our thinking and they do so because they are thought of as equals as trustees and not some sort of second tier. It is also the case that you don't have to be a youth-focused charity to gain benefit from younger trustees.

A less positive development has been the number of scandals and failures of governance in a number of high-profile charities. These failures have been on a range of issues from safeguarding to financial management as well as risk management and impropriety. They have been damaging to the sector globally and led to an understandable reaction from both governments and the public which has impacted on trust in the sector. This is especially disappointing as at the time of writing the need for charities and social enterprises to support communities appears to be growing just as generating income has become harder than ever.

All of these developments, combined with the impact of the pandemic, have meant that the nature of the role and the time commitment for trustees on charity boards has changed. Expectations, transparency and the logistical demands of the role are higher and the pool of potential candidates is also now much broader than before. At the same time potential trustees are tending to be more vigilant in their due diligence before they take appointments. A good thing.

Professional services firms

The professional service firms are a fascinating area regarding governance and it is a huge sector globally. Their complex structures combined with ever more challenging regulatory environments and demands for greater transparency are just some of the pressures forcing change. Add to this the challenges of achieving partner buy-in, containing risk, making timely decisions in the interests of the firm as a whole and ever broadening portfolios of services and it looks like a challenging time ahead for those responsible for their governance.

The stakeholder context is very different to public companies or the PE-backed world: the "*investors*" are the "*partners*", the regulators have oversight typically through their "*performance and conduct*" mandates and custom and practice has developed in each segment. For the bigger multi-service offering firms the very well-intended *"independence"* regulations can make it difficult to find board members or advisory council members who can do the job. This is especially the case for those firms offering audit services in the more developed markets. The firms ideally want people who currently serve on the boards of major organisations. As a consequence, finding one who is not on the board of an organisation audited or being pitched to by the firm can be hard.

The variety in scale and reach of firms and the fact that many have diverse sets of offerings, eg law and accountancy, means that there are a myriad of different governance models in practice from the *"kitchen table"* style to those aiming to mirror the principles and practices of large listed businesses

In some firms the number of partners runs into thousands and to those responsible for leading them it can feel sometimes like having all of the burden of running a public company without the benefits. The partnership structure clearly makes it challenging to have a traditional "*corporate*" governance approach so many end up having independent advisory boards or councils to supplement a partnership council which provides governance oversight on behalf of the partners of the firm.

As you might expect the leading firms in each sector tend to be more transparent about how they are run and governed, eg EY and Clifford Chance lay it all out on their websites. In general, the management consultancies tend to be less transparent. However, I suspect that this will change as a result of increased spending by governments on consulting services as a result of the pandemic and a number of high-profile issues.

Finally, I would say that if you wanted to become a member of a professional service firm board you'd better brush up on your knowledge of insurance. The frequency and level of claims over the last decade has increased significantly and, as a consequence, is now a major and regular topic for their boards.

Public bodies

Public body boards are another area where the landscape for boards is changing globally. Quite rightly, governments have a need to show taxpayers and users of services provided by such bodies that they are well governed in every respect. Those interested in serving on such boards are generally public-spirited and expect, and are prepared, to provide their skills and experiences for well below their market rate. However, in recent years in some countries, the UK being one of them, the growing asymmetry between fulfilment and the amount of work, risk and pure hassle has led to many people who would be able to add a great deal to such boards finding other ways to contribute to society.

In many countries government departments have also been appointing independent non-executives and although best practice is developing in this space there are many examples of this adding considerable value. The remit of these boards (see Useful links, page 411) generally makes it clear that they are advisory, eg the UK Code of Governance for such boards states:

> "Boards are advisory in the sense that they will provide advice to the department on issues within their remit, such as strategy and the deliverability of policies. They are supervisory in the sense that they scrutinise reporting from the department on performance, and challenge the department on how well it is achieving its objectives.
>
> Policy will be decided by ministers alone, with advice from officials. Boards will give advice and support on the operational implications and effectiveness of policy proposals, focusing on getting policy translated into results. They will operate according to recognised precepts of good corporate governance in business: leadership, effectiveness, accountability and sustainability.
>
> Boards advise on, and supervise, five main areas: strategic clarity, commercial sense, talented people, results focus, and management information."

The wise on such department boards will be well aware of where the power really lies and alert to the *"majority of one"* power of a minister. The chairing of these boards by Secretaries of State in the UK and the fact that the governance liability typically rests with the lead civil servant adds an interesting dynamic. In many countries, the UK included, the accounting officer is defined as: *"Those civil servants whom Parliament holds directly to account for the stewardship of resources within their department's control."* This can be disorientating for board members who come from other sectors where it is the board that is jointly and severally liable. Lest you think that this is therefore an easy ride, the *"court of public opinion"* is frequently capable of providing severe punishment for poor governance or decisions.

Most government departments are of the scale of large corporates and have common challenges in terms of retaining clarity of purpose, attracting and developing talent and dealing with rapid changes in technology, communications and expectations. However, the annual budget mind-set and the short tenure of ministers can often bring an overweight focus on the short-term or how the media might respond at the expense of the future.

For government and other public body boards the world has moved on considerably from the days where the investors tended to be simply the nation's taxpayers and national debt. A whole host of commercial funding, typically through public private partnerships, is provided to or through governments these days. So, it is just as important if you are joining the board of a government or public body to understand its financial dynamics as any other sort of organisation.

There are numerous types of public body boards, eg hospital boards and regulators. They will differ from country to country depending upon the degree of state ownership. In the UK public hospitals operate through the legal entity of Public Benefit Corporations known as National Health Service Trusts. These Trusts have unitary boards and are held accountable by a sector regulator called Monitor, the Care Quality Commission and the National Health Development Agency, as well as by a local council of governors. There is an extensive Code of Governance and this is commented on more fully in the section on codes (*see* page 76).

A major challenge for NHS Trust boards is striking the balance between what they need and expect of board members and being realistic and reasonable about the demands placed on people who take on these roles. In the first edition of this book, just before the pandemic struck I said that *"I have huge admiration for those who do (take on these roles) and for the commitment that they make out of public-spiritedness, given the volume of work, responsibilities and reputational risk that they assume."*

That admiration has grown even greater as a result of the events since. the resilience of character, quality of judgement and level of support from board members in health has been an inspiration. Rightly they have tried to ensure that the lion's share of praise goes to their teams, especially those on the front-line but I think it right that their contribution is also acknowledged.

Universities

University boards can also make for fascinating appointments. These are complex organisations with demanding stakeholders and a heavy regulatory influence in most countries. They are legitimately polymath in purpose, subject to a wide range of external influences and have an interesting mix of short- and long-term decisions to make. My time on the University of Warwick board was endlessly interesting and challenging. Not least because of the diverse cocktail of board members including faculty, students and people from a wide cross-section of society. At Warwick our commercial activities strengthened our ability to boost academic excellence and sustainability and that was seen as their purpose.

A frequent challenge for university boards is often their size. In an attempt to achieve diversity and satisfy the needs of a wide range of stakeholders they can often end up being too big. The common way to address the challenge is to use some of the sub-committees effectively as the real decision-making bodies, with the board as a whole then effectively confirming or endorsing their decisions. In the UK the finance and general purposes committee tends to be the powerhouse in this context.

The role of the academic board, often called a *"senate"* is also interesting and occasionally a source of tension with a university board. Senates are usually responsible for all matters academic including, but not always, authorising admission, degrees, honorary degrees as well as the discipline of students and faculty. The members of the senate will also see an important role for themselves in terms of upholding academic freedom and integrity and will generally be comprised solely of academics. Justifiably some would claim that it is such senates that have protected what is most precious about some of the world's leading centres of educational excellence in terms of academic freedom for centuries. At the same time many, including some of the same people, would claim that they have from time-to-time stifled innovation and protected under-performing academics.

University boards have had a tough time reconciling and balancing the wants and needs of their various stakeholders through the pandemic with stretched resources, significant uncertainty and limited room for manouevre. In the UK they have also had to deal with the severe disruption arising from BREXIT in relation to freedom of movement, research funding, the ERASMUS programme and the resultant negative perceptions about the UK's receptiveness to foreigners.

Media and social media

I thought long and hard about including these few paragraphs on the influence of media on boards. However, I think that it is very worth- while and I have experienced at first hand as a FTSE 100 Communications director in the past how this can be both tremendously positive and destructive. Of course, the media varies by country and by sector in terms of its vigilance, its attitude to boards and its quality.

From a positive perspective, a high-quality press, ie one which is vigilant, well informed and balanced, fulfils a very important role in holding boards to account when required and acting as a deterrent to poor performance or a lack of social responsibility. A press which gives due credit to success can also inspire others to create wealth and employment, to invest or to take on challenging public roles.

Sadly, the current environment for the press is not always conducive to quality. An age which demands instant response and analysis, where often journalists are freelancers being paid per article and where attention and retention spans seem to be decreasing has an impact on quality. Many publications or websites now just simply don't have the resources, institutional knowledge, process or time to research, to refine and to accurately and fairly report on an issue in a balanced way and put it into context.

There is also a big difference between healthy scepticism and cynicism. Naturally any board will know that it is an asymmetric game and that the standards by which you are held to account are not necessarily always being held by those who are holding you to account. The idea for the short piece on dealing with *"asymmetric sensitivity"* on page 102 was born out of a conversation with a journalist.

The highest quality journalists are adept at spotting someone with an interest in manipulating or using them. Sadly, as with board members, not all journalists are of the highest quality. There can be occasions where those with an interest or axe to grind will carefully feign knowledge or simply just have a hypothesis they are looking to prove no matter what.

I passionately believe that honesty is the best policy and that it is much better to declare an issue than have someone else do it for you. Yet, it can be incredibly disappointing if the response to honesty is disproportionate and sensationalist.

From a board perspective, when ensuring that the organisation has the right resources to deliver its vision and strategy the board must make sure that the organisation has an appropriately strong communications function whether that is in-house or outsourced. It also needs to place as much emphasis on internal communications as external. The role of the communications director and the pros and cons of having a fully integrated communications function are discussed on page 46.

Other than in dictatorships few people have had the possibility, power or capability to control the press. Even some of the mightiest organisations in history have failed at that game. The advent of social media has provided an additional set of communications channels. It has created another set of highly cost-effective channels and techniques to gain direct access to its stakeholders. This access can be used to engage, to inform, to gather intelligence and to build a stronger brand. Equally if there is a problem and an organisation isn't social media savvy or doesn't have the mind-set or capabilities it can amplify problems disproportionately and enable significant damage to be done.

These days there are a few important questions to ask before you join a board and some basic rules about social media once you are on a board. Before we join a board no matter what size or nature of organisation we should go back to the three P's ("*Purpose, People and Process*") and the 3 R's ("*Right strategy, Right resources and Right governance*"). We need to know what the organisation's perspective is on social media with respect to both supporting its vision and strategy as well as managing the risks involved. We need to know that it has an appropriate and realistic strategy for social media and that it has the right resources and governance in place to execute that strategy.

We can usually tell how savvy a company is by looking at what it has on the main social media platforms and by the way it talks about its social media presence. If it talks about the number of followers or connections then it tends to be fairly unsophisticated, if it talks about how it developed a presence in a market through social media before it launched there and got off to a flying start then that will give you a different feeling. If on "*Glass Door*" (*see* Useful links), a site that contains views of current and former employees about what it is like to work at the company, we spot that there is something controversial on there, then it is worth finding out whether they know. We also need to know whether the organisation is responding rather than reacting to negative comment on social media and whether its responses are proportionate.

As a candidate for a board position we ought also to assume that our own presence on social media will be looked at and be very conscious of what we have posted.

Governance advisory services

If you are on the board of a listed company then you will probably be familiar with a range of governance advisory services and used to seeing their reports just before your AGM. These are generally businesses but sometimes are campaigning groups. They tend to produce research and analysis and advisory reports to help shareholders vote on resolutions as well as a range of other services including proxy voting systems. They range from niche issue-focused consultancies to major international groups serving some of the world's biggest institutional investors.

The classic services provided by these firms are the company report prior to a company's AGM or specific issues-based reports, typically on a governance or responsibility issue. The pre-AGM report will tend to focus on advice on which way to vote on resolutions including a narrative based on relevant best practice and peer group practice to support it. However, it is also possible that it will include reviews and commentary on the governance of the company, including compliance with:

- relevant governance Codes, board composition, independence and attendance, auditor independence etc;
- remuneration both in terms of quantum and policy and practice in relation to performance, including pension arrangements, share incentives and the dealing in shares of the company by any of the directors;
- responsibility topics such as environmental, employee arrangements, health and safety and so on; and
- other relevant issues for the time period concerned, eg significant acquisitions by the company or bids for the company.

In my view they fulfil a useful purpose even if some can be superficial, obsessed with form over substance and consume large amounts of your investor relations or group secretariat team's time. Knowing that someone independent with a critical eye is looking at all of these things and has influence over the voting at your AGM is another helpful influence driving quality.

Directors' duties

Clearly, all of that goes before this in terms of the roles of directors or trustees must be placed in the context of the law and the duties of directors and trustees under law. I am not a lawyer but let me get my disclaimer in here. As the law is constantly evolving and differs from context to context you should not rely wholly on what follows and check things with either the company's or, when appropriate, your own legal adviser before taking action.

I've had the privilege to work with many lawyers who have delivered legal duties sessions for budding directors or trustees. They generally tend to follow the following pattern:

- scare the **** out of the gathering;
- build them back up with some sensible tips so as not to scare them off completely; and finally
- make sure that they remember to call their lawyer when they need to.

Three who get the balance spot on are Paul Dixon at Slaughter and May, Simon Witney at Travers Smith and Plimpton and Martin Webster at Pinsent Masons.

Paul uses the very good slide (*see* Fig. 1.8) on a *"Financial Times Board Director Programme"* course. It summarises four categories of things that you need to take into account when thinking about your duties as a director which pretty much transcend countries and types of organisations.

Before we take each in turn it is worth a moment to consider who is a director, as in the UK and in many other countries it is not as obvious as it may seem. Directors can be *"appointed"*, *"de-facto* "or *"shadow"*. The distinction being that those who are considered *"de-facto"* are those seen to act as a director and those considered *"shadow"* offer advice and instructions behind the scenes. Why does it matter? Because if you behave like a de-facto or shadow director then a court might consider that you have the same duties and responsibilities.

Statutory duties and obligations

The acts governing statutory duties will differ from country to country taking into account the relevant model of governance for the country as a whole and for the category of company in particular. For example, in the UK the model is for a unitary board, whereas for Holland it is for a two-tier system with a *"management board"* and a *"supervisory board"*. Things get a bit more complicated in Germany and Italy where, depending upon the category of company, it may be a unitary or two-tier system.

Figure 1:8 Directors' duties

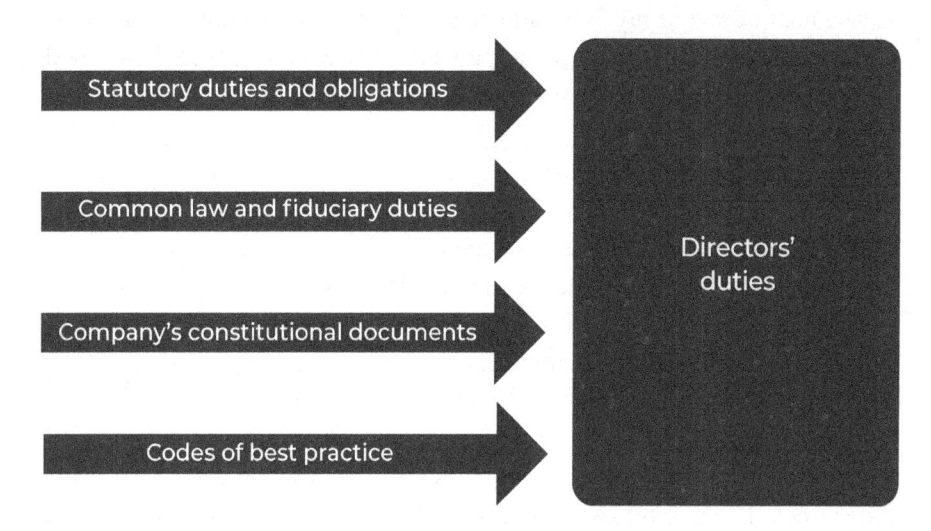

- Statutory duties and obligations
- Common law and fiduciary duties
- Company's constitutional documents
- Codes of best practice

→ Directors' duties

Whatever the system the Companies Acts tend to be left alone for a decade of two with only minor revisions before undergoing major reviews. Their content generally summarises the core duties and obligations and then clarifies definitions.

At the time of writing in the UK, where there is a unitary board system, the critical Act is *"The Companies Act 2006"*. The Act sets out seven duties for directors and these are the duty to:

- act within powers;
- promote the success of the company;
- exercise independent judgement;
- use reasonable care, skill and diligence;
- avoid conflicts of interest;
- not accept benefits from third parties; and
- declare any interests in proposed transactions or arrangements.

What is meant by *"acting within powers"* is simply that a director must act in accordance with the company's constitution (which includes its articles of association and shareholder resolutions) and must only exercise their powers for their proper purpose.

Considering the second one of these duties on promoting the success of the company, it is natural to wonder what is meant by success. Much to the amusement of one of my German friends the interesting thing is that in the UK it is left to the directors to determine exactly what this is in the context of their company. However, they are required to have regard to the following:

- long-term consequences;
- the interests of employees;
- high standards of business conduct;
- the impact on community and environment;
- fostering business relationships; and
- act fairly between members.

There's a similar issue with regard to the fourth duty. You may well wonder what on earth *"reasonable"* means as well as who gets to make the judgement. The answer to *"who says"* is effectively a court when it's all gone wrong. When it comes to what is *"reasonable"* the Act says helpfully in Section 174 that there are two tests, one objective and the other subjective.

> "The section provides that a director owes a duty to his company to exercise the same standard of care, skill and diligence that would be exercised by a reasonably diligent person with:
>
> a. the general knowledge, skill and experience that may reasonably be expected of a person carrying out the same functions as the director in relation to that company (an objective test);
>
> and
>
> b. the general knowledge, skill and experience that the director actually has (a subjective test)."

Conflicts of interest can be either direct or indirect. A direct conflict of interest might be when you have a direct personal interest in a decision, perhaps where you stand to make personal financial gain from a transaction or investment being considered. An indirect example might be where you are on the board of a supplier or where you are on the boards of both the acquirer and the target in an acquisition situation.

On avoiding conflict of interests, the key points are to:

- know what a conflict of interest is, which, for the purposes of the Act, is essentially a personal interest either directly or indirectly which does or might conflict with the company's interests;
- have a good process for declaring and communicating interests, in a timely manner;
- keep a register of interests;
- ensure that you don't take part in decisions where you have a conflict or, where allowable, gain authorisation to do so; and finally
- make sure that this is minuted.

The Act also covers *"indemnities for directors"*, allowing the provision for a company to provide a limited indemnity to a director in relation to the liability of that director to third parties. Such an indemnity cannot cover criminal and regulatory fines or legal fees in the event of an unsuccessful criminal defence and no indemnity can be given in relation to liability of a director to the company itself. However, and somewhat surprisingly, there is a provision to allow the company to pay a director's legal fees, even for an action brought by the company. Although if the director is unsuccessful in his defence the fees would be repayable by him to the company.

For those companies in difficulty there is one very important point in terms of duties and responsibilities. Where there is an insolvency, or a threat of an insolvency, the law specifies that the interests of the company are to be regarded as broadly equivalent to the interests of the creditors of the company. Once a liquidator is appointed their authority replaces that of shareholders and directors and the liquidator's obligation is to maximise returns to creditors. Therefore, a director in such circumstances should act in the best interests of the creditors.

The critical thing for directors is to anticipate such a situation and take expert professional advice ahead of time. Not just so that they can take the right actions but also do so in the right way with the proper accompanying records so that if they need to they can demonstrate later that they operated in a responsible manner and in line with their obligations. Given the complexity of insolvency law and the variety of approaches taken internationally I won't comment further here.

In the UK the Government also published a white paper for consultation in March 2021. It's title *"Restoring Trust in Audit and Corporate Governance"* was clear and although its major focus is on issues relating to audits and audit firms there is a suggested step increase towards a Sarbanes Oxley approach when it comes to directors responsibilities. The extract below makes this clear.

> Plans also aim to make directors of the country's biggest companies more accountable if they have been negligent in their duties – reflecting the level of responsibility that comes with holding such a position:
>
> - directors of large businesses could face fines or suspensions in the most serious cases of failings – such as significant errors with accounts, hiding crucial information from auditors, or leaving the door open to fraud;
> - under the UK's Corporate Governance Code, companies could be expected to write into directors' contracts that their bonuses will be repaid in the event of collapses or serious director failings up to two years after the pay award is made, clamping down on *"rewards for failure"*;
> - large businesses would need to be more transparent about the state of their finances, so they do not pay out dividends and bonuses at a time when they could be facing insolvency. Directors would also publish annual 'resilience statements' that set out how their organisation is mitigating short and long-term risks, encouraging their directors to focus on the long-term success of the company and consider key issues like the impact of climate change

It will be interesting to see how this plays out and where the balance is struck.

Common law and fiduciary duties

Again I am not a lawyer so please excuse my layman's description of common law as essentially all of the legal precedents and judgements that have been made in court. A *"fiduciary"* is a person in whom trust has been placed, eg a shareholder and a board member or a beneficiary and a trustee. With that trust goes the obligation to act in someone else's benefit.

Company's constitutional documents

The "*Articles of Association*" will be the core document governing this area for businesses and there are equivalent governing documents for charitable companies or charitable trusts (*see* below). It sets out in writing the rules agreed by the shareholders, directors and company secretary for running the company. The articles can be amended/updated but only by following a specific process which involves the approval of shareholders/members.

The UK and many other governments have produced "*model*" articles and details on the processes to be followed for amending or updating them are available online (*see* Useful links).

At time of writing the "*model*" articles for private and public businesses in the UK consist of five parts:

- Interpretation and limitation of liability.
- Directors' powers and responsibilities, decision-making and the appointment of directors.
- Shares and distributions.
- Decision-making by shareholders.
- Administrative arrangements.

The equivalent "*model*" documents for charities of various constructions follow similar patterns.

It is important if you are a director to ensure that the company's articles are up to date and it is generally the responsibility of whoever is fulfilling the company secretariat function to alert the board and produce the necessary resolutions to effect the change.

Another consideration is that of other regulatory requirements, eg "*the listing rules*" for public companies. In the Financial Services sector many countries have what is known as a "*senior managers' regime*"; in the Accounting and Advisory sector the "*independence regulations*" and so on. The final point with regard to legal duties is to make sure that the organisation has the appropriate level of legal advice. There may be times when the directors may need independent legal advice and in some situations, perhaps a bid for the company, the company will fund these subject to an agreed brief and limited amount.

Codes of best practice

Most countries have governance codes for different categories of organisations whether they be public bodies, listed companies, charities and other sorts of organisations. These are usually created and refreshed by the relevant regulators and often follow a major failure in governance in a high-profile organisation. Here we will look at the some of the key developments and codes in the UK; a large list of codes for other countries are available on the ECGI website at https://ecgi.global.

When it comes to the purpose of these codes the Governance Code for National Health Service foundation trusts in the UK makes the point well in its introduction:

> *"We bring together the best practices of the public and private sector in order to help NHS foundation trust boards maintain good quality corporate governance. We believe this is necessary if the needs of patients are to be met."*

A good example of a code that is highly relevant for the largest businesses is the FRC's UK Corporate Governance Code for public companies which are *"premium listed"* (*see* Useful links, page 411). *"Premium Listing"* is described by The London Stock Exchange as follows:

> *"A Premium Listing means the company is expected to meet the UK's highest standards of regulation and corporate governance – and as a consequence may enjoy a lower cost of capital through greater transparency and through building investor confidence."*

The nature of the Code is one of *"comply or explain"*, ie if you don't comply with an aspect of the Code you must explain why not, usually in your annual report. This approach, first introduced as a result of the Cadbury review (see below), has been picked up internationally by numerous countries but there are others, eg India and the US, which prefer what's described as a *"comply or else"* approach.

The introduction to the UK Code, at time of writing *"The Corporate Governance Code 2018"*, continues the Cadbury tradition by saying:

"The Code does not set out a rigid set of rules; instead it offers flexibility through the application of Principles and through 'comply or explain' Provisions and supporting guidance. It is the responsibility of boards to use this flexibility wisely and of investors and their advisors to assess differing company approaches thoughtfully."

The increased emphasis on purpose and culture in the Code reflected the wider debate about the role of business post the financial crash in 2007/8. The confidence demonstrated in the unitary board model and the credit given to the investment community for their role in the introduction to the Code is also interesting.

"The principle of collective responsibility within a unitary board has been a success and - alongside the stewardship activities of investors – played a vital role in delivering high standards of governance and encouraging long term investment."

We saw on page 50 a good example of one of these investor activities.

The structure of the 2018 Code is to focus on five areas:

1. Board leadership and company purpose.
2. Division of responsibilities.
3. Composition, selection and evaluation.
4. Audit, risk and internal control.
5. Remuneration

All of these are covered in this or the *"People"* or *"Process"* sections so I won't comment further here, other than to say that what happens in the largest and most high-profile organisations influences what happens more generally. There is a lot in this latest UK Code in terms of basic principles (eg appointment of directors) that is relevant to a much broader range of organisations and can be applied in a practical and relevant way.

One of the most useful things about the Code refresh was the statement and clarity of communication of the principles which should be applied to each of the five areas stated above:

"By applying the Principles, following the more detailed Provi- sions and using the associated guidance, companies can demon- strate throughout their reporting how the governance of the company contributes to its long-term sustainable success and achieves wider objectives.

Achieving this depends crucially on the way boards and companies apply the spirit of the Principles."

The statement places an onus on both boards and investors to exercise judgement and to be thoughtful. This brings a helpful balance to things and was most welcome.

Where we have got to with this Code is the result of three predecessor codes each shaping the landscape in this area in the UK and more broadly. Each one has built on the one before and they have pretty much remained intact throughout the various refreshes and updates. These were:

- **Cadbury** in 1992: The seminal work from the late Sir Adrian Cadbury, a former Olympic rower and Chair of Cadbury Schweppes plc, at the time a large global UK listed business. This set out the fundamentals and captured most of the key aspects of governance. It was widely praised and accepted and became the bedrock upon which everything else has been built. (*See* Useful links, page 411.)

- **Greenbury** in 1995: This was led by the UK's Confederation of British Industry. It was principally focused on remuneration issues following a period of political and press pressure on FTSE 100 salary packages, especially those in former state- owned utilities. Its Chair, Sir Richard Greenbury, was at the time Chair of Marks & Spencer then one of the most highly regarded companies in the UK. The Review was far more controversial and, given the nature of what it was trying to do, had numerous challenges in coming up with the right balance of principle and practicality.

- **Higgs** in 2003: The late Sir Derek Higgs, an investment banker, was initially charged with providing an update of the Code. However, his Review turned out to be far more than a simple refresh and update. The creation of the formal role of the Senior Independent Director, the work on diversity which led to the creation of the 30% Club and the emphasis on director development and training were all significant and have stood the test of time.

It is not that common internationally for large private companies to be subject to codes of governance but this may well change following the 2018 publication of the Wates' Review in the UK. The exact title was *"Corporate Governance Principles for Large Private companies"* (*see* Useful links, page 412). This was essentially a commonsense version of the codes for listed companies adapted to suit the private nature of the businesses. The primary target groups were both large Private Equity backed businesses and family and entrepreneurial concerns with dominant owners. The criteria were that a governance statement is required if the organisation has either more than 2,000 employees, or turnover (revenue) of more than £200 million and a balance sheet of more than £2 billion (or both), ie pretty large companies.

The Charity Commission in the UK and equivalent bodies in other countries have produced *"Codes"* and *"Best practice guides"* for charities. The *"Useful links"* section of the Bibliography contains a list of such codes with their corresponding website links. As with the UK ones, they generally cover the following: organisational purpose, leadership, integrity, decision-making, risk and control, board effectiveness, diversity and openness and accountability.

The two I tend to refer to most are *"The Essential Trustee: What you need to know, what you need to do"* and the *"NCVO Charity Governance Code"* (*see* Useful Links, page 425). At the charities I chair these form an important part of the induction pack. They are highly accessible and, as commented earlier the *"must"* and *"should"* distinctions are very helpful. One word of caution in the UK is that the devolved nations (Scotland, Wales and Northern Ireland) have their own Charity Codes. For public bodies in the UK there are various codes to consider. The central government departments have their own code (*see* Useful links, page 411) and there is a strong echo of Cadbury in it as this quote from the introduction on the website at time of writing demonstrates:

> "This code lays out the model for departmental boards, chaired by Secretaries of State and involving ministers, civil servants and non-executive board members. The code is accompanied by a guidance note, which provides guidance on how departments may practically implement the requirements laid out in the code.
>
> Boards help departments and government succeed in achieving their aims by encouraging good planning, managing performance regularly and raising delivery capability. They also help foster a culture of openness and good governance by providing a clear oversight structure.
>
> The code provides for a 'comply or explain' approach, whereby a department can depart from the code's provisions provided the reasons are explained in its annual governance statement accompanying the department's accounts.
>
> The principles outlined in the code will also prove useful for other parts of central government and they are encouraged to apply arrangements suitably adapted for their organisation."

The UK Government also has a code of governance for National Health Service foundation trusts (*see* Useful links, page 411). This code again is "*comply or explain*" in nature although there are some elements which are mandatory, ie your licence to operate depends upon compliance, because they are statutory duties. One of these is particularly interesting:

"The council of governors has a statutory duty to hold the Non-Executive directors individually and collectively to account for the performance of the board of directors."

As the council of governors selects the board and holds it to account, it feels as if this is where the fundamental power lies. Not exactly, as an organisation called Monitor is the sector regulator for health services and the independent regulator of NHS foundation trusts and they have a governance code for governors. Then there is the Care Quality Commission, the independent regulator of health and adult social care in England who also have a guide for governors. Finally, there is the National Health Development Authority which is responsible for overseeing the performance management and governance of NHS Trusts, including clinical quality, and managing their progress towards Foundation Trust status. So you have to enjoy complexity to be on an NHS Foundation Trust and to have considerable time for regulatory and compliance matters.

Having said all of that the NHS Foundation Code sets legitimately high expectations given the life or death nature of what these organisations do and it is written in a very accessible style.

Other than this complex governance architecture, other points of note in the Code are the emphasis on behaviours, the use of the inelegant politically-correct "*Chairperson*" word (Page 24), the guidance on what independence means and finally on what is expected in terms of managing relations with stakeholders.

The university sector looks relatively light compared to the health sector in many countries in terms of the complexity of its governance structures and the regulatory burden for board members. However, in recent years this seems to be changing: a new regulator in the UK, "*The Office for Students*" came into force in 2018. The unfortunately or perhaps ironically named TOFS, is:

> "*Designed to champion the interests of students, promote choice and help to ensure that students are receiving a good deal for their investment in higher education.*"

There has been much heated debate about whether this is the right name and approach for the sector's regulator. Although, clearly students are the main beneficiaries of the sector and, in recent years in the UK, they have been funding their own education (assuming they graduate and end up with jobs that can repay their loans) they are not the only stakeholders. Academics being just one other group that may feel they have a stake in the sector. The jury is out and time and the behaviour of the regulator, politicians and the universities will tell whether this was the right thing to do.

In the UK the main code of relevance is the Higher Education Code of

Governance issued by the Committee of University Chairs in 2014 (*see* Useful links) and guess what the academic sector has come up with, its own variant of *"comply or explain"* and *"must"* and *"should"*: it is *"apply and explain"* and *"must, should and could"*.

One thing I quite like about this Code is the section describing a set of core values for HE governance and these are:

- Autonomy as the best guarantee of quality and international reputation.
- Academic freedom and high-quality research, scholarship and teaching.
- Protecting the collective student interest through good governance.
- The publication of accurate and transparent information that is publicly accessible.
- A recognition that accountability for funding derived directly from stakeholders requires Higher Education Institutions to be clear that they are in a contract with stakeholders who pay for their service and expect clarity about what is received.
- The achievement of equality of opportunity and diversity throughout the institution.
- The principle that Higher Education should be available to all those who are able to benefit from it.
- Full and transparent accountability for public funding.

It also places important emphasis on the relationship between the academic decision-making body, typically the senate, and the board and on diversity and inclusion. Naturally it also has its own appendix on Taxonomy!

Section Two

People

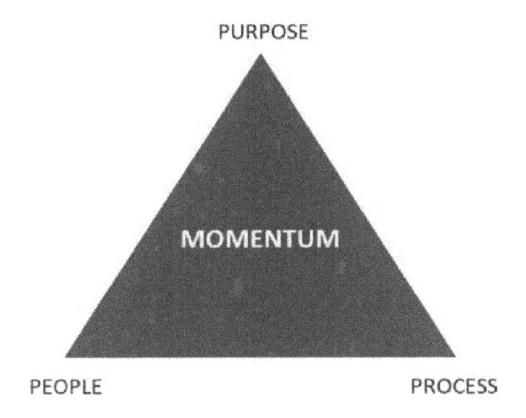

```
        PURPOSE
          /\
         /  \
        /    \
       / MOMENTUM \
      /          \
     /_____\
   PEOPLE       PROCESS
```

Introduction

The most brilliantly thought-through purpose for a board combined with superbly well-engineered processes are near to useless if you don't have the right team on the board working together and with others in the right way. So, having explored the key roles required on a board in "*Purpose*", this "*People*" section is essentially concerned with building and developing effective boards as well as the behavioural dynamics involved. The details on "*People*" processes, from recruitment to succession or removal and including board reviews are covered in the "*Process*" section.

We will start by looking at the importance of self-awareness, feedback, feelings and respect. After all it's very hard to influence people if they don't respect you and tough to build respect if you aren't self-aware and good at feedback and understanding and managing your feelings, especially when under pressure.

We'll then consider composition and board building including diversity and inclusion as well as the characteristics of effective directors and boards as a whole. After this, we'll explore a range of topics including achieving alignment, power and influence, common causes of dysfunction and dealing with it as well as managing cultural differences and conflict including removing directors. Finally, and more positively, we'll take a look at the subject of training and development for board members.

My own preference is for building boards step by step, trying to get ahead of, rather than lag behind the need, and to add only those of competence and character who will be additive both to the culture and to the dynamic of the board. I believe that it is a healthy attitude to think that your board is always in transition and to be constantly thinking about what else will help make us a better board. A strong and established core makes this much easier to do.

When working with dysfunctional boards, especially early on in my career in private equity (PE), I was frequently struck by how often the Chair and chief executive officer (CEO) were unaware of the impact of their own behaviour on others, or worse didn't care. It led me to think about my own behaviour and especially how I sought, gave and received feedback. I started to experiment and, as I was based in Yorkshire at the time, was able to go right up and down the *"polite"* spectrum in doing so. This involved being blunt and direct to the point of rudeness at one end to delivering elegantly-nuanced messages which bordered on the confusing at the other, as well as all points in between.

What I discovered was no surprise, that different people, situations and issues needed different approaches and that the same people required different approaches for different situations and issues. Atmosphere was also a really important variable. However, what remained constant was that when I thought ahead about what might work best, rather than just simply reacting in the moment, it tended to go a lot better.

At that time, I was very fortunate in having a tremendous boss at 3i, David Wilkinson. He taught me many tricks of the trade in dealing with rampantly entrepreneurial people, grumpy Chairs, dangerously charming advisers and other characters as well as the power of *"drippy, drippy, nudgey, nudgey"* informal feedback. The ability to give and to receive feedback is a core skill for directors and trustees. We will look at some of the forms that feedback can take from the instant response we might give through our body language to the more formal and aggregated (note not aggravated), annual review process.

Personal biases are covered in the decision-making section on page 236. We all have them, and it is an important part of self-awareness to know which ones we are most susceptible to and how we might be able to manage them. At the risk of being accused of exhibiting confirmatory bias, I was delighted when in 2015 I came across Erich Dierdorff and Robert Rubin's Harvard Business Review paper: *"We are not very self-aware, especially at work."* One of the most striking things in the paper was a chart (*see* page 92) which shows that teams who are highly self-aware are on average twice as effective at decision quality, co-ordination and conflict management as those with low self-awareness.

An important aspect of self-awareness is understanding how you make people feel. As the legendary writer Maya Angelou said:

"I've learned that people will forget what you said, people will forget what you did, but people will never forget how you made them feel."

That's as true in the boardroom as it is anywhere else. My gran gave me a fantastic piece of advice as a small boy which was that: *"It's really important to listen to what people say but it is even more important to listen to what they think"*. Trying to listen to what people think is a good step in being conscious of how you are making people feel. I loved cartoons which led to me constantly imagining what was in people's thought bubbles.

It isn't a very boardroom thing to talk about feelings but as research suggests that feelings transmit quicker than ideas and that feelings are an important driver of behaviour it seems worth looking at some relevant aspects of *"feelings"*. One of these aspects is how mood might affect performance.

Earlier on in my career, when I hadn't learnt that, I made many a mistake by believing that the power of the logic of an argument would win out as long as I kept repeating it. There is now a whole area of research into what is delightfully known as *"emotional contagion"*, both physically and through electronic media.

High performers in the arts and in sport and other aspects of life put a lot of thought and effort into being in the right condition and *"getting into the zone"* before a big event. Perhaps, we should do the same when making major decisions that affect not only our own livelihoods but also those of others. Greater awareness of the links between well-being, both physical and mental, are welcome. Matthew Walker's *"Why we Sleep"* is a good entrée into this topic if you haven't explored it.

Another aspect that I have found to be important to understand is what I have labelled *"asymmetric sensitivity"* (*see* page 102) which is where someone seems to demand far greater sensitivity from others than they are prepared to show or give themselves. Popular portrayals of high achievers often show this and the person may be fooled into thinking it is ok because of their status or the adulation they receive for their exceptional talent. The inherent hypocrisy is often lost on them and there are real costs in terms of it undermining their judgement, group alignment and their own long-term happiness as their talents fade.

The quality of relationships, cohesion and alignment of the board matters a great deal. So, as part of looking at the behavioural dynamics, we will also look at the key relationships between those on the board and the executive (exec) and other relevant groups. In a public company this will include the communications director and company secretary.

Getting the *"right"* board for your particular set of circumstances with the right levels of engagement and alignment isn't always easy. Avoiding the trap of recruiting the *"best looking"* board that we can which then fails to deliver can be tough. This is a common trap in start-ups, when recruiting new board members ahead of a stock market listing and also in the charity world. It is striking how some, so called, *"heavy hitter"* boards can lose the plot or just not turn up to do the job.

Sometimes we don't end up with the right board because we're using ineffective or unrealistic selection processes. The *"Process"* section covers selection and on-boarding directors from page 192. Other times it could just be that the nature, location, stage of development, market or financial position of the organisation is, or appears to be, unattractive to the sort of candidates that we need. Probably the most challenging issue is when it is the reputation or perception of the existing board or Chair that's the issue.

Even if none of the above applies, realistically we don't all have convenient access to the boardroom talent with the competence and character we might dream of. Yet being too modest in our expectations may well inhibit us from attracting the best and most relevant that we might be able to recruit.

Whatever the reason, if you have ended up with an inappropriate board member my experience is that the sooner you deal with it the better. Removing directors is far from fun. It is not something that most of us get much practice at. Doing it poorly can damage an organisation as well as reputations and cause considerable collateral damage. So, we'll also look at the issues involved in doing this effectively.

Having a galvanising purpose and being good to work with matters even more if you aren't able to offer people high status. In these situations, the people that you most want are those who genuinely want to make a difference. Perhaps you have a lot more to offer in that regard than a more established and high-status board where candidates may feel they can't add a lot. Being clear what you have to offer new board members is a good way of getting the balance right in terms of realism and aiming high as well as helping you to convert good candidates.

Highly effective Chairs and directors have the ability to manage both conflict and cultural differences effectively. They build atmospheres which bring out the best from a group of diverse characters, understand the differences between responding and reacting and have the ability to use their power to influence outcomes in a measured and inclusive way. We'll look at the characteristics that seem to drive such successful behaviour. When challenged to list my top three I invariably come out with *"good judgement, strong interpersonal skills and finely tuned antennae"* and I'll explain why.

You may have been lucky to work with, and learn from, those who are highly effective on a board. You might also have felt the consequences of, or had to tidy up from, those who operate at the other end of the performance spectrum. If so then, like me, you have probably found both types highly instructive.

There is a natural tendency to go for experience and situational experience in my view is far more important than sectoral experience. Yet, I have also had very positive experience in recruiting *"first time boarders"*, especially high potential young people with backgrounds, perspectives and talents that are very different to other board members. Just as with other forms of diversity, a board with a nice mix of experience may prove more effective than one whose experience levels are less varied.

No matter what our level of experience we will continue to learn. Overconfidence and complacency undermine judgement and ultimately performance so it's important to feel that we never have it cracked and are always open to learning something new either from experience, our peers or from formalised learning experiences.

At the Chartered Management Institute, where I have been a trustee, the CEO Ann Francke came up with the wonderful term *"the accidental manager"*. The aim was to try and provoke people to get more development and to think about the art and science of management as a profession for which you need preparation and development to be able to practise successfully.

The big gap in training for board members that existed at the time of the Higgs Review in 2003 has been filled by some excellent providers in many countries but in my view, with a few notable exceptions, the providers are more focused on what I would describe as *"knowledge transfer"* than *"developing board skills and behaviours"*. Peer group learning is particularly powerful and the opportunity to explore common challenges with others within or across sectors and types of organisation seems far greater now than it has ever been.

Finally, it's my experience that it's the people stuff that's the most enjoyable and frustrating thing about being on boards and when I think of the best Chairs, directors and trustees they have all been good at it, or at least at making me believe that they are!

Self-awareness, feedback, feelings and respect

As mentioned in the introduction to this section, the common disconnect and apparent lack of self-awareness of Chairs and CEOs of struggling companies left a big impression on me as a young PE investor. There were many contenders for the most dramatic example, but one really sticks in the memory.

This was where the CEO of a company, who was incredibly needy for praise and over-sensitive to challenge himself, used to call his highly competent finance director (FD): *"Mr Bean, the bean counter"* in front of everyone inside and outside of the business, even the FD's own staff. He also interrupted him whenever he made a comment on anything other than to do with the numbers.

The first time I observed this, after asking the FD following the meeting how he felt about it, I decided to raise it with the CEO over an already scheduled coffee the next week to talk about follow up to the board. It seemed to be something that was too important to let go and that it should be dealt with.

After first congratulating the CEO on yet another month's sparkling performance I raised it by saying I was a bit surprised at the way he introduced the FD at the meeting and kept interrupting him. Instead of listening and taking it seriously he interrupted very quickly and tried to brush me off saying: *"Don't be so ******g sensitive, it's just a joke, he loves it. Now Mr Money let's get on to the important stuff."*

I knew for a fact that this couldn't be further from the truth. The FD hated it and had asked the CEO not to embarrass him in front of others. In this case it was hard to believe that the CEO wasn't aware of the anguish he was causing his FD, but he seemed stunned when I told him how weak, insecure and silly it made him look to everyone else. Even more so when I told him that he was highly unlikely to get any further funds to grow until he proved he was better at developing his team.

In several African countries the 'Warwick in Africa' team and our volunteers have worked hard to reduce corporal punishment and one of the most effective of the many ways we try to do this has been to demonstrate that only weak teachers need to hit children. Bullying is unacceptable and many who bully have themselves been victims of bullying but are not always aware of the effect that it may have on them.

Dealing with it can be tricky and as bullies aren't often naturally receptive to feedback you may need to go up the scale, as I did with the CEO, by starting to help them to realise what they are doing, informing them of how others really feel about it and hoping that they realise quickly and adapt their behaviour. If that doesn't work then you reveal more, then appeal to their emotions to persuade and if all else fails have some form of sanction at the ready in case you need it.

What impact can heightened self-awareness have? Erich C. Dierdorff and Robert S. Rubin's Harvard Business Review paper: *"We're not very self-aware, especially at work"* contains the powerful and persuasive chart in Fig. 2.1. Essentially, they concluded that groups of highly self-aware people are roughly twice as effective when it comes to the quality of their decisions, their ability to successfully complete co-ordination tasks and in managing conflict.

The caveat to their work is that although the sample size was significant at 300 people in 58 teams, they were all from the same Fortune 10 Company. However, as you will see some of their conclusions are supported by other studies.

A starting point for them was the belief that people are notoriously poor judges of their own capabilities. They backed this up using the major study by Ethan Zell and Zlatan Krizan, published in 2014, as proof. This Study combined the results of 22 studies involving over 357,000 people and found an average correlation of only 0.29 between self-evaluations and objective assessments (a correlation of 1.0 would indicate total accuracy).

The implication of this for Dierdorff and Rubin was that:

"How other people see us or against objective data is essential for transforming self-knowledge beyond mere personal introspection into accurate self-awareness... The punch line is that with no external data, the results of self-knowledge assessments are presumed to be accurate, when instead they may reinforce inaccurate perceptions of ourselves. The net result can be harmful to development and performance and, as we observed, the effectiveness of teams."

Figure 2:1 Self-awareness

HIGH SELF-AWARENESS LEADS TO BETTER TEAM PERFORMANCE
A simulation shows that it affects decision-making, coordination, and conflict management.

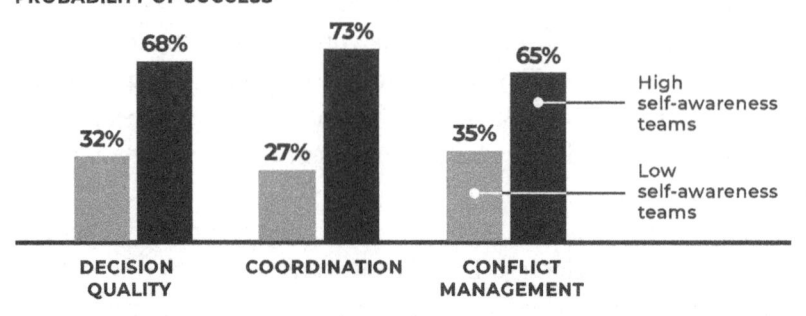

PROBABILITY OF SUCCESS

	Low self-awareness teams	High self-awareness teams
DECISION QUALITY	32%	68%
COORDINATION	27%	73%
CONFLICT MANAGEMENT	35%	65%

Source: ERICH C. DIERDORFF AND ROBERT S. RUBIN   HBR.ORG

This then led them to conduct a business simulation with data from an executive development programme with the 58 teams and over 300 leaders at the Fortune 10 company mentioned above.

They tested the extent to which accurate self-awareness was related to team effectiveness, evaluated across a number of business metrics like market share, Return on Assets, customer awareness, productivity, and so on. Levels of team coordination and conflict management were also assessed. In their words:

> *"What we found was striking. The most damaging situation occurred when teams were comprised of significant over-raters (ie individuals who thought they were contributing more than their team members thought they were). Just being surrounded by teammates of low self-awareness (or a bunch of over-raters) cut the chances of team success in half."*

Their recommendations for organisations were to: use self-awareness tools that are linked to performance, create a line-of-sight between self-awareness and personal job success and teach self-development skills in addition to self-awareness (eg error management training). On this latter point I think there is a nice link with Matthew Syed's thought-provoking book "*Black Box Thinking*" which is referred to in more detail as part of "*Decision Making*" on page 242.

The whole area of self-awareness, emotional intelligence and mindfulness is a burgeoning area of research and writing. Over two decades ago Daniel Goleman's blockbuster book *"Emotional Intelli- gence"* popularised this area of thinking in an organisational context. He essentially said that emotional quotient (EQ) was as important as IQ and that there are five elements to it: *"Self-awareness, Self-regula- tion, Motivation, Empathy and Social Skills."* This seems pretty easy to get your head around and a simple framework to use when you are thinking about your own EQ or when you are coaching or giving feedback.

So, what would be good ways to learn how self-aware you are and whether you have high EQ? Here are six things I have found to be good signs that someone has appropriately high self-awareness (ie isn't just a self-obsessed ego-maniac or neurotic). They:

- understand the importance of self-awareness and are keen to expand their knowledge on the subject;
- have a good understanding of their strengths and weaknesses, aren't over confident about their strengths;
- are constantly trying either to get better at their soft spots or team up with others who have complementary characteristics, so their weaknesses aren't an inhibitor to performance;
- are very aware of the impact that their body language, words and actions have on others and equally good, as my gran would have said, at interpreting what others' body language, words and actions are really saying, ie *"listening to what they think"*. Their antennae are superb and have noise-cancelling power to enable them to pick up the smallest of signals yet cut out the background noise;
- are excellent at encouraging, giving and receiving feedback with warmth, accuracy and in doing so genuinely come over just as someone who wants to help you or themselves get better at something; and finally
- know where they are and where others in their team are on the effectiveness and pressure curve (see below) and, as importantly, know how to move themselves or others along it when required.

Psychologists use a lot of mathematical principles and methods to prove their theories with statistics but also to convey their concepts visually. One of the simplest and most useful examples of this is the application of the *"normal distribution"* to the relationship between how effective we are and how much pressure we are under (see below).

Figure 2:2 Effectiveness and pressure curve

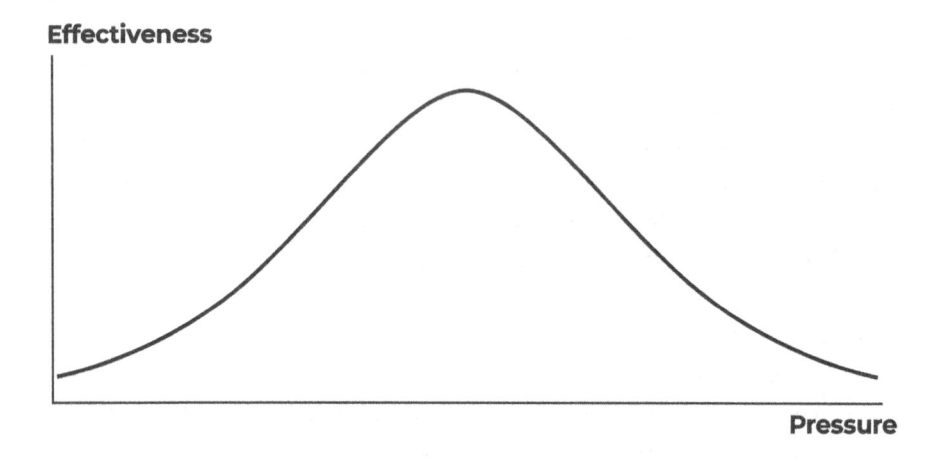

Effectiveness

Pressure

For my mathematical and physicist friends, please don't interpret this literally. It is simply to illustrate a principle and, of course, different people or groups have different tolerances to pressure.

Put simply, on the far-left hand side we're asleep and on the far right we are rushing around like a headless chicken. For those rare moments that we find ourselves at the top of the curve life is good, we have a strong momentum, we're getting lots done, we have time to think and to plan ahead and everything feels, and is, under control. As with a lot of things, if you understand where you are and what is causing the pressure then you stand a better chance of doing something about it. Frequently I have found that when it comes to boards the quality of relationships can sometimes create more pressure than performance challenges or external threats. Just think about how much pressure is caused when the Chair and CEO aren't seeing eye to eye or the CEO and chief financial officer (CFO) grate on each other.

We'll look at the *"Effectiveness and Pressure"* curve again in terms of Agenda setting (*see* page 202) and decision making (*see* page 219). Suffice to say here, that highly effective directors can use their good judgement to resist their natural instincts to pile on the pressure when things get tough for the exec and to increase the pressure when they sense that the exec might be getting overconfident or aren't responding quickly enough to challenges.

So, that's what I think might be good signs that someone has high self-awareness but what do the experts on EQ think? Dr Travis Bradberry, the President of TalentSmart, the EQ test provider, and author of *"Emotional Intelligence 2.0"* was quoted in an article for the World Economic Forum in 2017 as saying that *"90% of top performers have it, do you?"* and that you are more likely to have high EQ if you:

- have a robust emotional vocabulary;
- are curious about people;
- embrace change and are flexible and are constantly adapting;
- know your strengths and weaknesses;
- are a good judge of character;
- are difficult to offend;
- let go of mistakes;
- don't hold grudges;
- neutralise toxic people;
- don't seek perfection;
- disconnect (ie take breaks);
- limit your caffeine intake;
- get enough sleep;
- stop negative self-talk in its tracks; and
- don't let anyone limit your joy.

Pretty well all of these are obvious other than *"limit your caffeine intake"*. The reason Bradberry includes this one is because:

"Caffeine triggers the release of adrenaline, and adrenaline is the source of the fight-or-flight response. The fight-or-flight mechanism sidesteps rational thinking in favour of a faster response to ensure survival."

This, I think, is connected to the *"get enough sleep"* point and the link between well-being and performance. On the caffeine, I think his point is that if you were self-aware you would know that drinking too much caffeine would reduce your self-awareness and therefore not drink too much tea or coffee. You could, of course, be supremely self-aware, know that it impairs it a bit but be prepared to trade impaired self- awareness for a nice cuppa or cappuccino.

Another thing Bradberry asserts is that:

"Unlike your IQ, your EQ is highly malleable. As you train your brain by repeatedly practicing new emotionally intelligent behaviours, it builds the pathways needed to make them into habits. As your brain reinforces the use of these new behaviours, the connections support- ing old, destructive behaviours die off. Before long, you begin responding to your surroundings with emotional intelligence without even having to think about it."

Do the principles that apply to individuals apply to groups? I think they do. It is hard to find research on this, but I did find a fascinating piece of research which looked at the link between a board's EQ and its performance. The work *"Emotional intelligence and board governance: Leadership lessons from the public sector"* by Margaret Hopkins, Deborah O'Neill and Helen Watkins from the US, was published in the *Journal of Managerial Psychology* in 2007 and it was focused on school boards.

Drawing on some existing work, by Eugene Smoley (*see* Bibliography), on a model for school board effectiveness, they looked at what they called the practice domains:

- making decisions;
- functioning as a group;
- exercising authority;
- connecting to the community;
- working towards board improvement; and
- acting strategically.

Then using the model below, developed by Richard Boyatzis, they investigated the association between a range of 18 emotional intelligence competencies clustered into four groups and effective school board leader- ship. The data was drawn from existing and former school governors in two regions (*see* table overleaf).

What they found was that:

"After applying the emotional intelligence competency model to the practice domain action statements, we found that there are six emotional intelligence competencies central to effective school board leadership: Transparency, Achievement orientation, Initiative, Organizational awareness, Conflict management, and Teamwork and collaboration."

So, if we have a good level of self-awareness on those six things combined with a desire to strive for high performance we ought to be able to do a decent job.

Self-awareness	- Emotional self-awareness. Recognising one's emotions and their effects for accurate self-assessment. Knowing one's inner resources, abilities and limits. - Self-confidence. Having a strong sense of one's self-worth/capabilities.
Self-management	- Emotional self-control. Keeping disruptive emotions and impulses in check. - Transparency. Maintaining integrity, acting congruently with one's values. - Adaptability. Being flexible in responding to change. - Achievement orientation. Striving to improve or meet a standard of excellence. - Initiative. Displaying proactivity. - Optimism. Persistence in pursuing goals despite obstacles and setbacks.
Social awareness	- Empathy. Sensing others' feelings, perspective and taking an active interest in their concerns. - Organisational awareness. Reading social and political currents. - Service orientation. Anticipating, recognising and meeting customers' needs.

| Relationship management | - Developing others. Sensing others' development needs and bolstering their abilities.
- Inspirational leadership. Inspiring and guiding individuals and groups.
- Change catalyst. Initiating or managing change.
- Influence. Having impact on others.
- Conflict management. Negotiating and resolving disagreements.
- Teamwork and collaboration. Working with others and creating group synergy toward goals. |
|---|---|
| | Source: Boyatzis et al. (2002) |

Feedback

A key input to self-awareness is feedback and as board members we will be both giving and receiving feedback all the time and in many ways. Every conversation is a feedback session even if you are just listening. Facial and body language are big sources of feedback, the signals we transmit by how we say things can be as important as what we are saying. Then of course there are formal feedback processes. Sadly, many of these, like those used in board reviews (*see* page 158), have become sterile and over "*processy*" and not very useful.

The key points relating to feedback are that:

- exuding warmth, conveying genuinely that what you are saying is all with the intent of helping them and relaxing them rather than to point out failings, and being thought-provoking and motivational will all make people more receptive;
- remembering that feelings transmit quicker than ideas, there- fore your body language can be a powerful tool to create the right atmosphere to help someone be more receptive;
- it is how the person that you are giving or seeking feedback to or from interprets your body language that matters, so remember to try and listen to what they might be thinking: you can see this in the way they respond physically as well as verbally;
- the angle that you are sitting or standing is important: leaning too

far forward can be threatening, leaning too far back might be interpreted that you don't care;
- as people are prone to mirror behaviour, if your demeanor and posture appears warm and open, they are likely, other things being equal, to reciprocate;
- the way that we take notes can make a difference.

I think it is also the case that people are more likely to listen to your feedback if you have listened to theirs and followed up on it. Asking for feedback is a useful way of gaining the permission to reciprocate.

There are myriad of courses and articles on giving and receiving feedback and I am guessing that many readers will have been on a course or two on the topic and have their own favourite tips. An article I wasn't familiar with, until researching this book, was Jennifer Porter's *"How Leaders can get honest, productive feedback"* in the *Harvard Business Review*. Jennifer is CEO of Boda Group and her article was about how leaders can get better feedback. This is especially relevant for CEOs and Chairs where you are always anxious that what some people say might be what they think you want to hear rather than the truth.

Even when we want it we don't always transmit that. In *"Running Board Meetings"* I quoted legendary movie mogul Sam Goldwyn's famous quote:

"I want you all to tell me what you think, even if it costs you your jobs."

Jennifer lists ten key points for leaders to take note of as follows:

- Build and maintain a psychologically safe environment.
- Ask for feedback skillfully.
- Request both positive and negative data.
- When receiving feedback, give your full attention and listen carefully.
- Don't debate or defend.
- Own your reactions.
- Demonstrate gratitude.
- Reflect and evaluate.
- Make a plan and take action.
- Sustain progress and share updates.

She also advises against asking general questions, for example, *"What feedback do you have for me?"* preferring specific ones, such as *"What do you think that I can do to help build my relationship with X?"* All pretty obvious but when we reflect on what we do in practice we don't always do this.

The final thing to say on feedback is that it is always, always worth checking what has been said is what has been heard and discussing how you can help or be helped to take the most useful bits of feedback on board and adapt.

Feelings

Feelings can have a significant effect on our performance through affecting the way we think through or decide things, the quality of our relationships and how we solve problems to mention just a few. Various studies have shown this. One that I think sums it up nicely is the article by Nadine Jung, Christina Wranke, Kai Hamburger and Markus Knauff in *"Frontiers in Psychology"* in 2014. Their conclusion is as follows:

"Participants in negative mood performed worse than participants in positive mood, but both groups were outperformed by the neutral mood reasoners."

I'm not sure a lot of us are instinctive *"neutral mood reasoners"* and perhaps one reason why diversity on a board is helpful is that a diverse mix of moods may balance out to a neutral mood reasoning group. That is if you can avoid the grumpiest person in the room infecting others or as psychologists call it *"Emotional Contagion"* (*see* page 103). In the context of a board meeting it is the Chair's job to ensure that the joyous and gloomy voices in the room produce that balance rather than try and manage every individual to a state of neutrality.

"Never let feelings get in the way" is a common expression applied to *"seeing things as they really are"*, *"your judgement"*, *"having a good time"* and so on. Ironically these sayings arouse the feeling that feelings are a negative force. They can be but these quotes are really about managing your feelings rather than feelings themselves. I can think of many occasions where my feelings about something or someone have saved me from making a mistake on the basis of the facts presented or the views of

others. It seems important to distinguish feelings from judgement but for your feelings to be an important input to whatever judgement you are about to make.

In the real world our feelings and instincts as a board member are complex, spanning a range from *"danger, danger!"* to *"this could be fantastic"* and more often than not both at the same time. The *"Law of approach and avoidance"* (Kurt Lewin) states that our survival instinct means that we approach those people, things and events that we believe can do us good and avoid those that can do us harm (*see* page 138). Here the key word is *"judgement"* and high quality of judgement is one of the defining characteristics of the best directors. The ability to interpret all the facts and feelings and judge what might be the right thing to do and to do that consistently is the hallmark of a brilliant board member.

Feelings are also significant in the context of how others might feel about an action or decision and the influence that then has on how likely they are to help you in carrying it out enthusiastically and well. If you have ever been unlucky enough as an exec to have been left hanging about outside a boardroom waiting to do your presentation, then when you finally got in there you found that you only had half the time you thought you were going to get and that the non-execs are either exhausted by the previous topic or disinterested, then tweaked your proposal into something nonsensical and wished you well with the implementation then you will get the point.

It has been proven that feelings transmit more rapidly through human sounds than words. Marc Pell, Kathrin Rothermich, Paul Liu, Silke Paulmann, Hartej Sethi and Simon Rigoulot in their *2016 McGill University* paper stated that:

> *"It takes just one-tenth of a second for our brains to begin to recognize emotions conveyed by vocalizations. It doesn't matter whether the non-verbal sounds are growls of anger, the laughter of happiness or cries of sadness. More importantly, the researchers have also discovered that we pay more attention when an emotion (such as happiness, sadness or anger) is expressed through vocalizations than we do when the same emotion is expressed in speech."*

They gave the reason for this as being that our brains use *"older"* systems and structures to preferentially process emotion expressed through vocalisations. They believed that the speed with which the brain *"tags"* these vocalisations and the preference given to them compared to language, is due to the potentially crucial role that decoding vocal sounds has played in human survival.

The researchers focused on three basic emotions - anger, sadness and happiness - and were able to measure:

- how the brain responds to emotions expressed through vocalisations compared to spoken language with millisecond precision;
- whether certain emotions are recognised more quickly through vocalisations than others and produce larger brain responses; and
- whether people who are anxious are particularly sensitive to emotional voices based on the strength of their brain response.

What they found was fascinating but rings true, namely that:

- participants were able to detect vocalisations of happiness more quickly than vocal sounds conveying either anger or sadness;
- angry sounds and angry speech, however, both produced ongoing brain activity that lasted longer than either of the other emotions, suggesting that the brain pays special attention to the importance of anger signals;
- individuals who are more anxious have a faster and more heightened response to emotional voices in general than people who are less anxious.

This difference between the positive and the negative rings true and a good example of it is the asymmetry of feeling between the joy of being part of a group and the intensity of the feeling of exclusion when you aren't included.

On the subject of asymmetry, ever wondered about people who demand huge sensitivity from others but show so little themselves? Me too. What follows is far from scientific just some personal thoughts on the matter.

Self-awareness is usually at the root of it. You might simply not know this is how you come across and once someone with deft feedback skills lets you know then you can adapt quickly to suppress those unhelpful natural urges.

Wonky antennae might be another problem. Others may think they are giving you obvious signals, facially or verbally, but you just don't pick them up. Practising guessing what's in the thought bubbles as opposed to the words can help if this is the problem.

Higher than normal competitive instincts might be another factor (*see* page 143). The pursuit of winning and achieving one of our objectives can sometimes make us blind to the objectives and feelings of others. Again, try experimenting with other approaches, especially when you don't need to.

Often, people assume asymmetric sensitivity is a right of a more powerful position. Absolutely wrong. It isn't and to do so almost always costs you in the end so is definitely best avoided.

Being a little power tipsy and having an overly accommodating team could be another reason this happens. Think lions and lionesses. That sense of entitlement which is reinforced by others allowing it isn't helpful. Gaining buy-in might feel a bit of a waste of time if it's always given. Whether you need it not. Whether you have got it or not, before you start it is always wise to assume that you need to gain buy-in.

I've also observed that people prone to asymmetric sensitivity, have a tendency to project their feelings onto others. Psychologists call this "*psychological projection*" and explain it as a defence mechanism where we repress a weakness of our own, deny it exists and then attribute the weakness onto someone else. The classic example is where someone who is instinctively and habitually rude frequently accuses others of being rude.

Yet the biggest issue driving asymmetric sensitivity, in my experience, is simply poor judgement.

Emotions can also be infectious. Sadly, the description for the study of this, "*emotional contagion*", sounds less than positive and there are many examples in history of the destructive power of whipping up a crowd or it contributing to groupthink (*see* page 240). Yet "*emotional contagion*" can just as well be positive as anyone who had the privilege to hear Nelson Mandela or other great orators speak can testify.

Gerald Schoenewolf's definition of emotional contagion is:

> "*A process in which a person or group influences the emotions or behaviour of another person or group through the conscious or unconscious induction of emotion states and behavioural attitudes.*"

In a board context the Chair is responsible for managing the mood of meetings and the general atmosphere of the board outside meetings. The CEO and CFO are also key determinants of mood and can either help to create an open collaborative spirit with their board or alternatively a feeling of *"us"* and *"them"*.

Our feelings are also influenced by whether we feel that a process has been fair or not. We'll cover this more deeply in the decision- making segment of the *"Process"* section on page 156. Feelings of injustice can evoke strong emotions and also dominate thinking. Many times for the good but occasionally not so.

Respect

It is really hard to influence people who don't respect you, unless of course they are frightened by you or what you might do. In *"Power and influence"* (*see* page 120) we will read Warren Bennis's wise words that *"power is the ability to convert vision into reality"*. It has always seemed to me that respect is an important source of sustained and effective power.

As a Chair or CEO, you have the store of respect which goes with position but few of us would ever rely just on that to mobilise people to help us achieve our vision. We know that sustained success is easier if those who will turn a vision into reality feel, believe and own it. We also know that if we want to create a certain culture and have a set of values that will support what we want to do and will last beyond our leadership we need to be respected for living up to those values and demonstrating that culture ourselves.

If you want a culture of high integrity and which encourages openness and learning from mistakes, the board has to demonstrate collectively and individually that it not only practices what it preaches but that it is well known throughout the organisation that it does.

For new independent directors (IDs), who generally have few formal powers, aren't well known to the other board members and need to rely more on the respect in which they are held than the authority of the position, building respect is paramount to making a difference.

Naturally their track record and how they have been sold in by whoever recommended them can make a big difference. Yet in my experience in the PE world entrepreneurial CEOs are more interested in what you can do for them rather than what you have done for someone else.

IDs can build or lose respect as early as the due diligence phase. Really positive interactions with other directors and the exec team which strike the right balance of listening, skillful questioning and deft challenge can really help with the first outing in a board meeting. They can also lose respect in the first board meeting by falling prey to *"new ID syndrome"*.

At one end of the spectrum is the new director who is mad keen to make an early impact. They set aside the weekend before the board meeting to go through the papers and are likely to be the only one around the table who has read every line of every paper. What's more, to have a view on every item and, even more dangerously, the need to express it. Any recollection of respecting and managing the pie chart of their airtime goes out of the window in a desperate desire to show their diligence and usefulness. The result is that they risk coming over as too much in the weeds and not strategic enough, insensitive to the need for others to express their views and don't spend as much time listening, observing and reflecting and learning. It's important to remember that you are likely to be on a board for six years, so you need to pace yourself.

At the other end of the spectrum is what I call the *"Well I'm just the new kid on the block"* who doesn't say anything at all at the first board meeting other than to ask a few clarifying questions. Useful though these may be others may be left at the end of meeting wondering what value the new kid might bring.

The smart new ID prepares well, decides what the issues are and where they can make the biggest contribution, then manages their airtime to be able to do so. They also pick up any detailed points they may have ahead of the meeting and ask for feedback from the Chair after the meeting, knowing that asking for feedback is a good way of gaining a licence to give feedback.

Someone who has fallen prey to *"new ID syndrome"*, or perhaps just has lousy judgement might, if they spot a mistake in the management accounts, save it for the meeting, point it out, embarrass the CFO and feel that they have added value as the CFO will be more careful next time. The smart ID will just give the CFO a call ahead of the meeting, thank them for the high quality of the papers and gently say: *"I'm sure that you have already spotted the inconsistency on page X, not worth mentioning at the meeting. The only point that I would like to make there is about X."* In this way they have shown the CFO that they are on the ball, respected them and shown that they don't want to embarrass them and have given them notice and time to prepare for the bigger point.

Making useful contributions at board meetings is, of course, fundamental but far from sufficient to build respect. It is usually the useful things that you do outside the board meeting that give you the respect within it. Examples of this might be mentoring an exec, providing expert knowledge on an issue, helping with a review of something material and so on.

Composition and board building

There is both art and science in building boards and a series of important questions to ask before we start, namely:

- What's the best mix to achieve our purpose (or, if our purpose isn't clear, to help us gain that clarity)?
- What's the best size of board for our situation?
- How do we achieve a diverse and inclusive board with the culture that we want with inevitably a small number of people?
- How do we ensure that we have the right people for our sub-committees as well as the Board itself?
- Do we recruit potential Chair successors or not?
- Realistically, how attractive are we?
- What's our pitch to high-quality potential board members?
- How should we reward board members?

For new organisations it is generally best to start with the Chair. After all, if they are the leader of the board team it helps if they have ownership of the selection of the team, even if they are not the owner or majority stakeholder. They will know that they have to find a board composition that the owners or majority stakeholders are happy with and will probably, though not always, be judged on the performance of the board rather than its composition. We'll look at the characteristics of effective directors on page 110.

Microwaved boards are risky. For example, growth companies preparing for an Initial Public Offering (IPO) trying to put the board together that they want post IPO just a few months before they plan to list take quite a risk. Start-ups, boards built in haste for the primary purpose of looking good to potential investors, seldom are the boards that are really needed to drive success and sustain it. In my experience, adding one by one and adding only people you think will be additive to the culture that you are trying to build is the most effective way to build a strong board.

It also helps to have a feeling that the board is always in transition and unless you have coterminous appointments, where a number retire at the same point, it is easy to achieve for a board of six or more. Coterminous-driven refreshes can be helpful from time to time but more generally it is better to be continually adapting and bringing in fresh perspectives.

It seems as if increased churn has arisen from the pandemic driven by three factors. First, as visions and strategies have changed and therefore so has the blend of skills and experiences needed for the Board. Second, not all board members stepped up to the challenge and some even got in the way, so are being managed out. Finally, for others increased commitments elsewhere or the level and nature of work as well as risk has meant they have chosen to step down.

The framework below is one I use regularly when recruiting board members, starting with thinking about the board we have now to help ascertain the need. Having established what we need then the framework is also useful in the selection process when evaluating candidates.

Figure 2:3 Assessing team

As individuals	As a team
· Competence	· Gaps and overlaps
· Fit to role and others	· Cohesive
· Character/culture	

As fit for purpose	Good to work with
· Fit with strategy	· Integrity
· Resilience	· Professionalism
· Potential to develop	· Pleasant

When it comes to optimum size the research is inconclusive. A good summary on the topic comes from Yi Wang, Antony Young and Sally Chaplin in *"Is there an optimal board size?"* in *"Corporate Board: role, duties and composition"*

> *"This research quantitatively examines the determinants of board size and the consequence it has on the performance of large companies in Australia. In line with international and the prevalent United States research the results suggest that there is no significant relationship between board size and their subsequent performance."*

However, it is a biased sample as it relates to large public company boards, so they were effectively looking in a bounded range as few are less than six or more than 12.

They also quote other studies to reinforce the no optimum size view but raise some of the issues.

> *"Lipton and Lorsch (1992) contended that as the board increased in size, director free-riding would increase. Jensen (1993) also endorsed small boards because of the efficiency in decision making due to greater coordination and communication. Dalton et al. (1999) and Coles et al. (2008), on the other hand, argued that larger boards would bring more experience and knowledge which could result in better advice."*

In general, I have seen small boards of four or five work very effectively in growth companies or in social enterprises and boards of up to 12 work in public companies. University council boards tend to be much bigger and often over 20. This is too large and so in practice they make it work with a *"nucleus"* of members who do the heavy lifting and recommend to the wider group for approval and comment. The dangers of this are obvious.

In terms of getting the best mix, a straightforward approach is to produce a set of objectives covering what you need and want your board to have. Looking at the vision, purpose, strategy and culture and working out what skills and experiences would be most helpful to have to be successful is a good place to start in this. Then consider other aspects that are desired such as diversity and inclusion in its many forms. A lot of progress has been made in many countries on gender diversity, as noted on page 131: ethnic, social, neural and character diversity less so. The best Chairs will place a high priority on diversity and inclusion, will recognise that it is challenging to achieve but do all they can to do so. The fresh impetus of the "*Me too*", "*Black Lives Matter*" and other events and campaigns has provided fresh impetus. As has increased interest and growing expectations from investors and others.

If you are heavily regulated or your stakeholders have policies or strong views you will also need to take those into account. It is always important to start with what you think you need and then to look at what others think you need and then consider their view. There should be a match in terms of what is best for the organisation but this is not always the case.

In most cases it won't be starting from scratch. A skills, knowledge and experience audit of the existing members mapped against the need will highlight where the gaps are against your dream board team. It should also highlight where you may have someone who is now no longer a good fit. This is dealt with in the "*Removing Directors*" section on page 146.

When conducting such audits it is critical not to make it too mechanistic and to focus on the blend of characters as much as their knowledge, skills or experiences. So what characteristics should we be looking for and how do we achieve this through a natural evolutionary process rather than a disruptive spring clean every few years?

As a way of thinking about this Maslow (*see* page 223) can help us again.

The four central characters involved in developing the board and managing succession - the Chair, CEO, company secretary and the SID (who is usually Chair of the nominations committee) - all view it as a regular item which helps to create the right mindset.

With the right mindset developing a robust and realistic plan is straightforward. That plan needs to be owned by the board but the work will be driven by the nominations committee (*see* page 188). Strong feedback processes will ensure that their intelligence on the performance of existing board members is accurate and will inform their work.

A good nominations committee will also propose a robust selection process to the board and then manage that process, ensuring that there is the right level of involvement and engagement from both board and exec.

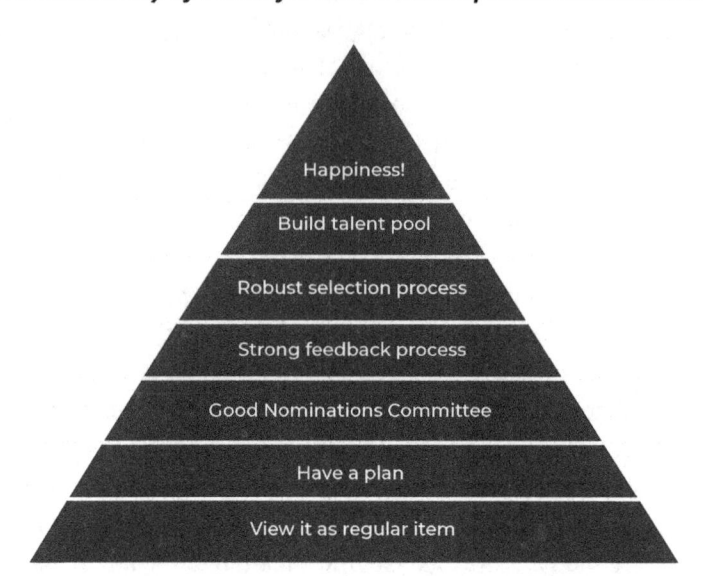

Figure 2:4 Hierarchy of needs for board development and succession

- Happiness!
- Build talent pool
- Robust selection process
- Strong feedback process
- Good Nominations Committee
- Have a plan
- View it as regular item

In public companies they will also be very mindful of the views of investors. It is always easier to appoint people that the board knows and rates. So, building a small talent pool in advance of need can be helpful as long as in doing so it doesn't fall victim to "*old boy*" or "*new girl*" network syndrome and risk objectivity and diversity being diluted.

The Chair and the Chair of the nominations committee will be the key people responsible for ensuring that the mindset is right and that the work is done to achieve this. In doing so they will want to add people to the board who have the right characteristics above and beyond, sectoral, functional or situational knowledge, skills and experiences. They will also ensure that there is the right level of buy-in and engagement from others especially the CEO.

In my mind there are three universal characteristics that highly effective board members possess (*see* Figure 2:5).

The word judgement is under-used and the importance of good judgement often not given the weight it deserves in selection processes. High quality judgement of people and situations is central to making good decisions and building relationships and influence. Yet we all know people who have great judgement but are incredibly irritating, so good judgement needs to be complemented with a high order of interpersonal skills to enable those inspired judgements to be brought to bear. People with both tend to have good levels of resilience and to be calm and measured.

Figure 2:5 Universal characteristics

- Good judgement
- Superb interpersonal skills
- Excellent antenna

Judgement is not a static thing: it can be developed and it can decay. That's why I think a good director also needs excellent antennae so that they are continually informing and developing their judgement and not letting fungus grow all over it. Getting out and about in and outside the organisation and sector, talking to people at all levels formally and informally will all help. Board members who display a strong sense of curiosity but do so with great sensitivity to management are often the best.

In addition to these universal characteristics you will want to know that board members have the specific core skills and knowledge relevant for the organisation, its strategy and the situation it is in and is likely to face as its strategy progresses.

There is good debate around the topic of introversion and extroversion. In a board context having a balance of introverts and extroverts contributes to neural diversity and therefore should be healthy, assuming that they can find a way to work effectively together. As with many things extroverts can be very useful in stimulating creativity and creating positive momentum. They tend to have a high need for stimulation. At the same time they can be dangerous in using that momentum to steamroller flawed ideas through or just simply be over-exuberant. The best talker may not have the best judgement or ideas.

Introverts can be incredibly useful at thinking things through while others are consumed with the conversation and then making brilliantly incisive interventions which turn decisions the right way. They also may make big contributions in one-on-one conversations outside the board, influencing the way that people think on an issue. They may be more likely to read the board papers thoroughly and less likely to take outsize risks. There are numerous examples of solitude being helpful to creative thinking: Edison, Van Gogh and Beethoven to name but three. However, there may be times when introverts really need to speak up and don't and others where because their share of the pie chart of airtime is so low that people think they aren't contributing or don't care and lose respect as a consequence.

In the western world it feels that there is a strong bias to extroverts. Susan Cain's book *"Quiet"* with its wonderful subtitle – *"Power of introverts in a world that can't stop talking"* is full of useful tips for introverts to increase their influence. Susan was a Wall Street lawyer and as an introvert found it hard to get her voice heard and have the influence that she felt she should have. Her 2012 TedTalk is highly thought-provoking. She feels that the time of the introverts is coming, although the rise of the noisy populists in society may mean it is a little way off yet.

Achieving all of your objectives and having the right-sized board can be tough even if you are a very attractive board to join; harder still if you can't offer high rewards or status. On that topic it is really important to be realistic and straightforward about how attractive your board might be to join. Beauty is always in the eye of the beholder and your challenges are someone else's opportunities. Happily, there are usually enough people who are keen to make a difference and feel that sometimes that is easier to do in a smaller organisation.

One of the most fulfilling experiences of my life was joining the Board of Leap Confronting Conflict in 2003. At the time I was approached to join the board of a number of high-profile, well-funded charities with tremendous boards. I kept declining the approaches as I found it really hard to see what value I could bring given the brilliant people who were already on the board. The headhunter, Janet Cummins from Charity Appointments got a little frustrated with me and in exasperation said:

"Look for goodness sake tell me what sort of organisation you are looking for."

My response was:

"Well something where I can make a difference. So, a cause I identify with (young people suffering from violence or poor educational opportunities). A charity that is doing great work in small scale and has an opportunity to create a lot more impact. Probably one that doesn't have any money, has a thin management team and no profile."

She then said:

"Are you serious? Because if you are I have just the thing. It's called Leap Confronting Conflict, I'm actually a trustee myself and think the work they do is incredible. They are a wonderful bunch of people but don't have the experience of scaling things. Your growth capital and venture capital experience could be really handy."

Shortly afterwards the then Chair, Pete Lawson and CEO, Helen Carmichael and I met in their offices, then a room at the YMCA building in Finsbury Park. They were refreshingly honest about all their challenges and issues but the more they talked about them and their model for the work that they did the more excited I became about the opportunity to make a difference and help so many youngsters manage conflict more effectively. I'd grown up in what was a *"conflict rich"* environment in Liverpool and could see the incredible power of the work immediately.

It was also clear that I would also learn an enormous amount and I can honestly say that Leap's work has had a profound effect upon me ever since. We've grown substantially and the team's work has had a major influence in the sector and most importantly for the tens of thousands of young people we have helped to have happier and more successful lives. As an aside and somewhat amusingly, the techniques for helping adolescents manage conflict more effectively are just as useful with CEOs.

Leap also provided a valuable antidote to life in FTSE 100 and PE land. I am convinced that I was able to perform better in my day job because of the things that I learnt through Leap, especially about chairing, managing conflict and staying grounded.

Happily, there are usually enough people who are keen to make a difference and feel that sometimes that is easier to do in a smaller organisation. That said you still need a realistic and compelling pitch and to think about things from their perspective. I remember one situation where, when asked how she thought a charity might be different to a business board, the CEO of a charity replied. *"I suppose the main difference is that, unlike a business, as a charity we have values!"* Honesty is helpful so, I suppose it was good to know what she actually thought but the fact that what she said might be felt to be insulting and stupid was clearly lost on her and showed a worrying lack of judgement.

When recruiting independent directors it is also important to consider whether you want the person also to be a potential successor for the Chair, SID or sub-committee Chair. Unless it is a sudden need to replace it should essentially just be part of the Board development and succession plan. The process is covered more fully on the following pages and on page 192.

Every board member depends upon the quality of the CFO. It is a critical appointment and one which requires considerable care in making. At a time when I was running 3i's people programmes, where we were developing pools of Chairs, CEOs, CFOs and IDs for portfolio companies and our management buy-in business in particular, I noticed that failure reports almost always noted that there was an issue with the CFO. So a colleague, Cindy Casciani (now at Equity Chair), and I then set about thinking about how we could improve our selection of CFOs. We thought that looking at the characteristics of the best CFOs in the portfolio might be a good place to start.

We recognised that context was going to matter a great deal. Matching for nature, scale and other aspects of the organisation was the easy bit. It was the other characteristics that we were interested in.

Quite quickly we realised that traditional approaches to interviewing and to referencing were not as effective as they could be as they often didn't test strongly enough for the things that mattered most. In addition to focus groups with CFOs, we ran a series of events with Chairs, CEOs, and IDs to gain their wisdom on the topic. One of the highlights of these was playing a 20 questions role-play game where as a selection panel you only had 20 questions to discover whether the person in front of you was the right CFO for your situation. We'll cover some of this in the *"Process"* section on page 155. Here we'll focus on the characteristics that we are looking for.

At the time we thought that a good way to present these characteristics was to take a Maslow's hierarchy of needs approach (*see* page 223).

Figure 2:6 CFOs – a hierarchy of needs

- CEO skills!
- Strategy
- Board skills
- Sales skills
- Management skills
- Technical competence
- Integrity

At the base is integrity, something you absolutely need in your CFO for the organisation to stay safe and survive. Then you need them to have the relevant technical competence for the nature of the business. Management skills are then important as they will have to manage a finance function, suppliers of services and projects as well as the interaction with other functions and business units.

Sales skills might not be an immediately obvious need for a CFO but when you think about the need to convince others of the importance of good budgeting, financial control, management of cash flow and forecasting it becomes more obvious. They will also have to be convincing with providers of finance and with other stakeholders. In major public companies the CFO will be spending a significant amount of time on investor relations.

Whether your CFO is on the board or not they will need to have the skills to operate at board level and to be able to interact with confidence. My general preference is for the CFO to be on the board and if you haven't got a CFO who has that capability then either develop or change them.

As with sales skills, strategic skills may not be as obvious a need. Yet if you want your CFO to be a strategic partner to the CEO, and not merely a finance functionary, then they will need to have a good understanding of strategy over and above financial strategy. The CFO will usually play a key role in the development of strategy. In a major public company the CFO will spend a reasonable amount of time explaining strategy to investors. To do that successfully they will need to have more than just an understanding of the company's strategy but also of strategic options and the strategies of competitors and supply chain.

At the top of the pyramid as an optional extra are CEO skills. You may want to recruit a CFO who could be a potential successor or insurance policy for the CEO. This could be a very good approach given the succession horizon of the CEO and the development time for the CFO are aligned. However, if this isn't the case then you need to be very careful as you may just simply be setting up a conflict.

Figuring out what the characteristics are is an important first step in working out whether you have the CFO you need or in embarking on recruiting a new one but how in practice do you work out whether an incumbent or candidate has what you are looking for.

An all-time favourite due diligence meeting, before taking a board appointment, was with the University of Warwick's FD, Rosie Drinkwater. I started the meeting, after pleasantries with the following question:

"As I haven't been on a University Board before it would be incredibly helpful if you could just talk me through the financial dynamic of the University."

"Sure", replied *Rosie*, *"Probably the best way to do this is to take you through our income statement so you can see the make-up of our income and key costs, then look at the annual cash flow cycle, followed by looking at the major items in our balance sheet. Finally, I think it is important that you understand the principles by which we manage the finances of the university."*

It was a brilliant answer: calm, clear, confident and detailed. Exactly, what you want from a CFO. The best bit though was yet to come. Over the next hour or so using a combination of her monthly financial dashboard and the Annual Report she described these things in stunningly simple terms (ie ones that I could understand).

The "*talk me through the financial dynamic*" question is useful not just in the context of due diligence but also when you are hiring CFOs. If the CFO can't do this then it isn't your problem it's theirs. For a CFO to be successful they have to be able to explain the way the finances work whether you are a financial person or not. I always use this question and it is best deployed with no advance notice. This combined with the selection panel carving up the job to ensure that you have the right blend of other characteristics usually does the trick.

A few other useful questions are:

- "Give me some examples of how you have managed the relationship with the Board, the CEO and the other members of the leadership team."
- "What's been the most difficult investor or bank issue that you have had to deal with?"
- "Talk me through the last management letter from the auditors of your last company and how you dealt with any issue in it."
- "What's your approach to dynamic budgeting?"
- "What do you think of our strategy compared to the competition?"
- "Describe what your dream team for our finance function would be?"
- To pick a current high-profile failure and ask them for their view of it and what they would have done as CFO in that situation.
- "How do you see the CFO's role in risk management and helping the board to establish its risk appetite?"

Aligning people

On page 12 we explored the alignment between the board and the exec. See Figures 1.3 and 1.4.

The same principles apply to other key relationships where strong alignment is required. These include the one-to-one relationships between the Chair and CEO, CEO and CFO as well as those involving bigger groups. For example in a major public company strong alignment between the Chair, SID, CEO, CFO, company secretary and communications director is critical.

It is the Chair's responsibility to ensure there is alignment on the board and the CEO's that there is alignment amongst the exec. Although the ultimate responsibility for ensuring alignment of both board and exec rests with the Chair, the CEO has an important role to play in helping them achieve it.

What do they need to be aligned on? Essentially it is what they are going to do and when and how they are going to do it; the key things being about organisational purpose, vision, values and strategy as well as the key challenges and opportunities and culture.

Figuring out what people need to be aligned on is far easier than getting them aligned. For those who believe in basic instincts and that *"sex, greed and fear"* are the primal motivations for humans to do anything, you may find that appealing to people's sense of excitement, their desire to get rich or achieve status or to avoid something seriously unpleasant may work well for you. The *"Money, money, money"* and *"RemCoCoCo"* and *"Falling in the Strid"* dilemmas on pages 329, 357 and 399 respectively provide plenty of fun around the greed topic.

As a mathematician by background I would instinctively prefer that logic had a key role to play in determining people's choices but life's experience suggests that the use of logic to decide what is the right thing to do is not always a popular choice. The *"Dilemmas"* section (from page 269) provides plenty of illustrations of logic bypasses and people making choices not exactly in their own interests. In describing how these dilemmas were resolved it also provides a wide variety of approaches to different situations where greater alignment was required to move forward.

Moving from the *"rabble"* state (the circle) to a highly-aligned, high-performing place (the triangle) see Fig 1.4 usually requires people to accept that there is a better place to be and some sort of galvanising goal even if it is simply not to go bust. It is also rare to move away from the *"rabble"* state and take all of the same people with you. Almost by definition if you are in a *"rabble"* state then, unless the Chair has just been appointed to sort it out, there is probably an issue with the Chair's ability to bring people together around a common purpose or sadly they may be the root cause of the problem. The *"Convo"* and the *"Boiling point with too many cooks"* dilemmas on pages 304 and 287 are two such examples from business and the social sector where both of these factors apply.

In majority-controlled PE situations it is easier to resolve this by changing the Chair. This can usually be done fairly swiftly and most PE firms have access to a bank of experienced Chairs who can move in and establish unity of purpose. In public companies if the institutions feel that there is this sort of issue they can calibrate their view with the SID and effectively give them the mandate to bring about change. In public bodies the regulator may be the catalyst for change.

In a family- or founder-controlled business or in a charity where it is either in a *"rabble"* or *"monarchist"* state it is much harder to bring about change as either the change required is with the person who legally or practically controls the situation or there is no focal point of power to decide. The *"Bones & Sons"*, *"The revolution"* and *"Boiling point with too many cooks"* dilemmas on pages 388, 375 and 287 respectively cover some of the practical challenges and approaches to resolving such situations.

When in a *"rabble"* state with a group or groups you may have to start simply by aligning one individual at a time and building a strong enough coalition to gain enough power to achieve the change you want to see.

Possibly one of the best portrayals of a successful transition from *"rabble"* to unanimous consensus was that of Henry Fonda's Juror number 8 role in the classic movie *12 Angry Men*. The film tells the story of a jury of 12 white men from different backgrounds deciding whether an 18 year old non-white man from a slum stabbed his father to death. Apart from being a masterclass in acting and a moving and brilliant movie, the character and technique of Juror number 8 is an inspiring example of how to achieve alignment when it looks impossible.

Essentially, 11 jurors shaped by their prejudices and prior experiences initially believe the young man is guilty. The strong voices in the room are in a rush and think the conclusion is obvious (*"Guilty"*). Those who haven't decided, other than Fonda, are prepared to go along with them. Fonda calmly intervenes and turns the conversation by saying: *"We are talking about someone's life here we can't decide in five minutes."*

This is a superb example of gaining people's attention and ensuring that they feel a deep sense of responsibility over their decision. Most board decisions aren't life or death but it is always important when people have lost sight of their responsibilities or the consequences to others of what they are deciding to remind them of the seriousness of what is being discussed. It also focuses people on deciding what is the right thing to do rather than taking the easy or expedient choice.

This, however, clashes with Juror number 7's position who sees it all as an inconvenience and just wants a quick decision so he can get to his baseball game. Juror number 7 presumes guilt, believes that's the mood of the room and so adopts a strong competitive position. *"You wouldn't change my mind if you talked for 100 years."* However, later on when it reaches 6 – 6 he suddenly switches in a wonderful example of the *"Compete-Avoid"* switch described on page 140.

Another thing that Fonda does is to demonstrate the power of humility. His line *"I don't know whether he is guilty or not."* shows great empathy with those who also haven't jumped to a quick conclusion. He then builds on this by getting people to put themselves in the young man's shoes. He thinks this is important as he wants to ensure there were no other possible explanations as to what happened. Humility and empathy combined are extremely helpful in gaining alignment if combined with the strength of personality or position which commands respect.

A part of Fonda's personality which is very helpful is his steady and calm disposition which is contrasted with the majority who are more emotional and expressive or the coldness of Juror number 4 who is probably the strongest intellectually and most logic-driven. Fonda has an assured, calm but strong voice which isn't dominant or weak.

He has a big impact on evidence-driven Juror number 4 by doing his homework and finding evidence that the knife which was used in the killing was more widely available than stated in court, thus injecting the possibility of another explanation for the murder.

Juror number 8's use of *"drippy drippy"* comments which build to get what he wants is also masterful. I guess today we would call that brilliant use of *"nudge theory"* (*see* page 254). He deftly deals with the considerable bias shown by others, not by arguing with them head-on but by letting them build their biases into preposterous positions which undermined their arguments. Bias is covered in considerable detail on page 236.

Most of us will recognise much from the film in board experiences that we have had over the years.

Achieving alignment has much to do with building power and influence and being able to manage conflict effectively, the subjects of the next two parts of this section.

Power and influence

As a starting point it is worth being clear what we mean by power and influence. More traditional definitions of power define it as the ability to control people or events. Influence is typically defined as the capacity to have an effect on the character, development, or behaviour of someone or something, or on the effect itself. Implicit in these definitions is that the more power you have the more influence you have.

As mentioned on page 104, management guru Warren Bennis came up with what I think is a better description of what power is in a board context, namely: *"The ability to convert vision into reality."* Part of its appeal is that you have a vision, something that you want to see happen or not. Another is that by saying you have the ability to convert it into reality there is the suggestion that you don't have to do it all yourself or necessarily control other people to achieve what you want.

You can be a powerful board member simply if the questions you ask lead the exec to go forward with something you would like to see happen or halt a course of action when they might not have otherwise done so.

Professor Linda Hill at Harvard Business School is an authority on the subject of power and has looked at the sources of power for individuals in organisations. In her 1995 work *"Power Dynamics in Organisations"* she categorised the sources of power into *"positional"* powers and *"personal"* powers (*see* Figure 2:7).

Formal authority conveys formal powers. For example if you are a Chair, CEO or CFO you will tend to have more approval rights than other non-execs, trustees or execs and therefore more power. However, those powers derived from the formal authority that you have are only useful if they are relevant.

Figure 2:7 Sources of power

Positional	Personal
· Formal authority	· Expertise
· Relevance	· Track record
· Centrality	· Attractiveness
· Autonomy	· Visibility

Linda Hall: Power Dynamics in organisation HBS 1995

Centrality relates to the power that you get literally from being at the centre of things, knowing what's going on, being involved in the important decisions and so on. The CEO and the CFO will tend to be the most central of the execs on a board and the Chair and SID the most central of the non-execs.

Autonomy is all about what you can decide on your own without reference to others. There isn't much of this these days with the checks and balances that exist in most well-governed organisations.

IDs and execs who aren't the CEO or CFO will generally have to rely more on their personal powers than their positional ones to achieve influence on a board. The most obvious two of these are expertise and track record. Although recently *"experts"* have come in for scorn from certain politicians, in most board settings those with demonstrable expertise and track records of success on certain issues will generally be respected and influence outcomes.

There are essentially two forms of attractiveness, *"physical"* and *"personality or charisma"* in this context. Physical attractiveness can convey power but as beauty is in the eye of beholder and there are significant cultural and other factors influencing what we consider to be attractive, it is far from straightforward. However, historical research suggests that height helps and for a time in the US the profile of the *"silver fox"* for males was helpful in a board context in conveying more power with men and women. These were those over six feet, with good heads of silver hair, strong jaws, good teeth and of athletic build. A look through the annual reports of S&P 500 companies in the 1990s and first decade of this century seemed to demonstrate this. The rise of the tech companies and other social changes are probably eroding the *"silver foxes"* dominance.

There doesn't seem to be an equivalent of the *"silver fox"* for women in terms of a physical profile conveying more power.

Another concept relating to influence is the *"Hill of Influence"*. I have to thank my friend Nigel Grierson for pointing me in the direction of this piece of work by Edward Muzio, CEO of Group Harmonics. The idea is that if you take a typical meeting a participant in it can choose to be involved in a number of ways and that will have an effect on their influence. Overall as Chair of the meeting you are likely to want active and even participation without anyone dominating over the course of the meeting.

Figure 2:8 Hill of influence

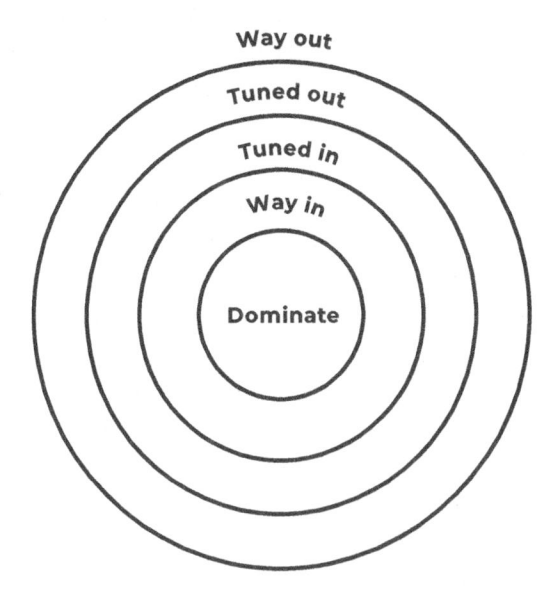

- Way out
- Tuned out
- Tuned in
- Way in
- Dominate

Source: *Iterate: Run a Fast, Flexible, Focused Management Team*
Edward Muzio, CEO, Group Harmonics

Edward describes the five states above to illustrate this using the analogy of a hill. Topologically, if you *"dominate"* you are at the top of the hill, bang in the centre of everything; whereas, if you are on the outskirts of the hill at the bottom you are *"way out"* with little influence. Perhaps you don't think the issue being discussed is relevant or you are thinking of other things. If you are *"way in"* then you have a lot of influence and are an active participant. If you are *"tuned in"* then you are listening and will be able to become *"way in"* when required or relevant. Yet remember if you stay completely "tuned in" but never get "way in" you probably won't be seen as one of the central characters. If you are *"tuned out"* then you aren't engaged and being further from what's going on you may find it hard to get in when you might want to.

He suggests using this model, which he also describes as *"talk up or shut up"*, as a tool to get people reflecting and thinking about how they engage in meetings. It is a useful analogy.

Smart use of body language is another way of increasing your influence. The main forms of body language relevant to board interactions are those to do with the face, posture, body movement, eye contact and voice. The most effective board members are skillful at using all of these aspects to increase their performance in terms of achieving the outcomes that they wish to see. Beware though, overuse or non-genuine use of such techniques can just as easily undermine respect.

Our facial expressions are highly effective givers of feedback and tools for letting people know how we are thinking and feeling. A smile or a scowl can change the mood instantly whether it is a deliberate act or an instinctive subconscious reaction. The ability to be inscrutable and not portray how you are feeling can be highly useful and is frequently deemed to be a great skill. However, the downside is that others may feel you are manipulative, cold and lacking in empathy or have something to hide.

An appropriate level of eye contact is important in showing respect by demonstrating that you are listening and paying attention. Too much and it can feel threatening whereas avoiding eye contact may indicate that you don't want to reveal too much or are anxious.

Eye contact can also be used to bring someone into the conversation. If a simple smile and look doesn't do the trick then using what is known as the *"finger switch"* nearly always does, even with those who are relatively introverted. The finger switch is simply turning the angle of your hand outwards and gently pointing to the person that you want to bring in.

There is a growing research base using facial imaging studies to support the idea that eye contact arouses our social brain and signals that communication is coming; also that a direct gaze does indeed hold attention. In her 2012 article *"Eye contact: Don't make these mistakes"* Jodi Schulz from *Michigan State University* in 2012 provides a number of tips for using eye contact effectively.

I haven't been able to find the research which backs up the 50/70 rule but it feels believable.

We can also use our posture in a meeting to show interest and other feelings. For example, a Chair leaning forward when the CEO is talking too much when others want to join the conversation gives a clear signal and usually the CEO gets it loud and clear. If not a simple lightly raised hand, the reverse of the *"finger switch"*, can be used to reinforce the message.

Leaning back from a forward lean to the neutral of further back is a good way of reducing tension and almost always results in others doing likewise because as humans we tend to mirror such actions.

Eye contact: don't make these mistakes

Use the 50/70 rule. To maintain appropriate eye contact without staring, you should maintain eye contact for 50 per cent of the time while speaking and 70 per cent of the time while listening. This helps to display interest and confidence.

Maintain it for 4-5 seconds. Once you establish eye contact, maintain or hold it for 4-5 seconds. After this time passes, you can slowly glance to the side and then go back to establishing eye contact.

Think about where you're looking. Maintaining eye contact is easy because you're looking at the other person. However, when you look away, do it slowly without darting your eyes. This can make you look shy or nervous. And don't look down; remember to look from side-to-side. Looking down can give the appearance that you lack confidence.

Establish eye contact right away. Before you begin talking, establish eye contact. Don't look down or look at something before you begin speaking. Establish eye contact right away and then begin talking.

Listening with your eyes is important too: Remember the 70 per cent rule (you should maintain eye contact for 70 per cent of the time while listening)? Communication happens with your eyes while you're listening just as much as when you're talking. Remember that while you're listening and maintaining eye contact, you should smile, open your face and look interested.

Practice. Eye contact will come easy to some, but if it doesn't for you, it's okay to practice until you become confident. You can look at an eyebrow or the space between the eyes and mouth. You can also practice with yourself in the mirror.

Jodie Schulz

Our voice is also important tool. Just think of the number of ways that you can express the words *"yes"* or *"no"*. On page 101 we heard that it takes just one tenth of a second for our brains to recognise emotions conveyed by vocalisations and that it doesn't matter whether these non-verbal sounds are growls of anger, the laughter of happiness or cries of sadness.

The use of non-verbal can be powerful but we can't get through a whole board meeting with laughs and grunts. The words we use and the intonation we give them are also important. One of the most important words that we will use is the word we use to join a conversation. If you filmed a classic engaged board meeting in the West you would probably find that it was, what can best be described as, a giant *"interrupt-fest"*. We tend not to leave a pause before we build upon or challenge someone else's point. To many other cultures this seems weird and disrespectful even if it isn't intended to be so.

Conventions differ and in some boards you raise your hand if you want to say something and wait for the Chair to effectively give you permission to speak. My own preference is generally not to be that formal allowing a conversation to develop but scanning the room to ensure that those who look like they want to speak are given that opportunity and those that don't are also asked for their views. Where I am not Chair I've found that a hand signal or simply saying the word *"I"* is the best way to get into the flow.

"I" is a very useful word as it is short and can easily be followed up with good entrée words into a discussion whether we want to follow up with a clarifying, probing, challenging or blocking question. For example *"I would be really grateful if you could drill down on the XYZ point please." "I would like to understand better what you think the competitors' reaction if we do this will be." "I wonder if you could remind me of the data set on that."* or, *"I don't think doing that would fit with our values, what do others think?"*

On the FT NED Diploma Ali Gill and Murray Steele do an excellent session on creating a culture of constructive challenge and using role plays to build experience of moving in and out of the zone of comfortable and uncomfortable debate with ease.

They describe the benefits of a culture of constructive challenge and the ability to ask good questions:

- helping people to solve their own problems and thus are empowering;
- provoking thought and insight;
- surfacing underlying assumptions;

- inviting creativity and new possibilities;
- generating energy and forward movement;
- channelling attention and focusing inquiry;
- staying with participants for a longer time;
- touching a deep meaning;
- evoking more questions and;
- encouraging engagement.

They then look at the three types of questions below. The key point being to have a clear motive in asking a question and not to get stuck in asking one type of question or simply reacting to what is put before you but to use all three types of question to ensure rigour:

Conceptual clarification questions

- Why are you saying that?
- What exactly does this mean?
- How does this relate to what we have been talking about?
- What is the nature of...?
- What do we already know about this?
- Can you give me an example?
- Are you saying... or...?

Probing assumptions

- What else could we assume?
- How did you choose those assumptions?
- Please explain why/how...?
- How can you verify or disprove that assumption?
- What would happen if...?

Probing rationale, reasons and evidence

- Why is that happening?
- How do you know this?
- Show me...?
- Can you give me an example of that?

- What do you think causes...?
- Why is... happening?
- Why? (keep asking it - you'll never get past a few times)
- What evidence is there to support what you are saying?
- On what authority are you basing your argument?

Finally, if you want to read more on power, Robert Greene's *"48 laws of Power"* provides an interesting tour of the topic with an entertainingly cynical eye.

Common causes of dysfunction

I love working with dysfunctional boards and trying to help them to become more effective. When you do a lot of this you look for common patterns and work hard to distinguish between symptoms and root causes. The *"Purpose"*, *"People"* and *"Process"* framework has proven to be a useful diagnostic for understanding where a board is. In applying it I have observed that the following are regular features of a board in bother:

❏ **Purpose**

◊ Lack of agreement or alignment on purpose of the organisation, the board, the key roles on it, sub-committees and its relationship with the exec, shareholders and others.

❏ **People**

◊ Composition in terms of matching what is needed.
◊ Quality of relationships (they tend to be either end of the harmony spectrum).
◊ Cohesiveness of exec team.
◊ Poor board and exec interaction and a lack of respect for the board from broader leadership group.
◊ Weak at managing conflict.
◊ Lack of diversity.
◊ Recognition privately that things need to change but no-one prepared to take the lead.

PEOPLE

❏ **Process**

- ◊ Rarely one process deficiency. Usually a number of process flaws and inefficiencies.
- ◊ Poor decision-making processes and buy-in.
- ◊ Lack of fit between agendas and real issues.
- ◊ Ritualised agendas.
- ◊ Poor board papers.
- ◊ Ineffective management of meetings.
- ◊ Big decisions taken outside of board meetings.
- ◊ Poor follow-through from board to action.

One of life's paradoxes is when what I call "*heavy hitter*" boards, lose the plot and an organisation collapses, despite it having what looks like the fantasy board. In "*Directors' Dilemmas*" I offered some personal views posed as questions:

- "*Is it because the board of heavy hitters is usually assembled for a big business?*"

    They are all busy people and the business is complex. They can't possibly be on top of all of the detail. They may miss the signals that there is a problem emerging.

- "*Is it because they always think someone else has the problems thought-through?*"

    The high degree of mutual respect they have for their board-room colleagues may mean that things fall between the cracks. Is everyone thinking "*It must be ok because Jane or Joe haven't said anything?*"

- "*Is it because their skills and experience are not relevant to the company concerned?*"

    They may be wise and wonderfully warm human beings but are simply not relevant to the issue of the particular situation.

- *"Does the arrogance that sometimes goes with a prolonged period as a big hitter numb their antennae?"*
  Persistent preening and grooming may dull the senses.

- *"Is too much focus placed on the CEO and FD in terms of information flow?"*
  If board meetings become a carefully organised show for the non-execs this is a possibility.

Finally, and perhaps the most difficult question:

- *"Is the heavy hitter's reputation deserved?"*

The final and obvious points on this are that a heavy hitter board by definition is less diverse as they are all heavy hitters and *"groupthink"* (*see* page 240) applies as much to heavy hitters as any other group. In 2019 Capita plc a FTSE 100 UK company made a bold move appointing two non-execs from within the business at more junior levels. The main reason stated in the announcement was to bring diversity of thought and to strengthen decision making. The two are paid the same annual fee and expenses as other non-execs and have equal authority in strategic decision making as other directors. This is clearly an experiment with their initial period of appointment being two to three years but a bold statement by the company.

Others have created "NextGen" boards to connect with more diverse thinking and challenge (page 134).

It's a bit dated now in terms of the examples used but the *"Paranoid Corporation"* book by William and Nurit also offers further interesting insights into how boards lose the plot. These two psychologists studied a series of high-profile corporate failures in the US and came to the conclusion that the failures were generally down to one of, or a combination of, two psychological illnesses *"Psychoses"* and *"Neuroses"*. Fig. 2.9 summarises what they meant and I feel their work still has relevance and resonates. Just think of whatever is the latest mess in your country or sector and you will probably see what I mean.

So, in terms of board building and composition, you need to ensure that you have a range of characters who are collectively not susceptible to neuroses and psychoses, even though some of the individuals inevitably will be.

Figure 2:9 Psychoses and neuroses

Psychoses	
"Illnesses in which contact with reality is lost"	
Examples	Symptoms
· Manic behaviour	· Expansive moods
· Manic depression	· Grandiosity
· Schizophrenia	· Excessive excitement
· Paranoia	· Low attention to detail and few hard plans

Neuroses	
"Disabling emotional disorders"	
Examples	Symptoms
· Neurotic behaviour	· Fear and self doubt Inability to act
· Depression	· Apathy, lack of commitment
· Intoxication	
· Obsessive compulsion	· Inability to do self analysis break out of unproductive cycles
· Post-trauma syndrome	· Shock, erratic behaviour
	· Victim mindset refusal to take responsibility for the future

William and Nurit: The Paranoid Corporation

Managing diversity, difference and inclusion

Considerable progress has been made in recent years in some aspects of managing diversity, difference and inclusion in organisations in many countries and sectors, most notably on gender. Yet it is not a tale of consistent and steady progress everywhere and progress has been at a glacial pace even where it has been made. As noted on page 4 it has taken the UK almost two decades to go from 6% of women on boards of companies to 34%. At that rate gender parity is still at least a decade away. In some countries, most notably the US and Russia, there have been high-profile examples of reversion to less tolerant and inclusive ideals.

In his *"Rebel Ideas"* book on the subject, published in 2021, Matthew Syed makes the point powerfully that diversity adds to collective intelligence, innovation and creativity. He emphasises the importance of relevance and the benefits arising from greater coverage of problem space and reduction in the risk of Group Think (page 240) if you get the right mix.

The hard evidence to support the argument is patchy but growing. Research from McKinsey in their 2018 *"Delivering through Diversity"* stated that

"Companies in the top-quartile for gender diversity on their executive teams were 21% more likely to have above-average profitability than companies in the fourth quartile. For ethnic/cultural diversity, top-quartile companies were 33% more likely to outperform on profitability."

Different together

At Apple, we're not all the same. And that's our greatest strength. We draw on the differences in who we are, what we've experienced, and how we think. Because to create products that serve everyone, we believe in including everyone.

Love them or loathe them, Apple Inc's statement of what it means by diversity and inclusion and managing differences is a good example of a progressive approach to the subject and one which is directly linked to their business. They also back it up with evidence through statistics and personal stories to show that they mean it and to compare themselves with others. Their current CEO, Tim Cook, has also made a very public stand on a number of issues to further evidence the company's commitment.

A board needs to lead on this issue, to set an example, to encourage diversity and inclusion and to be clear what it will and won't accept as acceptable behaviour. It is a complex area and there are many ways that difference can be defined. Most countries will have legislation in this area. The laws are typically covered under *"Equality"* legislation and are designed to eliminate unlawful discrimination, victimisation and harassment and more positively stimulate the advancement of equality of opportunity.

In the UK for example the Equality Act of 2010 is the main piece of legislation. This Act brought together a range of laws relating to different areas including gender, race, age, disability and so on. It defined a number of *"protected characteristics"*. These are: age, disability, gender, sexual orientation, gender reassignment, marriage and civil partnership, pregnancy and maternity, race and religion.

As noted above considerable progress has been made in terms of gender balance, although there is still some way to go, even in those countries which are advancing on the issue. Sadly, there has been less progress in other areas, eg on race, disability and in social diversity.

Sir John Parker's review of ethnic diversity on major UK boards in 2017 contains the following statement

"As at the end of July 2017, only 85 of the 1,050 director positions in the FTSE 100 are held by people from ethnic minorities. In fact, only 2% of director positions are held by people from ethnic minorities who are UK citizens, despite this group making up 14% of the total UK population (up from 2% in 1971). 51 companies of the FTSE 100 do not have any ethnic minorities on their Boards."

According to Sir John:

"Today's FTSE 100 and 250 Boards do not reflect the society we live in, nor do they reflect the international markets in which they operate. Whilst we are making good progress on gender diversity in the Boardroom, we still have much to do when it comes to ethnic and cultural diversity."

The Report made a number of recommendations to improve the position including that the FTSE100 should *"Go beyond one by (20) 21"* and *"that a lot more effort should go into developing the pipeline."*, something which the 30% Club has focused on in relation to increasing the proportion of women on boards.

A 2019 report in the UK *"Elitist Britain"* by the highly regarded Sutton Trust and the Social Mobility Commission analysed the educational background of 5,000 people in top jobs in business, politics, the media, public organisations, creative industries and sport. They found that other than in sport, these influential people were five times more likely to be privately educated than the average population. This problem is even more pronounced in many other countries around the world.

The Colour of Power reports by search firm Green Park reinforce this with respect to race. Indeed in Feb 2021 they reported that there were no black executives in any of the three top executive roles in the FTSE 100.

As far as I know there is no up to date report on the demographics of disabled, dyslexic directors or trustees and the many other forms of difference. I'd like to see more work in these areas.

I'm an unashamed idealist yet I recognise the practical challenges and effort that it takes to turn those ideals into reality. It can be really challenging when recruiting to meet your goals in terms of diversity, especially in smaller organisations where you don't have the pick of a much broader field. But it should never stop you trying and sponsoring and developing the role models who will inspire others and help you to recruit and develop more diverse pipelines. The way that Leap Confronting Conflict, the EY Foundation and ESSA have engaged young people from groups who don't normally have a say in things has been hugely beneficial to the organisations and well worth the effort.

Having a good policy and the best of intentions is not enough. You have to mean it, live it, evidence it and, most importantly, those people who come from groups considered to be different to the majority have to feel it.

One way an increasing number of boards are tackling generational diversity is through "*NextGen*" boards. These vary from boards composed of younger managers in the organsiation to boards with groups of independent but connected younger members relevant to the organsiation's business. Good examples of these are Gucci, Interbrand, the FT and the EY Foundation which I Chair. Although most of these NextGen boards are not accountable for governance sometimes the Chair will sit on the main board. In the case of the EY Foundation the Chair and the Vice Chair of the Youth Advisory Board sit on the main Trustee Board. NextGen boards terms of reference are typically to provide insight and challenge to the main board and senior executive.

An important aspect of difference is cultural difference. A book well worth reading on this topic is Erin Meyer's "*The Culture Map*". Erin is a Professor of Organisational Behaviour at INSEAD and has focused her work on understanding and managing cultural differences. Her view is that although cultural stereotypes are unhelpful, understanding cultural norms in a sophisticated way can be very useful. So, for example, although the cultural norm in the US is to be more extrovert than in Japan, not all Americans are more extrovert than all Japanese and there are many Japanese who are way more extrovert than many Americans.

Erin's research led her to identifying several dimensions of difference which matter in a working together context. For example the way we communicate or make decisions. Her research has also inspired the idea that cultural relativity matters especially when working with groups of numerous nationalities. This in part is because she believes that we can place ourselves along a spectrum in relation to each dimension. For example in communicating we may prefer a very low context form of communication at one end of the spectrum with simple language and brief points or a very high one at the other involving lots of nuance. So, the US, Holland and Australia are at the far end of the low context spectrum, the English may be considered by the Japanese and Kenyans at the other end of the spectrum to be very low context communicators but to the Americans and Dutch we are relatively high context and occasionally confusing.

While the focus of Erin's work has been on different regions and nationalities it seems to me to have application beyond as I don't believe culture is confined to nationality or region. Different sectors, functions and individual organisations even in the same sector, have different cultures.

Figure 2:10 summarises the eight dimensions which Erin feels are most relevant to organisational groups. I have presented them in this way because when working with boards where there are issues between people I have found it helpful to get the people involved to place themselves, and those that they are finding it hard to work with, on each of the spectrums. It is so often the case that when you do this the scales fall and people understand why it is that they find someone really frustrating to deal with.

We've covered *"Communicating"* above. In terms of *"Evaluating"*, in some cultures, eg Russia, Israel or Holland, direct negative feedback is not just acceptable but expected: whereas in others, eg Japan, Thailand or Indonesia, it is considered unacceptable and rude.

When we are *"Persuading"* people we may prefer a principles-based approach to putting our case. This is sometimes known as deductive reasoning where we derive conclusions from general principles. Alternatively we may prefer an applications-based approach sometimes called *"inductive reasoning"*. Here general conclusions are drawn from observing facts. The persuader may tend to say *"In my experience, ..."*. *"When we had the situation at the XYZ company we..."* and so on. According to Erin the Italians, French and Spanish tend towards the *"Principles-first"* approach, while the Americans and Australians tend towards the *"Applications-first"* end of the spectrum.

The *"Leading"* and *"Deciding"* spectrums are a little more obvious with those of an egalitarian persuasion, eg those in the Nordic countries, believing in consensus and buy-in and those who prefer more hierarchical approaches,

Figure 2:10 Cultural differences

Communicating	Low context	High context
Evaluating	Direct negative feedback	Indirect negative feedback
Persuading	Principles-first	Applications-first
Leading	Egalitarian	Hierarchical
Deciding	Consensual	Top down
Trusting	Task based	Relationship based
Disagreeing	Confrontational	Avoids confrontation
Scheduling	Linear	Flexible

Source: Erin Meyer INSEAD

eg the Chinese and Koreans, preferring command and control. This spectrum I think is especially interesting at the moment given the transformations happening in societies, technology and communications. There are huge pressures on boards from both ends of the spectrum. Staff, customers and other stakeholders are demanding more and more say in decisions and more and more transparency. At the same time with ever increasing expectations and lowering tolerance to failure, boards need to ensure there are strong control processes in place.

Interestingly, I was at something recently on the future of management and the feeling in the group was that age of "*command and control*" was dead. I challenged this as I really don't think that you can run an airline, a bank, a hospital or a distribution company in a completely egalitarian way. Moreover, I'm not generally a fan of "*either or*" choices. Life is generally more complex than that. Imagine the CEO of an airline gathering staff together in the morning and asking "*Who wants to fly the planes today, who fancies doing maintenance?*" and so on. The pandemic has also shown all too well the importance of well controlled and managed organsiations and the tragic circumstances which can arise from a lack of it.

At the same time these major organisations need to recruit highly talented creative people in parts of their organisations so have to be able to have the culture to satisfy a wide range of appetites for different leadership styles. It is also important to recognise that those who understand the importance of rules and for a high order of process discipline and are happy with those constraints have just as much right to feel listened to as well as to have the opportunity to have their views heard.

When it comes to *"trusting"* a task-based approach essentially means testing you. I give you something to do, you do it and if you do a good job I trust you enough to give you more and if you do a bad job that's it. It's pretty transactional. Taking a relationship-based approach means that I have to get to know you and build some sort of relationship before we can do business together. South American and Asian countries dominate the relationship end of the spectrum and Anglo Saxon ones, the other.

In *"Disagreeing"* the norm for Israelis, Russians and Germans is to get it all out there and deal with it while the norm for Ghanaians and the Thai is to deal with things quietly behind the scenes. Here the UK is in the middle.

The last spectrum *"Scheduling"* is very interesting in a board context and no surprise that the norm for the Swiss and the Germans are at the linear end of the spectrum preferring to do things in order and promptly. The Nigerians and Indians are at the other end of the spectrum preferring to do many things at the same time and being highly flexible as to timelines.

The central point in all of this is that understanding how you and someone else like to do things can help you pick the right approach to take with them, whether you are communicating, evaluating, persuad- ing, leading, deciding, trusting, disagreeing or scheduling something with them.

Managing conflict

Understandably, conflict is often viewed as a negative but it can also be a highly positive force for good in a board context. Conflicting ideas and personalities may be powerful stimulants to creativity and prove to be a strong vaccine against *"groupthink"* (page 240). Conflicts on boards can apply to ideas, interests, objectives, choices, personalities and other things so it is probably wise, given that and the nature of humans, to assume that conflict will arise at some point and focus on how to reduce the likelihood of negative conflict as well as how to manage it well.

Inner conflict can prove a driver of external conflict in that if we are uncomfortable either with choices we have to make or, for whatever reason, with ourselves this can bubble up and affect relationships with others. The simple choice of reading every line of every paper or skimming some and having more family time is a classic *"priority"* conflict we can have with ourselves. Of course, if we make the wrong judgement it can lead to conflict with others.

Kurt Lewin, the psychologist who coined the phrase *"group dynamics"*, did the pioneering work into force field analysis and did some interesting work on the nature of inner conflict. He categorised the types of conflict we may face in making choices:

- **"Approach-Approach"** - we want two different things, both of which we like (that have *"positive valences"* in Lewin's terms).
- **"Avoidance-Avoidance"** - we have to pick one or the other alternative, but dislike both (both have *"negative valences"*).
- **"Approach-Avoidance"** - we can either have, or subject ourselves to, one thing that has both positive and negative qualities; or
- **"Double Approach-Avoidance"** - we must choose between two things that each have both positive and negative qualities.

These sorts of conflicts are really to do with decisions and so are covered more fully in the "Decision" section (*see* page 219).

The only point on them I will make here relates to *"Vacillation"*, the inability to make a decision. I guess we have all come across life's natural vacillators or procrastinators. You may even be one. If you are, then you may find that others are incredibly frustrated by you from time to time but also find that you have saved them from the worst mistakes they might make through forcing them to give things more thought and time to make the decision when it comes to a tricky choice.

Two other psychologists Neal Miller and John Dollard did some interesting work on vacillation based on Lewin's categories of conflict. They conducted a series of experiments in which a hungry rat was on a runway with food at the end of it. In order to get the food the rat had to endure a shock.

They found in watching the rat that there was a *"vacillation point"*. When it was farther away, the rat tended to move toward the food or *"goal box"*. When it got closer to it, the rat tended to withdraw back to that *"vacillation point"*. They then drew two lines on a graph to represent that tendency that they called an *"Approach Gradient"* and an *"Avoidance Gradient"*. I can think of many meetings where I have been on full approach and then instinctively felt the gravitational pull of an *"Avoidance Gradient"*.

The main type of conflict I want to cover here relates to conflict with others as I think for board members, or for those working with a board it is managing conflict with or for others that will have the biggest impact on performance. That is assuming that you know how to manage your own inner conflicts, which is a big assumption I know.

The *"Managing cultural differences"* section above considered the nature of cultural differences. Figure 2:10 on page 136 is helpful when you think about where you might be on each of the spectrums and where others are as well. As we discovered on page 92 the degree of self-awareness we possess can make a material difference to our performance if we use that insight. Since we don't operate in isolation it must also be the case that gaining greater insight into others that we are working with must help as well if we have good judgement and interpersonal skills.

Understanding our instinctive preferences to dealing with conflict situations and those of others is really useful. The best test I have found for this is the TKI test constructed by Kenneth Thomas and Ralph Kilmann. I know, wonderful name for someone studying conflict isn't it? You can do it online or better, in my view, when together as a board as a whole. Although I don't have hard evidence to prove it, it is best to order the booklets and do it together, independently but at the same time, taking no more than 20 minutes. There are fewer attempts to game it this way and I think that a little bit of extra pressure is even more likely to bring out the instinctive choice.

Thomas and Kilmann proposed that there were essentially five ways to respond to a conflict situation: *"compete"*, *"collaborate"*, *"compromise"*, *"avoid"* or *"accommodate"*. Each of these has varying strengths of being assertive or co-operative, assertive in the sense of the extent to which an individual attempts to satisfy their own concerns and co-operative in the sense that they attempt to satisfy the concerns of others.

The descriptions of these five approaches below are highly relevant to board situations:

Figure 2:11 Managing conflict

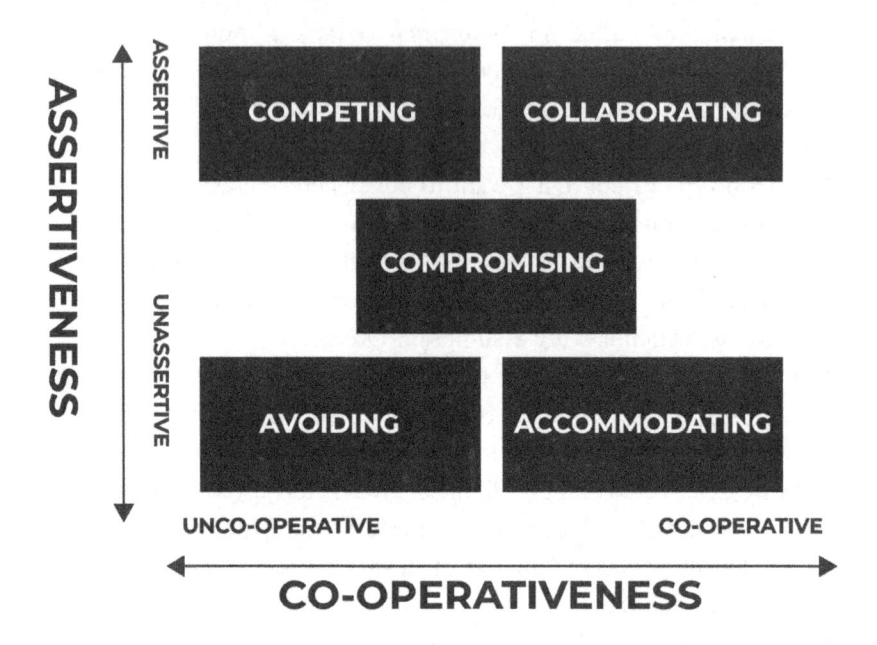

```
                  ASSERTIVE
              ┌──────────────┬──────────────┐
              │  COMPETING   │ COLLABORATING│
ASSERTIVENESS │              │              │
              │      ┌───────────────┐      │
              │      │ COMPROMISING  │      │
              │      └───────────────┘      │
              │   AVOIDING   │ ACCOMMODATING│
              └──────────────┴──────────────┘
                UNCO-OPERATIVE   CO-OPERATIVE
                    CO-OPERATIVENESS
```

In general when you test board members, exec or non-exec, they rarely have a rigid one mode response to all conflict situations and are capable of using all five. However, you do observe that most people tend to use a couple more than others. This can be driven by personality and the situations that they regularly find themselves in. Certain roles may attract you because of their nature and fit with your preferences.

I have found that when testing CEOs they tend to be high in "*compete*" and "*avoid*", prepared to die in a ditch over things they care about and avoiding things that they don't: an approach, if used consciously, which is known as "*picking your battles*".

Sophisticated CEOs may fool you in a meeting by throwing a veil of collaboration over the meeting. Perhaps starting it by saying: "*Morning everyone I am really keen to know what everyone thinks.*" If the team come up with the right answer then all is fine and happy. Yet, if they don't, then if it is something that matters a lot to them the "*compete*" switch goes on and if not it flicks to "*avoid*".

The best Chairs, non-execs and trustees that I have tested tend to have more balanced scores and have the ability to choose which one to deploy

Five ways to respond to a conflict situation

Compete
Assertive and unco-operative, a power-orientated mode. When competing, an individual pursues their own concerns at the other person's expense, using whatever power seems appropriate to win their position. Competing might mean standing up for your rights, defending a position you believe is correct, or simply trying to win.

Collaborate
Both assertive and co-operative. When collaborating, an individual attempts to work with the other person to find a solution that fully satisfies the concerns of both. It involves digging into an issue to identify the underlying concerns of the two individuals and to find an alternative that meets both sets of concerns. Collaborating between two persons might take the form of exploring a disagreement to learn from each other's insights, resolving some condition that would otherwise have them competing for resources, or confronting and trying to find a creative solution to an interpersonal problem.

Compromise
Is intermediate in both assertiveness and co-operativeness. When compromising, the objective is to find an expedient, mutually-acceptable solution that partially satisfies both parties. Compromising falls on a middle ground between competing and accommodating, giving up more than competing but less than accommodating. Likewise it addresses an issue more directly than avoiding but doesn't explore it in as much depth as collaborating. Compromising might mean splitting the difference, exchanging concessions, or seeking a quick middle-ground position.

Avoid
Is unassertive and unco-operative. When avoiding, an individual does not immediately pursue their own concerns or those of the other person. They do not address the conflict. Avoiding might take the form of diplomatically side-stepping an issue, postponing an issue until a better time, or simply withdrawing from a threatening position.

Accommodate
Is unassertive and co-operative - the opposite of competing. When accommodating, an individual neglects their own concerns to satisfy the concerns of the other person; there is an element of self-sacrifice in this mode. Accommodating might take the form of selfless generosity or charity, obeying another person's order when you would prefer not to, or yielding to another's point of view.

with that person in that situation on that day with that atmosphere in the room. In other words they can manage their instincts and are able to respond rather than react.

It is tempting to feel that some of the five are less positive than others but all will have their potential uses and costs. For example, if you are highly competitive you may be a huge asset in a turnaround or a crisis like the pandemic where to be decisive is essential and you have to carry out unpopular actions. However, are you sure that people are always telling you what you need to hear rather than want you want to hear as they want to avoid a competition with you.

If you are high in collaborating you may be brilliant at gaining buy-in but are there times when you take too long or use up too much energy in the process which could be used on getting things done.

Those high on compromising can gets things done quickly and generate goodwill through trading what they want for what others want. Yet sometimes they sacrifice principles for short-term gains and if they are a known gamer then people will respond accordingly which may not always be helpful.

Being high on avoiding may have value in situations where you might use up energy or social credits on something of low value. However, you may frustrate others because they can't tell whether you care, you don't seem to be engaged or appear too risk averse.

The fundamental point is to be aware of your natural instincts, use them wisely when they are appropriate and think hard about using other approaches when they aren't. Whatever the situation it is also easier if you have a good understanding of those you are in conflict with and how they are likely to respond.

The Thomas Kilmann thinking is helpful but not sufficient and there is another approach which I learnt at Leap Confronting Conflict which supports it really well. The acronym for it is FIDO which stands for Facts, Interpretation, Decisions and Outcomes. The idea is really simple. Be clear what outcome you want. Understand the choices that you have to make that outcome more likely and to inform what you think might be the best outcome and the choices you will need to make. Finally be clear what the facts are and what you are making interpretations on.

The situation we use a lot at Leap Confronting Conflict to help young people practise this approach is where you get stopped on a Friday night by the police. The outcome that you want is obvious, ie to be able to proceed along your way and not end up in the back of the van and taken to a police station. However, given the circum- stances, that may be a non-starter so you have to understand what the facts are. Could be you were just walking along on your own, haven't done anything wrong and are a decent and well-behaved young adult. Could be that you have a history of offences and are with a group of young people with similar profiles a few hundred metres away from where someone has just been stabbed. You also have to understand what you are interpreting from what the police officers are saying and doing and what they might be interpreting from what you are saying and doing.

You then have to think about what things you definitely have a choice over, eg what you say and when and how you say it, your body language and general demeanor. All of these things could affect the outcome and all of these things are influenced by how we feel and what we think others are feeling and thinking. Sadly they are also things that can be hard to control in an emotionally-charged moment where we feel threatened or simply just anxious. We may reach tipping point where we lose self-control.

There are numerous boardroom analogies to the police stop whether you are a CEO being challenged about a pet project that should really be stopped or an independent director who is losing respect for not doing their homework.

On the subject of tipping points and whether you are prone to a little catastrophe or not, there is one powerful illustration of Catastrophe Theory in action which has high relevance for boards. It was highlighted by mathematician Professor Sir Christopher Zeeman in his 1978 paper *"Catastrophe Theory"*. Chris, the founder of the University of Warwick's maths department, wasn't the first to study *"Catastrophe Theory"* or to coin the phrase. That honour goes to Rene Thom, but Chris did a huge amount to advance the subject and to make it more accessible. Indeed, today there is even the Zeeman medal for communication of mathematics.

Put simply, *"Catastrophe Theory"* is the study of small perturbations which lead to a catastrophic shift. A popular example of this is the bags of flour on a model bridge experiment. Bags of flour are placed on the bridge until eventually the last one placed on it causes the bridge to collapse.

As we go through one of Chris' most famous examples of *"Catastrophe Theory"* in the animal world below imagine that the board is the dog and the human is the exec, the punchline being that if you are an exec never ever get your board frightened and angry at the same time. Figure 2.12 sums this up.

So, what's the equivalent of bared teeth and flattened ears for board members, how can you avoid such catastrophic tipping points and what can you do when you start to see the teeth being bared or the ears flattening. Face, voice and body language tend give it away and most times it is obvious when the anger or fear becomes significant. However, as it is much better to spot it before it becomes serious, what might be the early signs?

A furrowed brow, a tightening jaw, intense eye contact, light reddening of the face or the person looking around the table to see if others are feeling the same discomfort are good signs. Changes in posture, especially leaning forward, and more formal and less obviously friendly language are also useful signals, as are someone starting to tap the table, shake their leg, scratch their face or head repeatedly or clench their hands or laugh sarcastically. All of these are signs of tension and anger rising.

Figure 2:12 Catastrophe theory: aggression in dogs

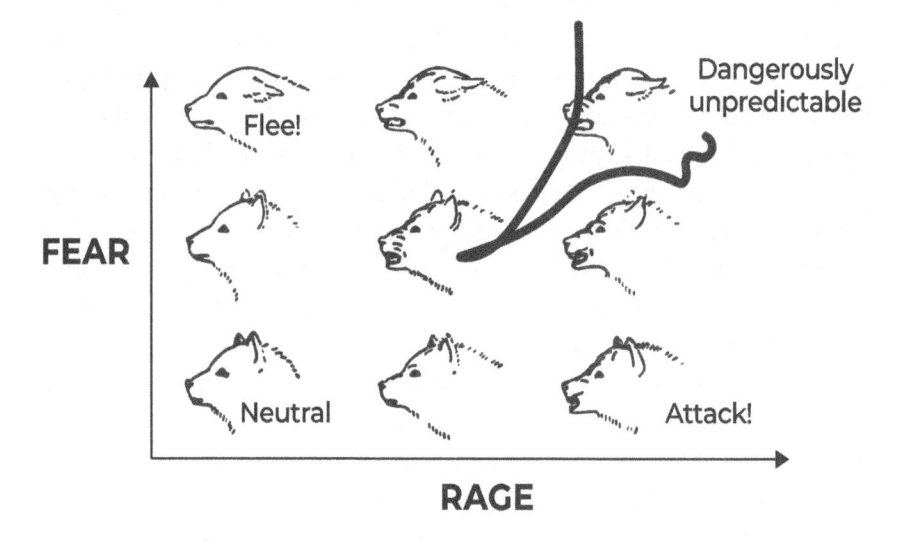

For early signs of fear instead of reddening they may start to pale. Errors in speech or in hearing can also be evident and varying speech tone or breathlessness are also clues. Twitching and avoiding eye contact are other signals. They may also be looking for reassurance from others that everything

Catastrophe Theory – an example

"I shall begin by considering a model of aggression in the dog. Konrad Z. Lorenz has pointed out that aggressive behaviour is influenced by two conflicting drivers, rage and fear and he has proposed that in the dog these factors can be measured with some reliability. A dog's rage is correlated with the degree to which its mouth is open or its teeth are bared; its fear is reflected by how much its ears are flattened back. By employing facial expression as an indicator of the dog's emotional state we can attempt to learn how the dog's behaviour varies as a function of its mood.

If only one of the conflicting emotional factors is present, the response of the dog is relatively easy to predict. If the dog is enraged but not afraid, then some aggressive action, such as attacking, can be expected. When the dog is frightened but is not provoked to anger, aggression becomes improbable and the dog will most likely flee. Prediction is also straightforward if neither stimulus is present, then the dog is likely to express some neutral kind of behaviour unrelated to aggression or submission.

What if the dog is made to feel both rage and fear simultaneously? The two controlling factors are then in direct conflict. Simple models that cannot accommodate discontinuity might predict that the two stimuli would cancel each other, leading again to neutral behaviour. That prediction merely reveals the shortcomings of such simplistic models, since in reality neutrality is in fact the least likely behaviour. When a dog is both angry and frightened, the probabilities of both extreme modes of behaviour are high; the dog may attack or flee but it will not remain indifferent. It is the strength of the model derived from Catastrophe Theory that it can account for this bi-modal distribution of probabilities. Moreover the model provides a basis for predicting, under particular circumstances, which behaviour the dog will choose."

Professor Sir Christopher Zeeman, University of Warwick.

is alright despite their anxieties. It might be that they also seem to be repeating themselves. The strategic toilet break is another good sign.

Removing directors

The topic of removing directors first began to interest me seriously when I took a call one morning from a recently-fired CEO of a 3i portfolio company. He wasn't someone I knew or had heard of before, but someone had suggested he call me and they hadn't had time to let me know before he called.

He started the conversation by asking: *"Are you responsible for training?"* *"Sorry, no."* I replied. *"But like all managers at 3i I get involved in delivering training. Sounds like you're pretty upset, and you might have an issue with us, what can I do to help."* *"Well,"* he said, *"let me tell you what happened to me yesterday."* He then launched into a rant about how he was fired the previous day and how awful it was.

After about ten minutes of what I thought was sensitive listening I thought that I had earned the right to ask a question, so I asked *"Would it be alright if I asked you a question?"* *"Sure."* he said. *"Well if I've heard you correctly, you aren't saying that it wasn't the right thing to make a change, it's just that you object to the way it was done."* *"Of course,"* he said, *"haven't you been f****** listening"*. I laughed and told him that although I couldn't have him unfired I could look into the situation to see what we could learn for other situations. Having got it all off his chest, he seemed very happy with that.

After finding out who was responsible for the firing, someone I knew very well and is a really decent person, I called him. As usual, I started the conversation with: *"Hi X how's it going?"* *"Well to be honest he said I had a really s*** day yesterday. We were removing a CEO who had badly underperformed and it all went pear-shaped. I really tried to be as sensitive as I could but it's the first time I have done it. I didn't have anyone with me and although I spent ages getting ready for it, a number of things came up that I didn't have answers for."*

The experience got me thinking and I wondered how good we were at removing directors, especially CEOs and Chairs. It felt like something that we should be good at given its importance to the individual and the momentum of the company, not to mention our reputation. So, I decided to find out who else had been fired from the portfolio recently and to get in touch with them and the Chairs and 3i people who had been involved to see what we could learn and then use what was learnt to construct a short training module on how to do it more effectively. Understandably the first person I rang who had been fired thought I was some sort of sicko sadist but when I explained why he was very open and following a pattern had a lot to get off his chest.

The learnings from this, my own experiences and further research then formed the basis of a short role play based course with the obvious title of *"Removing Directors"*. The key learnings driving this training where that very few people enjoy doing this and that preparation is paramount. Another important learning was that although people thought that they were putting in a lot of prep time they were confusing worrying with thinking. Worrying a bit is absolutely natural. We don't have to do this that often so may not have a lot of experience of doing it. *"Removal"* suggests an unplanned retirement or departure and an issue with the incumbent which they may or may not acknowledge or accept and finally it's personal.

So, what should we be thinking about in preparation? The issues will vary depending upon whether it is an executive or non-executive director, whether they are a shareholder or not as well as the context of the organisation and the specific reasons for making the change.

Whatever the situation I have always found the following checklist helpful.

- Ensure rationale for change is driven by what's best for the organisation.
- That Board and relevant stakeholders are aligned on the need for change, its timing and the way it is going to be done and communicated.
- Get the right legal, HR, regulatory and if relevant. Investor Relations advice so that you have the authority to make the change, are complying with the law as well as good practice and that you have the support in place to deliver what is needed.
- Decide upon the terms of departure and understand the financial and reputational implications.
- Agree the nature and process for succession. Is there an identified successor, will you be appointing an interim or conducting a formal search and selection process?

- Who is going to have the key conversation with the director being removed and when and where will it be?
- Role play the conversation with a colleague or peer and anticipate and be prepared for questions and reactions.
- On communications, have a detailed plan with consistent and clear key messages and remember sequencing is very important, especially for public companies or if the person has a high-profile.
- Finally, remember it is a human being and removal is rejection. They will be concerned about their reputation as well as any financial impact. Even if they have destroyed value or been personally difficult there is no upside in doing anything other than making it as smooth a process as you can for both the organisation and them.

Suffice to say that it is something that causes much anxiety, is absolutely one of those occasions where it is easy to confuse worrying about doing something with preparing to do it well and that very few people enjoy it. Generally, this is a matter for the Chair to take the lead on unless of course it is the Chair that is being removed.

Training and development

Governance codes tend to encourage training for board members rather than insist upon it. For example the UK Code for listed companies says

> *"All directors should receive induction on joining the board and should regularly update and refresh their skills and knowledge."*

They place the onus on the Chair to *"regularly review and agree with each director their training and development needs."*

Although I like the flexibility of this, I have always thought it a bit weak and that board training should start much earlier on in careers, especially for groups where the current pipeline is thin. Given the responsibilities we need to have the knowledge, skills and behaviours to do a good job. The most important preparation is experiential and there is a lot that is relevant in general executive training, but training on the specific things that you need to be a good board member can boost performance considerably. This is why I have been so keen to support and help create a number of programmes over the years, first within 3i and for our portfolio companies and board members and then beyond.

Historically, and still the case in many countries, an inhibitor to training was simply the fact that there were few courses or programmes available and those that were tended to be focused on knowledge and legal responsibilities in particular. This situation has changed consider- ably with many more choices available and a broader range in terms of content and style of delivery.

In addition to open programmes, many providers, including those where I am involved, eg Boardelta, Board Intelligence, Cranfield, FT Board Director Programme, Invest Europe and Winmark, offer tailored pro-grammes for specific companies or sectors, as do various trade associations.

Some, like FT BDP or the Institute of Directors, also offer formal qualifications such as the FT Non-Executive Director Diploma or the IOD Chartered Director and certificates.

Business schools and professional service firms also offer a wide range of other provision covering the span of relevant topics. The professional service firms also have networks to share experiences with peer groups which is another valuable contribution to development.

My personal preference is for those which offer a healthy mix of the practical and strategic and where the delivery is by experienced practitioners and there is the opportunity to learn with peers as well as those who are more experienced. In terms of content and delivery simulations, case studies, role plays, group work and high levels of interaction are more suitable than lectures or tales of how someone won the West in days gone by.

One of the good things to come out of the pandemic was the number of peer group sessions which sprang up either within or across sectors on specific issues. I was lucky enough to take part in a number of these and learnt so much from what others were doing to help inform the decisions of the boards that I am on.

As with other areas of training the quality of content and delivery varies enormously around the world and within any country. It is wise to do your due diligence before investing the time and money and to find out which are the most suitable options for you. Short knowledge refreshes or introductions are important, eg finding out the latest thinking and practice on cybercrime or artificial intelligence as well as legal or regulatory changes; so are deeper sessions on key roles and people issues.

Section Three

Process

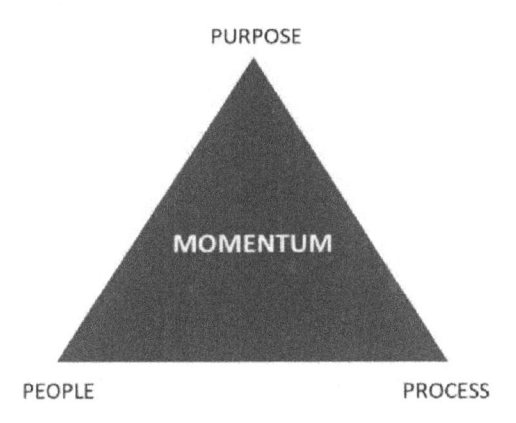

PURPOSE

MOMENTUM

PEOPLE   PROCESS

Introduction

Good plumbing is fundamental to helping many aspects of our lives go smoothly and so it is with a board. Talking about such hygiene factors might sound dull. You may also consider that the process stuff should all be dealt with by others. Yet the fact of the matter is that it is very hard to do our job as a board member in ensuring that there is effective governance if we haven't satisfied ourselves that the core board processes are effective. It can also be highly frustrating if the processes aren't good and end up wasting us a lot of time and energy.

So, what are these core board processes, how do we ensure that they are effective and how do we get the balance right between having the right processes in place and avoiding having either too much or irrelevant process?

Much depends upon the nature and purpose of the organisation and where it operates as well as its ambitions, eg whether it is a business, a charity or public body as well as the specific legal constitution of the organisation. If a business, is it public or private, private equity or venture capital backed or a family company? If it is a charity or social enterprise the legal structures vary across countries and there are generally a range of options. For example, in the UK there are four main types of legal entity (Charitable Incorporated Organisation, Charitable Company Limited by Guarantee, Unincorporated Association or Trust) as well as a more recent and increasingly popular option the B-Corp.

However, in general the core board processes tend to include those relating to:

- board effectiveness reviews;
- agreeing vision, mission, purpose, culture, brand and stakeholder strategy;
- terms of reference for sub-committees, advisory groups and the senior executive team;

- composition, recruitment and succession as well as removal of directors;
- agreeing agendas and preparing board papers;
- convening and managing meetings, including minutes;
- managing conflicts of interest;
- taking decisions of strategic importance, eg significant capital expenditure or mergers and acquisitions;
- approvals relating to other matters reserved for the board, eg the budget, remuneration, annual report and accounts and audit, as well as core company policies etc;
- communication within as well as from and to the board including relevant compliance requirements with public authorities, regulators, investors etc;
- processes for ensuring diversity and inclusion at both a board and organisational level.

Consequently, these eleven aspects form the structure of this Section and the aim is to provide some practical guidance on each. The largest single element, as you will see, being that focussed on decision making as it is the decisions that the board makes, including those about how it is to be governed, that will ultimately determine its success. References to the use of technology are made in the relevant section. As is the impact that the pandemic has had on board processes. Some of this impact has been to accelerate trends already underway and some of it more disruptive. Some of it may turn out to be temporary but there is no doubt that a lot will have a longer lasting effect.

It felt right to start with the processes for board effectiveness reviews on the basis that, in the majority of cases, readers will be thinking about existing boards and so thinking about that will help when it comes to reviewing other processes.

As elsewhere in the book where there are useful links to online resources I have flagged them and listed the links in the Useful links (*see* page 411).

In terms of what is meant by "*effective*" let's define it as producing the right output in a way that is considered both efficient and fair by stakeholders and produces the right results for the organisation. Taking out friction can also free up time, reduce grumpiness and boost motivation for executives (execs) as well as non-executives (non-execs) or trustees. Just think about the bad humour that can affect decisions if the board papers are late and are not of the quality board members expect. Especially when what was expected was never discussed and management have spent considerable time and effort preparing them.

From a legal and regulatory perspective all decisions must be made in the context of the director's statutory duties and obligations, common law and fiduciary duties, the company's constitutional documents and any relevant codes of best practice. These are covered elsewhere in the book.

Complying with the law meets a basic survival need but the organisation is also likely to have to comply with other regulations or codes specific to the nature of its activity, its form of ownership and the countries in which it operates. It also has to decide what its risk appetite is and where it wants to be on the spectrum of best practice if it wants not just to survive but also to sustain success and to fulfil its potential.

"*Relevance*" is a key word here and one of the board's first jobs is to decide what is the most relevant approach to governance and process as well as what resources will be required to achieve this given the organisation's current stage of development and its ambitions for the future. For small organisations processes need to reflect resources available and so a number of processes may well be better outsourced. It is generally best for the governance and process to be a little ahead of where the organisation is. By way of example it was tremendously helpful to Leap Confronting Conflict, the youth and conflict charity which I chaired, to be considered to be well governed and to win an award for it at a time when the sector was suffering. It helped us to secure investment as well as to save our time to focus on developing the organisation but, most of all, I am convinced it helped us increase our impact.

When considering joining a board the answers to your due diligence questions around board process might also reveal issues of real substance, eg around decision making (*see* page 219) and alignment (*see* page 12).

When describing the role of the board as "*right strategy, right resources and right governance*" on page 6, I referred to the importance of having the resource of good company secretariat and finance functions. Almost by definition if you are joining a board and the plumbing looks a bit ineffective you should be asking yourself the question whether you have got the right people leading these functions and whether they are being allowed to do their jobs.

In a public company the chief financial officer (CFO), company secretary and communications director is a critical triangle. Individual competence is not enough. These three need to have a very strong working relationship and command the respect of the board, the executive and others in and outside the organisation to ensure that all is as effective as it needs to be.

Since most process still involves people, another thing which matters is engagement in the process. If people feel a process makes sense, it is fair and efficient and it will do some good or prevent potential harm to the organisation then buy-in, although never guaranteed, is a lot easier to achieve. On the other hand, if it is poorly communicated or the benefits aren't clear then it is likely to be resisted either actively or passively.

"*Fair process*" is a fascinating area to think about and probably the most useful and accessible paper in our context is Renee Mauborgne and W Chan Kim's "*Fair Process – Managing in the Knowledge Economy*" (*see* Useful links, page 411). Their research was on the links between trust, idea sharing and corporate performance. Their central finding was that employees will commit to a manager's decision, even one they disagree with, if they believe that the process used to make the decision was fair.

In the paper they say that three mutually-reinforcing principles consistently emerged: "*Engagement, explanation, and expectation clarity*".

To sum up having the right processes is fundamental to survival, sustaining success and achieving full potential. As a board and as a director or a trustee, we need to ensure that we have the right plumbing and attitude to suit where we are and where we want to get to.

Board reviews

Motives for conducting board reviews vary considerably from the "*because we have to*" compliance-driven end of the spectrum, to the more confident and positively inspired "*because we want to get better*" at the other.

Effective Chairs tend to have the natural desire, combined with a sufficiently high coefficient of curiosity, to make them want to see if there is anything that they or their boards can do to improve. Possessing the confidence to allow someone else to provide an independent view and showing leadership throughout the process, they are happy to own responsibility for the review but let others manage the detailed work involved.

The best Chairs are genuinely interested in what other boards are doing,

Fair Process – Managing in the Knowledge Economy

Engagement

Means involving individuals in the decisions that affect them by asking for their input and allowing them to refute the merits of one another's ideas and assumptions. Engagement communicates management's respect for individuals and their ideas. Encouraging refutation sharpens everyone's thinking and builds collective wisdom. Engagement results in better decisions by management and greater commitment from all involved in executing those decisions.

Explanation

Means that everyone involved and affected should understand why final decisions are made as they are. An explanation of the thinking that underlies decisions makes people confident that managers have considered their opinions and have made those decisions impartially in the overall interests of the company.

An explanation allows employees to trust managers' intentions even if their own ideas have been rejected. It also serves as a powerful feedback loop that enhances learning.

Expectation clarity

Requires that once a decision is made, managers state clearly the new rules of the game. Although the expectations may be demanding, employees should know up front by what standards they will be judged and the penalties for failure.

What are the new targets and milestones? Who is responsible for what? To achieve fair process, it matters less what the new rules and policies are and more that they are clearly understood. When people clearly understand what is expected of them, political jockeying and favouritism are minimized, and they can focus on the job at hand.

Renee Mauborgne and W Chan Kim INSEAD 2003

are keen to learn and then apply that learning to their own board's circumstances. Most importantly they will ensure that any actions emanating from the review are taken with appropriate speed, especially those that may provide a degree of discomfort for themselves or colleagues.

Sadly, on the other hand, the last thing a weak Chair might want is a thorough inspection that risks shining a light on their own inadequacies. As a consequence, and as with many other things in life, those that least need board reviews tend to do them with the greatest enthusiasm whereas those that could benefit the most either try and avoid them like the plague or make them as sterile as they can.

Just as motives vary, so do the ways in which board reviews are conducted. At one end of the spectrum of approaches are the superficial, skimpy, somewhat informal and *"going through the motions"* reviews. At the other end lie those which become triumphs of process over substance, with reports as interesting as a manual for a dishwasher. In these, little attention is given to the real issues and to the opportunities for improvement and they are lacking in conviction to follow through.

As you can probably tell, I favour a balanced approach which is at neither end of these spectrums and which gets to the real issues and opportunities for improvement in a grounded and efficient manner to suit the size, nature and stage of development of the organisation. It also won't surprise you that in thinking of a framework for conducting a review I have a strong preference for a *"Purpose, People, Process"* approach which also reviews the board in the most relevant way for its context.

If you are on the board of a large listed business or a regulated organisation then you will also want to ensure that whatever way you conduct your review it is compliant with the relevant authority's regulation or best practice and that you have generated the necessary information to report in the manner expected. For example, the UK the Financial Reporting Council's (FRC) *Guide on Board Effectiveness* provides clear guidance on what it expects from board reviews as well as providing some helpful process points (*see* Useful links). If you aren't a major organisation or are not so tightly regulated then you have a lot more flexibility and a lot less need to report.

The art and science of board reviews has developed considerably over the last 20 years. Although the idea had been around for a while and many boards were doing them already, more formal board reviews, especially those considered to be *"independent"*, were only really gaining traction in countries with well-developed capital markets at the time we were conducting the Higgs review in the early 2000s. In many ways the public sector was ahead of business at that time when it came to board reviews and was certainly so in terms of where it was on the spectrum of formality.

In a general atmosphere of encouragement for greater transparency and disclosure from a range of quarters, there was also demand at the time to share the results of such reviews openly. The late Sir Derek Higgs, in his understated and ever canny way, advocated that encouraging greater use of independent board reviews as well as a more open approach to their findings might help to shake things up a bit, especially with regard to diversity and gender in particular. He felt that greater and better use of such reviews had the potential, through the *"spring cleaning"* which often follows a good review, to create more rigorous selection processes. The drive for him was all about performance improvement and that's why there was a complete annex in the report dedicated to *"Performance Evaluation Guidance"*.

The suggestion of the senior independent director (SID) role in large listed companies also provided a mechanism for gathering and communicating feedback on the Chair's performance and then dealing with Chairs who may otherwise find a way to carry on past their sell-by dates. The fact that the SID was someone who wouldn't be a candidate to succeed the Chair was obviously helpful in this regard.

As well as maximising the benefits of greater transparency he, we and the governance officers of leading institutions at the time, also noted that it was the change that took place as a result of a board review that was the biggest prize, not the description of the review in an annual report.

Quoting Sir Derek from his review:

"It is the responsibility of the Chairman to select an effective process and to act on its outcome. The use of an external third party to conduct the evaluation will bring objectivity into the process. The evaluation process will be used constructively as a mechanism to improve board effectiveness, maximise strengths and tackle weaknesses."

Looking back at FTSE 100 annual reports from those days and comparing them to those of today reveals that although there remains caution over disclosure, custom and practice has moved on a lot with more meaningful reviews being conducted and more importantly action taken as a result. The use of board reviews is also more common now in many countries for organisations which are not in the public eye as well as for those who don't have a regulator demanding one.

Many of the benefits of board reviews are obvious, in terms of clarifying roles, becoming more efficient, making better decisions, helping to define what skills and experience gaps you may have and so on. However, there are a number that are less so including:

- Understanding why your peers are performing better. Comparing how your board is composed and how it operates against peers can be illuminating.
- Unearthing and resolving, unspoken conflicts between directors, the board and the executive or between sub-committees.
- Supporting cultural change. If you haven't got the culture you want in the organisation around the board table it's going to be hard to achieve elsewhere. Moreover, if the board doesn't demonstrate the desired culture then it will undermine what you are trying to achieve. A good review will spot a gap between what the board wants and what it does and why that might be the case.
- Improving stakeholder engagement. Reviewing how the board interacts with stakeholders including shareholders, funders, regulators and others can often highlight opportunities to remove misunderstandings and for the stakeholder to gain greater confidence and be more supportive. (Page 171)
- Greater understanding and appreciation from the broader leadership of the organisation as to what the board does and how it does it. In a surprising number of organisations the only exposure that many of the broader leadership get is through a board presentation.

Yet, perhaps the most common benefit I find coming out of the work of Boardelta in this space relates to how the board and the exec are aligned and how they work together in practice. A review that doesn't cover this in my view is missing a major opportunity. For more on this topic see page 12.

Suggesting a review might also serve as a useful mechanism for a new Chair to ensure that they have ended up with what their due diligence suggested they would have. It provides a baseline for where the board was when they became responsible for it as well as from which to chart progress. It can also be useful in highlighting and providing the evidence to justify early changes that are required to the composition or operation of the board.

Finally, one other motivation for board reviews can be as a consequence of high-profile failures. For example, in the UK it is likely that the Grenfell Tower fire tragedy, the failure of Carillion plc and other situations like them have led to many stakeholders and boards in the Housing Association and business sectors wanting to review, with a little more vigour, whether their boards are as effective as they could be.

Not all reviews deliver a positive outcome. So, what are the pitfalls? Probably the best summary of the most persistent problem is summed up in this comment from a friend talking about a review he had much higher hopes of:

"Nothing changed as a result. The Chair was incredibly proud they had done one, he even bragged about it in the annual review. Then promptly put his beautiful 70-page report in the cupboard and did nothing to follow it up. Worse still, apart from me none of the other non-execs has ever mentioned it since. I'll be resigning from there as soon as I can."

In a word *"leadership"* is the main challenge. If the Chair doesn't feel like they own it and doesn't have the right motives then all the effort can feel wasted, one reason why whenever I am asked to help with one I ask what happened to the last review.

Another cause of problems is choosing the wrong person, team or firm to lead the independent aspect of the review. This is no different to the risk in selecting any other form of consultant. Do they have the relevant experience, character, skill and antennae to do the job at the level of the directors and exec? Are they just applying a cookie-cutter process and cutting and pasting and projecting general recommendations onto your situation? Will they command sufficient respect at the beginning of the process to encourage people to share the most useful things with them and then at the end so that their views will make a difference and will be acted upon. A wise Chair of the board or of a nominations committee is usually well up to the task of making the necessary judgements required to enlist the right support.

Whatever our motives for doing a board review the questions that naturally follow, once you have decided to conduct one, relate to how you are going to do it. These are likely to include:

- When to do the review?
- What should the review focus on? Compliance, composition and effectiveness being the most common.
- Who is going to lead and be involved in the review?
- Are you going to enlist the support of an independent expert or organisation to support the review or do it yourself?
- Do you want to review the board in the context of best practice both in general and in the sector you are operating in?
- What's the budget?
- Do you aim to conduct regular reviews?
- If so are you going to have a multi-year approach and a plan which focuses on different things each year as well as have some things which are reviewed every year to track progress?
- How will you involve the board, the exec, broader leadership and other stakeholders in the review?
- In what form do you want the output to be?
- Who do you want to share the results of the review with and how?
- How will you ensure any actions that the board agrees as a result of the review are followed up and implemented?

As with any other significant project it helps to have a definite timeline which induces momentum and has a clear end point. For this reason, it can help to begin a review at the start of a financial year whether you are a public organisation or not. Doing so should provide the time to conduct the review, implement the bulk of the actions and report on it all within one reporting cycle. The major benefit of which is that it encourages you to get on and gain the benefits of the review as quickly as possible. A secondary benefit of this approach is that it conveys a greater sense of purpose and dynamism to stakeholders. The financial year end provides a natural timeline both for achievement and reporting and is usually the point at which personal objectives are reviewed as well.

This approach is usually feasible as most reviews only take a couple of months in elapsed time to do. Some of the actions will be in the quick win category, others, usually those which will result in larger gains, might take longer. Whatever the balance of these you should have been able to implement a sufficient number within a year to be able to both make and demonstrate progress.

With regard to who is going to lead and be involved in the review, my preference is that the Chair makes it clear that they *"own"* the review and that the SID or Chair of the nominations committee manages the process. If it is a large listed business then, in line with the relevant regulators guide on best practice or regulation (eg in the UK the FRC), the SID who is often the Chair of the nominations committee or equivalent leads the process with the support of the company secretary and an independent specialist.

In considering the use of independent specialists there are a number of factors to take into account, other than those mentioned above. These include whether you have a well-developed and competent secretariat function which should be able to conduct the compliance aspects of a board review. You may want the independent specialist to review this work, but it should still save you cost. In my view the secretariat should be doing this anyway, so all the information should be close to hand.

In January 2021 the Governance Institute published their *"Review of the Effectiveness of Independent Board Evaluation in UK Listed Companies"* with 15 reccomendations. There are some interesting nuggets in the report including the fact that there is nearly full compliance in the FTSE 350 with conducting an external review at least once over a three-year period. It also states that two organisations undertook 40% of all externally facilitated review in the FTSE 350 in 2020.

The recommendations start with suggesting that The Financial Reporting Council (FRC) should consider adopting the terminology *"board performance review"'* instead of *"board evaluation"* when it next updates the UK Corporate Governance Code and the Guidance on Board Effectiveness. Although I like the link to performance I'm not sure about this as *"performance review"* has a suggestion of backward looking whereas evaluation includes the possibility of a forward look. They also suggest that the FRC should provide guidance on how to report on reviews.and that there should be a code of practice for independent reviewers which they should publicly sign up to .

The greatest value of an independent assessment apart from the objectivity they bring is that they are seeing numerous other boards in action, know the right questions to ask and process to follow as well as have a good ear for signals that those people being interviewed in the process are transmitting.

Agreeing the vision, mission, purpose, strategy, brand, values, culture and approach to stakeholders

Each of these elements combines to define the organisation and need to be consistent with, and reinforce, each other. That is why they should be considered together and once agreed upon, clearly and actively communicated.

Deciding what they should be is one of the most fundamental things for a board and a management team to determine. It is therefore critical to agree how it is going to be done, who is going to do what and when, as well as how each element will be reviewed and adapted if needed.

To get the semantics out of the way, this is what I understand by each of these headline terms:

Vision: What we want to see happen.

Purpose: Our contribution to making that vision a reality.

Mission: A description of what we actually do.

Strategy: How we are going to make it happen - which includes defining the operating model we are going to deploy to deliver the strategy as well as our ownership and stakeholder strategy.

Brand: What is in people's heads about the organisation.

Culture: The values and behaviours and style of the organisation upon which everything else depends.

Values: the basic and fundamental beliefs that guide or motivate our attitudes and actions.

Stakeholder: Anyone who affects or is affected by the organisation.

It is OK for these statements to overlap a little in a Venn like way, eg with brand and culture. How you want people to think about the organisation ought to be in line with the culture you are building. There is a more on culture on page 169.

You will know all of this is really working when the financial and market performance proves it and when research amongst key stakeholder groups confirms that what is in people's heads about the organisation is what you set out to achieve. You should as a board however feel it a lot earlier than that. Conversely, you will know it isn't working when the research is suggesting a gap between your marketing and the product or financial performance, staff churn rates are high or there is a chasm between your stated values and the actual culture in the organisation.

What people think about the company will be based upon a whole range of things from their own experience as a customer, supplier or team member to what others say about you and how you present yourselves in the many different settings that people come across you.

The organisation's context and stage of development, as well as the resources that it has at its disposal either internally or through advisers, will matter a great deal in deciding what the best process for agreeing things should be; as will the degree of robust insight that you already have or can gain access to on the market or area of social impact you are addressing.

I've found when you are doing this with an established organisation in a mature market you can often yearn for the clean sheet and lack of *"legacy"* that a new entrant might have. However, as a newcomer or creator of a new market you may look with envy at the resources and powerhouse market intelligence teams of the larger incumbents or their *"heritage"* in a space.

All visions and strategies combine a mix of evidence and judgement. Getting the balance right between rigorous research and intuitive and instinctive judgement is one of the best as well as one of the toughest bits of doing strategy. The better you understand the drivers of your market, as well as the likely reactions of customers, suppliers and competitors to different strategies, the more comfortable the process and the more likely you are to come up with a successful strategy. Yet if you just do the logical thing based on the information you and others have available, the risk is you end up with a boring *"me too"* undifferentiated strategy.

One of my favourite vision/purpose statements is that of Wikipedia, whose founder, Jimmy Wales, said:

"Imagine a world in which every single person on the planet is given free access to the sum of all human knowledge. That's what we are doing."

Incredibly clear and galvanising. The details might have been a little sketchy to those on the outside on how this would be achieved. Yet Wikipedia has moved from having no users, staff, contributors or content when it was founded in 2001 to being consistently one of the world's most popular websites since, with content in 285 languages and around 6 million articles just in English in 2020.

Few of us have Jimmy's incredible vision and most of us are likely to have more modest ambitions, resources or less transformational concepts to work with. Having been in private equity (PE) and venture capital (VC) for the bulk of my executive career and seen thousands of business plans for start-ups or transforming existing businesses the thing that I always looked for was the linkage between the vision, strategy, operating model and fit with the team's capabilities. All too often a grand vision is divorced from reality either in terms of the market or the capabilities needed to achieve it. The hardest feedback to give was when the founders' vision was compelling and their business and operating model looked wonderful but the team before you were not the one that was likely to turn it all into a successful reality. It is far easier to tweak a plan with a strong team than the other way around.

There will be a spectrum of choices to make on how to agree a clear and fully aligned vision, mission, purpose and strategy. A start-up or radical re-purposing of an organisation will require a different process from a *"touch on the strategic tiller"* for a highly successful organisation that has shown itself adept at anticipating change ahead. However, it is healthy for even the most successful organisations to adopt the characteristics of a more radical review from time to time to avoid complacency and missing major shifts in their markets. A technique like the *"birthday company"* where you imagine you didn't exist and had to start again today is an example of one of these.

When you distil it all down to what you typically need to do as a board and management team, no matter what the context, there are essentially seven phases to these processes:

Figure 3:1 Seven phases of agreeing a clear and full aligned vision, mission, purpose, strategy, brand, values, culture and approach

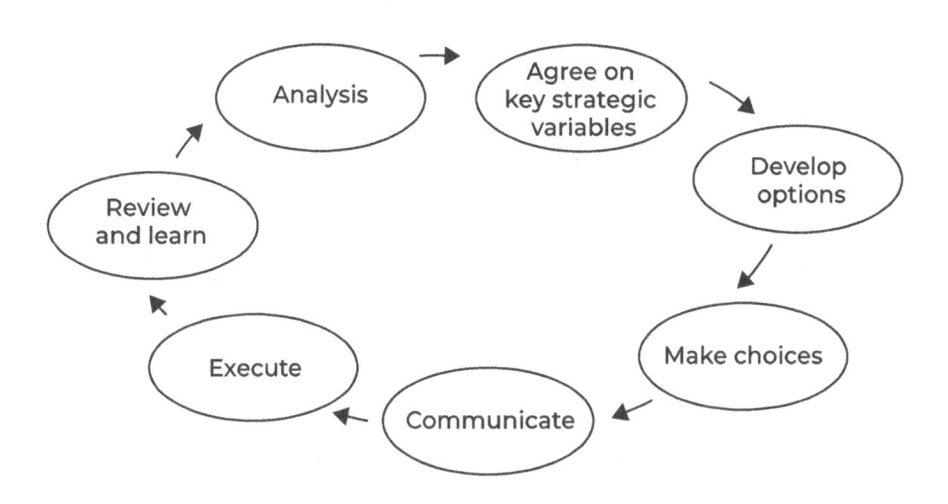

Analysis → Agree on key strategic variables → Develop options → Make choices → Communicate → Execute → Review and learn → (Analysis)

If you follow this then who to involve, when and how is the next thing to decide. Here I would usually incline to use the Bain RAPID® model principles (*see* page 229) to agree clarity over roles in the process and when and how they get involved. I would also be alive to the fact that, as with many other things, the joy of taking part and the feeling of exclusion if you aren't involved are so often asymmetric. Good strategies are often made to look foolish by poor implementation, insufficient resources to successfully achieve them or a lack of buy-in so I would tend to over-, rather than under-, invest in buy-in. That's why I believe having a thorough stakeholder strategy (page 171) is worthwhile.

On the subject of resources, a key role of the board in satisfying itself that the strategy is the right one is to test not just the capacity of resource but the capability of it and to be ever mindful of the *"Effectiveness and pressure"* curve (*see* page 94).

On the subject of effectiveness and pressure the pandemic has accelerated a shift that was already underway from classic *"Strategic bibles"* to *"Strategic frameworks"*. In an ever more uncertain world we need greater flexibility and to acknowledge that we may need to change our route in the light of emerging information. Yet we also need a clear direction at each stage of the route and to understand the consequences on reaching our destination.

The strategic frameworks I have been seeing and using have much greater emphasis on interdependencies, clarity over strategic variables and choices and set parameters within which to operate. They also have risk appetite more clearly apparent throughout and linked to this a lock step approach to investment rather than a calendar-based approach. There is obviously a strong linkage with the strategic framework approach and *"Dynamic Budgeting"*.

For this book the key concern is how the board and management interact over strategy. The driving forces in determining this should be that:

- the board have oversight of the process, the opportunity to provide input at relevant stages of the process, both individually and collectively, have final *"sign off"* of the strategy and a good process for monitoring and reviewing execution of the strategy;
- the management have support for the process, the benefit of the board's input throughout the process as relevant, clarity on what has been agreed as well as the mandate to execute the chosen strategy; and
- board and management own the resultant strategy together with the management responsible for its execution and the board for providing oversight and finally that;
- the board provides the right level of oversight and support in ensuring that there is or will be a high level of stakeholder buy in for the proposed strategy.

Where the quality of relationships is high then this is usually a straight-forward discussion. However, when relationships are not so good between the board and management, the Chair and the chief executive officer (CEO) or the management team themselves or if the process is not considered to be *"fair"* then this can be a tricky thing to agree upon. It is almost always better to sort out relationships before embarking on a major strategic review. Although I guess we have all been in situations where the process or the outcome of a strategic review has led to soured relationships.

Appointing a new CEO almost always leads to a strategic review unless you are very clear, eg in a PE situation, that you are recruiting a CEO to execute a strategy that has been set. Even in that case any high-quality CEO you appoint would want to validate the strategy before, or quickly after, they join before they start executing it.

When it comes to the use of strategy consultants and advisers the board needs to be crystal clear what they are being appointed for and why. Good reasons might be to provide objective insights, specialist expertise or process skills, additional capacity or access to the latest thinking or knowledge from the sector or other sectors of relevance. Less positive may be the desire to abdicate responsibility which you won't be able to do anyway or to cover your behind by being able to say *"well we used a blue-chip consultancy firm"*.

With regard to doing all you can to ensure that the process is felt to be fair and rigorous, the most important thing is that it is just that. This is not the same as everybody liking it especially if there are nettles to grasp and vested interests involved which there frequently are. As Chair, I like to know how each member of the board and management really feel about the process as well as the big strategic variables where choices will need to be made. It has always been worth a check. Most times its reassuring but occasionally you unearth some undealt with issues. I feel a lot more comfortable when there's a good passionate open debate and everyone has given their ideas and had their say on the process before we start. Renee Mauborgne and W Chan Kim's *"Fair Process in the Knowledge Economy"* paper for the Harvard Business Review (*see* page 156) picks this up well and their focus on *"engagement, explanation, and expectation clarity"* is helpful.

Many boards choose to have the most important discussions on strategy at awaydays. Often this is at the beginning or at the end of the process: at the beginning to gain the board's input and ideas and to get a sense of the broad parameters that the exec can work within and at the end to consider a range of well-formulated options and determine which one they want the exec to come back to the board with for a final recommendation with all the supporting information. There are some thoughts on the joys of awaydays on page 199.

Given the importance of culture and the interest in it from regulators and society as a whole, it is surprising how infrequently it appears as a decision item on board agendas. There will be the customary *"engagement"* reviews on an annual basis, market intelligence reports and brand reviews but these are not the same as a clear decision about what culture you want and how you are going to get it. Where CEO tenure is relatively short, eg in larger public companies or public bodies, there is also an additional challenge around building sustainable cultures. Is the CEO being recruited with the culture that the board wants in mind or is the board recruiting for someone to work out what the culture for the next phase of development should be?

In an established organisation an obvious starting point is to test whether the culture you think that you have is what you really have.

In recent years new tools specifically designed to answer this question have emerged. Examples of two organisations providing these tools and associated services are CultureAmp and iPhsycTec's CultureScope (*see* Useful links). CultureAmp comes from an HR management perspective with a range of tools around employee engagement, performance management, diversity and inclusion and so on. It has worked with over 2,000 organisations and has a focus on the technology sector. CultureScope, takes a broader perspective analysing the links between strategy, culture, talent and performance. Based on research with over 51,000 people in 61 countries it also takes an iterative approach which provides insight into the effect of taking actions to change culture in terms of behaviour culture and performance.

It seems really important to have a culture that will reinforce the success of the organisation and its brand. Over the years I have seen many what appear to be very happy organisations in their early stage and formative years find it really challenging to build a culture relevant for significant scale or broader international reach. Cultural tensions also emerge when the board hasn't made clear which things are core elements of the culture and which things are fine to be flexible over to suit local market or functional needs. Managing cultural difference is covered on page 137.

The board's approach to brand and values should be pretty much similar, starting with being clear what you mean by the words themselves (Page 164). Then, moving on to knowing what the current position on each is and, after aligning with the executive on how they should be developed, having an agreed and robust set of metrics to chart progress. Values drive culture and also what is in people's heads about your organisation and actions speak louder than words. How others describe your culture can sometimes also be a shock and far from the wonderful words in your annual report.

It has been interesting to watch how culture and values and brand reputations have been moving during the pandemic crisis. The MIT Sloan partnership with Glassdoor which studies what staff say about their employers published some interesting research in October 2020 on how some 1.5 million employees were rating their 500 employers.

The good news is that on average employees were significantly more positive about their companies than before the crisis. More interesting was the difference between those that had the largest increases and those that had suffered the biggest falls. The companies with the biggest gains seemed to excel on communications, employee well-being and agility.

In the top 50 companies, employees were nearly twice as likely to speak positively about how well their top team communicated during the first six months of COVID-19 compared to the preceding year. Central to this was the fact that 88% of them were more likely to write positively about leader's honesty and transparency.

It's no surprise that employers who walked the talk on doing all they could to support employee well-being both in terms of physical and mental health and safety were the most highly rated.

On agility what appeared to drive the positive scores were confidence that leadership was taking account of the rapidly changing external environment and taking considered action swiftly but not panicking. Employees appeared to value trying out new ways of working and then adapting as they went. The flexibility underpinning was important to them.

The crisis has been a tragic event but it might just be that one good thing to come out of it is that it has made it easier to see and feel who the organisations with strongly positive culture, values and brands are. When it comes to agreeing a stakeholder strategy the starting point is ensuring that there is alignment on what a stakeholder is, who your key stakeholders are, why having a formalised stakeholder strategy is helpful and what the objectives of it should be.

In terms of what a stakeholder is I will stick with R Edward Freeman's 1984 definition of *"Anyone who affects or is affected by your organisation"*.

The key drivers are usually value or impact creation, accountability and the expectations not just of individual stakeholders or groups of them but society more broadly. In private equity when saying why have strategy on this I would always lead on value creation with entrepreneurs by making it real and saying that

"Positively engaged customers, staff, regulators, suppliers, communities and others we engage with, creates way more upside and far less downside."

So that's why it matters but how you turn that into an actionable strategy and what's the board's role in all of this?

The first thing is to believe that it is a key responsibility of the board both in its oversight and supporting roles. It's tough to have the right overall strategy, resources and governance if you don't.

One of the most helpful things I have read on putting together a stakeholder strategy in detail is *"Stakeholder engagement – A roadmap to meaningful engagement"* by Neil Jeffrey & Prof Andy Neeley at the Doughty Centre at Cranfield. There are two charts from the paper which I have found especially useful (Figures 3:2 and 3:3).

The first I call *"Where are we and where do we want to be on the spectrum?"* which I think is self-explanatory.

Figure 3:2 Where are we and where do we want to be on the spectrum?

Crisis Management	Stakeholders Management	Stakeholders Engagement
Reactive	Proactive	Interactive
Vulnerable	Anticipate	Encourage
Episodic	Regular	Inclusive
Hostile	Defensive	Prepared to change

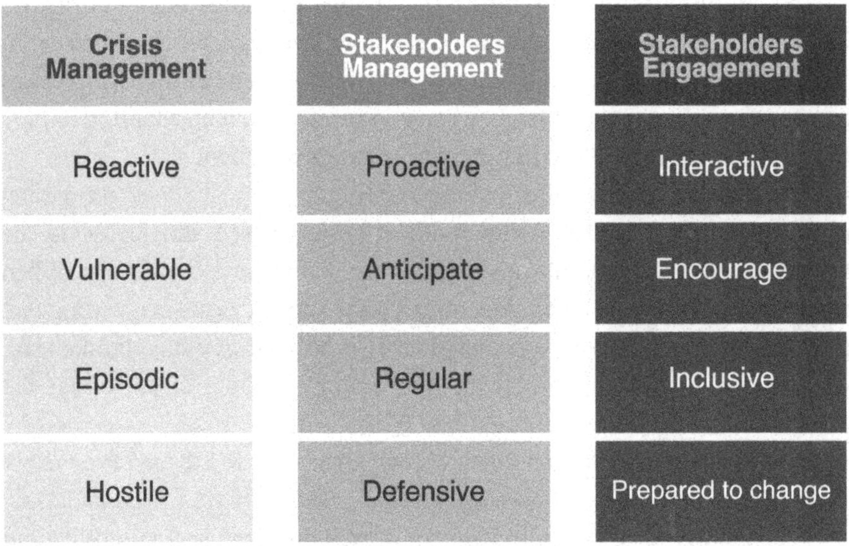

Neil Jeffery & Prof Andy Neeley Doughty Centre, Cranfield

The second, an example of which is below, is a brilliantly simple concept to bring focus and clarity and provide a framework for developing Key Performance Indicators to work out where you are today, where you want to get to and to chart progress along the way. They call it the *"Performance*

Prism" and understanding what your stakeholder wants and needs are as well as what you want from them is what drives it. I have used this with startups as as well as major listed businesses and its simplicity and clarity always helps.

Figure 3:3 The Performance Prism

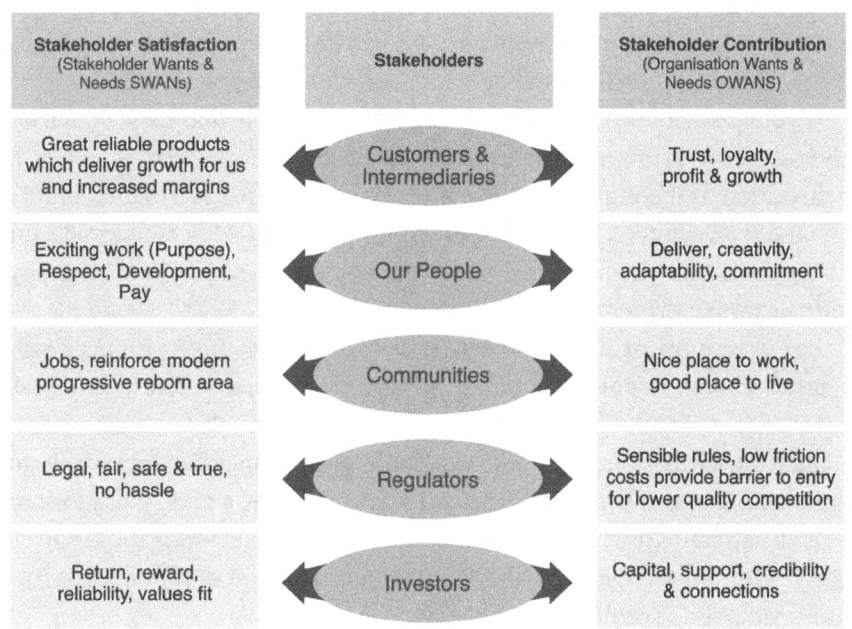

Stakeholder Satisfaction (Stakeholder Wants & Needs SWANs)	Stakeholders	Stakeholder Contribution (Organisation Wants & Needs OWANS)
Great reliable products which deliver growth for us and increased margins	Customers & Intermediaries	Trust, loyalty, profit & growth
Exciting work (Purpose), Respect, Development, Pay	Our People	Deliver, creativity, adaptability, commitment
Jobs, reinforce modern progressive reborn area	Communities	Nice place to work, good place to live
Legal, fair, safe & true, no hassle	Regulators	Sensible rules, low friction costs provide barrier to entry for lower quality competition
Return, reward, reliability, values fit	Investors	Capital, support, credibility & connections

For any approaches like this as with tracking culture getting good relevant and timely data is key and this is definitely an area benefitting from technological change and the ability to join big data sets up.

Terms of reference for sub-committees, the senior exec team and advisory groups

Having covered the roles themselves in the "*Purpose*" section, here we're going to look briefly at the process of agreeing, reviewing, adapting and implementing the "*terms of reference*" (TOR) that a board needs for its sub-committees and advisory groups as well as for the individual roles.

For an established and high functioning board an annual review is a good way of ensuring that there is an effective, interlocking and mutually reinforcing set of TOR that are relevant for the next phase of development as well as compliant with whatever regulations or codes the organisation wants or needs to comply with. In these situations, this is usually fairly light work for the board. The company secretary supports the Chair of the board or the sub-committee concerned in preparing refined TOR to recommend to the board as a whole for approval and adoption. Board effectiveness reviews normally include a review of TOR and recommend changes if required. A good company secretary will typically be part of a network of other company secretaries and be up to date with best practice.

If you are a public company or a regulated entity then in most countries it is really easy as the various relevant codes usually set out what is required. In this case it is therefore a simple matter of ensuring that your TOR comply with the relevant code and adding anything else you feel is appropriate for the nature of the business, the phase that you are in and to deal with any other factors that you think are relevant.

For a start-up or situations where a board needs transforming more significant work might be required. In these cases, there is likely to be less resource to do it. Yet even then by using model examples and advisors it shouldn't take too long to work out what's needed and then agree how to implement it in a relevant and practical way. In the UK a good place to start is the Chartered Governance Institute model TOR including for the exec (*see* Useful links, page 411): they have model TOR for corporate, not-for-profit, the public sector and sports governance.

Over time there is a tendency for sub-committees to grow in number and scope and it is healthy to give them the occasional prune. If you don't, they end up doing the opposite of what they are intended to do, ie to enhance board productivity. Where it gets tricky is where there are too many sub-committees or too much overlap in responsibilities either between the Chair and the CEO or between the sub-committees. Where, through Boardelta, I have helped boards to simplify things the hardest part tends to be persuading those who have grown to like their roles on sub-committees or the status it confers that it's time for change.

Given that there are model TOR online for most types of organisation and you will need to take into account your sector, nature of ownership, regulatory environment and country or countries of operation, here we will just look at some of the key points specific to each of the main sub-committees, the senior exec and advisory groups.

Audit and risk committee

The first key point is the trend to combine audit and risk committees although regulators in some countries and sectors prefer them to remain as distinct committees which collaborate closely. Where they are combined it is important to be clear whether the risk element is confined to financial risk or not and if it is not and encompasses broader categories of risk then the composition of the committee should reflect that. The rise of cybercrime and the emerging use of robots and artificial intelligence (AI) are changing the game in terms of control and risk and encompass more than financial matters.

Given the workload of an audit committee and the need for focus, views differ on the benefits of combining audit and risk. My own view is that given that other categories of risk do have a bearing on the control environment, asset valuations and other matters and discussing risk without including financial risk carries risk, it is generally better to combine and have a slightly bigger single committee than to have two distinct committees. In part the comment in Section 4 on *"Audit, Risk and Internal Control"* in the UK FRC's *"Guidance on Board Effectiveness"* (*see* Useful links, page 411) where it is talking about visibility statements, makes the point:

"The long-term success of a company is dependent on the sustainability of its business model and its management of risk."

Moreover, the Guidance doesn't appear to limit the audit committee's consideration of risk to just financial risk. It will also be interesting to see how reviews in the UK, and other countries in relation to moving closer to Sarbanes Oxley approaches, play out in terms of impact on audit and risk committees and directors' responsibilities more broadly.

As noted on page 15 it is not the responsibility of the committee that is being delegated but simply some of the work. The board has responsibility for overall oversight.

Following the financial crash in the late 2000s there has been a trend for regulators, especially those in financial services, to becoming more prescriptive about the composition of audit, risk or combined audit and risk sub-committees. Generally, they will want the majority of the committee to be independent directors and for them to be able to demonstrate relevant experience and competence in financial matters, including accounting or auditing.

They have become tighter on what they mean by *"independent"* and often have the power to approve the appointment of the Chair or members of the sub-committee and have put in place regular review processes including interviews with the sub-committee members individually. This increased rigour is understandable but can be a deterrent to strong candidates as much as the weak.

In the public sector, especially for organisations where lives are at risk, for example in health and transportation, the regulators may adopt a similarly high level of interaction and inspection.

In private and smaller businesses in sectors which are not heavily regulated the audit and risk committee can be relatively small and although it will have the same fundamental role the process can be much more straightforward: this typically means two or three people. In charities it is important to distinguish between someone who fulfils a treasurer role and the Chair of the audit and risk committee.

Along with the Chairs of other committees and, in their case, supported mostly by the CFO and their team, the Chair of this committee will also need to ensure that there is a good plan in place for the work of the committee throughout the year in order for it to balance doing its work with the appropriate degree of rigour, meeting the deadlines that it needs to and involving others to the appropriate extent.

Whatever the nature, size or location of the organisation the committee's relationships with the leadership within the company, with the key stakeholders, advisers and regulators will be central to its success. In picking the Chair of the committee, whether it is combined or not, it is important to select someone who not only has the technical prowess and experience required but also good judgement and a high order of interpersonal skills.

Audit and risk committee members will have to come up with their own views on matters and should not be overly dependent upon the exec, key stakeholders or auditors in forming these views. As a consequence, there will be times when they have to manage conflicting views and to reach, and be prepared to defend robustly, what they feel is the right judgement on an issue. Given that there is also a lot of work to do and a need to ensure follow-up on a wide range of detailed matters, they will also have high skills and the capability to both understand the detail but not get lost in it.

One of the most important relationships for the committee is the one that they have with the auditors. Selecting the right firm, lead partner and team is critical. Switching costs and the effort required to change before a planned rotation is high so getting it wrong can be expensive. Understanding independence regulation and having good process for approving allowable non-audit services is essential.

If you are a highly international organisation you also need to have a strategy with regard to which firms you will use in countries where your primary auditor can't serve you either because they don't have operations there or they have conflicts of interest. The major firms will either have operations on the ground or relationships in most countries and will have a preference to sell you a one-stop shop approach which has obvious advantages. However, few firms have pulled off the trick of having high quality in every market and so the committee needs to satisfy itself that the quality is as required.

Regulators vary in the level and nature of interaction with audit and risk committees. For some, most notably in financial services, the regulator might have an audit quality review process on top of other financial reporting requirements. As part of its role in ensuring that the company is complying with all financial reporting requirements the committee will be engaged in such reviews. In some sectors, such as financial services and in utilities, it may well be that you also have a regulatory sub-committee. If you do it will need to work closely with the audit and risk committee and may have overlapping membership.

Of all the relationships that the committee will have the five-way relationship between the Chair of the organisation, the Chair of the committee, the CEO, the CFO and the internal auditor is the most fundamental. The trust that they all have in each other and their level of respect underpins the success of the organisation from a governance perspective.

On the subject of internal auditors, it is generally accepted that they should report to the audit committee and not to the CFO. However, in terms of their administrative reporting line views vary. If you have a company secretary of the right experience and stature then that is a route that can make sense.

The relationship between treasurer and Chair of audit committee in the charity sector is another key relationship. Many charities have small finance committees, chaired by the treasurer, who oversee budgeting and reporting on financial matters and often provide support to the management team. As an important part of the audit committee's role is to scrutinise it is often the case that someone else Chairs the audit committee but the treasurer is a member of it.

A final point on audit committees is to note a dangerous trap that lurks for its members. Namely the danger that it is hard to reveal ignorance when you are all supposed to be experts. This is why it is helpful, if you have capacity, to have someone who is strong on financial matters but not an auditor or CFO.

Remuneration committee

Remuneration is a highly emotive, controversial and complex topic, rich in dilemmas and challenge. Being on a remuneration committee (RemCo) is therefore both fascinating and demanding, especially in publicly quoted businesses or organisations which have public money or significant public profile. This section is supplemented by the "*Money, Money, Money*" and "*RemCoCoCo*" dilemmas (*see* pages 329 and 357).

RemCos typically do the work and make recommendations to the board on the following matters where appropriate:

- overall reward strategy and policy as well as performance metrics to be taken into consideration;
- specific reward and incentives for the senior exec and, in some cases, the broader leadership group or highest paid group within the organisation;
- specific reward for the Chair and non-execs (trustees in charities are generally unpaid);
- selection and management of remuneration consultants and other relevant advisers (eg pensions, tax); and
- the remuneration report and communication of remuneration issues.

In recent years in some countries and sectors their brief has been extended, eg in the UK the FRC's *2018 Corporate Governance Code* (*see* Useful links) contains the following Provision (40):

The Code also describes an expanded remit for RemCos in the

communication of remuneration and, in particular, describing their own work:

> **"When determining executive director remuneration policy and practices, the remuneration committee should address the following:**
>
> ○ **Clarity** – remuneration arrangements should be transparent and promote effective engagement with shareholders and the workforce;
>
> ○ **Simplicity** – remuneration structures should avoid complexity and their rationale and operation should be easy to understand;
>
> ○ **Risk** – remuneration arrangements should ensure reputational and other risks from excessive rewards, and behavioural risks that can arise from target-based incentive plans, are identified and mitigated;
>
> ○ **Predictability** – the range of possible values of rewards to individual directors and any other limits or discretions should be identified and explained at the time of approving the policy;
>
> ○ **Proportionality** – the link between individual awards, the delivery of strategy and the long-term performance of the company should be clear. Outcomes should not reward poor performance; and
>
> ○ **Alignment to culture** – incentive schemes should drive behaviours consistent with company purpose, values and strategy."

Provision 40 and the description of the work above all makes sense, is hard to argue with and provides useful things to think about beyond the realm of major public companies. It is also quite a lot of work to do for what is usually a small group of people (two or three) in most organisations, even if they are well supported by a strong human resources (HR) director and effective remuneration consultants. This is why, increasingly, RemCos are co-opting people with strong technical expertise or experience of RemCo matters onto their committee who aren't members of the main

> **"There should be a description of the work of the remuneration committee in the annual report, including:**
>
> - An explanation of the strategic rationale for executive directors' remuneration policies, structures and any performance metrics;
>
> - Reasons why the remuneration is appropriate using internal and external measures, including pay ratios and pay gaps;
>
> - A description, with examples, of how the remuneration committee has addressed the factors in Provision 40;
>
> - Whether the remuneration policy operated as intended in terms of company performance and quantum, and, if not, what changes are necessary;
>
> - What engagement has taken place with shareholders and the impact this has had on remuneration policy and outcomes;
>
> - What engagement with the workforce has taken place to explain how executive remuneration aligns with wider company pay policy; and
>
> - To what extent discretion has been applied to remuneration outcomes and the reasons why."

board. I have found this an especially useful approach in smaller organisations.

A RemCo has to help a board not only to set the *"right"* level and structure for remuneration and to understand competitive realities to achieve its broader strategic objectives but also to be able to communicate what it has decided in a way that is felt to be *"fair"* and *"appropriate"* to stakeholders and to wider audiences. These three subjective words are at the heart of a RemCo's deliberations and its recommenda- tions to the board. But what do *"right"*, *"fair"* and *"appropriate"* mean and who judges?

The need for a RemCo to understand how others might see and feel about their decisions is fundamental to their work. Many critics of RemCos will argue that by their nature those who serve on RemCos will find this hard to do in practice. Although absolutely spot on in many specific cases this seems an over-generalisation and insulting to those who come from poorer backgrounds and spend considerable amounts of time with disadvantaged communities.

As to what is *"right"*, *"fair"* and *"appropriate"* this feels easy to state but harder to achieve in practice. The remuneration needs to be *"right"* from the organisation's perspective in that its investment in the remuneration will deliver the desired value or impact for an *"appropriate"* affordable and market rate. *"Right"* from the individual's perspective so that they will be highly motivated to deliver and consider it *"fair"*; and *"right"* and *"fair"* from the perspective of a variety of stakeholders, eg shareholders, regulators, peers and colleagues.

When it comes to *"fair"* this needs to be both in terms of the outcome and the process in terms of engagement, explanation and clarity of expectation (*see* pages 179 and 180). This is easier to do if you have a set of clear principles.

In BP plc's 2018 Remuneration Report, which ran to 22 pages, the following succinct description in the introduction is a good example of communicating this:

"The policy delivers remuneration in three parts: a market- aligned foundation of base salary, benefits and retirement provision; annual incentives based on measures that reflect our strategy, assessed against targets that require progressive improvement year-on-year; and a material opportunity to earn shares at the end of a three-year performance period, which is accompanied by a shareholding requirement to ensure our executive directors' interests align with your own."

Even when as clearly communicated as this attribution of contribution to success, timing and the roller coaster that represents share and commodity prices, not to mention the increasing frequency of high impact political and natural events, can make even the most rational of plans hard to defend with hindsight. The pandemic crisis will have a material impact on many remuneration schemes and is likely to result in many a dissonant bonus or payout as well rendering some schemes meaningless.

In PE-backed businesses the remuneration principles are typically to:

- pay a benchmarked market rate for salary and benefits;
- align interests with investors by enabling management to invest meaningfully in equity;
- align the broader leadership group through an option scheme which delivers on exit; and

- align other employees through a broader employee share ownership scheme.

The challenge here comes in modifying schemes when further investment is made or when there are departures.

If you are on the board of a PE, VC business or infrastructure or other types of investment funds then you may also have to deal with the joys of carried interest schemes. These schemes are designed to align the interests of those providing the funds with those who invest them on their behalf. For example, PE and VC firms make their money from charging a fee on the funds they manage and receiving a carried interest in the outcome of a specific fund (rates vary but 15-20 per cent of realised uplifts is typical as long as a threshold rate of return is achieved). As typically PE firms are partnerships, these profits are then shared amongst the partners. The timeframes of these schemes are usually aligned with the life of the fund which tends to be ten years in practice. This means that they need to cope with joiners and leavers. The additional challenges that transparency of remuneration brings alongside the fluctuations in values of investments is often a deterrent to PE firms listing.

In private companies, which tend to be entrepreneurially or family owned, there are a range of mindsets towards remuneration across a spectrum from what can best be described as from *"hired hand"* to *"shared ownership"* where employees have a significant stake in the ownership of the enterprise. Private owners can also sometimes get confused between what is reward as a result of being a shareholder and that of being an employee. Taxation systems can influence this, eg significant differences between the rate of taxation on dividends and remuneration or the taxation of pension contributions.

In public bodies, the challenge of competing for talent with other sectors, tight budgets and public scrutiny make serving on remuneration committees especially challenging. The health and university sectors globally are good examples of sectors which have been under siege over remuneration in recent years.

The university sector in many countries has seen an escalation of salaries for vice chancellors (VC), registrar or chief operating officers (COO), finance directors (FD) and, in some cases, top academics. A number of drivers have been responsible for this including significant growth in the size of the organisations, more global competition for talent capable of running such organisations, the economic success of such institutions enabling them to afford it and, on this topic, benign regulation.

From the individual institutions perspective if the university is thriving and increasing in scale and reputation it all feels like straight-forward paying for success and a good investment. After all a VC's salary in the context of such a big organisation is a very small cost and, given the size of the organisation is bigger than many commercial enterprises where leaders are paid substantially more, only fair.

However, others argue that the major growth of these institutions is really driven by demographics and increasing participation rates driven by government policies, economic development and availability of student loans where government takes the risk. So, it has little to do with the leadership of individual universities in their eyes. Moreover, they add, the risks are much lower for a university VC than a corporate CEO. After all they say, governments rarely allow a university to go bust, VCs in many countries are political appointments so may not have the rare experience that justifies the pay and few get fired by their boards on performance grounds. Add to this the political tensions around student fees, constraints on academic pay and shortfalls in university pension schemes in many places over many years and the issues arising from the pandemic and it isn't hard to see why remuneration has been an incendiary issue.

In the UK the Committee of University Chairs (CUC) issued *"The Higher Education Senior Staff Remuneration Code"* in 2018 (*see* Useful links, page 411) in response to some high-profile situations where there had been considerable unrest over the levels and nature of remuneration of VCs. The Code is just that, a code rather than regulation. The Committee is a representative body for Chairs of university councils (boards). The regulator is called *"The Office for Students"* which many people, especially academics, feel, despite its best intentions, is the wrong name as it suggests one, albeit very important, set of stakeholders dominates. Its guidance on remuneration at time of writing is a little thin (*see* Useful links).

In its Code the CUC focus on *"fair and appropriate"* remuneration, say what they mean by that and emphasise the importance of procedural fairness, transparency and accountability and being able to justify the decisions taken to protect reputations. You can almost hear the pain in various sections of the Guidance. That said the Code does have some useful advice and it is a good starting point.

For charities the issues for remuneration committees ought to be a lot more straightforward given the essential principles regarding remuneration tend to be simply paying a charity market rate for salaries and benefits, no bonuses or long-term incentives and not paying the Chair or trustees. However, if the charity has trading activities designed to generate sustainable and unrestricted income it may need to pay them more than the CEO of the charity even though this might be less than they could otherwise command.

This leads to the question of the link between remuneration and motivation. A paper from Harvard Business School in 2013 *"Does Money Really affect Motivation: A Review of the Research"* (*see* Useful links) by Tomas Chamorro-Premuzic asked a few straightforward questions, namely:

- **Does money engage us?**

    They found the most compelling answer to this question in a meta-analysis by Tim Judge and colleagues of research to synthesise the findings from 92 quantitative studies. The combined dataset included over 15,000 individuals and 115 correlation coefficients.

    The results indicate that the association between salary and job satisfaction is very weak with less than 2 per cent overlap between pay and job satisfaction levels. Furthermore, the correlation between pay and pay satisfaction was only marginally higher, indicating that people's satisfaction with their salary is mostly independent of their actual salary.

    However, they do note a paper from Nobel prize winner Daniel Kahneman and Angus Deaton *"High income improves evaluation of life but not emotional well-being"* which concludes that in the US, emotional well-being levels increase with salary levels up to a salary of $75,000 — but that they plateau after that.

    They also note unsurprisingly that studies show marked individual differences in people's tendency to think or worry about money, and different people value money for different reasons (eg as a means to power, freedom, security or love).

It is also likely to be the case that the pandemic has made people reflect on what really matters to them. and many other factors are present in the overall package, for example the opportunity to work from home.

- **Does it depend upon job level or country?**

In the Judge and colleagues study quoted above, they found that: *"Employees earning salaries in the top half of our data range reported similar levels of job satisfaction to those employees earning salaries in the bottom-half of our data range."*

They also found this was consistent with some engagement research conducted by Gallup in 2011 based on 1.4 million employees from 192 organisations across 49 industries and 34 nations. This Study reported no significant difference in employee engagement by pay level.

With regard to countries, the Judge and colleagues Study found that there were no significant differences between the US, India, Australia, Britain and Taiwan), a small number of countries but interesting nonetheless.

- **Does money demotivate?**

In answering this question, they say that: *"Despite the overwhelming number of laboratory experiments carried out to evaluate this argument there is still no consensus about the degree to which higher pay may demotivate"*.

Overall Tomas Chamorro-Premuzic's conclusion from reviewing the research was that: *"In a nutshell: money does not buy engagement"*.

If you serve on a RemCo then you are likely to interact with remuneration consultants and the ability to select the most appropriate firm and manage them is an important part of the job. Remuneration consultants typically provide a range of services covering exec and non-exec remuneration. Their work is normally focused on the board and the senior exec, but they may also advise on the organisation's overall remuneration policy. As senior level pay in the corporate, public and social sectors has become ever more emotive, the range of organisations commissioning such consultants is now very broad.

Clearly the scale of the organisation and the nature of its stakeholders will have a major bearing on the scale and complexity of services a board may require. These services normally include providing data and advice on:

- benchmarking with comparable organisations and insight into what will be acceptable to institutional shareholders, the media and others;
- design of remuneration policies for board and senior exec as well as the organisation overall;
- design of remuneration for specific groups or individuals (eg CEO);
- drafting remuneration reports for annual reports;
- liaison with institutional investors or regulatory bodies includ- ing organising and supporting consultation processes; and
- question and answer preparation for annual general meetings (AGM) or governance officer and media meetings.

Apart from these offerings consultants will suggest that they add further value by providing a degree of third-party legitimacy for the board's proposals. This is easier to argue if the remuneration consultant acting for the remuneration committee is different to the one advising the exec on remuneration for the organisation more generally. Some firms who serve both functions do so with separate teams to reduce this challenge over their independence. From the company's perspective, if this is the case, then you can lose a major benefit for using the same firm, namely that: *"they know the company"*.

There has been much debate about the role of remuneration consultants and their effect on pay escalation in public companies, universities and public sector organisations. One reason for blaming the use of benchmarking data is the ratcheting that occurs because most boards will want to argue that they need to pay top quartile to attract top talent. Exaggerating to make the point, the critics argue that each time the benchmarking is done 75 per cent of those in the group benchmarked will want to raise their remuneration to a level to get into the top 25 per cent.

In the UK, following a desire for greater transparency and concerns about the independence of remuneration consultants serving major listed companies, new UK pay regulations came into force in 2013 which required UK-listed companies to disclose previously undisclosed details of the consultancy arrangements in place for supporting their exec pay structures. A new requirement was imposed forcing companies to state whether and how the remuneration committee satisfied itself that advice received that assisted the committee's considerations was objective and independent. Another related to the disclosure of fees paid to remuneration consultants.

In response the top firms providing such services drew up a Code of Best Practice, (*see* Useful links, page 411) formed the "*Members of the Remuneration Consultants Group*" (RCG) and signed up to a set of best practice principles.

As with other forms of professional service, a few firms tend to dominate the top end in each market. Experienced Chairs and Chairs of RemCos will be well aware of the top firms and probably have relationships with them and preferences as to who to use in different situations. However, they will still go through a pitch process in order to legitimise their choice.

A smart board will consult key stakeholders to ensure that proposals are acceptable before putting them to a vote. Remuneration consultants can play a useful role here as they should be able to provide insights on the latest views of leading institutions as well as the voting recommen- dation and their reactions to other companies with similar issues to discuss.

On the subject of communicating decisions on remuneration, the remuneration report is a critical part of it and most remuneration consultants with support from the organisation's HR team should be able to produce a good first draft which meets regulatory and govern- ance code requirements. The tendency for reports mostly to be read online has enabled a more engaging approach to what historically were very dry styles of reporting. Many organisations have realised that they need to communicate less defensively on the topic instead of being on the backfoot waiting for challenges.

The final thing to say about the RemCo is the importance of getting the composition of the committee right as well managing its relationships well with the Chair and the CEO through the process. The senior or most experienced director or trustee is usually given the job and will have experience of other organisations' RemCos. They will have the appropriate blend of judgement, interpersonal skills and antennae to help the RemCo reach the right conclusions and make the right recommendations to the board as well as help to persuade others that they are indeed right. They will have a relationship with the Chair that ensures the Chair doesn't have to get too involved and with the CEO so that they can't.

Nominations committee

There are clearly many connections between this part of the book on nominations committees (NomCos) and the "*People*" Section (*see* page 85). I have tried hard to minimise replication through cross-referencing but it may be worth just a quick look again at what is in that Section before you start.

The role and influence of NomCos has grown considerably in recent years as many regulators and investors have realised a high-quality NomCo will provide the support a Chair and board need to build the best board they can, ensure that they have good succession plans and will achieve diversity and inclusion in its many aspects.

The description of the role of the NomCo by the UK FRC overleaf provides an example of the broader brief that NomCos have these days. It is not out of line with how regulators in other sectors and markets describe it and the approach taken across a broad cross-section of organisations.

If the Chair is the leader of the board team then it may be natural to think that the Chair of the organisation should be the Chair of the NomCom. However, the general principle for many is that the Chair shouldn't chair any of the sub-committees and the fact that one of the most important jobs that NomComs have is to support the process of managing the Chair's succession and board reviews, means that in practice NomComs tend to be chaired by the SID or the most senior independent director or trustee.

For major UK listed companies, it was stated clearly in the Higgs review that:

> *"The chairman or an independent non-executive director should chair the committee, but the chairman should not chair the nomination committee when it is dealing with the appointment of a successor to the chairmanship."*

Role of the nomination committee: UK FRC

"The nomination committee is responsible for board recruitment and will conduct a continuous and proactive process of planning and assessment, taking into account the company's strategic priorities and the main trends and factors affecting the long-term success and future viability of the company.

Appointing directors who are able to make a positive contribution is one of the key elements of board effectiveness. Directors will be more likely to make good decisions and maximise the opportunities for the company's success if the right skillsets and a breadth of perspectives are present in the boardroom. Non-executive directors should possess a range of critical skills of value to the board and relevant to the challenges and opportunities facing the company.

Diversity in the boardroom can have a positive effect on the quality of decision-making by reducing the risk of group think. With input from shareholders, boards need to decide which aspects of diversity are important in the context of the business and its needs.

Developing a more diverse executive pipeline is vital to increasing levels of diversity amongst those in senior positions. Improving diversity at each level of the company is important if more diversity at senior levels is to become a reality. Greater transparency about the make-up of the workforce could support this. This might cover a range of different aspects of diversity, including age, disability, ethnicity, education and social background, as well as gender.

Working with human resources, the nomination committee will need to take an active role in setting and meeting diversity objectives and strategies for the company as a whole, and in monitoring the impact of diversity initiatives. Examples of the type of actions the nomination committee could consider encouraging include:

- a commitment to increasing the diversity of the board by setting stretching targets;
- dedicated initiatives with clear objectives and targets; for example, in areas of the business that lack diversity;
- a focus on middle management;
- mentoring and sponsorship schemes;
- a commitment to more diverse shortlists and interview panels; and
- positive action to encourage more movement of women into non-traditional roles.

Diversity of personal attributes is equally important. The nomination committee will want to ensure the board is comprised of individuals who display a range of softer skills."

However, it is important to acknowledge that the Chair should have a significant input to NomCo matters other than their own succession. The latest FRC Code (2018) deals with this by saying:

"The Chair's vision for achieving the optimal board composition will help the nomination committee review the skills required, identify the gaps, develop transparent appointment criteria and inform succession planning."

Language which provides a lot of flexibility.

As well as considering the Chair's role in NomCo activity we also need to think about the CEO's involvement. It is a perfectly understand- able and a natural desire for CEOs to want to influence who is going to be on the board. This can be driven by very positive motives, ie they want the best board they can possibly get to help them achieve the vision they have agreed with the board. At the same time, it can be less positively motivated and simply be a desire to have a board that they will find easier to manage or may be softer on them.

CEOs, like Chairs, have an important and valid role to play in providing input to the NomCo about what they feel are the characteristics required in new directors. It is up to the Chair of NomCo to ensure that this is indeed input and not control and if they need support then the Chair, through their role as *"chief"*- CEO coach, should be able to provide it.

Before we cover board composition, recruitment and managing succession below there are a few other points to make on NomCos, especially given its wider brief these days.

The first of these is that if the NomCo is supposed to be so central in driving the board's diversity and inclusion agenda then, to the extent that it can be diverse itself given its small scale, it should practice what it is going to preach. This means being as diverse and inclusive as it can be itself and its members having "*diverse and inclusive mindsets*".

It is challenging in practice for small organisations and small boards to achieve what they would like to but it is always obvious whether they are trying or not.

The next general point relates to tenure terms and co-terminus appointments. As mentioned on page 85, I think it is a healthy state of mind to think that the board is always in transition and to have a balance of continuity and continuous refreshment. This is hard if you have too many co-terminus appointments. This is easily avoided, even in start-ups, if you start with a smaller board than you are going to need and add as you go to get to the size you want.

The issue of the timing of Chair and CEO successions and the ordering of them is another significant thing for NomCos to think about. Inevitably, life has a habit of ruining the best laid plans and so it will often happen that you simply need to get on and recruit a new Chair or CEO because of circumstance. However, except in understandable situations such as serious underperformance or major governance issues, most boards and stakeholders would prefer you to avoid changing both at the same time and for you to get the order right. It is much easier to achieve this if you have a plan.

The next point relates to the connectivity of the NomCo with other committees and the communications, company secretariat and HR functions of the organisation function. The NomCo and the RemCo (*see* page 178) should have a good level of connectivity as getting the remuneration right for exec and non-exec appointments is important. They will also be in discussion over both policy and specifics relating to departing directors as well as the remuneration report. In charities, where the trustees are unpaid, this focus will be more on the execs.

In relation to the audit and risk committee there will be common ground to discuss over key "*people risks*" as well as the relevant content in the annual report around governance, succession, people risk and so on.

Effective NomCos will also have interaction with the communications function over key appointments, both from an internal and external perspective. If it is a public body or public company then there should be a process in place for agreeing content, timing and nature of announcements both publicly and internally. The transition of a Chair or CEO is probably the most crucial of these and the ones which require the tightest logistical management.

They will also tend to have a close involvement with the company secretariat function in relation to the formalisation of appointments, induction, regulatory approvals, announcements and so on. In a public company situation both the communication director and the company secretary are also likely to be in communication with appointees or departees over agreeing statements, timing of announcements, question and answer with those joining or leaving and their respective current employers.

The nature of the role of the HR director varies considerably but one would expect the HR director to be involved in key people issues for the organisation, including the appointment or departure of directors. This may be a light touch in terms of providing technical advice or ideally more involved in terms of supporting the NomCo in organising processes, selecting recruitment consultants, induction processes and so on.

Board composition, recruitment and managing succession

Supporting the board on these three things, through leading the process, is the core of a NomCo's job.

On board composition this is generally to:

- Do the work in ascertaining what the "*ideal*" composition of the board should be given the purpose, vision, strategy, brand, values and culture of the organisation that has been agreed for the next phase of development.
- In doing so, to take into account input from the rest of the board and exec as well regulatory and stakeholder require- ments, the diversity and inclusion objectives for the board and the most recent board effectiveness review.
- Consider and develop a strategy and plan for the board to approve on how that ideal composition might be built over an agreed period, taking into account existing members tenure and the succession plan.
- Make the difficult judgement as to whether existing members, would qualify as part of the ideal composition.
- In conjunction with the RemCo, ensure that the cost of appointments and the process to make them is understood and approved by the board before any recruitment process starts.
-

On recruitment, once the plan, the roles to be recruited and the specifications have been approved by the Board, this is usually to manage the process on behalf of the board, from that point, including:

- organising and conducting a pitch by recruitment consultants; selecting them and agreeing process, terms and timeline;
- inputting to, and approving, all communications involved in the recruitment process;

- significant personal involvement throughout the selection process;
- ensuring the right level of engagement of other board members, the exec and key stakeholders in the process including gaining their approvals as relevant;
- being sure that there is rigorous and effective due diligence of individual candidates prior to offer as well as for onboarding, induction, development and review for those chosen;
- where relevant, supporting the company secretary in organising letters of appointment and gaining such regulatory approvals as required; and
- supporting the communications director in ensuring that there is effective communication of new appointments with key audiences both internally and externally.

On managing succession, this will typically include:

- with input from the board, the exec, key stakeholders and relevant advisers, producing a succession plan to recommend to the board for approval;
- ensuring that the plan includes consideration of developing the talent pipeline for both execs and non-execs or trustees as well as the board's objectives in terms of its vision, strategy, brand, culture and diversity and inclusion;
- supporting the delivery of that plan through its role in board composition, recruitment and diversity and inclusion; and finally
- having a contingency plan for key positions, eg Chair, SID, CEO and CFO.

In doing these things it will need to recommend, agree a process for and undertake a review of the skills, knowledge and characteristics against that ideal composition on an appropriately frequent basis. Synchronising this with the strategic development cycle or with major organisational events is helpful. For example, if the board has just agreed a refreshed strategy it is natural, as part of this or immediately following the decision, to then question whether you have got the board needed to support the agreed strategy. If the organisation is embarking upon a major acquisition or other major strategic shift or cultural change, again it is right for the NomCo to ask the board whether the board itself needs to change as a result.

The word "*ideal*" is helpful in this process as it is right to have a strong desire and aim to get the best board you can for what you want to achieve. However, it is rare to be able to find all of the things that you want within a small number of people at the specific time that you are looking. As a consequence, the NomCo has to understand the market and help the board in being realistic and understanding which elements it absolutely has to have and which it would be prepared to compromise on.

The underpinning processes which support all of these activities are an important part of the board recruitment strategy and plan that the NomCo will recommend for approval to the board. They are likely to be finalised after addressing the following issues and questions:

- The balance between internal support (eg company secretariat and HR) and external support (eg recruitment, and or board effectiveness consultants).
- Turning the analysis of the ideal composition and existing composition into candidate specifications for specific appointments to be made.
- Whether there should there be a "*batch*" or "*step-by-step*"
- approach to recruitment.
- Recommending a timeline and budget to the board and, once approved, ensuring that they are met and that progress is reported along the way.
- Recommending who is going to be involved in the process, when and how.
- What the blend of physical and virtual meetings should be.
- Ensuring that chosen candidates will add to the organisation's culture and will support its objectives in terms of diversity and inclusion.

As with many things the pandemic accelerated some trends already under way. Many of us, especially in international organisations were using a blend of physical and virtual meetings before and suddenly had to switch to all virtual. It was an odd feeling at first, appointing someone to a board without physically meeting, but we soon became more comfortable, adapted our interview styles and got on with it. I suspect we will go back to blend but the balance will shift to a higher virtual element.

Deciding the right balance between internal and external support is usually straightforward and determined by the resources the organisation has. The important thing is the NomCo is driving the process on behalf of the board and have control of it.

If there is a need to recruit a number then figuring out whether to try and achieve this in one go or to take a step-by-step approach is likely to be influenced by the current situation and the degree of stretch implied by the current strategy. If the organisation is performing well and the board and exec are stable then a step-by-step approach is often the route chosen. However, if the organisation is in crisis or has a major shift to make in a short timescale then a batch approach is likely to be more appropriate.

If you are going to take a batch approach it is worth recognising that it is generally harder to figure out whether people you don't know are going to work well together than those you do. Therefore, in going down the batch route you will need to place the right emphasis on considering the group dynamic. You will probably also, once they are recruited, want to hold a bonding event to accelerate the new board team-forming process.

Timelines for such processes vary considerably, especially if the organisation requires government or regulatory approval for the appointments it is making. Non-exec or trustee appointments are generally quicker than exec appointments as, typically, these don't require notice periods, negotiating terms take less time and the process tends to be less involved. For non-exec appointments three months is, in many cases, a reasonable objective from start to appointment. For senior execs the process can take six months to a year unless it is a crisis situation.

Interview processes remain highly variable, especially for non-execs or trustees and cover the whole spectra of formality, rigour and transparency. Ideally, I like to get external support and focus the search consultant on helping us to sharpen the process, take up the research load, provide access to candidates we wouldn't have thought of and conduct the long list interviews. In summary, to increase the effective- ness and efficiency of what we would have been able to do on our own. If you do this then you are focused on selecting from a small group of high-quality appointable candidates.

Whether you have the benefit of external support or not, it is always to helpful to view those involved in doing the selecting to think of themselves as a team, work out who will focus on what in interviews so that you can not only cover the desired ground but also calibrate views on the most important aspects without overduplication. The processes are both buying and selling in their nature and a weak and unimpressive or unbalanced process may deter the candidates you most want.

The *"Twenty Questions"* game can be really useful. In this context it is simply discussing together if we only had twenty questions to ask to discern whether the person before us is the one we want what would they be and then allocating the questions between us and deciding which ones a number of us ask to calibrate. By the way one of my favourite questions is: *"If I had the opportunity to talk to anyone that you have worked with over the years, what would be the most embarrassing thing that I would find out?"* This question will tell you what someone thinks is embarrassing, give a clue as to their integrity, openness and humility as well as to how resilient they might be. Over the years this has led to discovering deal-breaker facts about people as well as strengthening views on candidates and seeing them in a new light.

Chair and CEO selection processes are understandably more intense than others but it is increasingly common to find a second stage process for a non-exec or trustee taking a half or full day involving a variety of one-on-one and group meetings. Involving people from within the organisation beneath board-level and other key stakeholders is becoming more common.

One trap to fall into if you have a more intense selection process is that you then sigh with relief at having made a good appointment and don't put the effort in that you should to the onboarding and induction process. Regulators and Public Bodies will often have either a guide to what they expect of these processes or may even be involved in the process so that new appointees understand their obligations to them as well as what is expected. In the UK and elsewhere the Charity Commission and equivalent bodies also have a trustee pack to support this.

In planning onboarding and induction processes I like to think of it not as a one-off exercise but as part of how we ensure that all board members are well-informed about the organisation, how it works, what the big opportunities and challenges are and so on. It should also be a participative process and not a knowledge dump. The questions a new board member asks at this stage can be really powerful providing fresh insight and value.

By getting individual board and exec members involved in delivering onboarding and induction also serves the purpose of helping them to keep up to date as well. The process of preparing to explain something to someone less familiar is nearly always useful in making you think why something is the way it is or is done in the way that it is.

Diversity and Inclusion

NomCos are the obvious sub-committee to lead on Diversity and Inclusion given their focus on people and the fact that consideration of D&I issues is central to so much of what they do.

So, what is normally meant by D&I, what are the most frequently occurring issues for boards and what are the elements of a good D&I policy for a board?

"*Diversity*" generally describes the ways in which we differ and "*inclusion*" the way in which we manage those differences to ensure that people are treated fairly and equally no matter how they differ. Dimensions of diversity could be gender, ethnicity, sexual orientation, age, religious belief, disability and so on. Aspects of inclusion include policies designed to make the organisation welcoming to people with different dimensions of diversity and to ensure that people are treated equally no matter what their characteristics. Examples might include recruitment, promotion and other HR policies including board compo- sition and working practices such as flexible working hours and support for specific challenges to enable someone to perform well.

The most frequently occurring D&I issues for boards relate to board composition, decision making and culture.

In reviewing a broad range of board D&I policies it seems that the following are the key elements at a high level:

- Starting by understanding what D&I means and its relevance to the organisation's purpose and strategy.
- Setting clear objectives with timelines and metrics to track progress.
- Making the investment in time, money and reputation to achieve those objectives.
- Committing to a diverse and inclusive leadership and the communication and training and development required.
- Constantly reviewing progress and the landscape to ensure that it maintains a good understanding of the issues and that its objectives

and strategy for achieving them and the language that you use is relevant and up to date.

Having commented on the elements above then policies tend rightly to focus in on aspects of diversity and inclusion such as gender, ethnicity, religious beliefs, age, disability and so on. As has been commented in the introduction to the book several tragic events and campaigns arising from them have given fresh impetus to tackling deep and poorly addressed issues relating to D&I across the world.

In chairing the EY Foundation, I became aware of EY's approach to diversity and inclusion (*see* Useful links) which I think is pragmatic, linked to the needs of its business and delivered in a highly engaging way. We have adopted it at the EY Foundation and although there are lots of things we would like to be better at it has helped enormously. It essentially has three aspects:

- championing diversity at every level of the business;
- taking targeted action to level the playing field; and my favourite aspect
- creating a culture where different perspectives can thrive.

It is sponsored from the top, driven by the staff who have created a wide range of networks focused on specific aspects of diversity which are supported by the firm and underpinned by what I think is a very practical approach to inclusive leadership and working practices; all of which has taken substantial investment in development and communication. This includes producing a range of tools and training designed to understand default behaviours, tendencies and unconscious bias (*see* the "Isms" on page 244) as well as setting personal objectives and strategies to improve how leaders interact with colleagues and clients.

The key benefit for them has been in attracting talent and in strengthening teams. A fascinating feature of the approach has been how EY has used the nature of its business to reinforce what it is doing internally by taking positions on issues. Encouraging others means you have to deliver yourself or risk being a hypocrite.

Board awaydays

These events can be inspiring, catalytic, hugely enjoyable and lead to transformational change in organisations and much improved perform- ance. Yet, they can also be ritualistic, miserable, stressful and counter- productive affairs which make you realise that you really don't want to be on this board, work for the organisation or be with these people a day longer.

I once did some light research on how people felt about awaydays and as to what they thought were the secrets of success. Although what I found was a generally downbeat picture there were bursts of uplifting sunshine and some really useful thoughts and tips which are described below.

Be clear on the purpose of the awayday and what your desired outcomes are. Don't just have one because you always do at this time of year. Having to manufacture things to discuss because you have the date in the diary should lead you to think about cancelling it, asking whether you are poor at planning or whether you are simply avoiding a major strategic issue that needs discussing.

At the same time, most well-organised boards will have an annual board calendar, will want to plan ahead and will probably have a year of board meetings, including a possible awayday, in the diary.

A common driver for these events is to discuss strategy (*see* page 167 for the board's role in developing strategy). In practice the driver tends to be to gain the board's perspectives on a range of strategic issues or options with a view to the exec finalising the strategy for the next phase of development and then presenting it to the board for approval at a forthcoming regular meeting. Other drivers might include an event to bond a new or refreshed board, or to consider a major event such as a significant expansion or contraction, a merger or acquisition or perhaps a crisis. An awayday might also be a very good opportunity to review the outcome of a board review, agree actions and start to work on some of the issues emerging from it.

It might be tempting to save time and money, especially if you have a multinational board, to start the day with a regular board meeting. Obviously, there are circumstances where doing this is necessary and it can be made to work but doing so carries the risk that it places increased time pressure on both meetings. On top of that it can create an odd dynamic.

In convening the meeting and in setting the tone right at the beginning, it is important to be clear what the desired outcomes are. They can cover a wide range of possibilities. Taking one focused on strategy outcomes are likely to be to:

- ensure that the board and the exec have a well-informed and common view of the strategic opportunities and challenges, the key strategic variables and the main choices that the organisation has for its strategy for the next phase of development;
- gain the board, the exec and relevant advisers' input on those choices;
- narrow the choices down to a few options; and
- agree the parameters, responsibilities and work to be done by the exec before bringing a finalised strategy proposal to the board for approval and timescale.

There are advantages to having an awayday at the same point each year and planning sufficiently far ahead especially for a group of board members and execs based in different countries. However, it is also the case that there are advantages to only having awaydays when you have something important to discuss and the right time for that may not fit with the annual schedule.

My approach is to have a date planned in the diary but to be prepared to cancel it if it isn't needed or arrange an awayday on a different date if that feels the right thing to do.

A common format is to have an early dinner the night before partly to ensure a prompt start the morning afterwards and to build the right atmosphere.

Obviously, it isn't really an awayday if you do it in the office. The environment may not be conducive to the nature of what you want to do and the potential for interruptions is much higher. As a consequence, despite the increased cost, awaydays tend to be in off-site locations with environments that are conducive to broader thinking and also suitable for board bonding.

When researching with people how they felt about their awaydays, a common complaint amongst those dissatisfied with theirs was that they were in awkward places to get to and they rarely used the facilities that would have made it worth the journey and the expense. As a consequence, if you are going to use such a venue make the most of it.

It is important that all board members attend whether they are exec or non-exec. As to others, this will depend greatly on the alignment between the board and the exec that we explored on page 12. It is normal for other members of the leadership team including the company secretary and advisers to attend for specific items.

CEOs views tend to differ on whether all of the exec should be

present for all of the day or not. Some feel it is motivational and gives the board good visibility on succession candidates. Those who feel that only the execs who are on the board should attend may prefer to have their execs focused on delivery, want to avoid revealing lack of alignment amongst the execs or may not feel sufficiently confident in their colleagues.

In talking to other Chairs, the consensus seems to be that a balance needs to be struck so that the board has enough board-only time and that the opportunity to engage with execs is also taken.

Using an external facilitator for such days has advantages. Doing so enables the Chair and CEO to become true participants removing the burden of managing the time and content as well as allowing them more airtime to participate rather than orchestrate. Although Chairs and CEOs ought to be good at facilitating meetings, an expert facilitator will have a helpful level of neutrality and may be even better at it. If you are going to use one then they need to be:

- credible with the participants and experienced at the appropriate level;
- able to create an appropriate atmosphere which will be a blend of formality and informality;
- prepared and able to challenge participants (collectively and individually);
- able to maintain an objective and neutral approach; and
- have a clearly-defined process for running the day, which is flexible enough to deviate from it when right to do so.

Good facilitators who fit your specific requirements aren't always easy to find but a well-networked board will usually be able to get a number of recommendations of people who have successfully run sessions for peer organisations. If you don't have such recommendations, then your advisers should be able to suggest people. If you draw a blank there, then in a number of countries there are now agencies which have panels of facilitators who have experience of working with a wide range of organisations.

For smaller organisations cost may be an issue and you may, as many charities do, be able to secure someone on a pro- or light-bono basis.

Creating the right atmospheres is an essential ingredient for having a highly productive event. Generating a feeling that this is an important event with the right blend of momentum and reflection, creativity and pragmatism is something good Chairs, CEOs and facilitators take seriously and are good at delivering.

You know that you have achieved this if years later those attending refer back to it as a touchstone or with the fondness reserved for game-changing moments.

For an awayday to be successful there needs to be good follow up and communication afterwards, not just with those attending but, as importantly, to others. As with any other meeting of the board I like, as Chair, to know at the end of such a day that we have all agreed on what we are going to do, who is going to do it and have a timeline. The company secretary is the natural person to organise this record.

With regard to communication it is good practice for the CEO to send an email the next morning to their broader leadership team letting them know the key things discussed and what, if any, implications there are for them in terms of follow up, especially in communicating with their teams.

It is normal for the Chair to send a thank you email with appropriate feedback to those attending who are not on the board.

Finally, I always think it is worth doing a quick go-around at the end of such a day to gather initial feedback and gain the different perspectives from those attending on what has been agreed and how they feel about it.

Agendas and board papers

One of the many things that a Chair and CEO have to get right, together with the support of the CFO and the company secretary, is the process for deciding what goes on the board's agenda and when, as well as the form and content of accompanying board papers.

If the role of the board is to ensure that there is the *"Right Strategy, Right Resources and Right Governance"* for the organisation (*see* page 6), then it ought to follow that the agendas and papers for its meetings should be focused on items relating to these three things.

It all sounds simple, but in practice managing the *"agenda challenge"* can be tough, not least because there are so many things to balance including:

- The overall nature of the meeting and the content. These should fit the content and can vary considerably through the year. It's ultimately the Chair's job to manage this, with support from those relevant, at each stage from covering email to the minutes.
- Time spent in either the zone of comfortable or uncomfortable debate (*see* page 215). The Chair needs to lead the board in achieving the right balance both through the year as well as in individual meetings.
- Being thorough and not consuming too much exec time. This applies both to the content of meetings as well as to board papers.
- Strategic and non-strategic issues.
- Long and short-term issues.
- The necessary and the desired.
- What's for information, discussion and decision. In particular ensuring that board members are sufficiently well-informed to make the most effective decisions.
- Gaining visibility of the exec beyond the CEO and CFO in an efficient, as well as effective, way. Them just sitting in the room and not being allowed to contribute is counter-productive.
- Bringing in people from outside the board to present but avoiding *"death by PowerPoint"*.
- When holding meetings away from Head Office, maximising the impact and minimising the disruption to operations.

To name but a few.

Considering the points and Figure 3.4 below can be in helpful in trying to achieve the various balances required and also in ensuring that the rest of the board and the executive, not only agree how things should get on to the agenda and when, but also have opportunity to input to forming agendas in an efficient way.

Figure 3:4 Managing the 'agenda challenge'

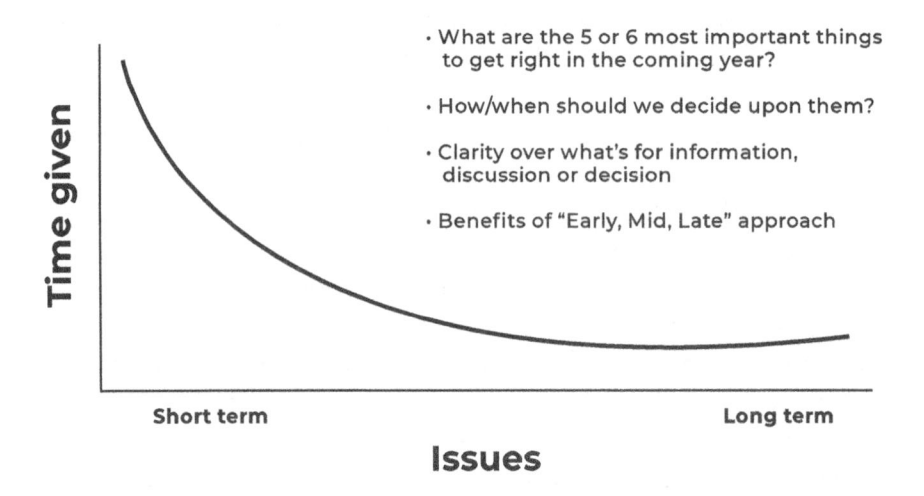

```
Time given
         |
         |·  What are the 5 or 6 most important things
         |   to get right in the coming year?
         |·  How/when should we decide upon them?
         |·  Clarity over what's for information,
         |   discussion or decision
         |·  Benefits of "Early, Mid, Late" approach
         |_____
           Short term                     Long term
                        Issues
```

The chart comes from research I did many years ago from looking at around 100 agendas from a range of companies. I made a judgement, from talking to the Chairs and company secretaries, of how much time was spent on each item and then crudely put them into *"Short"*, *"Medium"* and *"Long"* term categories. The conclusion, as the chart shows, was an inverse relationship between time given and importance. So often the time for major strategic decisions was squeezed through time taken up by short-term issues, including compliance and regular governance matters.

I make no claim that the analysis is robust scientifically. It was a narrow group of public and private UK companies and a relatively small sample and the precise shape of the chart was a little more wiggly than the smooth curve shown above. However, over the last 20 years since I produced it, and have been using it in training, it seems to resonate with people from a much broader range of organisations and is rarely challenged as representing the reality for many boards.

Frequently board agendas are packed with ritual items. Many directors, execs and non-execs, feel frustrated that big strategic issues often don't get the time they should. They and others also feel that they don't have enough opportunity to provide input to shaping agendas of how a matter is going to be discussed. All issues which regularly crop up in board reviews.

So, how can you change this?

A good starting point is by agreeing as a board and exec how to decide what goes on board and sub-committee agendas and to develop an agenda plan for at least a year ahead which has good synchronicity between board, sub-committee and exec meetings as well as with the company's reporting cycle. The company secretary and CFO are usually the execs driving this operationally. This may sound incredibly basic and almost insulting to suggest. Yet, all too often and especially with underperforming boards, I have found that this discussion hasn't been had.

It is usually straightforward to agree, as part of such a discussion, that we should start by agreeing what the most important things are, as well as the necessary things, and then which items need discussion and decision and which should go on the agendas to ensure that the board can make informed decisions. A lot of the informing can be done outside of the board but there is still a need, especially for decision items, to ensure that everyone is aware of the specifics.

Most boards usually have only five or six big strategic things to agree each year and allowing time in the board's calendar to have a discussion about what we think they are is usually highly productive. Given the pace of change, it is normally the case that in practice that two or three of them might actually emerge during the year so the other thing that is needed is to agree how, if something material does crop up, it will be dealt with. Much harder to do if the board calendar is already crammed.

Another principle is not to start out with a packed calendar. Remember the *"Effectiveness and Pressure"* curve from page 94. Frequency and length are important contributors to pressure. Too short or too frequent meetings and there's a risk of hasty decisions or matters which should be discussed by the board not being so: too long and concentration and focus may dissipate; a problem which magnifies when strategic decisions are at the back of the agenda. Too infrequent and the board isn't *"match fit"* or in the *"zone"*. Agendas are likely to be crammed and too much time is needed for catching up. The rise of Board Apps and the use of technology has made things a lot easier and many lower level decisions can be taken between meetings (*see* page 262).

It's the board's job to decide upon the frequency and length of meetings, although frequency is often pragmatically determined by the organisation's nature, including how international it and its board are as well as its stage of development. The deciding factor for both frequency and length should be *"what's best for the organisation"* and there is nothing to stop you varying it according to need. In practice this is what happens anyway, eg through periods of major transactions, events, or crises.

The most common frequencies are *"monthly"*, *"bi-monthly plus an awayday"* and *"quarterly plus an awayday"*. For quoted businesses the reporting regime in many markets tends to result in the bi-monthly plus an awayday beat. For start-up businesses with VC backing or start-up charities or social enterprises with Social impact investors monthly is the norm. For many public bodies and for established charities quarterly seems to be the typical pattern. There are pros and cons in all of them and one would expect the frequency to influence the length.

The pros of monthly meetings are that the board should be better bonded, informed and on top of the detail as well as better able to spot the need for, and to take, corrective action more quickly than with a less frequent beat; hence their popularity in the start-up and early stages of an organisation's life. The downsides of monthly meetings are that they may become too operational and that the consumption of senior exec time, most notably the CFO, undermines the benefits. In PE or VC investments the risk is that they become overly focused on the monthly financials and on investor catch up. However, I have seen many fine examples of the monthly interrogation saving a company. As ever it is a question of balance.

The benefit of the *"quarterly plus an awayday"* model, is that it reinforces focus and concentrates on the most strategically important topics. The cons might be that too much time is needed catching up, that the volume of *"necessary"* items which have built up crowd out the strategic ones and if there isn't a strong Chair they just become an even more crammed version of a monthly one.

The *"bi-monthly plus an awayday"* approach has a lot going for it in terms of avoiding the cons of either monthly or quarterly meetings and working well with those organisations that need to report quarterly to a Stock Exchange or Regulator.

In agenda planning it is also wise to consider more than one year in framing things. For example, if you are an organisation subject to regulatory review you will inevitably have things for the board to decide in the years before the next review. If you are a charity with a big multi-year funder then it is wise to ensure that the board reviews, if required, how replacement funding is being raised well ahead of need.

As well as deciding what these most important decisions are, you should also Figure out when would be the best time to discuss them, who to involve and whether it is right to use an *"Early"*, *"Mid"* or *"Late"* approach, or not, for each of them (*see* page 230).

The most important strategic items should form the backbone of the agenda plan and, ideally, they should be spread out so that there is a good mix at each meeting. Once the timing for these has been allocated then is the time to add *"the necessary"*, ie all the necessary governance, compliance and other matters which a board must review and agree. It is also essential that the board understands the financial position of the organisation before taking decisions.

The reason for doing it this way round is that there is usually more flexibility as to when most of the *"necessary"* items can be done. If you have the basic structure in agendas of *"Strategy"*, *"Resources"* and *"Governance"* you can spread the various items through the year. Often the governance items, including the formalities, are dealt with first.

It is also a good idea for each board meeting to have a good balance between items for information, discussion and decision and effective chairs, CEOs, company secretaries and CFOs will be take this into account. On that point, one device many Chairs use now is to have a tick column grid where the columns are *"Information"*, *"Discussion"* and *"Decision"*.

A good process, and one which many boards adopt these days, is to have the discussion referred to above in terms of strategic items and agree a broad outline for the period ahead and then check towards the end of each meeting whether any changes are required to the plan in the light of changed circumstances or decisions now taken.

There are people not on the board or in the senior executive team who also might have useful suggestions to make in terms of what the board should be discussing. As Chair I find it helpful to canvass views of the broader leadership and of advisers as well as the board and senior exec continuously and informally. I am also keen to learn from peers as to what they have on their agendas, whether they are in similar organisations or not. One of the great privileges of a career in PE was being able to see trends in other sectors and learn from other organisations, big and small across the world.

Key stakeholders, shareholders, regulators, governments, major funders may also have views on what the board should be discussing as well as on the frequency and length of board meetings. If you have a syndicate of investors it is normally the job of the lead investor's representative to canvas the views of the other investors and communicate a combined and united view on frequency, length and nature of content and, in good time, any input to specific topics they feel should be discussed at forthcoming meetings.

On length, views vary. Personally, unless you have a very international board I favour a 2-3 hour approach with only two big decisions being taken. It tends to keep things focused, energised and allows enough time for proper discussion on the major decisions. However, if you are flying board members in from across the world it might be your frequency is less and so legitimately each meeting might be longer. The trap though is to overdo this. It is perfectly reasonable for those who have travelled further to do things outside of the board meeting in the location which will add value.

Experienced Chairs appreciate the benefits of a good covering email to accompany board papers and a reinforcing introduction at the start of meetings, to focus the board's attention on the key decision items and ensure the priorities in terms of use of time are clear. They may even, in the email or in the agenda itself, set an expectation of the time allowed for certain items without being too rigid about it.

A few other practical points in setting regular board meeting agendas are worth thinking about including:

- Ensuring, if you can, that if you have external presenters to the board that they go on first or early in the agenda. They are much more likely to be on time this way, not have their time compressed and have the board at its most attentive. Impressing external presenters is not the primary purpose of having them there but I know, and have experienced myself, how demotivating it can be if you are kept hanging about, have your time chopped and then enter a room of board members grumpy or tired from a preceding item.
- That agendas should also take into account location. If the board is meeting at a divisional unit then it will typically want to use the opportunity to learn more about that unit, to reinforce their market position by holding some form of event and perhaps also take advantage of being there to strengthen or open up key relation-

ships. I have seen brilliant examples of this as well as car crashes. Success usually depends upon the planning and the engagement of whoever is the senior local person.
- Would this meeting be better as a physical meeting or a virtual meeting. Clearly during the pandemic few of us had a choice. So, we upped our game on holding and participating in virtual board meetings and gained and lost in the process. As we emerge, we will be able to choose again and to find the right balance through the course of a year. The forced experiment has accelerated what I think was already a trend to a blended model which is likely to be more effective and better for the planet but retain some of the powerful benefits of physical meetings.
- Linked to the previous point how can you maximise the use of board apps to make *"time together"* as productive as possible (Page 262).
- When synchronising with sub-committee meetings it's obvious that the relevant sub-committees meet before the board. My preference, logistics allowing, is for this to be a week before the board papers are circulated so that there is time to properly incorporate their recommendations into the board papers. Obviously during the peak of a crisis, as evidenced by the pandemic we may not always have that luxury.
- Awaydays are covered more fully on page 198, but one important point of linkage here is that it is generally not a good idea to start an awayday with a regular board meeting, tempting though that might be from a logistical perspective (*see* page 199).

If there is one frustration that crops up more than most in board reviews, even for the most effective boards, it is "*the board papers*". I may be old fashioned on this but I feel that there is value in the rigour of having to prepare a detailed paper for the board and there were many times throughout my career where doing so gave me a different perspective on something. More than that, producing the paper helped enormously in constructing a more robust rationale for what was being proposed.

I also learnt early on from a wise Chair, the Late Lord Cuckney, when he Chaired 3i, that:

"Neither you nor the board may know what they need to know until you do this properly and research the topic thoroughly."

He, like many other effective Chairs, also didn't feel that the rigour of a paper was proportionate to its length. As with speeches it generally takes longer to prepare a more powerful short one than a long one.

Going back to board reviews and to comments on board papers, this composite comment is a good summary of what you frequently hear from independent board members where they are frustrated:

"We need to review the way we do board papers, they're too long, consume far too much management time, and are full of stuff I don't really need to know or see."

A mirroring exec composite comment tends to be:

"I don't know why they need all this stuff, it's a time killer, they don't appear to read them and they never appear grateful for all the work we put in."

Typical factors driving these remarks tend to be that:

- As with some other matters, there might not have been a "real" discussion about what the specific point of the board paper was, ie was it for information, to stimulate discussion to gain input or for decision. Moreover, it may not be clear what the exec want from the board.
- Ironically, I have observed that this tends to happen more when there is a policy, usually written by the company secretary or CFO on *"the way board papers are done here."* The problem being that the result of the laudable aim of having a house style means that the house style might make lots of common sense in abstract but sadly only occasionally fits the specific purpose required.
- A lack of recognition that it is perfectly legitimate for papers to have different styles for different purposes.
- There is a lot of feedback on specific papers but no discussion or

agreement about what the desired house style should be for certain categories of paper.
- If you go back to the Venn approach to interaction between the board and the exec (*see* page 12), then they are either operating in parallel universes or trying to do each other's jobs. The heavy use of the word "they" is a good clue that this might be the case.
- Sometimes it is simply that the focus of a review of board papers is too heavily weighted on the ineffective ones rather than highlighting the best and learning from those.

I find this little checklist helpful when thinking about board papers. The following additional points may be helpful in addressing some of these challenges:

Figure 3:5 Board papers

- **Purpose** - *"Information, discussion, decision"*
- **Format** – *"A house style"*
- **Clarity** - *"This is what we want from the board"*
- **Timing** – *"When ready or as part of board pack as whole?"*
- **Facts and interpretations**
- **Who?**

- As a board member I make a deliberate point of highlighting in meetings the papers that I and others have told me they think are the best and following up with feedback to the CEO or CFO on the rest.
- If you are the CEO, then depending upon the nature of the Chair's role in the organisation and their appetite, consider asking the Chair to review all draft papers before they are finalised. It's something where I am Chair I am not only happy to do but also find helpful as part of my planning and preparation for the meeting.

If you do this you need to be very careful not to get too much into the weeds. It should be in the spirit of constructive feedback.
- If the need for a paper arises in a meeting then test whether it is really needed and if so agree what the point is and in what form and length you want it to be.
- Before commencing work the Chair should agree with the CEO, CFO and company secretary what papers are needed, their intended purpose and discuss what might be the headlines.
- Where relevant also consider asking a board member to be a "*board paper buddy*" to the exec responsible for producing the paper. This doesn't mean straying into exec territory. It simply means a follow-up meeting to give views on what sort of things the board might like to see covered in the paper and an email/phone exchange to review a first draft and provide input.
- Consider some training for those who produce the most. There has been some interesting work done by Board Intelligence (BI), the various Institutes and Associations of Company Secretaries and others on this topic (*see* Useful links, page 411) and several of them run useful workshops.
- Master what I call the "*AOB game*". 'Any Other Business' on an agenda should be reserved for those things which have arisen since the formal agenda and accompanying papers were distributed. Occasionally dominant CEOs may try to use AOB to gain a decision on something which they may be anxious about discussing in too much detail but is worthy of a proper paper and thorough discussion. Good Chairs can recognise this and will deal with it effectively.

In closing this exploration of agendas and papers it is worth remembering that good due diligence questions to ask before joining a board are: "*What is the process for deciding what goes on the agenda?*" "*What goes to the board and what is delegated to the executive?*" and "*Can I see the last year's agendas and papers please?*" The response to these questions should provide a very good perspective on where you are starting from, as well as help you get up the learning curve.

Convening and managing meetings

The first book I wrote on boards, *"Running Board Meetings"*, was stimulated by attending a really badly run board meeting. The structure of that book was really simple, *"Before"*, *"During"* and *"After"* and was based on observations from masters of the art of running board meetings as well as those who found it more of a struggle.

We have covered much of the aspects of *"Before"* elsewhere in this book but there are three topics not covered elsewhere and these are the convening of meetings, managing the meetings themselves and the gripping topic of board minutes.

The convening of the meeting ought to be simple if you have a plan for meeting dates and an accompanying agenda plan. Convening each meeting should then simply be a matter for the company secretary to organise and the Chair to confirm with the covering email accompany- ing the Board papers, ideally the week before. Yet life is rarely that simple and there may be many other reasons for a board meeting or call outside of those which are regular or planned, eg for a major transaction or event or during a crisis.

Again, the use of technology and Board Apps has made convening these unscheduled meetings so much easier. Even before the pandemic we often found ourselves *"dialling"* or *"Skyping"* or *"Zooming"* into board calls from all over the world. The use of *"Doodle"* or other *"polls"* to establish who is available when has also sped up the convening process and the board apps helps with the process of approving the fact that we should have a board meeting.

All of this requires tech savvy and responsive board members. The Chair has to cultivate this culture and show leadership through their own behaviour, as does the company secretary. Sadly, as with any other exec or board member, they are not all equipped to do this. Not everyone has passed the pandemic test in this regard. It is surprising that this is rarely discussed in interviewing board members (*see* page 192) when it is so critical to a fully-functioning board. It can be as important a development need as someone gaining greater financial literacy. More organisations ought to offer tech training for board members.

When it comes to managing meetings, the focus is rightly on the Chair and their chairing skills but, as with other things, it is the responsibility of everyone around the table to ensure that the board meeting is effective. To use the sporting analogy, the captain will lead the team but at numerous points during the game individual players will step up, show leadership and can turn the outcome of the game without the captain's direct involvement.

Chairing skills still remain an undervalued and undertrained area of development in my view. Learning by doing is of course highly valuable, as is watching the masters of the art or seeing someone who is ineffective and being able to figure out why. However, I think, despite the considerable increase in development opportunities, for those considered to be in the pipeline for board positions there is still nowhere near enough on chairing skills. Perhaps this is because people feel that these aren't necessary for a first appointment as an independent director as they will be needed later. I strongly disagree with this view, better-developed chairing skills will help you support the Chair, will help you chair a sub-committee and have considerable use generally.

The question as to what are good chairing skills often arises. On page 111 I said that I thought that there were three fundamental characteristics of effective directors and these related to *"judgement, interpersonal skills and antennae"*. Effective Chairs need an abundance of all three.

These days with more virtual meetings they and other directors also need to be what I call *"tech dexterous"* as well as *"Tech savvy"*. It is one thing to know what to do and how to do it. Quite another to do it. Especially if, like me, you are mildly dyslexic and find the visual sensory overload of all of the faces, slides, board papers and chat challenging. I have had to work hard to learn new tricks, invest in a few more devices and got there but I really feel for those great directors, of all ages, who are finding this shift even more challenging. It's back to diversity and inclusion again.

To ensure that the right people are on the board and that they will be discussing the right things in the right way means a discussion with the CEO, CFO and company secretary beforehand to agree objectives for the meeting; who will introduce the various topics; and if there are non-board member presentations, ensuring that they understand what's needed and have been given the support they need to deliver it.

Regarding objectives, this could range from: *"We really want to test this decision to destruction before we go ahead with it"* to *"We need to get Joe far more engaged in this meeting"* or a common one *"The CEO needs to talk less and let other executives play a fuller role"*.

Every board member should have their own objectives for the meeting and these are not simply about the outcomes they would like to see for the decisions to be made. Building or strengthening a relationship with another board member or executive may be goal or perhaps contributing to changing the balance or tone of the meeting from what might be anticipated.

With those objectives set then thinking about the pie charts of board time and your own how you might use whatever slice is yours will help.

Effective Chairs are determined that decisions are robust, that groupthink (page 240) is avoided and that the CEO and other execs are motivated to carry out the decisions of the board. Something, by the way, one should never assume. They will introduce the agenda well, usually through linking to the covering email; set expectations in terms of time and focus; and then use these opening remarks as a point of reference throughout the meeting. Most importantly they will remember throughout that their job is to Chair the meeting and not to "*be*" the meeting.

They will also work hard to manage the balance of "*Effectiveness and Pressure*" (*see* page 94); time in the "*zones of comfortable and uncomfortable*" debate; have the discipline required to get through the work in good time while enabling discussions to flow naturally; and be at the right depth and balance in terms of input from those around the table, especially the more introvert.

They will do this by using their judgement and antennae and through their interpersonal skills, as well as maximising the impact of their airtime. It's more challenging in a virtual setting, hence the need for more work beforehand.

They can use a mix of body language such as the "*finger switch*" (*see* page 124) and non-verbal vocalisations. A downbeat "*Hmmm*" with a frown can be as deadly as a warm "*Hmmm*" suggesting enthusiasm can be uplifting. They will also deploy effective bridging comments throughout the meeting such as "*I think Mary's point links superbly with the next item on the agenda.*" As has been said earlier technique will differ for virtual meetings.

Being adept at managing conflict, having the ability to foster healthy creative conflict, to make the most of difference but at the same time to achieve alignment, are important skills for a Chair and they are discussed in more detail on pages 120 and 137.

This means, on occasions, skillfully "*avoiding*" conflict in the meeting because they judge it is more effectively dealt with later, perhaps on a one-to-one basis or with them as the resolver. Equally it might mean adroitly surfacing an issue which is bubbling underneath the surface and they judge that now is the time to *"Out it and sort it"*.

Finally, at the end of each item and at the end of the meeting they will be good at summing up and ensuring that everyone is clear what decisions have been taken, what the consequences are and what follow-up is required, including how they will be communicated inside the organisation and externally. As part of this they will ensure that the company secretary, or whoever is taking the minutes, has captured the key points, decisions and actions accurately and clearly. Minutes are covered in more detail below.

As noted above managing video or tele-conference meetings is more challenging and again is an area where I think there is an opportunity for more training. The assumption seems to be that by the time you get to be a Chair or a director you are highly proficient at video or conference calls. Sadly, this is all too often a little optimistic. It is also the case that the nature of a board meeting is just different to the majority of virtual or conference calls we have as execs which tend to be focused more on projects, operational matters or communication of something.

Two questions raised often during the pandemic *"zoom boom"* were around the quality of decision making and whether board meetings were becoming too operational. On decision making my view was that there were benefits as well as disadvantages, most notably on the upside the more introverted felt more comfortable putting comments in the chat function than interrupting and it seemed easier to get short contributions from internal or external experts on a matter. On the downside the lack of social time for the board meant that sometimes how people felt about things wasn't always picked up as easily.

On the too operational point, some of this was due to the nature of the crisis and some due to the nature of tools we were using to have the discussion. It was absolutely vital in my view as a Chair to ensure that we took the right amount of time to ensure that everyone had their opportunity to input. It meant a lot more calls before meetings to ensure that we would cover all the bases and more afterwards to ensure that we had.

There are numerous systems which create an environment which is about as close as you can get to an in-the-room experience, but the reality is that most people seem to be using the now brand leading products.

If it is a physical meeting the Chair needs to work hard to ensure those not physically present have equal opportunity to contribute.

Over the years I have found the best way to achieve this is to email or call those not physically present, as well as those who may be absent, for their views ahead of the meeting so that I can draw them in at the right point and convey their views if they are unable to attend. I've also found that when *"going around the table"* if I simply alternate those physically present with those on the line it helps. Leaving those not present until last is not nearly as effective. It's also important to call those who couldn't attend the meeting to debrief.

Effective Chairs ensure that follow-through and linkage to subsequent meetings and events is effective. They will also be good at giving feedback, not just during the meeting through body language and their own input, but also after the meeting in individual conversations with board members and with the exec team.

Board minutes

Unless you are slightly odd or are in danger of insolvency, I doubt that this will be the part of the book that you couldn't wait to read. However, the subject of board minutes is very important and not just when the organisation is in danger of failing or facing serious legal action.

Investors, acquirers, regulators and others, including in some cases creditors, may, depending upon their authority or balance of power, request to see copies of the minutes. So they matter and when approving the minutes of any board meeting you attend you need to ensure that they are not only an accurate record of what happened, but they will convey the fact that the board is making reasonable decisions in the best interests of the organisation and its stakeholders with the information it had at the point of making them.

When helping boards through Boardelta it is often really instructive to look at the previous year's minutes. They can give you a good feel of how strategic the board is as well as how organised and efficient they are.

Practices vary according to type of organisation, the culture of the organisation and the capability of the person recording them. They cover the span from the comprehensive including a verbatim record of the discussion at one end of the spectrum, to a simple list of who was there and not, as well as decisions made and actions to be taken as a result at the other. Unless they are required to do so according to their articles of association or they are a public body where it is stipulated that they do, in my experience most boards tend to follow a path in the middle, noting the relevant paper and highlighting the major reasons for the decision as well as key points against.

The process for agreeing minutes is important and an effective Chair will feel a sense of ownership of this. A good simple process for doing this is as follows:

- The company secretary produces a draft set of minutes together with an action grid as soon as logistically possible, but ideally in the same week as the meeting.
- This draft is circulated to the Chair, SID and CEO for comment.
- Any resulting changes are agreed with the Chair and CEO then the minutes are circulated as a final draft to other board members for approval.
- If there are any changes required as a result of this broader circulation the Chair will endorse them.
- The final minutes are then either put on the board app (*see* page 262) or circulated.
- A good company secretary will follow progress of actions and alert those responsible for them and, when relevant, the Chair and CEO if they appear in danger of diverging from the timeline.
- Then in the covering email to the next set of board papers the Chair will note "*With regard to the minutes of the previous board meeting all actions have been implemented [with the exception of item X.X which will be completed by XXX].*" This will save time at the meeting.

In recent years the use of email to express reservations has become more common either before or after the board meeting. As emails are admissible in some countries as evidence in court this can be seen by some directors or trustees as a useful covering mechanism.

However, I think this needs to be done sparingly and when it is a matter of real strategic importance where you have a fundamentally different point of view. If you are really against something then it is better, despite the discomfort, to vote against it. Decisions involve making a judgement on the basis of the information you have. Your liability is likely to be joint and several and being seen to be constantly trying to cover your behind and undermine that will also undermine your credibility and respect which are key to your ability to influence.

When there is real risk that the organisation may fail then the board should be advised by an insolvency practitioner and an experienced lawyer in these matters. It is normal in these situations for one or both to be present at board meetings and to provide "*live*" advice in respect of the conduct and content of the meeting as well as the minutes.

Decisions and approvals relating to other matters reserved for the board

As Socrates said:

"It is easier to win an argument than to make the right decision."

As we explored earlier, in the section on the purpose of a board, making decisions about vision and strategy, resources and governance is fundamentally what boards do; a far from easy task for many reasons. I prefer the word "*making*" to "*taking*", not simply because it is more constructive but because it sounds more like a creative and rigorous process than taking which might imply a snatch at what might work. Whether we are into the "*making*" or "*taking*" style of decision making we always need to be careful of the dangers of yielding to the most eloquent rather than those with best judgement, as the legendary philosopher Socrates hints at in his wonderful quote.

There are a number of excellent books on the topic of decision making and as this is an enormous subject, I will make suggestions to enable you to dive deeper on a particular topic should you wish. There are also a range of other books that I have found useful and interesting over the years (*see* Bibliography).

If I had to pick only one of these books I would choose "*Thinking, Fast and Slow*" by Daniel Kahneman. It is an utterly brilliant book about how we humans make decision: "*Fast*" relating to those decisions we make instinctively and "*Slow*" to those where we use some sort of process. It may be a bit of dense read in the early chapters, but it is well worth the patience as much of the robust wisdom that follows is likely to increase your self-awareness and influence your approach profoundly.

Far from being a comprehensive tour of the subject this chapter will look at the business of making decisions from a board member's perspective, focusing on the following:

- the nature of board decisions;
- who should be involved in making decisions and how;
- their timing;
- the process of making such decisions;
- aspects of communication and implementation once a decision is made; and finally
- reviewing and learning from decisions.

When considering any decision, we need to be clear about exactly what decision it is that we are making, its nature, where it fits within the overall objectives of the organisation, how it might be linked to other decisions and what the broader consequences of what we decide are likely to be. We also need to be clear who we are going to involve and how. The tough bit is making the decision itself which should include consideration of when would be the best time to make it and how it is going to be made, communicated and implemented.

In making decisions we should also consider the likely reactions from others whether they be stakeholders or competitors and what our consequential responses will be. We also need to recognise our biases, both individually and as a group, and to manage them effectively so that we gain from both the power of human intuition as well as the opportunity afforded by objective evidence.

A director's ability to contribute to making good judgements on matters which are relevant to the board and which can be implemented successfully by the exec, is much more than a core competence. It defines our success in the role and is something that we must do rather than simply something that we can or might do.

The best boards are proactive in ensuring that they anticipate the decisions that they will need to make as well as getting on and taking the decisions that are needed now. They are also good at reflecting on decisions made and learning from those that go well and those that don't (*see* page 256). A big opportunity for many boards is to spend a little more time reviewing decisions, not to feel good or bad but simply to learn.

"*Contribute*" is also an important word here because, as we have discussed in the section from page 111 on the characteristics of the most effective directors, it isn't enough just to have good judgement. You also have to have the interpersonal skills and respect within the board to enable those judgements to influence the outcome as well as have the antennae to pick up on a vital piece of information to inform those judgements in the first place or add value to those of others. Being *"irritatingly right"* risks not being listened to or being avoided. Imposing our views on others, even if we might be right, almost always comes at a cost. As canny directors know, asking questions is usually a lot more effective than expressing opinions. Knowing what to say, when and how to say it are likely to be the most frequent decisions that you will make.

As in most situations the directors will be jointly and severally liable for the decision that the board takes, it shouldn't ever be about the decision of one person, even if that one person is the majority share- holder, but of the group as a whole.

Decisions are neither homogenous in their nature nor in their impact. So, different types of decisions probably need taking in different ways. This combined with uncertain information and frequently unpredictable outcomes all adds to the challenge. A perfectly good decision based on the information that a board had available to it at the time the decision was taken can be made to look a stinker by subsequent events or poor implementation. In general, I don't think enough time is given to ensuring that the board is happy with the implementation plan. Doing so often uncovers something which requires additional costs or time to be budgeted and impacts return.

It's easy to understand why this is the case given time constraints and the fear of stepping into exec territory. In practice I have found this latter point to be more of an excuse rather than a reason. It is easily dealt with if it is clear that the point is simply to be comfortable with the plan and not to get involved in delivering it. I suspect we can all think of acquisitions or international expansions which made sense strategically but have been value destroyers because of poor implementation. The learning from *"early-mid-late"* approaches to big decision making on page 230 is one way of dealing with this.

Understanding the specific context and consequences for the organisation and for others from the choices that we might make is critical to success. This means putting in the work as well as being *"actively"* open minded rather than just being open minded.

All of the above is easy to say but tough to deliver consistently in practice. Especially so considering some of the inherent challenges and the fact that there are humans involved. Here we'll look at some of these challenges, both structural and personal, as well as a number of the approaches that can be used to increase our chances of success. Page 111 in the *"People"* section contains some tips for when selecting directors to figure out what their approach to taking decisions is likely to be. It's often felt to me that the art and science of director selection doesn't always put enough weight on this even though track record should be a strong indicator.

There is a growing debate about the possible uses of AI with respect to boardroom decision making and so I have included a short section on this on page 262.

Finally, in this introduction to the topic I should mention that there are thirteen dilemmas for you to practice on in Section 4: *"Dilemmas"*. They are dilemmas because, like most of the decisions a board takes, they are far from *"no-brainers"* and are where all of your choices tend to have as many risks as gains associated with them. These originate from my second book *Directors Dilemmas* and have been updated and there is an introduction to them on page 269.

Nature of decisions

The nature of decisions that a board has to take varies in significance, complexity and degree of difficulty. It can be really challenging to ensure that enough time is spent on what appear to be the little or routine things which if you don't do properly can trip you up, create reputational risk and consume a lot more time if not dealt with properly at the appropriate time. Yet a more frequent challenge is spending enough time on the big things which will really determine the organisation's success and then considering them at the right time and in the right way.

Abraham Maslow's brilliant *"hierarchy of needs"* concept, first published in 1943, is widely used today in many contexts and has application in the boardroom. The concept is straightforward in that it simply orders the various needs that a human might have in a hierarchy of five sets of needs as the diagram below summarises.

Figure 3:6 Hierarchy of needs

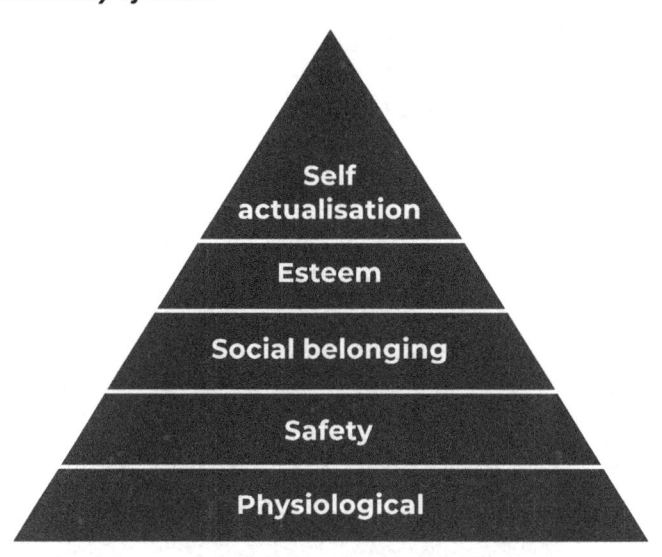

Physiological needs are the many requirements for survival, food, water, shelter and so on.

Safety needs come next and these include things like physical security, financial security and basic health and well-being. I like to think of this as keeping alive and well.

Social belonging, according to Maslow, recognises that humans need to feel a sense of belonging or acceptance among social groups.

Esteem satisfies our need for respect, recognition and status.

If we have all that, Maslow said that we then look for *self-actualisation* which he described as the desire to accomplish everything that one can, to become the most that one can be. Today, I suppose that we would call that fulfilling our potential.

Applying this to the many sorts of decisions we might want to take on a board we could simplify this into to three stages: *Survival, Sustainability and Fulfilling potential.*

Survival - The decisions that ensure our basic survival and ensure that we have the money and other resources that allow us to survive as an organisation.

Sustainability - Making the strategic decisions that ensure that we can survive into the future.

Fulfilling potential - Making the important decisions that will ensure that not only will we survive and thrive but absolutely maximise value or impact for our stakeholders.

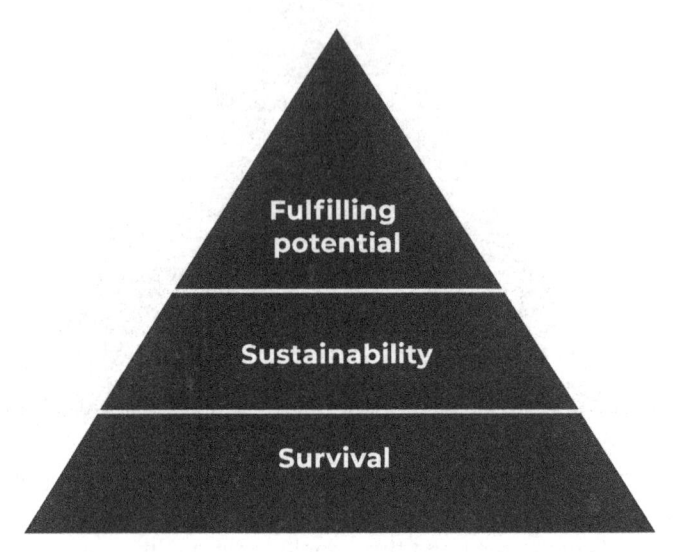

Figure 3:7 Stages of types of decisions taken on boards

```
            Fulfilling
            potential

           Sustainability

              Survival
```

The Board apps which have emerged in recent years and are described on page 262 can help a lot to increase productivity and allow more time for discussion on the big issues in the physical meeting. That is as long as you don't get tick happy, that you concentrate and have the courage to turn a non-discussion item into one you feel merits discussion.

My early career was in operations research in the industrial gas and chemicals industry. One of the most frequently used tools we were deploying at that time, especially to solve logistical challenges, was Linear Programming (LP).

LP was incredibly kind to me and helped me to solve a number of tricky problems that we had, not just in terms of the maths but also in terms of understanding the consequences for a whole range of people involved. As a result, I have carried my own little interpretation of the principles of LP with me to this day and have used them in so many ways, especially when emotions are high, information is uncertain, people aren't quite sure what they want and resources are constrained. These principles are that:

- It's ok to have multiple objectives. Indeed, it is usually easier if you accept this and focus on being clear what they are.
- You really need to understand your constraints and the relationships between things not just quantitatively but qualitatively as well. This helps you take account of varying tolerances and appetites, eg to the key elements of risk and return.
- You don't need to define everything perfectly.
- Never waste the data from a poor outcome. Use it to improve the model.
- A certain amount of iteration is healthy: a lot better than a binary *"Do you want to do this or not?"* Yet beware of over-iteration. Too much of good thing can paralyse you.
- Counter-intuitive solutions may actually be the best.
- Purely logical solutions can be really hard to sell sometimes, especially to those who appear analytical.

Another important point on the nature of decisions is the subject of what goes to the board and what goes to the exec. Inevitably it is a matter of judgement but whenever I have this decision to make with the CEO, I go back to the role of the board (*see* page 6) and the role of the exec (*see* page 10) to inform our decision. I would also go back to the discussion we had as a board on what the board and the exec's roles are and how we were going to work together, as that should have considered this point. There should also be a formal schedule of matters reserved for the board.

In my experience the most effective and appropriately confident CEOs will err on the side of caution and ensure they have strong board endorsement even if they might not technically need it. Weaker and less confident CEOs can be at either end of the spectrum: some wanting everything endorsed by the board to cover themselves and others

avoiding getting a board view in case they say no.

It is in the nature of all decisions that there is a level of risk and a board needs to be *"risk alert"* at all times. An important aspect of the audit and risk committee's role is to help the board to ensure that it is aware of the major risks facing the organisation and that they are being managed and mitigated in an appropriate manner (*see* page 175). The categories of risk are broad from basic commercial risks, external threats, legal risks and so on. All of these can, and should, have an influence on decision making, yet they may each have different levels of significance in terms of impact and likelihood in the minds of individual board members even if it looks as if they do on a risk matrix.

One category of risk that all directors or trustees need to be conscious of at all times is legal risk. This risk is both personal and organisational and is best mitigated through having the right legal team both in-house if you are sufficiently large to have it and from outside as well as having your antennae up for legal risk at all times. Occasionally though bad decisions are made for fear of legal consequences. The appearance of a humanity bypass has the potential to do considerable damage through a loss of market position and damaged staff engagement.

There may be occasions, perhaps in a merger or acquisition situation, where the directors need to take independent legal advice. This should be straightforward if provisions are in place through their appointment letter, there is a list of allowable firms to use and an agreed budget from which to pay such fees.

Some categories of decision, because they are a regular type of decision, develop a standard process or ritual of how they are made, eg the annual budget, capital expenditure, approval of mergers and acquisitions and core policies etc. I think it is important as part of the discussions about "*How we work together*" to discuss how these decisions will be made and to regularly review whether the way agreed is the most appropriate.

The final and most important point to make about the nature of decisions is that, for the moment, these decisions are made by humans and not machines and so it is essential to take into account the human factors. As you will see much of this part of the book on "*Decisions*" is devoted to these factors and is supported by the "*People*" section (*see* page 85)

Dilemmas

The most important decisions rarely tend to be no-brainers with an obvious choice. They are much more likely to be dilemmas where each choice has as many risks as gains associated with it. The definition of a "*dilemma*" in the Oxford Concise Dictionary is:

> "*A situation in which a difficult choice has to be made between two or more alternatives, especially ones that are equally undesirable.*"

In *"Directors Dilemmas"*, first published in 2000, I spoke about a childhood memory and how a fascination with aviation led me to think about dilemmas from a very early age.

"Planes were an endless source of amazement and as I watched them fly over to head into Liverpool airport or see the contrails in the sky above of planes heading out across the Atlantic, I wondered How they got up there? How did they navigate? How did they land so precisely? Who was on board?

Then one morning in primary school the teacher told us about a terrible crash the night before:

'The pilot had made his approach a little on the low side and as a result crashed into a building close by. We should pray for the dead, the relatives and especially the pilot.'

The accident left a deep impression on me. The overwhelming thought that occurred to me then and reoccurs to me now every time I hear of an accident is how horrendous it must have been for the pilot. What must have been going through his mind before impact? One little mistake and suddenly he was facing not just his own imminent death but the horrible responsibility for the deaths of others. Imagine the awful horror of those last few moments when he knew what was going to happen but was powerless to do anything about it.

Clearly pilots have to possess skills, nerves and judgement to match their responsibility. They are also critically dependent upon the skills of many other professionals. Who knows where it came from, but one day I started to think about the comparison between pilots and directors.

The analogy has only partial relevance, the nature of the passengers and the equipment is different. In most situations it is livelihoods rather than lives that are at stake for the director. Temporary loss of control or poor navigation is rarely as catastrophic.

This musing then stimulated the thought that it might be worthwhile to go and revisit some of the dilemmas I had seen or been involved in. Perhaps looking at them in more detail and maybe finding some new ones to explore might come in handy one day. After all who knows what new dilemma might be just around the corner? A little go in the boardroom simulator might be helpful."

Due to popular demand, in this book I have included a few of the dilemmas from *"Directors Dilemmas"* and updated them and also added some new ones so that you too can have a little go in the simulator (*see* page xv). As you will see after a description of each dilemma there is an exploration of the issues involved and how you might go about deciding what to do, as well as what the person actually did in the real situation. It is also made clear that what actually happened may not have been the best thing to do in all cases.

In all of these situations it was important to understand whether the decision presented the real decision or are we really taking others? The correct framing of a decision combined with careful consideration of the consequences normally sorts this out. Your vision, mission, purpose, strategy and values ought to be the frame for all other decisions to be made within. So, having a good process for agreeing, monitoring and adapting these fundamental things is at the heart of all decisions.

Who should be involved in decisions?

The well-known saying that *"None of us is as smart of all of us"* is powerful and encourages us to seek insight from the boardroom team and beyond before we take a major decision. No-one has a monopoly on wisdom and those who are often credited with genius have simply been fantastic at absorbing and synthesising the views of others. Without the input and stimulus of others they wouldn't be nearly as brilliant.

The *"wisdom of crowds"* described so well in James Suroweiecki's bestseller of the same name is compelling. The basic premise is that aggregating the judgement of many consistently beats the performance of the average member of the group. Yet we also know, that in large organisations in particular, seeking the views of too many and having too many potential blockers can result in poor decisions, decisions not being taken when they need to be or a lack of ownership and accountability for a decision when it is finally taken. It also may not be practical to seek a wide range of views given the timescale. Think of being on the board of a financial institution the morning after the Lehman's collapse in 2008.

The management consultancy business Bain & Company developed an approach to decision making for clients called RAPID® which I quite like.

As you can see from Fig. 3.8 this approach is all about bringing clarity to people's roles in the decision-making process. I suspect it also helped them to gain swifter and easier adoption of ideas generated by their work.

The benefits of the RAPID® approach are obvious even if you need to have some tough discussions at the beginning of the process about who gets to be in which group. Much better to resolve these conflicts at the start than the end of the decision-making process or worse during implementation. More can be found online about this approach (*see* Useful links).

As we make the decision it helps to have everyone pointing in the same direction, ie deciding in the best interests of the organisation. At the same time, we also want genuine diversity of thought, the confidence to challenge and to have different perspectives. How are we going to get that balance right?

Figure 3:8 Bain RAPID® approach to decision making

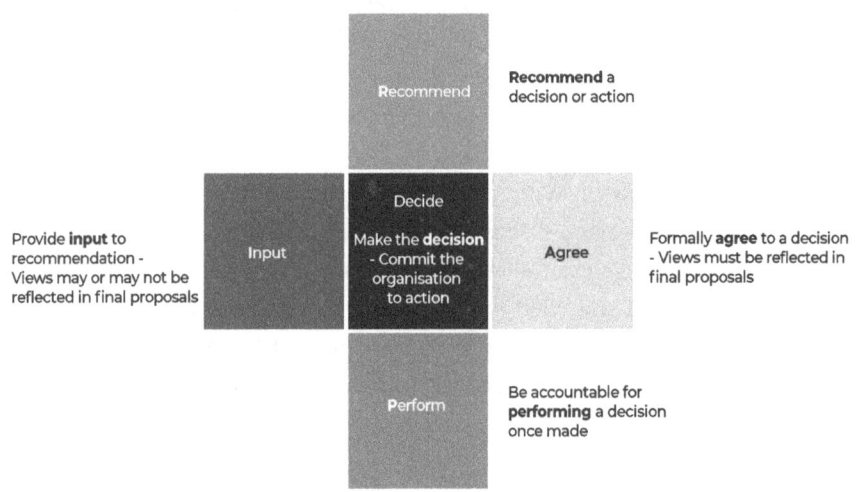

Recommend — **Recommend** a decision or action

Input — Provide **input** to recommendation - Views may or may not be reflected in final proposals

Decide — Make the **decision** - Commit the organisation to action

Agree — Formally **agree** to a decision - Views must be reflected in final proposals

Perform — Be accountable for **performing** a decision once made

Source: Bain & Company

Getting the board composition right is only part of the answer to this question. Making the most effective use of advisers and others, inside and outside of the organisation, will also help, as will creating the right atmosphere for the type of decision being made which is not just the job of the Chair. The CEO and other board members have a responsibility to do this as well.

When to decide

A consequence of crowded agendas for many boards is that decisions on key matters are often taken in one sitting. Yet many decisions are too important and complex to decide in one go. Over the years I have developed a liking for what is probably best described as an *"early, mid and late approach"* for the bigger decisions which avoids the dangers of what I call the *"Binary - Do us a paper for the next meeting"* way of taking decisions. It is even more powerful when combined with the RAPID® approach set out above.

In summary the idea is that for big decisions that don't need to be taken urgently you make the decision over a number of meetings in the following way.

- **Setup paper**
  This essentially describes the decision that needs to be taken, how it fits within the current vision, purpose and strategy and what the proposed *"early, mid and late"* approach being proposed is in this case as well as timeline and who might be involved.

- **Early**
  A short discussion with supporting paper beforehand where the board considers and discusses what are the issues that need to be taken into consideration in the decision and confirms who needs to be involved and what the process will be from here.
- The objective is to achieve alignment on issues and process and agree approach for this decision, perhaps using a framework like the RAPID® (page 229).

- **Mid**
  A longer discussion with supporting paper which this time:

    o confirms the issues and any others which have arisen since last meeting;
    o recommends consideration of at least two options;
    o has a list of points requiring input from the board; and
    o provides outline implementation plans, risks and risk mitigation strategies for each option.

The objective this time is to produce a preferred choice together with parameters and clarity over what will be required in the paper/presentation at the next meeting.

- **Late**
  Ideally a shorter *"finalisation"* meeting where the formal decision to proceed with the preferred option is taken. This time the emphasis is on the board being satisfied that not only is it the right decision but that they endorse the implementation strategy and resourcing plan to deliver it.

I like this approach because it reduces the risk of many strategic decisions where they are excellent choices but made to look a stinker because not enough attention was given to implementation. I'm also a bit of a *"Muller"* in that I like to reflect and gather calibrating information. It's my belief that looking at a decision from different perspectives is hard to do in one *"wham bam"* style go.

Remember the *"Effectiveness and pressure"* curve on page 94. In a decision-making context, there are lots of things which cause pressure; some of the common ones are listed in Figure 3.9 overleaf. These are mostly obvious and reinforce the need for thinking ahead so you can try and make the decision at the best time and in the right way with the best information and insights available. The less obvious one, until you think about it, is to do with the quality of relationships. For fear of normal distribution overload, I won't add another one on board harmony and effectiveness. The point is obvious: too much harmony results in groupthink and complacency and too little results in lack of consensus and chaos.

Sometimes pressure builds without you noticing it until you reach a tipping point. In the *"People"* Section on page 143 we looked at the application of Catastrophe Theory to the behaviour of dogs and board members. As a quick reminder, Catastrophe Theory is the study of small perturbations which lead to a catastrophic failure.

Some people know it as the putting bags of flour on a bridge until the last bag makes it collapse. Although not always, organisational failure is frequently a result of lots of bad decisions rather than one giant misjudgement.

So how can you avoid this *"creeping up on you"* danger? The history of financial markets and dominant market leaders who fail suggests that smart

Figure 3:9 Pressure in decisions

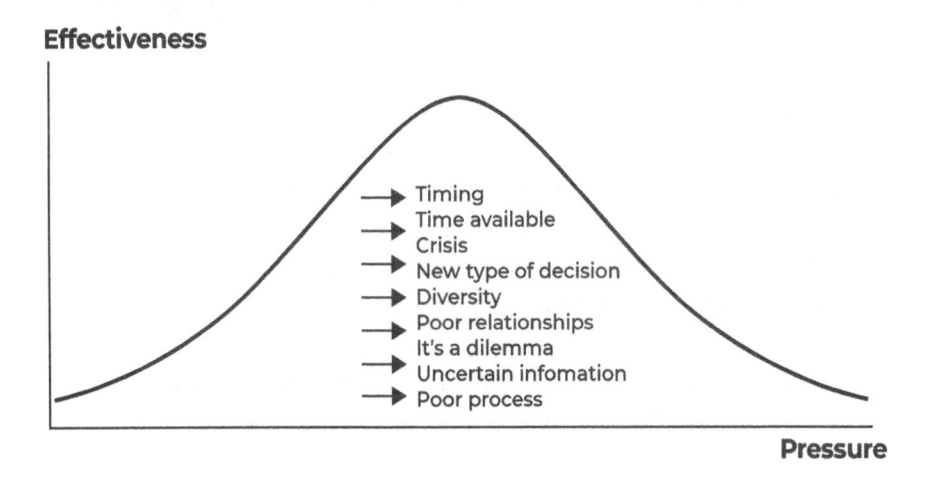

Effectiveness

→ Timing
→ Time available
→ Crisis
→ New type of decision
→ Diversity
→ Poor relationships
→ It's a dilemma
→ Uncertain infomation
→ Poor process

Pressure

people often have a poor ability to spot it despite being able to attract top talent and being so well-resourced.

There are probably three things which can help you avoid it and they are knowing what stress you are under, knowing what the causes of those stresses are and having the self-discipline to correct. It's tempting to just confine this to matters financial. We shouldn't, although I do think that the way much financial information is presented in board packs doesn't help us avoid the creeping problem even when there are trend analyses of KPIs all over the place.

Much better in my view to stand back at regular intervals to check out your organisational health from the perspectives that matter most and in a way that captures the fundamentals. What is our financial, market, staff, supplier, partner, regulator position and how is it trending. I know we think that's what we might be doing in each board pack and it is imperative that we keep on top of the detail but so often the depth and range, as well as the amount of detail, we receive as board members can blind us to the big picture.

Financial implications

Understanding the financial implications of board decisions is fundamental for board members. Decisions need to be put into the context of the organisation's current financial position and its commitments, overall financial strategy, financial dynamic as well as the wider environment in which it is operating. The financial impact of decisions matters.

Does this mean that everyone on the board needs to be a financial expert? In some cases, eg banks and other large complex financial institutions, it might well, especially to meet regulatory requirements. More generally however, it doesn't. But it does mean that no matter what your level of financial literacy, you need to make sure that you understand the key financial aspects when taking a decision.

Why? because you have the same responsibility, in most countries and types of organisation, as those who may be more expert or experienced. Delegating detailed verification or inspection to the audit and risk committee is normal and proper. Making sure that there are enough people on the board who have strong records in financial matters is sensible. Yet in most settings you'll still be responsible for financial conduct, whether you are an expert or not.

However, if you want a board with balance and a desire to achieve real diversity and inclusion then you have to accept that not everyone should be a financial expert. This is challenging as, at the end of the day, as noted above, you cannot delegate your overall responsibility for the decisions you take to either a committee or an executive.

On page 41 we looked at the issue of knowing whether you have the right CFO, including the importance of them being able to explain the financial dynamic to you in terms that you understand no matter what your level of financial literacy. Getting the right CFO is crucial but you still need to be diligent, vigilant and curious and to understand the basics.

Three fundamental things to understand in any decision, from a financial perspective, are its likely impact on the income statement, on cash flow and on the balance sheet. I use the word "*likely*" as one of the obvious traps for board members is to believe that the numbers presented are all fact or are what will happen, rather than the execs best estimate of how they think that things will turn out. As part of the testing of any proposal, the underlying assumptions, as well as risks and potential upsides and downsides, will also need to be discussed.

Greater confidence is provided when the CFO has a track record of accurately forecasting income, costs and cash flow and in demonstrating that the financial controls are in place to deal with the inevitable variances. A good CFO will also ensure that the board understands the true and specific cost of capital when considering individual investment proposals, as well as how that might impact future cost of capital. Over-leveraging a project can have a material impact on the cost of capital for future projects.

If the organisation is a public company then, like it or not it, the board will also have to consider the impact of decisions on its share price and capacity for paying dividends.

A charity will need to consider the impact on its unrestricted and restricted reserves. If it is using restricted reserves then it will need to be within the scope agreed with the provider of those funds. If it is unrestricted then it will need to be sure that the investment leaves the charity with sufficient unrestricted reserves to meet its reserves policy which should include any requirements of the relevant regulator.

No matter what the nature of the organisation you also need to determine, before any investment is made, as to whether this is the best use of funds to achieve your strategic objectives. Inevitably it tends to be a judgement over the board's appetite for risk and return. In a charity or social enterprise, you will also need to consider the return in terms of impact. What I call the "*impact bangs per buck*".

If you are not especially experienced in finance you can supplement briefings from the CFO with sessions which are run by most firms of auditors on financial matters for boards. Many of the training and development programmes (*see* page 148) also include segments on finance for board members.

Making decisions

By the time the board paper arrives for a decision often the decision has been made and the board meeting is about refining it. Yet, this is not always the case and I like to think as Chair that for every major decision we are about to take there is the possibility that we might not want to do it after hearing the views of the board and having a proper discussion. Otherwise, why have the meeting?

The atmosphere for decisions will influence the outcome and it is the Chair's job as well as the CEO's to create the right mood before the decision is taken. That mood needs to be supportive and challenging, warm and friendly but objective as well as both trusting and testing. As a mental image I imagine the triangle on page 13 with all the arrows inside pointing in the same direction but with enough degrees of difference to avoid groupthink.

A part of building the right atmosphere is how the paper for the decision is positioned. As a fait accompli then the board may feel manipulated or taken for granted and respond negatively. Alternatively if the execs aren't clear what their preferred option is the board may consider them weak or that the particular decision not worth making.

When the time arrives to make a decision there are a number of words that I always think about and I use "*5C*" as a way of remembering them: these are: "*calibrate*", "*choices*", "*constraints*", "*consequences*" and "*conviction*".

- "*Calibrate*": Does all the information that we have stack up and is it internally consistent? Are we clear what is fact and what is interpretation?
- "*Choices*": Do we really understand the choices that we have? There may be more than those presented.
- "*Constraints*": Few boards have the luxury of making deci- sions with unlimited cash, unrestricted access to talent and no opportunity cost. Most choices are unlikely to be equally beneficial to all of our stakeholders' objectives. So, what are our constraints and what are the consequences of relaxing them?
- "*Consequences*": More generally, have we thought through all of the consequences of what we are deciding? Have we factored in realistically what the competitor reactions to our decisions might be?
- "*Conviction*": Some decisions require a higher level of conviction than others. What degree of conviction do we need to have for this one? Is it likely to be divisive? Low levels of conviction for big decisions often result in death in implementation.

Before the meeting, when reading the papers, I will have thought a lot about "*facts and interpretations*" ("*F's*" and "*I's*") and ask myself: "*Are the facts and interpretations in the paper clearly distinguished and is there a good balance of each. Does it fit with my experience and the current view of the way things are likely to develop? Is what we are being told internally consistent? In short, does it feel real?*"

One trick I use is to write little *"F's"* and *"I's"* beside key points in a decision paper. If it's light on *"F's"* I think *"Oh F!"* and if it's light on *"I's"* and simply a set of facts, I think the same. The best papers are a healthy balance of both. If it's all *"F's"* it is likely to be backward looking and if it's all *"I's"* it tends to be flaky. I also mark little *"A's"* on the paper where I think I am being a deliberately anchored.

If you were looking for a good book on this topic then the late Hans Rosling's *"Factfulness"* is well worth a look. Hans was a wonderful man who was brilliant at explaining complex statistics and demographic trends and what they might mean with great clarity and humour.

Another issue that can be a challenge when making a decision in the board meeting is that occasionally we confuse worrying with thinking. It is natural to worry and a little bit of worrying is fine but worrying is nowhere near as useful as thinking.

Recognising bias and managing our instincts

Figure 3:10 Types of bias

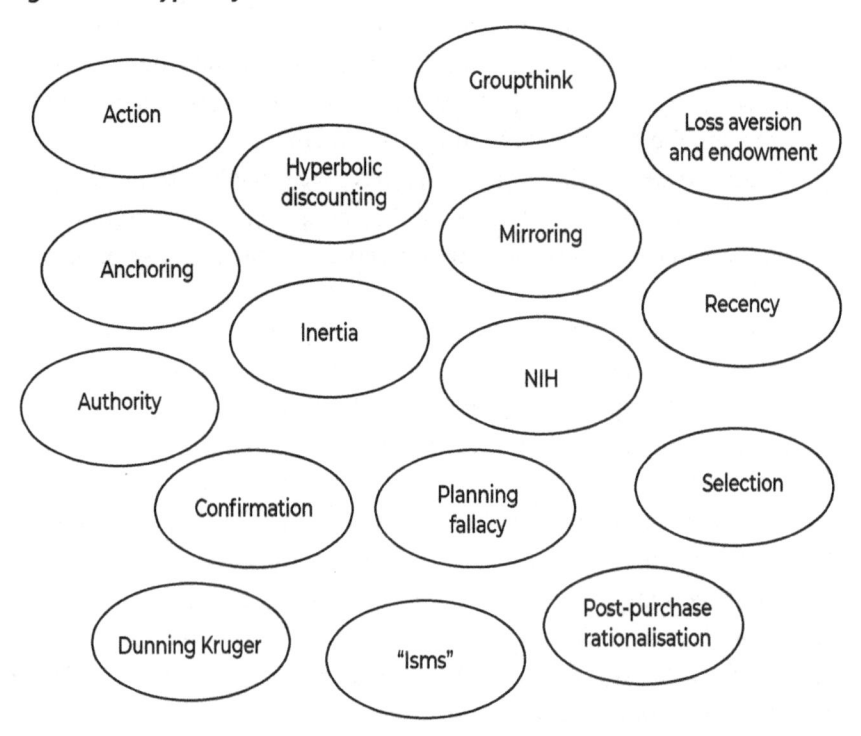

The importance of self-awareness in decision making was powerfully proven by the Harvard Business School research (*see* page 92). To remind us, groups with high levels of self-awareness are around twice as effective at making decisions as those with low self-awareness.

When it comes to decision making one vital thing to be aware of is our inherent biases and those of the people in our group. The chart above shows just some of the biases that we are vulnerable to. Probably the most dangerous is the bias-blind spot bias where we might think we are so smart or so good that we have no biases whatsoever. It's often mixed into an unappealing cocktail with one of the "*isms*" (racism, sexism …) and easy to spot when the victim says something along the lines of: "*I'm no racist but……*" and then proceeds to demonstrate dramatic bias.

The chart has some, but by no means all, of the common biases we are susceptible to and is followed by a very brief description of each.

Action bias

Although we may have very good reasons for getting on and acting on something swiftly, action bias relates to our desire to act when there are no such reasons. It may be driven by a feeling that if we do we are in control of events. It was named action bias by Anthony Patt and Richard Zeckhauser in the *Journal of Risk and Uncertainty* in 2000. It is obviously related to loss aversion bias (*see* below) and, as with all of these biases, it is a question of judgement.

The pressure that others exert on us to act may further stimulate action bias as "*do nothing*" can be perceived as being weak or prevaricating. A good example of this is described in the excerpt from the abstract of a paper by Michael Bar-Eli and colleagues on "*action bias among elite soccer goalkeepers*" and the case of penalty kicks:

Another driver of action bias may be overconfidence or perhaps the result of experiencing a run of negative outcomes before as a result of inaction.

Anchoring bias

About the best illustration of anchoring bias is the "*Redwoods*" experiment described in Daniel Kahneman's brilliant book "*Thinking, Fast and Slow*". The experiment was designed to show how when trying to decide something

> "In soccer penalty kicks, goalkeepers choose their action before they can clearly observe the kick direction. An analysis of 286 penalty kicks in top leagues and championships worldwide shows that given the probability distribution of kick direction, the optimal strategy for goalkeepers is to stay in the goal's center.
>
> Goalkeepers, however, almost always jump right or left. We propose the following explanation for this behavior: because the norm is to jump, norm theory (Kahneman, D., & Miller, D. T. (1986). Norm theory: Comparing reality to its alternatives. Psychological Review, 93, 136–153) implies that a goal scored yields worse feelings for the goalkeeper following inaction (staying in the center) than following action (jumping), leading to a bias for action. The omission bias, a bias in favor of inaction, is reversed here because the norm here is reversed – to act rather than to choose inaction. The claim that jumping is the norm is supported by a second study, a survey conducted with 32 top professional goalkeepers. The seemingly biased decision making is particularly striking since the goalkeepers have huge incentives to make correct decisions, and it is a decision they encounter frequently."

our choice can be heavily influenced by the anchor of a recent frame of reference.

Daniel split groups of people into two sets with different framing questions before asking them what they thought the height of the tallest redwood tree was. Those in the "A" groups were asked whether they thought that the height of the tallest Redwood tree was greater than or less than 1200 feet whereas "B"s were asked if they thought that it was greater than or less than180ft. A few people generally think it is a trick question and think it is exactly 1200 or 180 feet but that isn't the most interesting thing. The most interesting thing is that "A"s consistently give an average height of 844ft whereas for "B"s it is only a third of that at 282ft, whereas the actual tallest (at time of writing of his book) was between both groups responses at 379ft. Investment bankers, plumbers, estate agents and IT providers have never needed to read Daniel's book but the rest of us might.

The important thing here is to recognise the vulnerability and just ask yourself how you are being anchored. Most management teams will anchor you at the beginning of a paper. It's called making the case and it doesn't necessarily mean that they are malevolent in any way. They are just using the numbers or frames of reference that support their case.

As I said earlier, my way of dealing with it is to put little "*A's*" on the paper where I feel I am being anchored.

Authority bias

Put simply authority bias is where we attribute greater weight to the opinion of someone who is in authority (eg Chair, CEO or CFO) or who has authority on a subject, eg a lawyer. Authority can be derived from position or respect and this is another example of a bias where it is a question of degree and balance.

It's a tricky one as we appoint and pay people who have greater or different experience or expertise to provide us with different perspectives. So to suggest that we might then ignore them sounds foolish. I have also seen examples where people completely discount the views of those in authority and of experts. The point I guess is to never take any view at face value even if it is from someone you regard very highly and never ignore a view from someone who you may have less respect for.

As a non-exec or trustee who has limited formal authority this means in order to achieve influence you need to build respect within the group. (*See* page 104 for ways in which to achieve this.)

Confirmation bias

"*So, you'd say she was a really good CFO then?*" A classic confirmation bias question when referencing. Fine if it's a summary statement at the end of the conversation but not as an opener.

Many years ago, when I was working at the PE firm 3i I conducted an experiment to separate the referencing of board members and management teams from the person leading the deal. The results were significant and obvious in that we found that someone whose job it was to reference and wasn't anchored in the desire to do the deal or bond with the team being referenced tended to be more objective and had no prior judgement to be mis-proven. Given the good quality of my colleagues there were happily not many occasions which resulted in a "full stop" although there were some. In most cases the value came from understanding the individuals better as well as the team dynamic and in many choosing a different Chair or non-execs to support them. Our expectations were also much more realistic and we had richer content that we could use for feedback, coaching and development.

Confirmation bias is something those of us with a lot of experience may be more susceptible to. Our store of situational experience which we can find incredibly valuable most of the time can fail us when we presume too quickly that this situation conforms to our expected norm when in fact we should take a bit more time to realise that it doesn't.

Dunning Kruger bias

This bias is essentially linked to low self-awareness and bias blind spot. In their wonderfully titled 1999 study, *"Unskilled and Unaware of It: How Difficulties in Recognizing One's Own Incompetence Lead to Inflated Self-Assessments"*, and their even sharper worded 2003 follow up, *"Why People Fail to Recognize Their Own Incompetence"*, Dunning and Kruger from Cornell University identified this rather sad bias.

Wikipedia will tell you that their work was apparently derived from looking at the cognitive bias evident in the 1995 criminal case of McArthur Wheeler, who robbed banks while his face was covered with lemon juice. He believed that the lemon juice would make his face invisible to surveillance cameras. This bizarre belief was based on his misunderstanding of the chemical properties of lemon juice as an invisible ink.

Dunning and Kruger put a lot of this bias down to poor or incorrect self-assessment of competence as well as a person's ignorance of a given activity's standards of performance. Their research did however indicate that training in a task, such as solving a logic puzzle, increases people's ability to evaluate accurately how good, or bad, they are at it. For a light-hearted description of this bias you may want to look up the Dunning Kruger song on Youtube, which formed part of an Incompetence Opera at the 2017 Ig Nobel prize awards.

Groupthink bias

Regularly when post-mortems of catastrophic decisions are performed we often wonder *"How could they have possibly thought that?"*, especially when we think that this was a group of competent people with good intent. We can be staggered by such a heavy hitting board losing the plot so badly. The brilliant expression "*groupthink*" feels so instinctively right in summing up these situations.

Yet it is somewhat ironic that such a deeply-rooted phrase, and one which we think we all know the meaning of, has been one that the academic community has struggled so hard to measure in practice. The fundamental challenge typically being one of attribution. Was the appalling decision really due to groupthink or was it simply a lack of diversity in the group in the first place.

Irving Janis from Yale is credited with coining the term in 1971 as a result of studies he was undertaking on group dynamics and, in particular, the decision making which led to a number of US military fiascos or crises, such as the Bay of Pigs.

For Janis groupthink was essentially:

"The tendency of groups to try to minimize conflict and reach consensus without sufficiently testing, analysing, and evaluating their ideas."

The suggestion being that the pressure to conform inhibits the thinking of the group, deters those with different perspectives from either contributing or being listened to, biases the group's views on the evidence that it is presented with and promotes simplistic and stereo- typed thinking.

However, as noted above, for some groupthink is just a symptom of lack of diversity of thought within a group and an entirely predictable outcome. For others, no matter how diverse the group, once you are in it you become vulnerable to groupthink. Moreover, we might wonder is groupthink just tribalism for posh people!

Janis identified three conditions that led to groupthink. He considered the first to be the most important but that groupthink was only likely to happen if one of the others was also present.

- Overly high group cohesiveness - which dominates individual freedom of expression.
- Structural faults - which could lead to the group being insulated. These might include a failure in leadership or what I would call a reality by-pass.

- Situational context - perhaps where the group is under extraordinary pressure or following a string of success or failure which affects confidence.

Many of the ways in which Janis suggested that groupthink might be avoided while at the same time having a high level of cohesiveness are more vividly expressed in lateral thinker Sir Edward De Bono's book "*Six thinking hats*". Sir Edward was of the view that: "*Thinking is the ultimate human resource.*" but also that: "*Most people, convinced that they are competent at thinking (like humour and sex), make no efforts to improve*". In the book he proposed a way for any group to improve the quality of its thinking and effectively reduce the risk of groupthink. All you need to do is give each member of the meeting six different coloured hats and then confine each stage of the discussion to thinking from the perspective of a single colour with the colours being as follows:

> - *White:* Neutral and objective: Let's look at the facts.
> - *Red:* Emotions. Let's consider the emotions of the various groups involved and affected by our decision.
> - *Black:* Gloomy and negative: Let's look at all the downsides.
> - *Yellow:* Sunny and positive. Let's consider the upside and all the benefits to everyone involved and affected by our decision.
> - *Green:* Grass vegetation. Let's ensure we have some creative time in the meeting and encourage ideas from everyone.
> - *Blue:* Cool and the colour of the sky which is above all else. This is concerned with control of the organisation of the thinking process and also the use of the other hats.

The hats are, of course, metaphorical and it is the principle of focusing on one aspect of the discussion at a time and getting people out of their functional or representative positions that matters.

Another way of inhibiting groupthink is to encourage a "*black box mindset*" as described in Matthew Syed's "*Black Box Thinking*" book (*see* "*Reviewing Decisions*", page 256). Encouraging a culture where failure is looked at as much as success and where learning from the lessons of failure is natural can help reduce complacency and over- confidence.

We also have to acknowledge that humans are tribal and recognise when the joys and benefits of a strong team spirit start to shift to the dark side and edge towards that vulnerable and dangerous land of groupthink.

In a board context the four most important ways to avoid groupthink are to have a Chair who is absolutely terrified by the prospect of it, a CEO and management team that loves to have their best ideas given a good tyre kicking, a board that has genuine diversity of thought and, finally, a succession plan that involves a regular change of member- ship.

Hyperbolic discounting – *"Instant gratification"* bias

Hyperbolic discounting or, as I like to less grandly call it, instant gratification bias is simply the situation where we have a preference for something we can receive now rather than something we can receive later, even if the one later would have more value to us after applying a sensible discount for time. Research has shown that humans do have common sense in tending to discount the value of a later reward by a factor that increases with the time to receive it. Mathematicians or behavioural economists typically model this using what is known as exponential discounting, ie using a time-consistent model of discounting. However, a number of studies have shown that in practice we can easily deviate from this and put even higher discounts than might be rational on future rewards. Because of the resultant shape of this when modelled mathematically it became known as hyperbolic discounting bias.

Interestingly those who are particularly susceptible to this bias might also reveal a strong tendency to make choices that are inconsistent over time – they make choices today that their future self would prefer not to have made, despite knowing the same information. Then they may overcompensate the other way from time to time in order to try and achieve balance.

Inertia bias

This is a close cousin of loss aversion bias (*see* below) and is when we fail to act when we should or fail to update our view of things because we either can't be bothered to check that they are still true or ignore the signs or hard evidence that they are out of date.

The rise of low-cost operators which has hit many established operators in sectors from airlines and fashion to hotels and supermarkets is a good example of this. Superbly well-resourced organisations with highly experienced market intelligence functions somehow failed to spot or to act in time; not because they were full of lazy or dull people, often quite the reverse.

Inertia bias doesn't just affect strategy it is also prevalent in taking difficult decisions with regard to people, partnerships, physical facilities and much more.

If we go back to the chart on alignment in the "*Purpose*" Section on page 13 both the circular "*All pointing in different directions - Rabble*" state and the linear "*Monarchist*" state are especially vulnerable to inertia bias. This is because in the "*Rabble*" state the board and the exec are so preoccupied with fighting each other they either fail to see the threat coming or do but can't agree what to do about it. In the "*Monarchist*" state as few are prepared to challenge the monarch if they are satisfied with the status quo then the others go along with it. Whereas for those in the "*Triangular*" state, where they are all pointing in the same direction but there are enough degrees of difference to produce a healthy creative tension and restlessness, the risks are considerably lower.

"*Isms*" bias

The most obvious of these are racism and sexism: other parallel prejudices include regionalism, religionism, homophobia and social class. I won't provide an exhaustive list I'm sure the category is obvious and hope you will forgive me if the one that you may have suffered from is not on above list.

The rise of nationalism, fundamentalism and fear of other "*isms*" seems to have become a major problem in many societies and it would be odd to think that whilst it is an issue in society at large it won't be in the occasional board member or the board as a whole. There is a big difference between respecting difference even when it is uncomfortable and resenting it. I have always liked the Charles De Gaulle quote:

> "*Patriotism is when love of your own people comes first; nationalism, when hate for people other than your own comes first.*"

The Chair's job is fundamentally to ensure that they have a board with the right values and that means one which is "ism" free. They will also want to ensure that the organisation does all it can to, not just respect diversity and inclusion but to actively promote it and make the most of the strength that it brings. As part of due diligence before taking a board position it is always wise to ask for copies of the key policy documents which should include one on diversity and inclusion.

Loss aversion and endowment bias

This bias simply refers to the fact that numerous studies (eg Kahneman & Tversky, 1979) have shown that many, but certainly not all of us, would prefer to forego a potential profit even when the expected outcome is positive when we perceive that there is some risk of loss. Classic boardroom loss-aversion situations are decisions relating to new products or markets, acquisitions or capital investment.

Loss aversion is also relevant when considering reputation especially when it is others who get to gain most on the upside but us who might suffer most of the downside becomes a reality. This bias can be exacerbated in societies where there is a hostile and aggressive press. FTSE 100's who avoid capital returns that might take them out of FTSE will argue that the damage from falling out of the FTSE 100 isn't worth it, but rarely is this quantified.

This instinctive bias can also be source of tension between a board and the exec team. The situation where a board will happily agree acquisition criteria and even give a management team a license to hunt within the criteria but then turn down every target presented is probably a symptom of an excess of loss aversion. Unless of course it is really a lack of confidence in management to manage the investment well, in which case why give them a hunting licence? It can also be a source of tension between board members where those with higher risk appetites can be frustrated by colleagues even if they accept the need for diverse thinking.

For a Chair and CEO, the best avoidance strategy is to understand when recruiting board members what their appetite to risk is and also to ensure that diversity of risk appetite is given sufficient weight in considering board composition. As a fallback if there is a good process of decision review a board that has been overly conservative can be coaxed to take a little more risk. However, this will be nothing like the pace of pull back if such a review suggests too racy a risk appetite.

Naturally, given herd instincts loss aversion is likely to be at its height during bear markets and less when times are good. In my experience few can call the bottom with precision but most of us have a good sense of when it's hot or cold.

Endowment bias can be explained by loss aversion in that this is where we might place a greater value on things we own than their market value perhaps because of their significance to our personal track record or reputation or an emotional attachment. The classic corporate example of this is the reluctance to sell an underperforming division that has some historical or personal significance to current board members, eg the division the CEO made their name in.

If you want to learn more about loss aversion bias, endowment bias and prospect theory (the behavioural model that shows how people decide between alternatives that involve risk and uncertainty) then a good place to start is *"Thinking, Fast and Slow"* by Daniel Kahneman. For access to a further range of papers and resources the website Behaviouraleconomics.com is well worth a look. At time of writing there is also a very handy and accessible guide to cognitive biases on Wikipedia (*see* Useful links).

Mirroring bias

Selection processes are the natural habitat of mirroring bias which is simply our instinct to like people like ourselves. *"old boy"* and *"new girl"* networks thrive on mirroring bias and can be known to be resistant to even the most apparently rigorous processes. A good example of this is the ancient practice of the wearing what I call the *"process cloak"* for a *"shoe in"*.

The first step in this process is an announcement including the following words: *"The board has appointed XYZ (search firm) firm to support the board in conducting a rigorous selection process"*.

The second step then involves the Chair or the CEO strongly recommending a friend for the role but saying, *"of course I will respect the process and let the nominations committee get on with it"* and then doing exactly the opposite.

Mirroring bias is not only confined to selection: we also have a natural tendency to mirror the behaviour of those we respect. At its most basic level this might simply be adjusting our posture to reflect theirs or picking up patterns of speech or mannerisms.

"*Mirror imaging*" is another form of mirroring bias and refers to when we assume that others think like we do.

Mirroring bias can sometimes be used very positively though. Many a wise Chair has lowered the temperature of the room when required by leaning back and then watched others do likewise and done the same in reverse when a little more heat is required.

NIH (Not Invented Here) bias

This bias is simple to describe and to observe and is closely related to groupthink (*see* page 240). Here a group is instinctively resistant to ideas from outside. There are numerous examples of this in business where once market leaders have been felled by insurgent innovators.

Board diversity and being actively open-minded is probably the best form of defence against the build-up of NIH bias. The difference between being actively open-minded and just open-minded is that instead of simply being prepared to change your mind when someone presents a compelling alternative viewpoint, you go out looking for different views to enrich your thinking about what is the best thing to do.

Board members who are actively open-minded in my experience tend to have much more effective antennae.

Planning fallacy bias

This bias is another one which that legendary pair Daniel Kahneman and Amos Tversky first highlighted in 1979. Essentially this is where our predictions about how much time will be needed to complete a future task display an optimism bias and leads us to underestimate the time needed. They also showed that this can happen even if we know we have form and know that we have underestimated the time taken to complete similar tasks before.

Interestingly the bias only seems to affect our own predictions about our own tasks. When outside observers predict task completion times, they show a pessimistic bias, overestimating the time needed.

In 2003, Kahneman and Lovallo proposed an expanded definition of planning fallacy bias as the tendency to underestimate the time, costs and risks of future actions and at the same time overestimate the benefits of the same actions.

Post-purchase rationalisation bias

When we buy a consumer item large or small, whether we have spent a fair bit of time selecting it or whether it is an impulse buy, we may often "over-own" our choice, telling others what a great choice it is, even though we have yet to experience its true performance.

The board equivalent of this is the bad choice of capital investment, acquisition of new CEO or FD that we extol the virtues of to the market before having to unwind or fire later. Those who have had a lot of merger and acquisition experience may be more familiar with the term "Buyer's Stockholm Syndrome". The idea being that you become a prisoner to the deal and as with so called Stockholm Syndrome develop a dependency and bias towards the thing or people who have captured you.

Why do we take this unnecessary risk in bigging up something or someone when we don't need to? Sometimes it is to justify a choice we are unsure of in a Shakespearean *"He doth protest too much."* like way. On other occasions it could be due to a desire to stick to a commitment. More typically it is that getting a big capital investment or deal done involves a lot of selling and internal anxieties are suppressed to gain the buy-in required. The deal mantra becomes an earworm and hard to wash out.

The *"Principle of Commitment"* and its corollary the *"Consistency Principle"* was established by Cialdini in his book *"Influence: The Psychology of Persuasion"*. It describes the way in which people want their beliefs and behaviours to be consistent with their values and self-image. We tend to view consistency as an attractive social trait associated with good qualities such as being trustworthy and stable or rational. As a result, we will try to act in ways that are consistent with our initial action or thought, so that when we commit to something or someone, we stick to it. We also try to behave in ways that are consistent with the image we have portrayed to others and with the public image they have of us. This latter point echoes very strongly with those of us who have witnessed car crash acquisitions.

How do you reduce the risk of this bias? Experience helps, and a canny

Chair will often council an exuberant CEO or board in a deft way to ensure that their choice delivers before they shout too loud.

Recency bias

Recency bias is a very common low-level bias that can have a material effect on decisions. Essentially it is where we place greater value on things or evidence that has been gathered recently over that gathered before. A classic illustration of this is the anecdote by the CEO at the beginning of a meeting or start of a presentation. We are naturally all interested in the latest evidence and if it is personalised it will also be more memorable. However, it could be just one customer, supplier or shareholder experience and not be at all representative.

It can be hard in a fast-moving world to strike the balance right between robust evidence that was carefully gathered and analysed over months and today's breaking news. This is nothing new. Thomas Bayes theorem based upon updating beliefs on new evidence dates from the mid-1700s. It was sadly published after his death so he didn't get to see the profound impact of it. Indeed, it probably really wasn't until the 1950s that his work started to have more profound impact as significant computing power gave it new life and greater practicality. In our modern world we take SATNAV and many other everyday processes such as the stock control of our supermarkets and on-line stores for granted, many of which are fundamentally dependent upon Bayesian statistics and recency bias.

The rise of AI is already influencing decision making at operational levels and may well soon make an appearance in making strategic decisions (*see* page 262). In the meantime, even the best boards can avoid unhealthy recency bias by having their antennae up, their calibrators on and to ask the right questions to ensure that the right balance of information is considered.

Selection bias

Selection bias relates to using selective information and, in our context, is when we use selective information to make our case and either fail to find other corroborating information or worse fail to disclose that which might be unhelpful to our cause.

One of my favourite examples of selection bias is told really well in the story of a legendary mathematician's intervention in a discussion about the American B-17 bomber during the second world war. To cut a nice, but long, story short Abraham Wald had escaped from Nazi Germany in 1938 to the US and ended up helping the US Air force. The B-17 was considered critical to the Allied Forces plans to win the war and thousands were planned to be built. However, the early attrition rate was very high.

The USAF board delegated a senior trusted member to review the situation urgently and come back to the board with a recommendation (which might include cancelling the programme). At the board meeting the General gave short and powerful presentation with graphics (overheads at the time) which showed where the planes were being shot (Figure 3:11).

Figure 3:11 Abraham Wald: selection bias

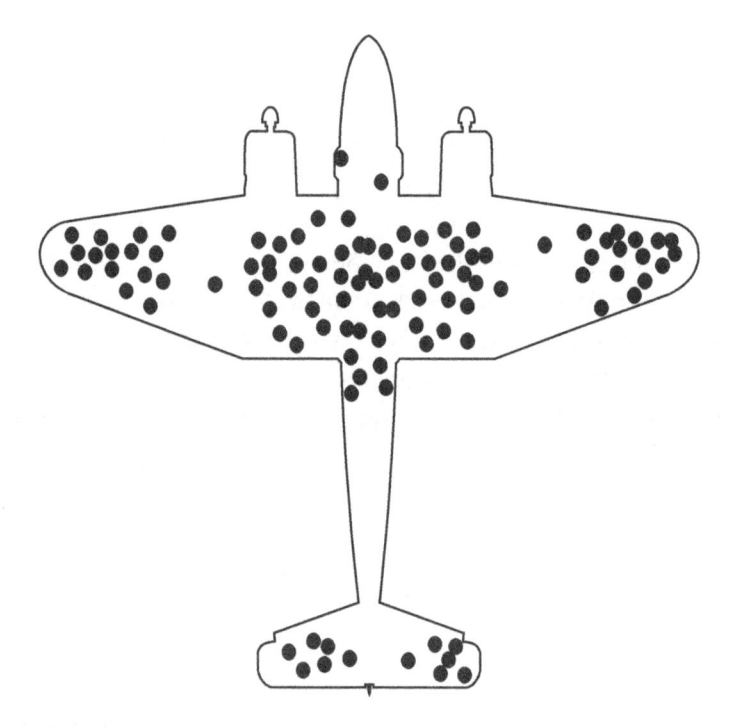

The conclusion was obvious, he said, and that was to invest in more armour for the wings and tail planes. He did however note that this would result in reduced payload and therefore there would need to be a budget increase to fund a purchase of an additional few hundred B-17s to deliver the same planned payload. Abraham apparently asked an equivalent form of that good old non-exec standby question *"Could you just remind us of the data set please?"* The General replied to the effect that these images obviously can only be of returning planes. Whereupon, Abraham proved another important point for non-execs,

"The first question is just to get you in the conversation it's the supplementaries that get you there" by asking whether it could be that, as there appeared to be no shots in the engines or cockpits of returning planes, whether it might be more productive to invest in more armour for the engine cowlings and under the cockpit as well as stronger glass for the cockpit windows. In this way a lot less armour will be required, payloads won't suffer as much and fewer additional planes will be required. Game over.

Rightly, large numbers of decisions are taken on the basis of market research, focus groups and other ways of seeking reliable evidence upon which to decide. A bit like overreliance on spreadsheets. We don't always test enough just how robust the evidence really is and can become phased by the data or the way in which it is presented.

Data phase and The Zebra puzzle or Einstein's riddle

This refers not to a bias but to another challenge driven by our instincts. The Zebra puzzle, or Einstein's riddle as it is sometimes known, is a pretty

straightforward logic puzzle. For maximum effect I like to spring this on groups of directors or exec teams that I am working with, usually when they have just conquered something quite challenging and complicated and are enjoying the warm glow that goes with it. I typically get half of the group to do it individually and the rest as a group.

The puzzle is as follows and it can be solved in a few minutes.

- There are five houses.
- The Scot lives in the red house.
- The Greek owns the dog.
- Coffee is drunk in the green house.
- The Bolivian drinks tea.
- The green house is immediately to the right of the ivory house.

- The Brogue-wearer owns snails.
- Brothel creepers are worn in the yellow house.
- Milk is drunk in the middle house.
- The Dane lives in the first house.
- The Birkenstock-wearer lives next to the person with a fox.
- Brothel creepers are worn in the house next to where the horse is.
- The Slipper-wearer drinks orange juice.
- The Japanese wears Havaianas.
- The Dane lives next to the blue house.

So, who drinks water and who owns the Zebra? Give it a try.

If you found it trickier than it looked don't worry, you are not alone. There is a lot we can learn from the Zebra puzzle and it has real relevance to decision making in the boardroom.

Most people, whether they are trying to solve it as a group or individually, will instinctively start by jotting down some knowns, ie coffee is drunk in the green house. They quickly realise that a matrix might be handy and start to figure out what the variables are. Rarely do they deliberately decide what variable should be in the rows. Simplifying assumptions are made but not often acknowledged, ie the houses are in a row in a street not randomly scattered in a wood or in a crescent.

The groups seldom start by thinking and talking about how they might solve the problem together, individuals seem to try to start solving it then share with the others and usually people defer to the person who is confident enough to suggest how to do it. Rarely does a group get one piece of paper and draw its empty matrix on it and get everyone to fill in the missing bits.

If you have done another exercise earlier on in the day which is insolvable you will also get some saying that the Zebra puzzle has no solution. For some reason I have noticed this happens more when I call it Einstein's riddle! A sort of recency and anchoring bias cocktail! Time pressure also helps to get people in a muddle. It's a good example of using the "*Effectiveness and Pressure curve*" described on page 94. Increase the pressure enough and a group of intelligent people can find a straightforward logic problem just all a bit too much.

The solution, as shown below, is really straightforward: this is a classic grid puzzle with a few variables: (houses, colours, nationalities, types of animal, drink and footwear). So, pick one to go horizontally in the grid (eg houses) and the others to form the rows.

	House 1	House 2	House 3	House 4	House 5
Colour					
Nationality					
Animal					
Drink					
Footwear					

Then look for the definites relating to the columns, eg milk is drunk in the middle house, the Dane is in the first house. Then look for the connections to what you have now tabled, eg the house next to the Dane's house is blue. Then go for the inferences, eg green and ivory are next door so first house can't be either of those; nor can it be red as the Scot is in the red house. So, the first house must be yellow. Be clear what assumptions you are making: the houses are in a row not circle!

Repeat the process and answer pops out as:

	House 1	House 2	House 3	House 4	House 5
Colour	Yellow	Blue	Red	Ivory	Green
Nationality	Dane	Bolivian	Scot	Greek	Japanese
Animal	Fox	Horse	Snails	Dog	ZEBRA
Drink	WATER	Tea	Milk	Ojuice	Coffee
Footwear	Bcreepers	Birkenstocks	Brogues	Slippers	Havaianas

If you enjoyed doing this and want to try a few more exercises to test how logical you really are, then "*Introducing Logic - A Graphic Guide*" by Dan Cryan, Sharron Shatil and Bill Mayblin is a terrific little book containing many more.

Reducing complexity, boiling it down to the basic choices that you have got, doesn't always come naturally. One person famous for finding ways to do this was the Italian physicist Enrico Fermi (after which the famous Fermi nuclear research Labs in Chicago are named for his work on the first nuclear reactor). Fermi is also well known for his famous and entertaining estimation techniques which enabled him to make pretty good approximations to things with little data. He did this by focusing on the most significant factors in a problem so that he could find the likely answers to more sophisticated analysis later and get to the heart of the problem quickly. I've seen many a good independent director use this technique when trying to make sense of an overwhelm- ing market analysis with simply too much distracting data.

On the subject of human behaviour in decision making, it would be remiss not to mention *"Nudge Theory"*, given its popularity and prominence in recent years. There's a debate about whether the nudge name is simply a packaging up of behavioural science techniques based on *"positive reinforcement"* and *"suggestion"* that were around for years. Indeed, the term was around for a while. However, there is no doubt that the publication of *"Nudge: Improving Decisions About Health, Wealth, and Happiness"*, by Richard Thaler and Cass Sunstein brought it to prominence and nudged many politicians across the world into a different way of trying to influence their populations. A good example of it in action is the use of opting-out clauses rather than signing-up.

The fact that humans don't always behave rationally, that small frictional costs can have significant impacts on their choices and that we are susceptible to suggestion often underpins the use of Nudge Theory.

It is natural to think of the use of Nudge Theory in relation to decisions the board is taking and applying it to the behaviour of customers and other stakeholders, ie those not on the board. However, it has another quite powerful application and that is in the relationship between the exec and the non-execs or trustees. It's natural for smart CEOs to nudge and to use the power of suggestion, your susceptibility to recency bias with a little story, or to highlight an irritating little friction cost in the option that they don't want you to choose.

Communicating and implementing what has been decided

Making the decision is an important step but in order to ensure that the decision is carried through and implemented successfully will have much to do with how it is communicated and executed, especially to those responsible for implementing it.

The first and obvious step in this process, which is the responsibility of the Chair, is to ensure that the board itself is clear what has been decided and who is responsible for it being implemented. Since most of decisions of the board are communicated to the organisation and then implemented by the exec then overall responsibility for the successful implementation of these decisions naturally falls to the "*chief*" exec or whoever he delegates that responsibility to. The rest are likely to be driven forward by the Chair, the CFO, a sub-committee or another director.

As mentioned on page 259 many boards now communicate more broadly following their meetings than was traditionally the case. This communication is normally swift, a summation and in larger organisations through a cascade process starting with the senior exec team, followed by the broader leadership team and then flowing through the organisation. It may be supplemented by a short email or video message from the CEO. Done in an engaging way it can be a powerful tool to support implementation, alignment and make the board feel closer to those leading and working in the organisation.

If you are going to do this the narrative has to be clear on what has been decided and why and what this means for people.

In terms of the implementation of decisions, the board's key role after taking the decision and satisfying itself that the right resources and governance are in place to maximise the chances of success is one of oversight and support. It needs to know how things are progressing and whether they are within the parameters agreed. It needs to know if there are any issues so that early action can be taken to support the exec in achieving whatever the objectives are or change course.

The terms used to ensure things are on track and describe progress often seem to have analogies with journeys: "dashboards", "traffic lights", "accelerators and brakes", "take offs and landings", "critical paths and way points"; especially when they go wrong: think "de- railed", "runaway train, "car crash" and so on.

The process of reporting combined with effective oversight from the audit and risk committee ought to deliver what the board needs in terms of oversight. This is underpinned if the CEO is progressive and focused on delivering successful outcomes, the CFO is strong and as a pair they have a peer or partnership style of relationship.

As a part of the responsibility they have to key stakeholders (page 171), the Board will need to consider for each decision and its subsequent implementation what, when and how it intends to engage and communicate with stakeholders throughout the decision process. This may range from the blindingly obvious as it is a regulatory obligation to do so to things which are less clear. For example, it isn't difficult to decide for a listed company on something price sensitive or for a public body something which is an obligation to disclose to a regulator.

If the organisation has a good communications director then they will have the plumbing in place and be suitably plugged in and prepared to provide timely support. When performing that role I had a whole library of draft announcements for things I hoped would never happen, just in case. The fact that we had debated the issues with the Chair, CEO and relevant others and come to what we felt was the right form of words in each case beforehand helped enormously on the occasions where they were needed at short notice and under pressure.

Reviewing decisions

It is surprising how few agendas contain serious reviews of major decisions taken whereas unsurprisingly a large amount of time is given over to reviewing progress, status updates and so on, for major projects. This has always seemed odd to me.

In Matthew Syed's brilliant short book *"Black Box Thinking"* he starts following a tragic event in a healthcare context wondering why the famous black box approach in aviation hasn't been taken up in many other walks of life where it would seem to have just as much relevance, outside transportation.

The overall objective of black box thinking in aviation is to reduce accidents and make flying as safe as can be. The safety performance of aviation is quite staggering and it is widely accepted that black box thinking has played a major role in this. In 2018 there was one fatal accident for every 2.5 million flights.

The principles of black box thinking are straightforward; namely that:

- Comprehensive data is captured by the legendary and almost indestructible "Black Box", as well as these days through live data capture transmitted back to the ground, that can be analysed in the event of a failure to identify the factor or more usually factors which caused the event.

- This analysis is carried out by independent experts as well as the organisation and people directly involved.
- Most importantly there is a culture of transparency supported by regulation, no matter what your status.
- The intention is that whatever is discovered is communicated with appropriate speed and weight so that everybody else using that equipment or process can make changes as rapidly as possible.

Sadly, I wrote this section on a flight from London to Toronto which was supposed to be a flight to Halifax, Nova Scotia. It is sad because my intended flight was due to be on a new Boeing 737-Max but due to two fatal accidents this new plane has been grounded for several months. The Boeing Company was in the middle of a huge crisis. Investigations were proceeding, allegations were being made over disclosure and action following the first accident. It will be interesting to see once all of this has been concluded whether there has been a departure from black box thinking at an organisation that was thought to have it at the heart of its culture.

In my view culture has been just as important as process and technology in the success of black box thinking.

The approach can be used as much to identify success factors as failure factors. Early on in my career, before Matthew's book, I benefitted significantly from this. I had just taken over 3i's recently launched *"management buy-in"* (MBI) activity. The business was focused on building a pool of talented CEOs and matching them with acquisition opportunities which had the potential for significant value growth. The idea was very popular and literally hundreds of CEOs clamoured to take part. There was a rush of investment but quite quickly it appeared that there was a terrible rate of failure not so much in businesses going bust but in reaching a position quite quickly where it was obvious they had destroyed value and were highly unlikely to ever recover it.

I was appointed with the classic brief of sort it out or shut it down. There were well over 100 investments so the obvious question was where do you start? The instinctive starting point as a mathematician was to analyse all the factors involved in doing one of these deals and look for correlation with failure. After assembling all of the original investment papers, performance reviews and, sadly, a large number of failure reports, it was clear quite quickly that there were more failures than successes but that there were some big successes as well.

There was a lot of pressure to find a quick answer. Yet it also seemed just as important to place as much emphasis on trying to identify non-financial factors as much as the financial ones and also to start by looking at the success factors for those that were performing well. Doing these two things would obviously take a lot more time. Taking a risk, I resisted the pressure and decided that this was such a big problem that it needed a thorough and comprehensive analysis rather than a quick snatch at an answer, even though there were plenty of obvious quick wins at every stage of the deal process. Ironically thanks to my relationship with my boss David Thorp and the Group FD at the time, Brian Larcombe, I was given the freedom to do this.

As we poured through the non-financial factors for the successful ones we noticed that the strongest common factor was that in the successful deals the CEO coming in involved some of the existing management team in the equity and in producing the value creation plan. It didn't take long then to identify that this had rarely happened in the unsuccessful deals. The rest is history as they say and the hybrid "buy-in management buyout" (BIMBO) was borne. A second major factor was that where an independent and highly experienced Chair was introduced early on in the deal they again significantly out-performed and were far more likely to have the BIMBO characteristic. The business was quickly transformed through fundamentally changing the model and being able to monitor progress as a result of black box thinking.

In general, I don't think enough comprehensive analysis is done of successes and failures and this is one area where the combination of big data and AI may prove to be a game changer for boards, especially in analysing capital investment, new products, mergers and acquisitions, organisational restructuring as well as understanding the true impact and how it is created in the charity and social enterprise sector. It is too easy in the absence of robustly produced data and analysis, especially when it concerns non-financial factors, to snatch at a convenient and sometimes self-serving rationale.

For a decision review process to be effective in an organisation, the Chair and the CEO need to lead the creation of a culture which is focused on identifying success factors and driving out failure whether at a minor operational level or major strategic one. For an industry or sector to achieve greater success regulators and Ministers need to do just the same. Especially so in sectors where a constraining and unhelpful blame-game culture exists. You can usually identify them easily by the language. For example,

"We are going to stamp this out, hold those responsible to account and make sure that this never happens again."

is very different to,

"We've learnt a great deal from this experience, we now understand how to significantly reduce the chances of it happening again by doing X, Y and Z."

A final point here, I wonder what the effect of risk committees changing the balance of their work to increase the amount of time they spend encouraging the board and the exec to better understand success and failure within the organisation and in its sector. It just might increase its predictive capability and avoid having to wait for an organisational disaster and the ensuing investigation to make positive change.

Board communications

It is the Chair's and the CEO's job together to ensure that there are effective communications within the board and within the exec as well as with each other and between the board and the exec and with key stakeholders including shareholders and or funders, the broader leader- ship and staff, suppliers, strategic partners, customers, regulators, where relevant local communities, and so on. It is a classic point to go in the Venn diagram of alignment on page 12.

When communications are working well it can provide a big boost to the culture, to the productivity and to the quality of decision making as well as to the enjoyment of being on a board. On the other hand, it can be a real challenge to do the job effectively if communications are poor.

In larger organisations to do this they will need the support of the communications director. In smaller ones they may well be doing the vast majority of this themselves. Whatever the scale of the organisa- tion they will need to be careful that even though there is inevitably a lot to transmit that *"It's not all transmit!"*. A crucial part of communication is listening and organisations that are strong on communication tend to invest time and resources in listening. Histor- ically, this was through market research functions and, as the name suggests, through research with key groups in order to understand their motivations and preferences.

A good example of the power of listening and encouraging people across the organisation to engage with the board is what should go on the agenda. Over the years numerous informal conversations that I have had with staff members, customers and strategic partners have resulted in things going on the agenda. Simply asking people what they think should be on the board's mind is often enough.

Probably the most striking example of this was a conversation with a young person in the lobby at Leap Confronting Conflict many years ago. When I asked him that question he said "sexting". At that point I had never heard of it but was horrified by what he told me was happening. I was in for a catch up with the CEO. We discussed it immediately and decided that we should have it in the agenda for the next board meeting and that the team should prepare a proposal on what Leap could do to help young people realise the dangers of sexting and how they might deal with it. Other examples have come from the factory floor, customer visits and a variety of other interactions. It is also doing things like this which keeps your antennae alive and in tune.

With the advent of the internet and other communications technology, the dramatic changes in the nature of information flows, the accessibility of information and the explosion of social media boards and cultural change smart boards have become acutely conscious of the importance of commu- nications and the opportunities and challenges associated with it. They have also realised that it is not something you can completely delegate to others and it is something that they have to be actively engaged in.

Boards have some obvious things to communicate. For the organisation to achieve its purpose and strategic objectives and to build the culture it wants to as well as ensure sustainability it also needs to make sure that it communicates effectively. The effectiveness of communications rarely appears on a board agenda; surprising given how critical it is and its relative importance to other topics that do appear regularly on agendas.

I remember the shock amongst journalists when I became Communica- tion Director of 3i Group and asked them how effectively we communicated with them as I wanted to know and to tell the board. They didn't hold back and as a result we learnt a great deal, changed a lot in what we did and in the way we did it and as a result we consistently had the highest rated press team in the industry. That didn't mean that they were soft on us when we had bad news to communicate, but it did mean a fairer hearing and more opportunities to get our side of the story across than those given to those less respected.

In general, I think that there is a major opportunity for boards to be much more proactive in communicating within and outside their organisations. This can be at a very basic level, eg ensuring that people know who is on the board, what they do, how they interact with the management and so on. Sadly, in some organisations all most of the staff, including the broader leadership group, know about the board is what they get paid.

On the subject of communication with the broader leadership, it is hard to make a judgement on the suitability of potential leadership candidates if your only interaction is through a selection process. A Chair, supported by the NomCo, has to make sure that the board has visibility of the broader leadership team, especially those who have potential to be CEO or CFO, over a long period and in a variety of settings.

In public companies or bodies and in heavily-regulated industries one issue that emerges frequently in connection with the non-execs or trustees is communication with the investment community, regulators and the press. This is especially sensitive when performance is chal- lenged or there are relationship difficulties between members of the board. If you have ever seen a media article, usually at the weekend, which goes along the lines of: "*it is believed that several of the non-execs and institutional shareholders are unhappy with the new strategic direction, the performance of the XYX subsidiary or country...*", then you can have reasonable confidence that either an activist fund manager, an adviser or investment banker or a non-exec has been talking.

I and the other FTSE Communications Directors could usually work out who it was from the expressions the journalist fed back when they were calling for corroboration. It is also the case that this sort of behaviour is not just confined to non-execs. Chairs and CEOs are just as prone when under pressure or when they want to get rid of someone they feel is either not delivering or making life uncomfortable. All of this is simply human nature.

The Chair must lead in creating a board culture which minimises these risks. On appointment and in the letter of appointment it should be clear what the organisation's policy is on communications with the press, investors, regulators and other relevant groups. The Chair needs to reinforce this. Savvy Chairs who have been around enough and are held in high regard do.

No matter what size the organisation and the board is, I think someone from the board should be involved in the selection process for whoever is leading on communications. In start-up and early-stage organisations, powerful communications can help to build credibility and gain funding or business and recruit the talent you want. Who knows, your reputation may also depend upon them doing a good job.

Finally on communications, in describing the ideal characteristics of a director I picked three things: judgement, interpersonal skills and antennae. It's my belief that all three of these are needed to be a good communicator and to be a highly effective director or trustee you need to be a good communicator.

Use of technology to increase board efficiency and effectiveness

The revolution in technology, particularly relating to communications technology and decision making, is having a growing impact in the boardroom, as elsewhere. The disruption arising from the pandemic to the way we work and the need to make decisions under greater uncertainty, urgency and pressure has accelerated trends already underway creating the environment and need for more radical changes.

The communication technology aspects and apps currently available are largely about changing the way we work. Although they have felt seismic since 2019, when we look back in a few years' time, they may not be as profound as the impact of technology on board decision making.

We're probably all familiar with the brand leading virtual meeting tools and there is a huge amount available on virtual meeting technique. The dominant apps in this space at time of writing appear to be Diligent, Board Intelligence and Boardpacks by eShare (*see* Useful links). These are now used by organisations of all sizes and across a broad range of countries and sectors.

They typically provide a range of functions for directors or trustees and company secretaries from basic administration to online voting, knowledge resources, including libraries of papers, and minute and induction packs and in some cases (eg Board Intelligence) access to broader organisational data.

Once a board gets familiar with the tools, they generally work well, save a lot of logistical hassle and are better for the environment.

They have helped enormously through the pandemic and there has been a step change in their adoption. The application of technology to board decision making is a more complex matter. As with the communication it is nothing new. Access to information as well as the ability produce and present analysis has evolved over hundreds of years and will continue to do so. The *"Big Data"* era is just the latest phase. As is *"social listening"* the ability to assemble and analyse social media.

Boards have also been using technology knowingly or otherwise to mitigate risk. For, example, in the organisation's cyber-crime defence and supply chain systems. I think we have moved to a stage where the board through its audit and risk committee needs to ensure it has the right strategy and oversight mechanisms in place on these issues.

Debate and experimentation is now underway in relation to the role and application of Artificial Intelligence (AI) and machine learning in board decision making. At this stage we are in the foothills of an interesting climb. AI is making its presence felt in lots of other areas of specialisation which have hitherto relied upon the experienced experts or groups of them, for example pilots, lawyers, engineers and surgeons.

In their interesting 2019 article *"Artificial Intelligence in the Boardroom"* the UK Financial Conduct Authority (FCA) said that:

"Boardrooms are going to have to learn to tackle some major issues emerging from AI – notably questions of ethics, accountability, transparency and liability."

And that:

"These are not matters that can be ring-fenced in a department, whether that be IT, legal, or customer service – that would be to abrogate boardroom responsibility and to leave an organisation exposed at the very top."

This implies that even if your implicit strategy is that you are going to wait to see how the pioneers get on with it, you need to do that consciously. The linkage to risk appetite and capabilities is obvious and should be taken into account in board and c-suite recruitment even if you have a *"Get ready"* rather than *"Go for it"* strategy on this.

I suspect the first step for most will be AI assisted decision making along the lines of the *"Satnav"* analogy I used on page 167 in relation to strategic frameworks and budget decision making.

Algorithms are an essential ingredient in AI and like many things are dependent upon the wisdom of those who define them and the reliability of the data that feeds them. Algorithms and AI don't create bias but they can be highly effective transmitters, amplifiers, and reinforcers of it

In *"Superforecasting - The Art and Science of Prediction"* by Philip Tetlock and Dan Gardner, which is about why some people might be better at forecasting events than others and the wisdom of crowds, they state that:

> *"When you have a well validated statistical algorithm you should use it because the evidence of over 200 studies has shown that in most cases statistical algorithms beat subjective judgement."*

The key word here is *"validated"*. As we saw in the summer of 2020 with the use of algorithms in producing proxy exam grades, just like an airline accident there is usually no one cause of failure but disaster arises from a combination of factors. The analogy of pilot error, poor design, not knowing where you really are and equipment failure and is all too obvious.

Access to big data underpins the success of a lot of AI as does the ability to break down complex problems into a series of smaller ones and the computing power to search for relevant, but not obvious, data points. Imagine a capital investment tool that was able to test the assumptions being made in a proposal against data from previous relevant capital investments and other useful data points such as what others in the industry are doing, to calibrate the information being used to decide. Imagine an acquisition decision-making tool that analysed all the acquisitions the company has made and those in the sector, looked at success factors, tested assumptions, considered things without human bias and so on. Imagine how much easier the black box thinking referred to on page 242 would be.

Still on data and this applies to non-AI decision making equally, one thing to acknowledge is that we tend to only use a fraction of the data or knowledge that we have. In his thought provoking book *"Dark Data- Why what you don't know matters"* David Hand explores the topic of overlooked data in decisions.

Big Data and AI technology may be the tools that enable us to tap into that data we have but don't use. Alternatively, they may overwhelm us with too much data and overcomplexity. Yet again why we need data and tech savvy directors with good judgement and antennae.

When it comes to being data savvy, if this is an area you feel less comfortable with then David Spiegelhalter's excellent book *"The Art of Statistics"* is a worthwhile read.

My interpretation from all that I have experienced and read on this topic is that it seems more likely that in this first tentative phase of AI in the boardroom it will be used to augment rather than replace or automate board decision making. AI could easily be applied on minor governance decisions, such as approval of minutes, or more significant ones, such as approval of directors, by using email content analysis algorithms. Yet these will only produce minor operational gains. The big wins are likely to come from better strategic decisions being made.

Could AI improve decision making for the most important decisions such as major capital investments or mergers and acquisitions? I not only think that it can but that it eventually will and the prospect of it doing so is both exciting and a little scary at the same time. I have no doubt however, that much money will be lost in the early stages of introducing AI generally and in the boardroom. There will also be many ethical dilemmas to resolve along the way. However, as was said on page 235, the best decisions are a good combination of fact and interpretation. If we have much more reliable evidence and tools to help us gather better evidence and interpret it more powerfully then there ought to be value in exploring whether AI can help in the boardroom as much in our operations.

Section Four

Dilemmas

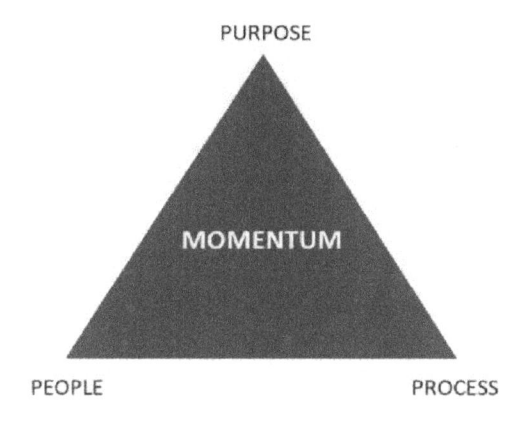

```
        PURPOSE

        MOMENTUM

PEOPLE            PROCESS
```

Introduction

In the introduction to this book on page xiv I noted that:

> "As a board often makes it biggest contribution when the choice isn't always clear this has been supplemented with a reprise and refresh of some of the most popular situations from an earlier work, "Directors Dilemmas", as well as the addition of some new ones. There are few *"no-brainer"* choices for boards and those that look like they are prove often to be illusory.
>
> All of these "Dilemmas" are real but sufficiently disguised to protect confidentiality. After a description of the situation, each has a short summary of the issues, the choices that you may have and then a description of what actually happened. The outcome may of course not always be the best."

The nature of dilemmas

The roots of success in dealing with any dilemma are the judgements that we make and our ability to bring those judgements to bear. Understanding the nature of dilemmas and having a few general principles for dealing with them might help us to increase the odds of making the right choices. So, before getting into the specific situations let's consider those two points starting with the nature of dilemmas.

According to the Oxford English Dictionary a dilemma is:

"A situation in which a difficult choice has to be made between two or more alternatives, especially ones that are equally undesirable."

As directors we seldom confine ourselves to the literal or are objective about the likely levels of pain. As a consequence in our world a dilemma tends to be:

"A tricky spot with no immediately obvious conclusion, where all the alternatives seem to involve some degree of pain and where the level of pain that might be involved may not be clear either."

Dilemmas occur for a whole host of reasons but in my experience four typical drivers are:

- confusion over the purpose or role of the board, the executive (exec) or an individual role;
  the fact that there are humans involved;
- changed situation; and
- money or status.

Lack of clarity over the purpose or role of the board and how it interacts with the exec and other bodies such as sub-committees will produce a steady stream of dilemmas, not just for its members but for all of those engaging with them or affected by their decisions. This topic is covered in detail in the *"Purpose"* section starting on page 1.

The fact that there are humans involved provides much of the enjoyment of being on a board as well as most of the frustration. The nature of human behaviour and motivation and our ability to find conflict even in the calmest of spots will also guarantee a regular supply of dilemmas to deal with. If you want to know more about the science behind this, Robert Sapolsky's book *"Behave"* is a good place to start. The *"US versus THEM"* chapter in particular is worth a read in this context.

The opportunity that making decisions provides for things to become personal combined with even the subtlest of misalignment of objectives produces the ideal compost for the dilemma plant to thrive. The *"People"* section starting on page 85 contains a range of topics relating to the human aspects of boards, including the importance of self- awareness, biases, managing difference and conflict and much more.

Changed circumstances are another fertile environment for dilemmas to occur. At a base level it can simply just be incredibly difficult sometimes to work out what the right response should be even if you can see it coming. If our thoughts and responses are diverse, which is something we want, then by implication we won't all deal with change in the same way and we are not all necessarily going to perform as well in a changed situation as we did in the previous circumstances.

We don't all recognise reality at the same rate and it can be harder to face up to a gradually growing issue than a sudden externally-induced shock such as the Crash. At the same time, I remember being struck by how well different colleagues at 3i reacted to the Lehman's crisis and the ensuing crash in the markets, some stepping up superbly to a massive shock and others, let's say, a little more windy.

When it comes to money or status, these two powerful motivators can be very positive drivers of behaviour. The desire to give your family a better life or to reach the pinnacle of whatever your career is can produce extraordinary performance. At the same time greed and hunger for power can be incredibly destructive. When it comes to dilemmas their cause and solution can often be found through understanding motivation and what objectives can do to behaviour, both good and bad.

Dealing with dilemmas

Having understood the nature of dilemmas, what might be some general principles for dealing with them. In the original *"Directors Dilemmas"* I noted a favorite quote from Albert Einstein which was:

> *"Out of clutter find simplicity, from discord find harmony and in the middle of difficulty lies opportunity."*

These were Einstein's *"Three rules of work"* and I think that they are highly relevant for dealing with dilemmas. They remind us that simplifying problems, by definition, makes them easier to solve, that it's harder to solve a problem when everyone is at war with each other and that when we may feel threatened it is important not to lose sight of opportunity.

There are four questions that I find it helpful to bear in mind when faced with any dilemma and these are "What? How? What? How?":

- **What**'s the dilemma?
- **How** am I or are we going to decide what to do?
- **What** am I or are we going to decide to do and when?
- **How** am I or are we going to communicate what I or we have decided to do?

Figuring out how the dilemma has arisen may help in understanding what the real dilemma is and to be able to see beyond what might simply be symptoms of a deeper problem. The four natural drivers above may be a useful place to start.

Looking at whatever the issues are from the perspectives of others involved also aids objectivity. Observing rather than participating is helpful in this regard and thinking about what might be in the thought bubbles of others especially so. If you are normally actively involved going quiet can also signal to others that you're uncertain about something.

Heightened self-awareness will also be helpful when it is a situation where you may be contributing to the problem or need to step up and help solve it.

As all dilemmas are inherently about choices, an important part of deciding how you are going to resolve the dilemma is understanding, agreeing and aligning objectives and being clear what choices you have. Thinking rather than worrying, responding rather than reacting and differentiating between facts and feelings can be critical to making the right choice. Yet the best solutions aren't always driven by logic. Sometimes you just have to make a judgement about what is the right thing to do with that person, or group of people, on that day with those issues and with that atmosphere in the room. Being able to articulate why with a well-reasoned argument should help but persuading others to do what you think is the right thing to do isn't always as easy as that, even if they understand the case for it. The *"Decision-making"* section which starts on page 219 has a lot more on this.

Communicating what you have decided to do, like any communication, is easier to do if you understand the people you want to convey your messages to, are clear what those messages are and then deliver them effectively. A good relationship and being held in high regard will help as people will be more open to listening.

We can't microwave relationships so we also have to recognise that sometimes the message may be better delivered by someone else. The best directors have no problem with this as their focus is on achieving the desired outcome and they are good at avoiding saviour syndrome when difficult moments arise.

In summary, dilemmas can be incredibly challenging but resolving them can also often be the most satisfying moments you have as a director or trustee.

The dilemmas which follow cover a range of situations and I hope that they are both fun and thought provoking. They are far from exhaustive, so if you have another tricky situation please do let me know and who knows it may make a future edition, disguised of course.

The dilemmas discussed are as follows:

1. Dave's dreaming is disturbed - *How involved do you want to get?*
2. The departing director - *Going with dignity*
3. Boiling point with too many cooks - *A charity forgets its purpose*
4. The radio-controlled finance director - *Goes for a spin and has a little bump*
5. Convo - *The star falls to earth*
6. Reserves - *The long and the short of it all*
7. Money, money, money - *Six short remuneration dilemmas*
8. RemCoCoCo - *"But it's my company!"*
9. Journalistic licence - *"They're all out to get me"*
10. The revolution - *A palace coup*
11. I wish we'd told them earlier - *What to tell my analyst*
12. Bone and Sons - *A family at war*
13. Falling in the Strid - *An entrepreneur gets confused about money*

Finally, I have thought long and hard over whether to change all the colloquialisms used in the Dilemmas, but have erred on the side of keeping them as they convey an element of the character. I therefore apologise if you are unfamiliar with a word or phrase and have to go online to find its meaning in your region.

Dilemma 1:

Dave's dreaming is disturbed

Dave, a busy Chair of a number of companies, is musing contentedly in his garden. He has just returned from a four-hour drive back from a board meeting at his most recently-acquired Chairship at Aceco.

"What a smashing evening. For once, home on Friday in time for tea. The garden looks great and Sarah seems very jolly tonight. Expect she can't wait for this time next week. Guess we'll be halfway there by then. Wonder what a three-week holiday is really like?

"Funny, we were halfway across the Atlantic this time last year on our way to that amazing retirement weekend Globeco laid on for us in Florida. Still, 20 years flogging around the world sorting out messes for them, they should have been grateful. Must write that 'Retirement Relief Counsellor' a note, smarmy idiot. Just to think I almost fell for that, what was it he called it, ah yes the FLP, a 'Future Life Plan'.

"Two months' holiday with your partner, time to reflect and get to know each other again. Two months' hyper-networking to get yourself into the new opportunity superhighway. Then, a highly recommended refresher visit to me to reorientate the plan. In a year's time you'll have built the ideal balance in your life. A day for your partner, a day for golf and a portfolio of interesting but not too challenging consultancies and directorships.

"Complete tosh!

"Sarah did seem a bit fed up when we had to cancel the cruise so I could chair Ritco. She's obviously right to be a little brassed off that we've not had a Saturday together so far this year. But at least everything's under control now. The holiday will be a great chance to make it up to her. She needs a break as well, she's been so busy with her Events Company. It's really taken off quickly.

"Ritco's been such good fun, great team and if that whizz-kid venture capitalist Paul has got the numbers right, I reckon I'll make as much from that as the 20 years at Globeco. He's all right, Paul. I'm sure I wouldn't have got Wimco without the glowing reference he gave me on Ritco. Aceco looks to have got off to a cracking start as well. Best managing director (MD) I've seen in ages, that Ian. I'm sure we'll be able to build a good team around him in time. Probably ought to start with the finance director (FD). Wurry by name and worry by nature."

Dave's dreaming is suddenly disturbed. Sarah calls:

"Dave, Daaave, it's that Jim Wurry on the phone again. Says it's urgent. Must be, he hasn't even had time to get into Uriah Heep mode. Please don't be long, dinner will spoil."

"Hi Jim, what's up?"

"I'm afraid I've got some terrible news, Dave. Ian's had a brain haemorrhage this afternoon and Helen [his wife] has just called me to say they don't think he's going to pull through. I'm sorry to disturb you, but I thought you ought to know. To be honest, I'm really not sure what to do. It's hit me hard as well. I suppose I need to take charge now. Ian and I were off to Atlanta on Sunday to close a deal."

What would you do now if you were Dave? What are the issues?

Dave has several things to consider. How deeply involved should he get? Should he leave it to Wurry or does he need to own the problem? How much time does he want to devote? What about his other directorships? The logistics of home and where Aceco is located are far from easy. Wurry's on the phone and he needs to give some sort of initial response. Do the rest of the board know? If not, how should he let them know and when? What should he do about the trip to Atlanta? What should he say to the institutions? After all, they own a majority stake between them. Who is going to inform the company's advisers and what should they be expected to do to help? Then there is the matter of the holiday. What does he say to Sarah when he puts the phone down?

The MD and his family have their own concerns. How ill is he really? Dave only has the naturally-pessimistic Wurry's description to go on. What support do his wife and family need immediately? What was Ian's role? MD's roles differ from company to company. Are there any other things that he was working on that need to be dealt with?

The business itself will face some new challenges. Is there a contingency plan already prepared? How damaging is the loss of the MD at this critical stage? Is there any temporary or permanent successor from within? Wurry doesn't feel like a natural leader and it sounds as though there are issues with him in his current role.

If it isn't known whether Ian is coming back or not, is it appropriate to start recruiting? Should they get an interim manager in? Could they if they wanted to? What's the company's financial position? Is their key man insurance in place? How does the company manage public relations? What public relations issues are there now?

How to decide?

What are the facts? Given Wurry's disposition, he may want to check. Dave is unlikely to know Ian's prognosis, which is fairly critical to any decisions that are taken. He is reliant on Ian's wife for this.

Dave will also have to determine what it is he can decide on his own as Chair, what things he must put to the other directors and what he needs to discuss with the institutional investor. He needs to decide whether he needs to seek their guidance on whether he should develop a plan and make a clear recommendation. He also needs to think about how much time he's got. How can he create space and relieve the pressure, particularly on Wurry? Luckily, he has got the weekend. Gives him some time to prepare communications and to talk with people who are bound to be upset.

Dave may also be thinking about other people he knows who have been through this situation before. If he does know someone, a quick call to see what they did could prove well worthwhile.

There is a need to exercise control, introduce calm and provide an *"It's OK, we can work through this together."* sense of security to those unsettled. For Wurry, this is vital. He is on the phone and needs a response now.

Dave also needs to decide whether Atlanta is a red herring or not. A decision on going is needed and he will have to find out whether a week's delay will have an adverse effect.

The views of the institutional investor will be important. Should Dave contact them, or Jim? Does this need doing over the weekend? Will whoever it is ask them what to do, or make a recommendation?

What to decide?

Let's look at some of the options.

"Not now Jim, I'm having my tea." A little insensitive and irresponsible perhaps.

"This must be very distressing for you, Jim. I don't think it would be a good idea for you to take Ian's role. I think I should until we can get a proper replacement." Almost as bad.

"OK, Jim. I think you're right. You should take over. I'll come and see you on Monday and we can decide what to do." Irresponsible and negligent. The cynical may think that this option is OK because he could always be fired later if he doesn't work out.

"I'll be there as soon as I can. It'll take me four hours. Let's meet for breakfast at the hotel. We can both sleep on it. I'd particularly like you to think about internal communications; you know the people best and how they're feeling." Very supportive, makes no commitments and buys time to think what to do. Dave probably plans to assume control with a view to recruiting a new managing director, assuming there is no internal candidate. At this stage, Dave will delay the decision on Atlanta.

What to say to Sarah when he puts the phone down? *"Sarah, it really is awful news this time... I know this may jeopardise the holiday but I'm Chair. I don't think Jim can cope on his own. They need me."*

The decision over whether anyone should go to Atlanta and, if so who, can be made when the directors get together.

How to communicate it?

First of all, who needs communicating with? There are lots of people. Sarah, Wurry, Ian's wife, the other directors, institutional shareholders, key advisers, key customers and suppliers and the public relations company.

In what order? The order matters as well as who talks to whom. In this case it is reasonably straightforward. He has to speak to Wurry – he's on the phone – then to Sarah, to Ian's wife, the other directors, and the lead institutional investor. The decision over who should speak to the staff can be made when the directors get together. Given that, of the directors, Dave is likely to be the most effective communicator and he is Chair, it probably should be him. However, it may be a good thing for Wurry to do.

For most of these conversations, he will have to have given serious thought beforehand to what he is going to say. He probably won't need much beyond a brief statement of the facts and what the board proposes doing.

How to say it? Remember, Jim Wurry is likely to be losing his mentor and his friend, someone he's been through a lot with. His normal anxiety level will be heightened. The Chair will be looking to reduce the pressure for Wurry rather than increase it. Uncertainty will no doubt raise it, as will telling him to relax.

Using the common purpose to galvanise is entirely appropriate here: "We owe this to Ian and his wife. It's what he would have wanted."

If Ian dies, then many of the staff will understandably want to grieve. They may need a symbol, however simple, to help with this. A special edition of the company newsletter, a memorial service, a plaque, or a collection and donation to his favourite charity – whatever is appropriate and sensitive to his family.

Honesty about the process of replacing Ian will be important. Getting the other directors' input to the brief for the headhunters may help gain commitment.

What did Dave do?

This situation in some ways is one of the easier dilemmas for highly-committed professional chairmen to deal with. This is because of the high sense of ownership and responsibility they generally feel for the board and the future of the business. Dave had no doubt that he had to assume control of the situation, that any other priorities he had, whether they were domestic or commercial, were lower than this one for the next few months. He was certain that his wife Sarah would understand and be supportive. Absolute conviction is the hallmark of those who sort things out.

After Wurry had finished speaking, he paused for a moment and said in the most genuinely sensitive of tones:

"Jim, I'm extremely grateful to you for letting me know. I can appreciate what a terrible blow this must be to you. You two seemed joined at the hip. It's an awful shock. How are you feeling?"

Wurry talked for a while and was naturally very upset. He intended visiting the hospital after he had spoken to Dave and would go into the office the following day to prepare for the Atlanta trip and write the necessary communications to staff and so on. Dave was very careful to sound supportive throughout. It was obvious that Wurry was terrified at the prospect of being the front man and his proposal to become MD was more out of duty than desire.

Dave then told him that he would come down to Aceco later that night and suggested that they meet for breakfast the next morning. He asked if Wurry could give him the mobile number for Ian's wife. He told him that he wanted to call her and convey his sympathy and offer to have the company arrange for relatives to be put up at the local hotel if necessary. Dave might not have done this had he not met her before and felt some rapport. He also asked if Jim could contact Ian's secretary and ask her to come in the next day; there was bound to be a lot to do. He suggested that they shouldn't decide on what to do about Atlanta until they'd chatted it through the next day.

What did he tell Sarah?

"Well, this time it's serious. Ian's had a brain haemorrhage and isn't likely to make it past the weekend. Wurry sounds gutted. Not surprising
– they were as close as you could get. Poor bloke needs some help. I think I should get down there for the morning. What do you think?"

"You've got no choice, have you? I think you should get a car to take you. You're not driving yourself. I'd take you but I've got the event tomorrow afternoon."

Sarah didn't mention the holiday, but the next day, when it was clear to Dave, the holiday was postponed for him. Sarah's sister went instead.

Dave took Sarah's advice and booked a car for the journey. This was a tremendous way of reducing pressure. During the journey, he spoke to Ian's wife to convey his sympathy and to ask what logistical support she needed. He bought tickets and arranged travel for relatives.

He used Ian's assistant to do this; she was a real trooper.

Dave then called other directors to let them know what had happened and to ask if they could attend a short meeting at 5 o'clock the next evening to discuss the situation. Unsurprisingly, all of them agreed. Dave was glad Wurry had given him that handy little sheet of all the directors' numbers when he joined.

At the meeting with the directors, Dave started by thanking them and offering sympathy. He then set about building a galvanising purpose

"*What Ian would have wanted, we must show we're in control*", etc. He told them that he would be taking over as chief executive until either Ian recovered or a successor from outside was appointed. They agreed on this instantly, it has to be said with some relief. The fact that he made it clear that the successor would not be from within immediately reduced the pressure again, particularly for Wurry, who was terrified at the prospect of being in charge. Having got that agreed, they then spent some time agreeing and planning the communications.

On the Monday morning, Dave told the institutional investors and the managers briefed the staff. A short statement was prepared for all staff. As it was clear by this stage that Ian wasn't coming back, this contained a sensitively written tribute to him.

They decided that the trip to Atlanta could be postponed a week and that Wurry and the sales director would go. They informed the other side of the deal, who were perfectly understanding.

Sadly, Ian died a few weeks later. It took nearly nine months to recruit his successor who turned out to be highly effective; not quite as capable as Ian, but the company has prospered. So, the MD died but the company didn't.

What about Sarah? Well, she forgave Dave instantly. After all, she knew what he would do. He did make it up to her later. The institutions were very impressed by the way Dave had handled a difficult situation and particularly by his commitment.

Dilemma 2:

The departing director

You are a longstanding independent director of LPJ.

The three directors who founded LPJ, Liz, Paul and John, have much to be proud of. Their business has grown from start-up six years ago to sales of £20 million. Profits are healthy at over 10 per cent net. Until recently, the team have got on very well together. They have shared the many highs and lows during LPJ's formative years. However, the stresses and strains of growth are starting to show. John, the sales director, and Paul, the operations director, just don't seem to be able to agree about anything anymore.

Liz, the managing director (MD), has performed extremely well, driving through the change and holding the team together through a major expansion. However, it's obvious that this has been at a cost and the team has reached its limit. She is a wonderful mix of visionary and manager and is capable of running a much bigger operation and plans to do so. Liz is convinced that LPJ will double in size in the next three years. However, her analysis is that the business has outgrown Paul and although he's done a great job so far, he is finding it hard to keep pace with recruitment, planning and control, and it's time to face reality and make a change.

Liz, Paul and John invested £150,000 from savings in the first couple of years to form and fund the early development. Liz has 30 per cent of the equity, Paul and John each have 15 per cent, you've got 5 per cent and a well-known venture capital company has 35 per cent. They've done well and the business could easily double in value from here.

Happily, you are seen as a trustworthy, reliable confidant by all the team and Liz has asked you to chat to Paul to get a feel for how she might best handle it. She wants to do everything she can to treat him well. You're sure John will be delighted to see Paul go, but equally sure he may be difficult over the terms of Paul's departure. One area where you think there is bound to be difficulty is in valuing Paul's equity. You and Paul have a regular chat a couple of times a year. Fortunately, one of these is coming up.

The chat with Paul got off to a great start. You didn't even need to raise the issue. As open and naturally engaging as ever, Paul raised it first:

> *"We've always had a good, straightforward relationship, and I would welcome your input on something really important."*
>
> *"Yes of course, Paul. What?"*
>
> *"I guess it must be pretty obvious to you that Liz and John want to expand more quickly than I do. To be honest, I'm not sure I'm cut out for what they've got in mind. I think it's best to recognise reality and for me to go before John and I cause any damage! Given the recent approaches we've had, my equity must be worth at least £4 million. That and a decent pay-off should be more than enough for me. I'm sure I can count upon your support to make sure John's not too difficult over things. He seems to be getting more and more aggressive by the day. Frankly, I'm a bit worried he might stitch me up. I recognise my own limitations but he does seem to make a meal of them. It's not as if he's Mister Perfect. He just seems better at presenting his problems."*
>
> *"Liz is bound to be embarrassed over things. She's been great all along. I want to make it as easy as possible for her, but I'm not going to let John force me out on the cheap. We all know he's extremely effective, but I reckon Liz will have to keep a close eye on him."*

How should you, the independent director, respond to Paul and then resolve the dilemma? What are the issues?

The key issues relate to Paul, John, Liz and you. Starting with Paul: are his performance and potential really below those required? Should he really be going? Can he be trained for the larger emerging role? If he is underperforming, or even if he isn't, is it right that he should go? How does he go with dignity and in a fair way? Does he need to go immediately or can there be a suitably long period to withdraw to give time for his successor to be recruited/promoted and handed over to. What's the likelihood of getting someone better than Paul? Are they readily available? Would they be attracted to LPJ? How should LPJ select an appropriate search firm and so on?

With regard to John: is he as good as he thinks, and as good as is needed? Or is he just the next problem waiting to happen? If he isn't a problem, how do you balance John's and Paul's views over equity value?

There are several issues relating to Paul's equity. How will it be valued? It is after all a minority stake in a private company and the company is not being sold. If a successor for Paul is to be recruited, will the replacement be offered equity at the outset or later? Has the company got the cash to buy the equity in, or are external funds required? What do the Memorandum and Articles of Association say about equity transfer? What about the investment agreement with the institutional investor? If there are good and bad leaver provisions, what is Paul in these circumstances? If the reason he is going is to do with his potential, and his performance to date has been fine, then it sounds like good. If he is seriously underperforming in his current role, then obviously not. Occasionally this issue highlights the fact that none of the directors is appraised in a conventional sense or has objectives.

You need to be clear what your role in this is. Are you the key resolver, the honest broker? Or perhaps you should be Liz's main supporter. She is Chair, after all. Liz's role also needs discussing. Is she showing sufficient leadership? It sounds as though she is within the business, but is the board operating as a board? Should she continue to be Chair and MD? Or is now the time to separate the roles?

Apart from these, there may be other, more fundamental issues. Is it appropriate to review the whole strategy for ownership and for the business? What is best for the owners may not be best for the business. Armed with this review, the suitability of the current team will be clearer. It may be that the best option is a sale of the company.

You also need to find a response to Paul, which gives you time and Paul comfort without false hope.

How to decide?

This is a situation where the Chair, ie Liz, needs to take charge and be the key character in resolving the situation. However, you have a major supporting role. Agreement to any solution is needed from all parties, especially Paul, John and the institutional shareholder. Finding out what Liz, Paul and John really want will be critical. It may not be what they say they want.

Liz will need to determine the likelihood of recruiting someone stronger than Paul to replace him. She also must decide whether it is appropriate to undertake a proper review of the business, its prospects and its management.

This could result in highlighting weaknesses in the rest of the team. It could prove necessary in any event if external capital is required to buy Paul's equity. Asking the institutional investor early on for an indication of the likelihood of raising capital might provide some useful input.

Clearly, with regard to an immediate response to Paul, you have to be brief and non-committal and, to give him comfort, he needs to be told that things will be dealt with properly and fairly.

What to decide?

Undertaking a review of the business will buy time and also introduce a measure of objectivity into the situation. However, given the description, it would seem that the likely outcome will be for Paul to go and for an external successor to be appointed. In the process, a fair value for his equity will need to be arrived at and it is likely that external funds will be required to fund its purchase and planned growth within the business.

You need to exercise your authority; you appear to have the respect of all concerned, which gives you pivotal influence. You may want to reinforce Liz's position and use the situation as an opportunity to send signals to John about acceptable behaviour if he is to develop. Liz and you will want to find a way for Paul to depart with dignity with a fair value for his equity. The starting point will probably be to get it valued as per the Memorandum and Articles of Association with the help of the auditors and the support of the institutional investor. The key will be whether Paul accepts that the value is on a minority basis. He may of course wish to keep some of his shares in the company. Depending on how the relationships develop, this could be acceptable to the others.

If extra capital is required to fund Paul's equity, then it might be worth considering raising growth capital at the same time, given Liz's plans to double the size of the business. The extra capital could prove helpful in attracting top talent. With regard to attracting top talent, a decision will be needed over Paul's replacement's equity position. Keeping some equity by for the new person to purchase at the end of a probation period on terms and performance agreed at the outset would be wise. Share options may be an alternative.

The final decision, if Paul is to be replaced externally, is to choose a search firm. You are likely to have had experience of this, so will know that it is important to organise a proper pitch, be clear about what the search firm will actually do and on what basis it will be paid. Your initial response to Paul is brief:

"I can understand how you feel, Paul. I think the best thing is for me to reflect on what you have said and then have a chat with Liz. In these situations, it is very important that things are done properly and fairly. I can't imagine Liz will want to do anything otherwise, either. So why don't you leave it with us for a few days and then we'll see if we can recommend a way forward?"

How to communicate it?

The most important relationship at this point is that between Liz and you, the independent director. If you are at one then, given the respect you both appear to be held in, an amicable solution should be forthcoming. Consequently, you may decide to start by having a long chat with Liz, during which you need to face the issue of her own position.

You need to discuss the issues raised above and then recommend a course of action to the others. Before you have this discussion with Paul and John, you will most likely want to consult with the legal and accounting adviser and probably the institutional investor to ensure that any recommended process or solution is feasible. If you feel external funding will be required, this is essential.

When you make your recommendations to Paul and John, you should be entirely even-handed in their communication. To do otherwise jeopardises the trust you have built up and endangers a solution.

In this case, it will be very important that key communications are also written, ie use confirmatory letters. To communicate orally with no record will inevitably cause problems later. To communicate solely in writing is inconsistent with amicable solutions.

What did the independent director do?

He had a long chat with Liz first. Because of their relationship the discussion about her own role went well and indeed she raised the issue first of separating the Chairship from the MD role.

They both felt that it was right for Paul to go and that John probably could grow a lot further with the company if properly directed. Liz and the independent director agreed that a proper review of the business would be worthwhile. Liz quickly warmed to the idea of a properly constructed board and raising enough new money to reduce the financial stress of growth.

The review was carried out in three parts: a market, a financial and an operational review. It was felt that with it, it would be much easier to arrive at a value everyone could accept. It would also help in determining the right amount of money to raise and it would be likely to confirm the independent director's view that there was nothing wrong with current operations, hence making it clear that the issue with Paul was to do with potential. A firm of consultants did the market and operational review and the auditors did the financial review. They were also asked to give an independent view of value calculated as per the Memorandum and Articles of Association.

While the review was being done, discussions were held with John and Paul and a good job was done of getting them to appreciate each other's strengths and positions. Interestingly, the independent director decided that he didn't feel he was the right person to be Chair, but with their help he found a selection of possible candidates for the role. This helped considerably with fundraising. It also reinforced his position as the honest broker.

One thing that he and Liz did at the outset, which helped enormously as they went through, was to write a short board paper setting out what they thought the situation was, the issues, the options, the objectives of the board and a recommended process for resolving the dilemma. They also made sure that all of the directors had access to good legal advice.

So how did it work out? Well, after a shaky start with John, the objectives were achieved. These were to strengthen the board, clarify the strategy and raise £10 million for the business, as well as to get Paul going on a high and receiving a good value for his shares. The extra cash for the company proved the turning point for John. Three headhunters pitched to find Paul's successor, who took six months to find and work his notice. He has worked out well, in fact so much so that he is the natural successor to Liz rather than John. The new Chair fitted in well and the company continues to prosper. The directors are currently contemplating a sale to a leading US business in their sector.

Dilemma 3:

Boiling point with too many cooks

MatFriend, a London headquartered maternal health charity was founded 20 years by its Chair Fred Frender. Fred put up $100m to found MatFriend and was chief executive officer (CEO) for first 13 years. He decided to step up to Chair eight years ago and brought in the current CEO, Victoria Forbes, five years ago after her two predecessors left rather abruptly following disagreements with Fred over strategy.

In addition to the $100m from Fred, the charity has been highly successful at raising money from others. These have included former colleagues of Fred, his former employer, Foundations and Corporates, as well as through general fundraising activity. Most of the board are major donors or are representatives of major funders.

After a strong start Victoria is becoming increasingly frustrated with Fred and with the board. She has a background in a high-volume service global corporation and this is the first charity role she has undertaken. So far, she has stayed the course, won Fred's and the board's respect and admiration and has tried valiantly to get the charity to be more focused, to reduce high staff churn as well as lower the number of risk incidents on a variety of matters including safeguarding and harassment.

MatFriend raises money in the US and Europe and then spends the majority of it in a number of African countries through a mix of direct delivery and grants for both research and a range of other things. It is a UK-registered charity, regulated by the Charity Commission with legal entities and regulators in 20 other countries. Some of these are where it operates (eg Malawi, Kenya, Uganda, Mozambique, Sierra Leone, Liberia etc) and others are where it raises money (ie US, Switzerland, UAE).

In addition to the main board of 11 trustees of MatFriend there are local governance boards in each country where it has a legal entity as well as advisory boards in 20 of them. It then has a group of eight advisory boards on different themes. There are also board sub-committees (Audit, Nomina- tions, Remuneration, International Strategy, Med- ical, Investment, Regulatory and Fundraising). There is some overlap of members on these boards but in total this involves just over 250 different people.

Victoria's first year at MatFriend was a nightmare. She couldn't believe the lack of focus and process yet how high the governance load was. Simply attending the various meetings already in the diary for her was challenging as she was expected to be at every country board meeting. The financial reporting was what she described as a collection of raw data dump. Treasury management was non-existent and it was very hard to get a sense of how much cash was really committed to grantees in aggregate or how much of the funding due was actually committed rather than loosely pledged.

Gradually over the last five years through changing the team, most notably through a new chief financial officer (CFO) and chief operating officer (COO) she has gained a much tighter grip on finance and operations and made the whole organisation more focused and purpose- ful. However, she remains disappointed that she has not persuaded Fred to reshape the architecture of governance and to give more autonomy to those responsible for implementing decisions. After an exasperating conversation with one of the more pompous country Chairs who kept referring to her as "*Young lady*" she has decided "*Enough!*".

You have just joined as a trustee and have been asked to become a member of the Audit Committee. On the morning that your 200-page board pack arrived with a similarly weighty set of Audit Committee papers you had a call from Fred. He rang you to say that he was highly embarrassed that Victoria had let the board papers go out with an additional paper that he hadn't seen proposing a radical review be conducted of the governance and decision-making processes. The paper states that the objectives of this review are to simplify decision making, give far greater autonomy to the executive and to reduce the number of committees and boards by two thirds. She proposes a budget of £50,000 to fund the project as well as two consultants with a track record in this space to pitch for the work.

Fred tells you that he is really disappointed in Victoria and that although she got off to a great start has found the job increasingly challenging over the last 18 months. He's been getting feedback from some of the country chairs that she can be impatient and brusque with them and that her style is increasingly an issue. "*She even contradicted me in a pitch for us to go into a new space the other day and as a result she blew it.*"

The addition of the governance paper without his approval is unforgiveable in Fred's view and he can't see how she can carry on as CEO. As a result, he tells you that he would like to have a board call in two days to formally approve Victoria's removal, for him to become interim CEO and for the appointment of a search firm to find a permanent successor. Fred ended the call by saying *"I'm so sorry to have sprung this on you with you being so new. I know that it will be difficult for you to contribute to the call in any meaningful way but wanted to speak to you in advance."*

You express surprise but think it best to reflect on the call before reacting and after putting the phone down start to think about what to do?

Further detail on the key characters

Fred Frender - Chair

Fred is a medical doctor with a PhD from John Hopkins who spent the bulk of his executive career in the medical devices research team of a major corporate. He lucked out with the invention of a jackpot diagnostic device for which the company he worked for gave him a royalty share. This ended up making him $200m by the time he was 40 and, in his words, *"Is still the gift that keeps on giving"*. At that point he decided to keep half as well as any future income for the family and to use the other $100m to set up a charity to support maternal health in Africa starting in Malawi. Fred is considered by many to be a genius and one of the most creative innovators in the devices space. Yet at the same time he can be surprisingly resistant to change.

Victoria Forbes - CEO

She was first of her family born in the UK, a year after the family fled from Uganda at the end of the 1960s. Her parents dream was for her to either be a lawyer or a doctor. Victoria excelled at the local state school in East London and thrilled her parents when she chose to do a law degree at Oxford. However, in her final year she decided that she didn't want to be a lawyer after all and accepted a place on the graduate programme of a large consumer goods company. She discovered she was really good at marketing and just five years later accepted a marketing director role for a major product group of a global conglom- erate. Her rise up the company was rapid and her last role was Group Managing Director for Europe, Middle East and Africa for the compa- ny's highest growth business unit.

The switch to the charity sector caught many by surprise, especially her boss, but such a move was something she had been planning for a while. When the headhunter called with the MatFriend opportunity, at first she thought it was a little soon but the more she learnt about the charity, the more intrigued she was and the more attracted she became. The headhunter was very open about the issues and the reasons for the two previous CEOs appointments not working out. Almost the more the headhunter talked about the challenges the more compelling it became to Victoria. She had always excelled at everything she did and in terms of scale MatFriend was less than a tenth of the size of her business which was in 50 countries.

Victoria had never spent what she earnt and had amassed a significant amount of savings and investments as well as paid off her mortgage at 45. There was always a hankering to do something in Africa, more than the short business trips and safaris she had been on. She was also starting to find the travelling and constant interruptions to holidays from the Group CEO were reducing her family time. Despite her hugely supportive husband Tom who is a successful writer and had taken the major load of looking after the children she was thinking that perhaps a move to run a significant charity might be a lot less stressful and give her a lot more time at home.

You Mary Starr

As a high-profile paediatrician with a glittering career in private practice and academia you have long been an admirer of MatFriend's work. Indeed, over the years they have funded some of your most impactful research. You plan to retire soon and so when you got the call from Fred to ask if you would be interested in joining the board the timing seemed perfect.

You have served on various medical advisory boards but not on the main board of a charity before. You had met Fred and Victoria a few times before and thought that they had complementary skills with Fred being the creative driving force and promoter and Victoria the implementer. Fred's call has therefore been a bit of a stunner.

The rest of the board

Apart from Fred you have met three of the other nine trustees as part of your selection and due diligence process. All stars in their field, they have been on the board for a long time but unlike you are major donors. You were struck in your conversations with them at how positive they were about both Fred and Victoria and the quality of their relationship. Yet one of them in crystal cut *"Downton Abbey"* English had said that *"Naturally, occasionally sparks fly but a little creative tension is a good thing don't you think my dear?"*. Another one equally politely advised you to buy a new pair of reading glasses but added *"Don't get too worried about the quarterly "War and Peace" arriving in your in-box. A lot of it is just summaries of the regional boards and sub-coms which you don't need to read."*

You haven't met the others yet but from their profiles there seems to be excellent diversity in terms of gender, ethnicity and nationality as well as field of expertise. There doesn't appear to be a formal Deputy Chair or Senior Trustee but you have picked up that Fred seems to have particularly high regard for Martha, a leading German scientist and business woman. You heard she has a very strong character and brings a sharp no-nonsense focus to discussions. Her frequent use of the word "concrete" has become a bit of an in-joke.

The issues

The most pressing issues here are what to do between now and the board call and then how to play the call itself. The relationship between the CEO and the Chair appears to have reached breaking point but is it as irretrievable as Fred says it is. He has made it clear what he wants to do and there is no suggestion of a debate but is he right and what do the other board members really think.

From what Mary knows she is likely to feel that the cause of this, as Victoria has suggested, is the over clunky governance architecture and practice combined with Fred's reluctance to change it. However, being new she might also be wondering what else is lurking beneath the surface. Does the charity really deliver the bangs per buck it should in terms of impact, is the stated strategy what is really being implemented and how happy are the rest of the team. A host of other thoughts may spring to mind, including what she thinks might be the biggest issue of all, Fred.

Maybe Victoria hasn't played it as well as she could have, even if she has lasted a lot longer than her two predecessors. Perhaps she has been a bit naïve about the challenges of running a significant charity, a common misjudgement. She doesn't look to have built sufficient allies on the board to support the changes that she feels are necessary, even if Fred is somewhat change resistant and suffering from a severe bout of founder's syndrome. Her frustration also seems to have got the better of her and either way she has taken a huge risk, calculated or not.

Having said all of that, from what we know, Victoria has a big point and a good Chair would have taken it on board, dealt with it despite the personal discomfort and enlisted the support of the board to find a pragmatic transition to a more effective governance model. The ultimate responsibility for a situation like this has to be the Chair's. A highly effective Chair would have tried hard to avoid reaching such a point, especially if they have been there twice before. You might also argue that the board should have seen this coming and wonder what they were doing to try and deal with it.

Being a newcomer makes this situation even harder for Mary. There is only partial information and few facts to go on at this stage. She is unlikely to have enough familiarity with the people to be able to listen to what they think as well as what they say. Moreover, they don't know her either so whatever she says she will need to be sure they hear what she means. A conference call with 11 people where you can't see the body language makes all of this tougher still.

Knowing where the power lies will be another issue. In crises it isn't always obvious. She may have the power that a fresh, objective and less vested voice brings or alternatively perhaps the lack of it for having not had the opportunity to establish personal credibility with them yet. Mary's instincts are likely to play a bigger role than her analytical prowess. An instinctive response for some may be to feel that they have the convenient excuse of not knowing enough to make a judgement and that it might be best to keep her head down, to leave it to the others and then go with the prevailing view.

As a top surgeon Mary had always admired military field surgeons and those in the trauma area for their bravery in making judgements on limited information rather than on having a detailed analysis of the underlying causes of the problem before having to decide on what to do next. This seems to be one of those tricky situations where she is well and truly in the field and will have to make some judgements before she has the ideal data to hand. She has very little time to calibrate what she has heard and will naturally want to avoid being seen to be undermining Fred. Integrity, trust and keeping confidences are so important to respect and therefore to influence.

If she decides not to wait for the call but instead to find out more from others, who should she speak to. By coincidence the board pack contained a fresh board and executive directors contact details sheet with everyone's numbers. If there is ever a time to take advantage of others greater tolerance to the ignorant questions of a newcomer it might just be now. Yet, it's quite a bit of work to call nine others, it's far from risk free and Mary might wonder how Fred and the other trustees would feel about her doing this.

She might also wonder about finding an excuse to speak to Victoria or the finance director. It is always easy to call ahead of a board once you have the pack to provide the excuse to ask a few clarifying questions that you don't want to take up whole board time for. Harder though to speak to Victoria without giving the game away and risk her feeling later that Mary has been disingenuous.

With regard to the call strategy, as a decent person respecting her rightful share of the *"pie chart of air time"*, Mary will recognise that she will have very little time to ask questions, make points or to challenge. One advantage of speaking to others first is to gain a better understanding of the points that they would like to make and to share them between you. On top of that you are likely to gain a sense of where the consensus is.

Conference calls are inherently difficult for proper discussions as you do have to take it in turns if you want to avoid an *"interrupt-fest"*. Fred may or may not be the consummate conference call Chair and with that number of people on the call it may be hard to make more than a couple of points. Given that should she send Fred a carefully considered email beforehand setting out the points that she would like to make on the call.

If Fred gets his way on the call, then with its profile MatFriend should be able to attract the sort of CEO that Fred is likely to want but will they be what the charity really needs. Losing Victoria could be a big blow to morale and Fred has never had the process skills to directly manage what is now such a large and complex organisation. Fred may also be sensitive to the circumstances of Victoria's predecessors' departures and want to avoid it looking like he is the problem.

Mary has been asked to join the Audit Committee but if she feels strongly about the importance of making the right choice for the next CEO and dealing with Fred's succession as Chair over the next few years then she may decide to ask to be on or to Chair the Nominations Committee instead.

Finally, most smart people encountering a fresh dilemma will have a think about who they know who may be able to provide a little wisdom on the topic. This is all very new, it's highly confidential and hard to share but we all have a few people we can trust absolutely to hold a confidence. There are other issues but let's leave it there and now consider Mary's options

What are the options?

Before the call, the first choice is whether to wait for the call or take some action beforehand.

Let's deal with *"no action"* before the call first. This may seem the least risky in the short term after all you are so new you could easily be forgiven for keeping your head down and going with the majority view. Yet doing that could easily be a decision that you may regret perhaps even as soon as the conference call begins but more likely later. Why?

Well because your ability to influence the outcome may be enhanced considerably by taking action. That may be redundant if the outcome is going to be the right one anyway but what if it isn't and you then feel later that you just let it happen or more significantly it isn't the best thing for MatFriend. That after all is what your duty as a trustee is all about – to act in the best interests of the charity. A tough call either way but one Mary has to make.

If she senses that *"no action"* just doesn't feel right for her then what things could she do before the call? As discussed in the *"Issues"* above she could ask for a proper conversation with Fred or call all or some of the board to get their take on things. She might also risk it and speak to Victoria without revealing Fred's plan. If she decides to speak to a number of trustees then which ones and how should she play the conversation to ensure she isn't seen to be causing trouble? Martha sounds like a good place to start given the brief description she has of her and in terms of how to play the conversation as long as she comes over as genuinely wanting to understand the situation better to inform her judgement then she should be fine.

When it comes to the call itself how does Mary maximise her air time? Clearly this depends upon what action she has taken beforehand. If Fred presents it as a "*fait accompli*" and the rest of the board are compliant then she is down to asking questions to reassure herself on areas of concern or the implementation plan and that overall Fred and the board are doing the right thing.

If Fred presents it as a "*fait accompli*" and the board are less sure then she will need to make a judgement about what she thinks is best. Her new more impartial voice may have more power especially if she is effectively the swing vote. In this situation her instincts may be telling her to listen first and then contribute and it is perfectly reasonable for her to ask to hear the views of those who have been on the board for some time before expressing hers.

Fred may start by asking for each board member's views on Victoria before going through why he feels his course of action is necessary. He is more likely to do this and choose the order of contributors if he is confident that there will be support for his proposal. In this circumstance Mary again will naturally want to go last.

What happened?

In summary this was a difficult birth to trusteeship for Mary but she played it brilliantly and this is one with a surprisingly happy ending. Remember though, as with all the other dilemmas where the director achieved a good result not everything about the way they did it here will work in a parallel situation.

Mary's instinct was not to react immediately to Fred's initial call but rather to reflect and seek the wise counsel of a mentor who she could absolutely trust to keep the confidence. Right from the call her feeling was that the issue was Fred and that although Victoria needed to be a lot more streetwise she was fundamentally a very strong CEO and absolutely correct in her analysis. However, at the same time Mary felt very uncomfortable making such a snap judgement on a set of issues which were this critical. She prevaricated a little about speaking to her mentor and decided to sleep on it.

The next morning, she awoke with a strong conviction to act but to do so cautiously. She emailed her mentor, a distinguished and canny Chair of a major corporate with a lot of experience in the charity sector but not in the medical field. As luck would have it he was free for a coffee just before lunch. When they met Mary set out as clearly and as dispassionately as she could what she thought the issues were as well as a couple of thoughts on how she might respond. Her mentor didn't know Fred or any of the other MatFriend trustees but quickly grasped the situation and through some excellent questions, about why her instincts were leading her to want to be proactive and speak to as many of the other trustees as possible, gave her the confidence to feel that this was indeed the right thing to do despite the effort and the risks entailed in doing so. He also asked her to try out her script with him, helped her hone it and from Mary's descriptions of the trustees guided her to start with Martha.

After some initial hesitancy on Mary's part and caution on Martha's her first call went well. Martha's instincts as sharp as ever made her ask Mary why she was really calling half way through the pleasantries. Martha thought that Victoria was spot on but her reluctance to discuss it beforehand and bottle it up was a big mistake. "*She has more support from the board than she thinks she has*". Martha felt that the time for change was long overdue and despite the fact that she thought the world of Fred he should think about passing on the Chair's baton. Martha warmed to Mary during the call and warned her to be careful of two Trustees in particular who would view any suggestion of disagreeing with Fred's view as treason.

The other five calls she was able to make that day, except for the two that Martha had warned her of, followed a similar pattern. Sadly, one of the two was the Chair of the Nominations Committee who said that he was fully behind Fred and he had already had a word with his favourite headhunter so that they could get ready.

Feeling that there was likely, although not certain, to be enough of a majority on the board to slow Fred up in despatching Victoria without proper discussion Mary then sent Fred an email and suggested that she see him as early as possible the following morning to share her concerns about their conversation about removing Victoria and some thoughts she had for the board call later that day. Fred was surprisingly relaxed about the idea believing that he had the board in his pocket and that Mary was simply being an anxious novice.

When they met Mary stunned Fred with a smart, sensitive and unmistakenly clearly-worded summary of how she saw the situation and her thoughts on what the trustees would welcome on the call. After preparing him by saying that what she was about to say would be uncomfortable for both of them, she told him that as a newcomer she had called most of the trustees to gain their views before making up her mind on what she thought. As expected she said *"there were a range of views but a consensus"*. This consensus, from all bar two, was that now was not the time for Victoria to go, even though she had made a serious error in putting the governance reform paper in the pack without discussing it with Fred or the Chair of Nominations Committee. The general feeling Mary said was that Victoria was *"Spot on in her analysis and the general direction of travel with regard to the solution."*

Fred's mood shifted considerably and he found it hard to conceal his anger that Mary should have done this *"behind my back"*. Mary said calmly and warmly that she appreciated that this was tough to hear and that she knew she had risked their relationship but that she genuinely didn't know what trustees might say and felt her first duty was to the charity and to find out. She said that she had an enormous regard for him and felt that there was a good way through this which despite the discomfort and embarrassment would leave the charity in a much stronger position.

Her suggestion was that he called the trustees individually and ask them to give it to him straight and then to use the conference call to agree on what feedback he should give to Victoria ahead of the board meeting and how they would take the issue of transforming the governance model forward in a way that was inclusive but delivered the step change that most of the trustees felt was necessary. Surprisingly Fred was a lot more compliant than Mary feared he might be. There was something about the warmth of her approach, the calmness and the irrefutable logic as well as the genuine respect she showed him. Reflecting on the conversation she realised that all that experience of having difficult conversations with parents about life and death and trying to balance clarity with compassion was very useful training. As was the importance of taking verbatim notes when under pressure.

Fred regained his composure for the call, startled Mary by thanking her for an incredible intervention that morning and said that she had made him reflect on his decision to remove Victoria. He said that having said this he still felt the level of disrespect that Victoria had shown in sending out a paper of that nature without sighting him was regrettable and that in the spirit of giving her balanced feedback he would be telling her this in his one to one the day before the board meeting. He also suggested that he would tell her that although her paper would not be discussed in detail in the meeting they would discuss the need for comprehensive governance review with a focus on decision making and including succession planning as well as who from the board should lead that process and what principles they wanted to apply in conducting it.

Once she had got over Fred's ticking off on respect for the Chair (ie him) and focused on the overall outcome Victoria was thrilled. Fred was very mature about the whole thing especially once he realised that Mary was right when she had tweaked Oscar Wilde's famous quote and said: *"To lose one CEO looks unfortunate, to lose two looks like carelessness and to lose three looks like you are the problem!"*.

Martha led the review which came up with a pragmatic step by step approach to governance slimming and decision quality enhancing. After two years most of this was in place, Martha became the next Chair, Fred became Founder Emeritus and Mary became Chair of the Nominations Committee. A couple of years later with performance dramatically improved a successor to Victoria was appointed from within.

Dilemma 4:

The radio-controlled accountant

It is now three years since Danny was appointed as Finance Director (FD) to a small charity which has a social enterprise activity selling equipment to its beneficiaries. He's done a good job in the eyes of the board who have found him far more compliant and reliable than his predecessor, who seemed to embody all the worst characteristics of the species and none of the good.

Danny enjoys his job and can always be relied upon to have that spreadsheet ready, that scenario analysed and unrestricted reserves to hand. However, you and the rest of the board are a little worried that while healthy surpluses have been reported in the last few years and reserves have grown and salaries increased, the charity's cash position has deteriorated. For a while this was put down to growth in working capital to support expansion of the social enterprise activity. Sadly, a recently-appointed Trustee, has been asking some tricky questions at the board. He has suggested that the pricing policy and stock position need independently reviewing.

The result of this review has shocked the board. Surpluses have been overstated and the current stock value is totally unrealistic. There is considerable concern over the real reserves position. Worse, there is significantly more off-balance sheet financing than was thought. The charity has been in breach of covenants on the financing relating to some equipment purchases, though the bank seems unaware. The Chief Executive (CEO) has challenged Danny, but his reaction has been as helpful as ever: *"If you'd like me to tell the bank, I'll do so right away."* The Trustees are embarrassed and all agree that they should have recognised the situation earlier.

You are the recently appointed Trustee and the only one with commercial experience. The Chair, who is a man of high integrity, wants to fire Danny today. The CEO is extremely nervous about doing this. They both appear to be looking at you for leadership on what to do and to come up with a solution. Danny, ironically, is the one who suggested there be a new Trustee with commercial experience in the first place and was a key factor in your selection in preference to someone else.

How should they recover? What are the issues?

There are a range of issues involved. First, is Danny's overstatement deliberate, incompetent or both? What about the rest of the management information? How good is that? Is there collusion? Who else is involved if there is? Why is the CEO nervous of firing Danny? Confidence will be rocked among the top team. The judgement of all of the directors will be questioned. What will be the effect on morale throughout the company?

If there is an Audit Committee, how did it miss it? What was it doing? What about the auditors? What did their last management letter say? Is there an issue with the auditors?

This is a defining moment. How the charity recovers will determine its future.

You may be wondering about your own position and questioning some of your own judgements. Thoughts may turn to the impact on your other appointments, the additional time you are likely to have to spend, and your own credibility.

How to decide?

Those who have experienced these situations will know that letting an incompetent and potentially fraudulent FD continue in the role for a moment longer is foolish. At least not having a finance director isn't adding to the damage and getting the facts out of Danny appears a dubious place to start.

What you need is to find some way of creating space with the bank to enable a confirmation of the true position of the company to take place. In this particular situation you may also be trading whilst insolvent, which has serious implications for all of the directors.

For this situation you will need excellent legal and accounting advice, yet there may be an issue relating to how it might be paid for. The accountants should feel compelled to help if there is any question that the last set of audited accounts was inaccurate. The bank and others may have supplied additional credit on the basis that they represented a true and fair view.

If you cannot persuade advisers to help, then the horror of having to appoint an administrator may become in reality the only option.

The key to deciding what to do is the severity of the company's financial position.

What to decide?

There are a number of decisions to make. Dealing with these in turn; the first concerns whether to fire Danny or not. It is difficult to see any argument for keeping him in place. To knowingly carry on with an incompetent or fraudulent FD, particularly given the risk of insolvency, would be most unwise. Consequently, he should be suspended immediately pending a thorough investigation and fired when the evidence supports the decision. The protests that it will undermine credibility at the bank because you'll need to come clean, or that you will lose his knowledge of what has actually happened, are weak. You will have to be honest with the bank immediately anyway and his knowledge is clearly suspect.

Will you report the matter to the police? Many don't in the belief that not doing so will enable the matter to be kept quieter. The damage that such a disclosure might do through undermining confidence in the company would loom large in the mind of any director. However, the forensic skills and experience of commercial fraud detectives may enable them to get there quicker than anyone else. You also have a duty to report a crime if you are aware one has been committed. But what is Danny's crime? It may not be clear whether he has stolen money for himself or whether he has used the money to secure banking facilities under false pretences. Some directors fear being drawn into criminal proceedings. The decision is obviously a personal one for the Trustees involved. The charity's lawyer should be able to provide a view on this subject and would generally advise notifying the police in almost all circumstances.

You need confirmation of the financial position as soon as possible. How do you get it? In this case you will probably need to borrow someone from the auditors. However, as we have already discussed, they don't appear blameless either. The bank may insist on an independent firm. This will be all very well if there are the funds to pay for it.

This brings us on to what to do about the bank. You must come clean, but it is better to do so with a plan. The bank will be looking to see that the situation is under control and that there is a better prospect of recovering their debt within this plan than by appointing an admin- istrator at the outset. Coming up with a plan without the facts is tough, so the key part of it is to buy enough time to establish what they are. This might even include loans to the company by the directors, an injection of funds by shareholders, a freeze on payments to suppliers and other crisis measures.

How to communicate it?

Who needs communicating with and in what order?

- Your fellow Trustees.
- The company's lawyers.
- The accountants.
- Danny.
- Relevant staff.
- Other key advisers (insurers etc).
- Shareholders.
- The bank.
- The police.

Depending upon the exact circumstances, there may also be a need to inform customers of the social enterprise. And you may feel it appropriate to inform some of the major donors.

A brief and accurate statement will need to be prepared for external purposes along the lines of:

"The board has discovered several accounting irregularities and has suspended the Finance Director pending a further investigation. We have appointed X to confirm the current financial position and will provide an update as soon as possible."

Clearly, this won't suffice for major donors with outstanding commitments or those the charity is currently bidding with. For these a more detailed explanation of what has occurred, what the implications are, and what the board is proposing to do about it will be necessary.

With regard to how to communicate the news to Danny, the Chair should be the one to deliver it. In this case, it would be wise to have this conversation in the presence of the company's lawyer and to have prepared a written notice of suspension and the justification for doing so. The meeting should be kept brief. Danny should be given the opportunity to rebut the allegations and advised to consult a lawyer. It will be very important to do this as calmly as possible – difficult when you may feel you have in front of you the person who might have destroyed your life's work. Your lawyer should make a careful record of the conversation and, if at all possible, get Danny to sign it as being an accurate reflection.

What did the Trustee do?

In this specific case, the new Trustee resigned immediately and the charity failed shortly afterwards. He was a director of a plc and very concerned about the collateral damage to the plc's reputation, even though he had only just joined. It would be a long haul to sort out the problem and, in his view, there was a low probability of survival. He knew the bank concerned well and also that neither trustees or donors would have or would be prepared to provide any additional cash. He had to decide one way or the other. He was extremely upset about his own due diligence on the company:

"I didn't meet the Finance Director before taking the appoint- ment. Something I will never repeat. I knew the Chief Executive as a former colleague. The charity had a good reputation and although it looked a little stretched, appeared to have potential."

In another similar case, in a business this time, the independent director formed the view that a rescue was more feasible, she seized the moment and got a mandate through the insecurity of others. The reason why she did that was that the company's market position was much better and, more importantly, it had a stronger balance sheet. In her assessment, it was therefore much more likely to withstand the shock. The shareholders put up sufficient funds for the company to trade, a new FD was recruited and the company overcame the problem.

Dilemma 5:

Convo

Convo is a south coast food manufacturing business, founded ten years ago by its Chair and chief executive officer (CEO), Archie Cresswell. Archie is an infectiously enthusiastic and effervescent process engineer who has grown Convo from nothing into a £60 million turnover business. In the process he has been awarded a CBE and has developed a profile for the business far in excess of its size. Convo has also won a Queen's Technology Award, together with a string of industry prizes.

The business manufactures a mix of own-label and branded products for the major UK multiple supermarkets. It wins customers on the strength of its highly innovative way of processing, preparing and
presenting its products.

Three customers account for 70 per cent of sales, the balance being smaller retailers and an exciting but somewhat volatile French agent.

Archie's former employer, BigFood Company, supplies most of the processing plant. It also owns 40 per cent of Convo through its initial support of Archie. Archie, his finance director (FD) Paul Tate, and the other two executive directors (execs) own 15 per cent. Five per cent has been granted in employee shares. The balance is held by an institutional syndicate that invested five years ago to fund the building of a new plant. It did so in anticipation of a float three years ago.

The business has a public aura of success but the institutions are clearly becoming concerned, hence your recent appointment to the board. You can understand some of their increased anxiety and have decided to jot down the following analysis.

The company's strategic direction is making it increasingly reliant on its few key customers. It also seems to be moving it closer to competing head on with global players such as Unilever and Nestlé.

The cash-generative growth years fuelled by a high-margin environment are over. Surplus cash has been invested in developing new brands and building plant capacity. The recent construction of a new head office/warehouse complex has exacerbated the problem through cost overruns and disruption to deliveries. The retailers have been unsympathetic; so have the institutions with regard to deferring dividend payments. Convo is up to its overdraft limit of £8 million.

You feel that the business has outgrown its management, which is largely inbred. Financial controls are poor; management information is overelaborate and tends to cloud rather than highlight key issues. You are not convinced about the profitability of two of the eight key product groups. Management is demoralised by constant changes in strategic direction by the mercurial but much-loved Archie. His board, as you can see from the profiles below, is an interesting mix.

The relationship with BigFood has become strained and less productive for Convo. Convo had to become far too involved in the detailed design of the latest machines and in fixing the considerable number of teething problems on installation. BigFood's new CEO has allegedly been questioning the strategic sense in holding minority investments. That said, you are suspicious that BigFood might be interested in acquiring control on the cheap. The Convo board is divided into two (if not three) camps and there is much gathering of interest groups before board meetings. BigFood's board representative has become ever more vocal and disparaging in his remarks.

This and next year will probably be loss-making, given the margin squeeze from the retailers and the fact that the latest equipment is still producing at costs much higher than budgeted. There is no possibility of a claim on BigFood.

Despite all of the above, this fundamentally remains a business with enormous potential in its market and it has a deeply committed and talented workforce.

All partners (other than BigFood) seem to be looking to you, as the only independent board member, to take the lead and catalyse the situation.

Note. The Articles of Association for the company give BigFood two board votes, the institutions two board votes and the management one vote. There is no casting vote for the Chair. There are no compulsory purchase provisions for departing directors who are shareholders, except in the case of termination for cause as stipulated in the service agreement of the individual director concerned. In this instance, an executive shareholding may be compulsorily purchased at valuation.

Board profiles

Archie Cresswell (45), Chair and CEO

An extreme workaholic. He loves the company – it's his baby and he knows every single employee on a first-name basis. Over the years, despite his ego, he has never paid himself adequately and 18 months ago the board insisted on awarding him a 100 per cent salary increase and forced a three-year rolling contract on him. He seems a straight-forward, open chap who can see that all is not well. He dominates the company, is strongly defensive of his own position and feels let down by his team. Beneath a seemingly naïve and homespun exterior, he can prove wonderfully adept at playing off the two shareholding factions (BigFood and the institutions). Domestically, he is supported by a strong family who think the world of him and his achievements, even though he neglects them.

Paul Tate, FCA (42), FD

A local man who qualified with a minor firm in the next town but got bored with auditing. Two years after qualifying he moved into broader commercial management, mostly in trading and commodity businesses. When Archie set up Convo and asked him to be FD, he was flattered and thrilled, considering the prospect hugely exciting. He did, however, have to gear up and borrow from his father-in-law to invest at the start and in subsequent rounds. A natural over-complicator who will often miss the central point, Paul is, like Archie, a workaholic and is having severe problems at home. He and his wife enjoy the reflected glory of being part of the Convo success story and, despite a relatively low income, are big spenders.

Terence Foster, PhD (38), technical director

A brilliant food technologist who pioneered the first, and still most successful, Convo product. He has always worked with Archie and has an undying loyalty to him despite growing frustrated at the difficulty in finding cash to enhance the plant. Financially and commercially unaware, he is very much the brains of the team. He hates formal presentations to investors, but is always thrilled at the prospect of showing visiting buyers and the local university round the plant. He dislikes any general management activity.

Heather Brigland, MBA (41), commercial director

Joined only two years ago from Unilever after an earlier spell at Bain and a career break. Brought in to bring more rigour to strategic thinking and planning, she has never been able to break into the core team of Archie, Paul and Terence. Heather is considered and treated very much as an outsider with no influence at the board. This is a real shame, as intellectually she makes excellent points, and if she were listened to would add a great deal. However, she often tends to blow it by missing trivial practical points. She also seems to be perpetually trying to alienate René (see below) by scoring points.

René Faux (45), BigFood representative

Joined BigFood as a graduate in France the same year as Archie. They didn't meet until they both got their first general manager jobs. Initially they got on well, but they once sat on the same project group and fell out violently over a redundancy programme. René's career faltered and he has been deeply envious of Archie's independence and very visible success. However, recently he feels he has been gaining ground and, with two highly successful acquisitions behind him, has risen to prominence within BigFood. He only got the board representation job at Convo when his predecessor, a former mentor of Archie's, retired. There is nothing more he would like than to put Archie in the position of having to report to him or give up his business. Archie dislikes René with a surprising intensity.

Angélique Beaulieu (32), BigFood's second representative

René's associate. She tends to be quiet but has remarkable insight and presence when she does join in the conversation. René is slightly irritated by her ability to say what needs saying in a few well-chosen and charming words.

Clive Maxwell (37)

The board representative from the lead venture capital investor. Convo is his star investment and he's done much trumpeting of it inside the institution. He's becoming increasingly uncomfortable as he is out fundraising himself and it isn't going that well. His boss has made it clear to him that if the fundraising falls through because of problems at Convo, he won't have a job.

You – the independent director

A seasoned campaigner with experience of five appointments in young food companies, all of which have experienced growing pains. You love a problem. That's handy!

What are the issues?

There are a whole series of issues relating to Convo's financial position, strategy, people, board structure and ownership. Your own position sounds pivotal. Convo's institutional investors are relying on you. Yet, what real authority do you have? You're the newcomer; you have no equity; what is your motivation? If you need external help, where will it come from? Who will pay for it? The company?

On the financial front, Convo has run out of cash. There is a mismatch between the financial structure and the requirements of the business. Capital investment appears to be funded from cash flow. Financial control is lax and there are questions over the accuracy of the financial position.

With regard to the strategy, have they got one? It looks mighty confused if they have. They seem to be competing in world markets but operating as a little local company. Dependency on BigFood is an obvious issue.

Convo has a clearly dysfunctional board and management team. Archie looks to be the main problem. His style and capabilities are a poor fit for Convo's current stage of development. He has not built a strong or cohesive team around him. There are also many individual issues apart from Archie. The FD looks out of his depth and under considerable stress, Heather is demotivated and not able to do her job, René's antipathy to Archie is getting in the way and so on.

There are diverse objectives among Convo's shareholders. Some don't appear to have objectives for their shareholding and there seems little communication between them. The link with BigFood is a major issue and one that threatens the survival of the business. Any change will be difficult to achieve, given the current voting structure.

It looks as if the board hasn't been well advised. Convo's advisers may have gone to sleep in the warmth of Convo's earlier success. On the other hand, they may have been frustrated in their efforts and given up. It will be important to understand who they are and what they think.

How might the current situation have been avoided?

The board needed changing as the business developed. A key point was the institutional investment. This provided an excellent opportunity to appoint an independent Chair, almost essential in co-owned situations like these. Retaining the Chair and CEO roles and doing them both well through such a period of growth is extremely difficult, even for the most talented of people. To try to do so without cohesive ownership is to attempt the impossible.

Should the FD have been replaced earlier? This looks like a no-brainer. Are the independent directors appropriate? With the exception of you, they all have vested interests. Should René have been put in such a role, given the personal animosity between him and Archie? Have the institutions been diligent or negligent? It looks as though they are suddenly awakening. The financial structure needed changing to reflect the company's need for cash as it grew. Did the institutions and BigFood recognise this?

A major capital project, ie the new building project, has been poorly managed. Does Convo manage other projects well? Is this just an isolated incident? Is it now sorted out or are there still problems?

The voting arrangements were almost set up to allow Archie to divide and rule. It is difficult at any time, but the voting position could have been more easily addressed when times were good.

How to decide?

Who do you turn to for advice? How do you maintain your honest broker status? What extra information do you require in order to decide what to do? What do shareholders want? Do you think it really does need more money? Do you think you have persuasive powers over Archie? Can you get BigFood and the institutions to act together? These thoughts will be going through your mind before you can decide on a strategy for resolving Convo's problems.

So, the first step must be to gather as much knowledge on the priority issues as possible. Consultation with the shareholders will probably be key to developing a solution. Before taking responsibility for sorting it out, you will need direction, a mandate and possibly some money from the shareholders. Asking the bank for views on what to do may result in panic.

This may be a situation where you need to come to a speedy decision over how much time you can allocate. To sort this one out will require a major time commitment. Determining the exact financial position is essential. External verification of this is an imperative.

The next step will be to build alliances to enlist as much support for whatever solution you come up with, particularly if this involves you becoming Chair of Convo.

What to decide?

Let's look at the options. You could do nothing and let them sort themselves out. After all, what's the upside – you have no equity? But what about your reputation with the institutions? To turn and run, even if sensible, is unlikely to enhance it. Presumably, when you took the appointment, it was clear that it might be a situation requiring increasing commitment. Some people like to wait until the situation reaches crisis point before they act. This one has.

Forcing an immediate sale to BigFood, a trade buyer or a manage- ment buy-in is another option. All look difficult to achieve, given the current shareholding split. Moreover, Convo is not in an easily buyable state. Any purchaser would need to be very confident in their knowledge of what they were buying and their own management capability. This would presumably be reflected in the price.

Firing Archie is a possibility. There is no obvious successor so his replacement would have to come from outside. The impact on employees, suppliers and customers, given his charisma, needs to be taken into account and managed. Will shareholders support you or consider it too risky? How would you compensate him for loss of office? Does his service contract contain anything to make this course of action difficult in practice? What about his shareholding? Who would tell him? Would you replace him as Chair and recruit a CEO?

You could redirect and restructure management and raise cash for a limited period. Removing the FD, re-establishing financial control and giving Archie greater direction may be all that is needed. As a part of this, you may be able to persuade BigFood to swap René for someone who doesn't have any personal issues with Archie. To do any of this, you would need a strong Chair. Could it be you? Even if you regroup, has Convo a viable future as an independent entity? You may just be stabilising the business before a sale.

Whatever route you choose to adopt, the voting structure means that you will need the support of two of the key constituencies. The most powerful combination is BigFood and the institutions.

How to communicate it?

Considerable diplomatic skill will be required to resolve this situation. In trying to bring BigFood and the institutions together, René mustn't be alienated. However, getting closer to René might have an adverse impact upon your relationship with Archie. Another thing you need to do is to ensure that there is greater communication between the different parties and set a new standard. Do you need additional contacts at BigFood and at the institutions to achieve this? Again, you need to be careful you don't alienate René and Clive by appearing to go over their heads.

Getting Archie to look to you for support and guidance would also be helpful, so you need to strike up a good friendly rapport with him and not appear to be a threat. To get anywhere you will need to be confident and assertive but not aggressive in your communication style. Asking good questions rather than making assertions will probably win the day. With Archie, painting pictures of the likely outcomes once you have established a good rapport may work.

What did you, the independent director, do?

You decided fairly quickly that the business had outgrown the management, especially Archie and the FD. To you, a sale was the only real solution.

However, you also thought that to attempt to achieve this in the short-term would be madness. Convo had a tremendous reputation in the market. Its competitors and customers seemed unaware of the difficulties within. Trying to sell Convo in distress would destroy this illusion. So you decided that the best route forward was to stabilise the situation in order to buy time to make the best judgement.

You asked the lead institution to make an introduction to René's boss, which it did along the following lines:

> *"As you know, the independent director has been in place a short while now. He has formed the view that some urgent action is required at Convo. I think you would find his detailed analysis of the situation very interesting. He is one of the most impressive turnaround Chairs we know. The reason I am calling you directly is because one of the things he is most concerned about is the relationship between René and Archie Cresswell. They seem to have developed an intense dislike for each other, which could potentially undermine Convo. He has asked me if I could talk to you to arrange a meeting for you and him so that he can share his views with you and also get a feel for your objectives for your shareholding in Convo. I think this is an excellent suggestion. For the moment, it might be helpful not to raise this with René until after you have heard what the independent director has to say."*

The BigFood co-divisional Chair was intrigued and agreed. René was due for a promotion, so he thought it might be interesting to find out how he was doing at Convo. He then picked up the phone immediately to René and asked him for a report on the current position at Convo, without disclosing why. René was a little put out and not quite sure what to write.

You got on very well with BigFood's divisional Chair. Between you, you agreed a strategy involving appointing you as Chair. You decided to fire the FD and appoint an interim director from the auditors to establish what the exact financial position was and to restore financial control. As you sensed that the business might be able to find cash from within, you ignored the issue of the cash shortage, believing that until you knew the exact position this was a premature discussion. An operations director would be appointed beneath Archie, allowing Archie to focus on selling the company once it was in a stable position. You both also agreed that you would obtain the institutions' agreement and then break the news to Archie.

You rehearsed your conversation with Archie several times with Clive. You decided that you needed to get Archie to face reality and then paint him some pictures of the possible outcomes. In the short time you had known Archie, you realised that the two most important things to him were his reputation in the industry and the well-being of his staff. He was not motivated by money at all.

You told Archie that the business was out of control and likely to fail. You also told him that until recently the institutions and BigFood had not been communicating effectively, but now they were. The pictures you then painted were obvious. One involved Archie's reputation in tatters; in the other, control was restored and the company achieved a high-profile sale. Initially, Archie brushed off the problems and tried to persuade you that it would be all right. You then went through the analysis you had given to BigFood and the institutions and what they proposed to do. Archie quickly realised that with 80 per cent he had little choice.

"Why don't you just fire me, then, if you think I'm so awful?" asked Archie.

"Because the company is you, Archie, and you are the best possible seller of it. The best person to ensure as many of the jobs are saved as possible. We really need you."

Archie was persuaded, but only if he could remain as Chair in title. You then took a gamble that many wouldn't. You agreed, but warned Archie that if he didn't keep up his end of the deal, you would have him removed. Archie then relaxed and was about as committed and loyal to the agreement as you could possibly imagine. The institutions and BigFood reluctantly agreed, but only on the basis of your reputation. Financial control was quickly restored by appointing an interim director from the auditors. Costs were reduced and working capital management improved to the extent that, although it was tight, no extra cash was required.

You managed the board meetings and set the agendas. You also ensured René and Archie had few opportunities to disagree. Eighteen months later, the company appointed an investment bank to market it. Six months later, it was sold to an American competitor that had no presence in Europe. Archie is now its president of worldwide marketing. He's a little regretful but in no way broken.

If you want to take this dilemma further, you might like to try out these subsequent challenges:

1. Having stabilised the position, you decide that management has to be regrouped and that Archie has to go. You have obtained the attached summary of his service contract. The institutions are behind you but you haven't discussed it with BigFood yet. *What board process do you need to go through and what difficulties do you foresee in implementation?*

2. Instead of removing Archie, you decide to adopt a gradual approach and persuade Archie to bring in a new managing director beneath him, together with a new FD to replace Paul Tate. After 18 months, Archie falls out with both of them. You remain impressed with the changes they have made. *What would you do now and what board process do you need to go through to implement your decisions?*

3. The financial position deteriorates significantly and the business needs an injection of £5 million. The institutional investors have been asked and they have resolved that they will only put this money up if there are management changes. BigFood is prepared to provide the money without changing the management, but insists on acquiring control at a depressed rights issue price. Archie refuses to open up the bidding to outside parties. *What would you do now?*

SERVICE AGREEMENT
ARCHIBALD CRESSWELL ('the Executive')
AND
CONVO LTD ('the Company')

Position:	Managing Director or in such other capacity as the Board of Directors or the company ('the board') may determine.
Period:	For three years from 31 March 2019 until 31 March 2022 and thereafter unless and until determined by either party giving to the other not less than 12 months' prior written notice.
Remuneration:	Salary £250,000 per annum inclusive of all director's fees subject to an annual review on 31 March in each year. The Executive and his family are to be entitled to private medical insurance. In addition, 10 per cent of salary will be paid annually into a private pension fund. The Company will also pay for life assurance cover equal to four times salary.
Expenses:	All reasonable expenses incurred by the Executive in the discharge of his duties will be reimbursed.
Motor car:	BMW 730i fully expensed.
Restrictions:	For so long as the Executive owns shares in or is employed by the Company, he will not compete with any food businesses of the Company or its subsidiaries, solicit customers or entice away employees. If his employment is terminated, the above restrictions apply for 12 months following the date of termination.
Termination:	The Company can terminate, without notice, if guilty of material or persistent dishonesty, misconduct or serious breach of obligation, if incapacitated by illness or mental disorder or subject to bankruptcy. In such an event, the Executive can make no claim for compensation.
Suspension:	If allegations arise out of serious breach of obligations, the Board can decide to suspend the Executive.
Board appointments:	Upon termination of this agreement, the Executive resigns his directorships.

Dilemma 6:

Reserves – the long and the short of it

Sam, the Chair of PovToGlow, a small Charity with income of £9m this year, has just emerged from the most tetchy Board meeting she has chaired. *"I really didn't see that coming at all."* she confided in her best friend Julia that evening. *"They almost came to blows. I am going to have to get behind the tension. I can't believe it's really all about something as esoteric as the level of our unrestricted reserves."*

This is Sam's first charity appointment after a highly successful business development career in a large corporate. Everything has gone swimmingly since she was appointed 18 months ago but she is clearly stunned by today's outbursts from her colleagues around the Board table.

PovToGlow was founded ten years ago by *"Rags to Riches"* entrepreneur, Benny Torwell. Benny had made his fortune in property but had never forgotten his roots. He lived in a beautiful old manor house on a hill overlooking the council estate where he was born. Benny had felt that there was a desperate need in his local community to help people in poverty, especially those who had never experienced anything else, by giving them some skills and a bit of cash to start their own micro business. *"I always want people to feel that we are there for them if they need us."*

He used his connections in the property and building trade to provide training and experience and donated a large rambling old building for them to practice on and to create a valuable asset for the Charity in the future. Today it is a vibrant and thriving social enterprise hub. Benny's connections with local industrialists also helped greatly and he was able to enlist the support of the local business community to support a range of PovToGlow experiences both with funds and volunteers as well as using their facilities.

Benny was almost 70 when he founded PovToGlow and his plan was to let his daughter, Tracy, run it for a few years under his tutelage and then, if it proved sustainable, recruit someone from the charity sector to run it when Tracy had proved she was ready to lead the family business. The Charity got off to a tremendous start as Benny and Tracy proved a powerful combination. Sadly though, two years in Benny had a severe heart attack and died a year later.

Despite this tragedy, Tracy's natural entrepreneurialism, huge energy, resilience and determination to fulfil her father's dreams for PovToGlow meant that instead of stuttering following the death of its Founder, PovToGlow grew from strength to strength. Her much older cousin Pete had become Chair and he had been a real source of calm and encouragement to Tracy.

Three years ago, Tracy became Chair of the family's property company and decided that it was time to fulfil her dad's original plan to bring in a charity professional and take PovToGlow to the next level. Daisy, her successor as CEO, has proven more than up to the job. Her strengths in marketing and operations have enabled PovToGlow to double its impact with only 50 per cent more income and she has been very popular with staff, beneficiaries and local community officials. Tracy remains closely connected through her role as Patron and has been excellent at giving Daisy space but supporting her when required.

When Sam took over from Pete as Chair last year she was struck by how thrilled he was that Benny and Tracy had built something which was really making a difference locally, wasn't dependent upon the family anymore and was so well run. *"Benny couldn't have wished for more, well apart from being alive to see it"*, he had quipped at his retirement party.

"So, who was arguing?" asked Julia. *"Claudia and Bert mostly."* Sam responded. Claudia, was a real coup to land as a Trustee and has been a big driver of increased income through the series of celebrity fundraising dinners she has organised. Sam knew her vaguely before- hand, was impressed by their interactions and had thought that having such a powerful and impressive female role model would inspire the young women PovToGlow was supporting as well as bring some fresh dynamism to the Board.

Claudia is in her early thirties and something of a local celebrity, having been brilliant at school, landing a first in Natural Sciences at Cambridge, a scholarship to go to Harvard Business School and becoming the youngest Managing Director (MD) of a business unit at the investment bank MorganCiti. She's on numerous *"Power"* and *"Rising star"* lists. After having recently married a Premier League football star, during the week she lives in their flat in Chelsea. Last year they bought a large house close to the manor that Benny lived in and Claudia has loved spending weekends in

Essex, especially in restoring the gardens to their former glory. Olaf, her husband is usually able to join her there on Sundays.

Sam is delighted that Claudia has been a lot more active than anticipated given how demanding her day job is. She has also provided some very constructive challenge to the Board in particular around its ambition. From Claudia's perspective the Board is far too cautious and, as she put it at a recent Board meeting: *"We just need to go for it. Our model works we have proven that over a decade. We should be a national Charity and twenty times the size. Seems like a no-brainer for me."*

Bert, a former managing partner of a small local firm of chartered accountants will be retiring as a Trustee and Chair of the Audit Committee in two years. He and Benny were very good friends. Benny relied upon him to give Tracy wise counsel and to ensure that the Charity was always under control and he admired Benny's combination of entrepreneurial flair and grounded approach to financial matters. He remembers Benny's wise advice fondly and regularly used one of his sayings: *"It is much easier to be bolder in our work when we are cautious with our cash."* as a touchstone to guide his coaching of Tracy and Josie.

Bert respects Sam and Tracy enormously. However, although he doesn't mean to be, he can come over as a little misogynist and occasionally patronising. At the same time and somewhat ironically, he is easily wound up by Claudia who he considers to be both patronising and ignorant. Out of earshot he sometimes refers to her as *"Little Miss Glamthropy"*. Another favourite saying of his is that: *"Perhaps we need another woman on the Board called Prudence."*

From Bert's perspective, although he admires Claudia's work on boosting the fundraising income from her dinners, there is considerable cause for caution over other streams of income. He senses that the landscape is becoming more challenging and there is growing evidence to support his view. Some of the Charity's multi-year corporate funders haven't renewed given the softening economy. Others have tailed off, having been acquired or restructured or choosing to focus their corporate responsibility activities on national programmes. There are also a number of new charities in the poverty alleviation space operating locally which has made competition for funds more intense. Bert has also noticed that the number of regular direct debit givers has been on the decline and that the growth in contactless payments has hit the tin collections income. At a previous Board meeting he proposed a thorough review of PovToGlow's income and fundraising strategy.

The spark to the flame at the last Board meeting was Claudia's proposal, as Chair of the Development Committee, that PovToGlow changes its reserves policy from *"Holding a minimum of 6 months' running costs in unrestricted reserves"* to *"three months"*. *"That's all the Charity Commission needs us to have anyway. After all we are starting from the position of having well over a year's costs in our current account and considerably more than that in our endowment funds"*, she added before concluding with: *"And what's more at the rate my development Board is going the team will find it hard to grow at the rate the money is coming in."*

Bert had been simmering for a while but when Claudia uttered the words *"My Development Board"* this was just too much for him. Reaching boiling point, he decided to remind her that *"It's not your Development Board it is the Charity's sub-committee."* He then went on to remind everybody of the principles that Benny and Tracy had adhered to and the great contribution that Josie the Finance Director (FD) was making and which had led to PovToGlow's strong financial position. Then to finish encouraged Claudia to *"Actually read the Charity Commission website where it makes no mention that 3 months is enough. What it says is that there is no single level, or even a range, of reserves that is right for all charities. Any target set by trustees for the level of reserves to be held should reflect the particular circum- stances of the individual Charity. To do this, trustees need to know why the Charity should hold reserves and, having identified those needs, the trustees should consider how much should be held to meet them."*

Josie, PovToGlow's understated but highly effective FD, is univer- sally popular. Despite being seen as a tough cookie from the perspective of staff and suppliers she tends to be somewhat over deferential with the Board. She, like a few other members of the management team who were present, was unsettled by the conflict and whereas some of her colleagues were almost cheering Claudia on in wanting to go national she was deeply anxious about taking more risk. Josie has been in the wonderful position during her eight years at the Charity of never having had a cashflow problem and would like to keep it that way. She's also been a little unsettled by Claudia's constant offers of mentoring support and introductions to social impact investors.

"What about Daisy?" asked Julia. *"Did she join in or keep her head*

down?" Sam said that she had given Daisy a signal when Bert flared up indicating that she and Sam would chat later and she should not join in the debate during the meeting.

What would you advise Sam to do if you were Julia? What are the issues?

It is important for her to separate out the various sets of issues. The *"Purpose, People and Process"* model is a helpful place to start. An obvious first issue and the one that has caused the flare up is the differing appetite for risk around the Board table from Claudia's *"Let's go for it"* zestful approach to Bert's desire for *"Prudence"*. Yet, as in this and so many situations like it, this is not the only issue and it may be symptomatic of deeper challenges.

There is clearly an issue over what the Board sees as the purpose of PovToGlow. From what we know there doesn't seem to be any challenge over the core focus being on poverty alleviation or on how it does that, but there is over where it does it and on what scale. For example, does it want to stay a focused local Charity or build upon its powerful model and go national? Going national might deliver huge impact well beyond what Benny envisaged and be of great service to the nation. Yet, has PovToGlow got the Board, team and other resources to do this and how would the model translate to communities were it is less deep rooted?

Additionally, given the focus on poverty alleviation and in helping people who have precarious incomes and lives, it could be argued that ensuring PovToGlow is financially strong is an important part of its purpose. As Benny had said: *"I always want people to feel that we are there for them if they need us."* Would that be put at risk if PovToGlow was too expansive? In summary, is the issue over reserves simply a symptom of the deeper issue that the Board hasn't agreed what the purpose of PovToGlow is?

Another purpose point may be to think about the purpose of the Audit Committee. Do its terms of reference include consideration of financial and other risks? If they do then it could be worth renaming the Committee to *"Audit and Risk"* to reflect that and to raise the level of thinking about risk. If they don't, then it is worth thinking about whether they should. The detailed work of considering risk and making recommendations to the Board, as well as defining what the key risks are and how they should be mitigated and managed, is a key part of an Audit and Risk Committee's role.

Determining the right policy for the level of reserves for any charity is fundamentally a Board decision, financial strategy being an important element of strategy as a whole. For restricted reserves, ie those funds which have been given to a charity for a *"Restricted"* purpose (eg to be spent on a specific programme) but haven't been spent yet, the issue is easy. You need to keep them in reserve. For other funds which have been given on an *"unrestricted"* basis (eg those from general fund-raising), the Board can decide on the level to hold in *"unrestricted"* reserves and what it would be appropriate to spend. Most charity regulators try and guide the charities under their regulation to adopt a balanced approach. This means holding sufficient unrestricted reserves to ensure sustainability whilst at the same time maximising the impact of the funds given to the charity to fulfil its charitable objectives.

The specific nature of the Charity's income should also have a bearing on the level of reserves to keep. If you have a range of large multi-year grants with reasonable contributions to core costs or you have significant social enterprise activities (eg retail operations) which deliver good steady unrestricted income, then you are likely to need less unrestricted reserves than if you are dependent on a narrower or less secure range of income streams.

From a personal perspective I like to have a lot more than three months unrestricted reserves as it provides greater resilience, ability to plan and to take opportunities as they arise. It also makes it easier to do the right thing for the long term as well as to make the Charity more attractive to high quality talent and partners.

When it comes to the people, there are clearly a number of issues apart from Claudia and Bert's style and the way they conducted themselves at the last Board meeting. These include whether Pov- ToGlow has the right Board and Executive (Exec) team to meet its purpose, whether they are working together in the right way and whether they are strategic enough. It doesn't feel like either group are at the optimum point on the alignment spectrums on pages 13 and 14.

There are clearly talented and committed people around the Board table and they may be a more diverse group than they were. However, the corollary to diversity is that you have people with different views and so you need to have an effective way of reaching agreement which balances different appetites to risk and styles of interaction. There are obvious cultural differences in the PovToGlow Board and Sam will no doubt be thinking about how she retains the value of the creative tension that this brings in a way that delivers a positive Board team dynamic. Given her experience she will be very alive to the distinction between the power of diversity of thought and the dangers of increasingly divergent and strongly held thoughts.

Sam may also be thinking about the impact of this on Daisy and Josie and also whether Daisy, in particular, should be more involved than seems apparent in driving the direction. Having decided to calm things down in the meeting, help Daisy keep her powder dry and not get involved in what was an emotive discussion, Sam was determined to ensure that Daisy would play a key role in resolving the conflict with Josie's support.

There may also be a thought in Sam's mind as to how did she allow it to get to this point and for the issue to erupt in a Board meeting. At the same time, she may see this as an opportunity, having got everything out in the open for her to show leadership and to bring the Board together around a clear goal for the next phase of development.

When it comes to process, the key point here is to ask what the right process should be to review the purpose of PovToGlow and then as a consequence for developing and agreeing its strategy for the next phase of development. Given the likely division around the Board table on agreeing this Sam may feel it helpful to have some independent support. Alternatively, she may feel she is able to do this herself and in doing so she may be able to make a significant contribution to the Charity. Many Chairs of charities feel that it is they who are the guardian of the founder's wishes and the driver of the *"objectives of the charity"*.

On this latter point if she hasn't looked at the *"governing document"* since joining it is well worth Sam reminding herself, and then the Board, as to what the Charity's charitable objectives are. These describe and set out what the purpose of the Charity is but provide flexibility in that they don't say what you do day to day. Most charity lawyers will advise you to draw these up fairly widely but it may well be in PovToGlow's case that Benny might have specified the geographic area in which PovToGlow would work. *"Objectives"* can be changed if there is the power of amendment in the governing document or with the approval of the relevant charity regulator, eg the Charity Commission in the UK.

The next process point may be to do with what has been noted above in terms of the way in which the Audit (and Risk) Committee operates and interacts with the Board. Ideally the debate over risk appetite shouldn't flare up as a consequence of two directors having what appear to be diametrically opposed views. It should really arise as a result of detailed consideration by the Audit and Risk Committee with the FD and management and a proper paper being put to the Board for information, discussion and then decision.

Trustees would reasonably expect such a paper to include a detailed financial analysis of the consequences of such a policy change including forecasts of the impact on the Charity's income, cash flow and balance sheet statements as well as any impact to its investment policy. For example, does its risk appetite for investment of endowed or other funds need to change as a result of a less conservative approach to the level of unrestricted funds to be held? In addition, does the ability to access such funds need to change for contingency purposes?

How to decide?

In a situation like this, with strong and able personalities, the natural way to reach a decision over a matter related to strategic direction is through a process led by Sam as Chair and Daisy as CEO which involves the entire Board and the Exec. The objective of such a process being to result in an aligned overall purpose and strategy which includes clarity over the degree of ambition and risk which is both acceptable to the Board and has the right Exec and other resources in place to deliver it.

There may be no immediate financial pressure to resolve this situation but given its potential to cause significant damage to relationships on the Board and its possible impact on the Exec, Sam and Daisy are likely to want to deal with this swiftly. They will want to get control of events and come up with a process to reconcile Claudia's ambition with Bert's prudence and take into account the view of other stakeholders, not least others on the Board and the Exec team as well as Tracy in her capacity as Patron.

The classic three-step approach an experienced chair would take in such a situation to achieve this would be firstly to gain people's immediate reflections on the situation, secondly, together with the CEO, to come up with a recommended process for approval by the Board as a whole and then finally to execute that process. It is probable that as part of that process there would be a Board awayday preceded by a significant amount of pre work to explore options and to assess the consequences of each option. It might also be a consequence of doing all of this that the Board decides that additional Board or management expertise might be needed to execute its preferred choice.

What to decide?

In this case the "*do nothing*" option seems irresponsible and is likely to lead to indecision, frustration and greater conflict. For Daisy and Sam to pick one side or the other without further discussion amongst the Board or the Exec also seems unlikely to result in the best result for PovToGlow. Even if they did that and were fortunate in making the right strategic choice, implementing it may be challenging given the divergent views.

So in this situation the Chair and CEO should grasp the nettle, resolve the conflict and more importantly help the Board to determine or recommit to the purpose and strategy for the organisation. Deciding what the reserves policy should be will then naturally fall out of those decisions.

How to communicate it?

Both Sam and Daisy will need to strike the right balance in their communication with the Board and Exec. They will need an assertive but deft touch to ensure that it is the Chair and CEO leading the process but that people feel that they are appropriately involved and that their views are heard.

Sam will also need to give constructive feedback to both Claudia and Bert about their interactions at the Board. It will be easy to thank them both for bringing something which was probably simmering beneath the surface to the forefront. Easy also to make them aware of the impact of the way that they made their points on others. Assuming that she is highly regarded by Bert and Claudia then this ought to be fairly straightforward for an experienced operator like Sam.

One thing both Sam and Claudia will need to ensure is that any talk of a "*Boardroom bust up*" is avoided.

What did Sam do?

Sam found Julia's questions and the reflections she had on her answers very helpful and combined with a conversation with Daisy the following morning she quickly resolved what to do. Daisy had been a lot more positive than she might have expected her to be. An indication of this was Daisy saying that "*It's really helpful to get all this out Sam. It's absolutely the right debate for us to be having. Maybe not quite in that way but I'm sure that we can sort it out. Bert and Claudia may have been at either end of the spectrum but I feel that most of the rest of us are somewhere in between. We think we could be more ambitious but we don't want to overreach ourselves."*

Daisy had another suggestion and that was to use a consultant who she had used in her last Charity who helped her develop a new strategy. *"Ian was terrific with both Board and Exec and although it was clear that the Chair and I were driving the process he fulfilled a very useful function in gathering views providing a good independent balance of those views and facilitating an awayday which allowed the Chair and I to play a full role as participants rather than facilitators."*

As Chair, Sam really liked this idea and liked even more the fact that Daisy was stepping up so assertively. Together they agreed that Sam would gather in the initial thoughts of the Board on the situation and Daisy would do likewise with her Exec. Then both would say after having gathered initial feedback that Daisy in consultation with Sam would prepare a paper for the next Board on a way forward to resolve the debate over PovToGlow's ambition and appetite for risk. Sam also set up a meeting with Ian to assess whether he was right person to help if the Board decided to go down this route.

Sam had coffees with both Bert and Claudia early the next week and also called the other Trustees to gain their reflections on the Board meeting. Bert was a little sheepish to begin with. He apologised for overreacting before Sam was able to give him that feedback but was still clearly very agitated by Claudia's *"Complete and utter lack of respect for what Benny had in mind when he founded PovToGlow. There's no way he would have wanted it to be a national Charity. He lived and worked around here all his life. If we became national who knows someone might decide not to continue providing support round here. They might argue perfectly legitimately the need is greater somewhere else."*

He also found Claudia's lack of caution regarding reserves deeply troublesome. *"I've seen this before Sam. There's a big difference between these City types who manage vast amounts of other people's money through computer screens and those of us that are responsible for making sure everyone gets paid every week. I know she came from a poor background and I really respect how well she has done. She is astonishingly clever and she has been a huge asset for us, no denying, but she does seem to have long forgotten where she came from and to be getting a bit carried away with herself. Must be hard to keep your feet on the ground as a WAG."*

Claudia, realised that she had been a bit high-handed with Bert but her competitive instincts combined with her ambition took over when she met Sam for coffee and she was far less contrite than Bert as illustrated by her welcoming remarks. *"I am so glad that we could have this coffee Sam. It was really kind of you to come down and see me and I'm so sorry that we only have half an hour now. I'm guessing that the little tiff that Bert and I had last week was the last thing you needed. I know I could have put it a lot better and I am so sorry for that but really what a dinosaur. Still I'm sure with your help he'll come round to our way of thinking. I know he retires soon but he is obviously very close to Tracy and as I see myself as your natural successor one day, I wouldn't like him to poison the well for us. To be honest I also wondered why Daisy went missing in action and assumed you had some reason not to slap him down. Seemed to me you both should have stood up for me and been a bit more assertive with him. I'm sure that you will have a good reason to keep your powder dry but it did make me wonder whether we have the right CEO to grow as quickly as we need to but that's a longer conversation."*

Sam discovered new Bert-like feelings for Claudia that she hadn't anticipated. *"******g cheek"* she said to her friend Julia that evening, adding *"but it did make things a little easier to decide"*.

She also had a very illuminating chat with Josie who had been silent on the topic of reserves at the Board. Sam was torn over Josie feeling deep respect but also that she may not be the right CFO for the future. Josie told her that although it was true that Claudia had generated significant income from her dinners, the costs in holding them meant that the profit on each one was a little variable and some of them had actually lost money. On the train home to Lincolnshire Sam reflected that the issue of reserves policy wasn't a major feature of most of her follow up conversations. *"Mustn't lose sight of it but it is far from the major thing I have to deal with."* she mused.

When Daisy and Sam met the following week they quickly agreed as CEO and Chair that Daisy's proposal was the right way forward and they issued a joint email to the Board and Exec setting out what they proposed to do. They agreed that de-personalising it was important and in their communication thanked both Bert and Claudia *"for their contribution to helping us to have this discussion now"*.

Her meeting with Ian went well and he was all Daisy had described:

smart, measured and skilful. A date was set for the awayday in eight weeks and in the intervening period the Exec consulted widely and came up with three core options for the Board to discuss. Ian was also able to persuade one of the UK's leading authorities on poverty to come and start the day with a tour of the "*Poverty Landscape*", how it was likely to develop, who were the major players in the space and where the gaps were.

The three core options were the classic ones of: "*Carry on with our current focus and approach*", "*Deliver a step change in impact*" and "*Expansive growth*". The implications for each in terms of investment, the risks involved and the likely impact and other consequences were presented with great clarity and all Trustees and Execs, as well as key stakeholders, had the opportunity to input into the process.

During the preparatory work it had become clear that PovToGlow would need to at least treble its income in three years to have a similar level of activity in the nearest two towns. They also realised in looking at similar charities elsewhere in the country that their model was indeed amongst the best and that there might be a way for others to adopt it without PovToGlow incurring the costs of setting it up or running it. Josie's suggestion of setting up an advisory service to help people set up and run the PovToGlow model might be a low-risk way of achieving national impact as well as generating unrestricted income for Pov- ToGlow to deploy locally.

They also discovered during the process of establishing what further room there was to increase impact locally that there was more than they had at first thought: firstly as a result of a significant influx of disadvantaged families who had been moved from London boroughs to new local, less expensive social housing and secondly because of the growing increase in the number of elderly people in poverty a group that PovToGlow had not previously focused on.

Although Bert was right to be cautious over the vulnerability of existing income it turned out that he was a little too pessimistic in this. Ian facilitated the awayday with an assured and deft touch enabling everyone to have their day and reach consensus. The moment Claudia had realised that the national option wasn't really a runner she became less interested. Six months later she announced her retirement from the PovToGlow Board on becoming Chair of a new international Charity funded by a billionaire and focused on women's empowerment.

On reserves, ironically the decision was that they were indeed a little conservative. In reality PovToGlow had almost two years unrestricted reserves available in accessible liquid assets. This was due to Josie, with Bert's agreement, classifying all income yield on properties as restricted for maintaining the value of assets. The Board agreed to move to an 18-month policy in order to strike the balance between being prudent in line with the Founder's wishes and maximising impact.

The other thing that Sam had decided to do shortly after the awayday was to strengthen the Board and, in particular, to start by recruiting two new Trustees: the first as the eventual successor to Bert and the other someone with extensive experience of developing social enterprise income through advisory services.

Things have worked out well for PovToGlow it has grown its impact consistently year-on-year and interestingly Claudia still refers to it, when giving speeches, as a Charity in which she helped to transform ambition!

Dilemma 7:

Money, money, money

This is a series of six dilemmas to do with remuneration.

Money 1

You are a Non-executive Director (Non-exec) of a small quoted company capitalised at around £250 million. There is a well-con- structed Board comprising a part-time Chair, a Chief Executive Officer (CEO), three other Executive Directors (Execs) and two other Non- execs.

The company has a discretionary bonus scheme. The Chair recom- mends awards to the Remuneration Committee. The Committee is made up of the Non-execs and the Human Resources (HR) Director. Although not a formal member of the Committee, the CEO attends every meeting to provide guidance. He is, however, always absent from the meeting where his own salary is discussed.

A takeover bid is in the wind and the Execs want their bonuses guaranteed at the capped maximum for the year ahead. They also want to avoid having to make an announcement about this to the Stock Exchange when the bid is announced. The Directors therefore want a non-formal but effectively binding understanding from you as Chair of the Remuneration Committee.

What should the Remuneration Committee do? What are the issues?

Why is there a possible takeover? Has the company underperformed? Who are the likely acquirers? It sounds as though they think the acquirer will remove them. What leads them to think this, or that their bonuses wouldn't be paid by the acquirer if they stayed?

What is the remuneration history? Have the Directors been paid appro- priately in the past? Have they been reasonable in their demands or permanently trying to get more? Are they proposing for the bonus to be pro-rated so that if the bid arrives halfway through the year, they will receive half of it?

Does the performance of the company to date suggest that they would be likely to receive the maximum? This might be hard to assess if the year has just commenced.

What is the scale of the bonuses under discussion? Do they relate to a longer-term performance scheme or solely to the year under discussion? Does the level matter? Is it the principle that is at stake?

How will the Execs react if the proposal is rejected? Some may consider their relationship with the management an issue. Clearly, accepting their proposal will be more likely to strengthen it than not.

Others will feel this has nothing to do with it; for them it is a simple matter of corporate governance.

There is an issue of process as well. The Non-exec shouldn't give a view either way or make any promises without discussing the matter with the Remuneration Committee. To do so will undermine its authority. It is not a good idea for the CEO to be attending all the Remuneration Committee meetings and this may be the ideal opportunity to set some new ground rules.

What do they mean by 'non-formal but effectively binding'? A side letter or verbal promise? How enforceable are either?

How to decide?

There are probably two key drivers of the decision here: first, the performance of the business and the reasons for a possible bid; secondly, whether or not you think it is morally acceptable to guarantee a bonus, given that it appears to have been intended to be linked to performance. You may also feel that such an undisclosed arrangement is not appropriate for a public company. Some might try to compromise and avoid a fight by linking the bonus to the price at which the business gets taken over, ie linking it to shareholder value. This is generally only relevant where there is a clear objective to sell.

You will also need to consider how the other members of the Remuneration Committee will react. You'll face another dilemma if you disagree, but they are more relaxed.

Most decent Chairs would reach for their lawyer in these circumstances.

Even if you know what is right commercially, the manner in which the process is conducted is crucial to a successful outcome.

What to decide?

The first decision is whether you feel the issue should be put to the Remuneration Committee. Even if they personally felt it was totally unacceptable, most Non-execs would probably decide to do this. Why? Because it makes the decision non-personal and because this is exactly the sort of issue the Remuneration Committee should be discussing. If no scheduled meeting was due to take place in the near future, a special meeting should be convened.

You then need to decide how the issue is framed for the Remuneration Committee. The most straightforward way is to ask the CEO to write a proposal stating the reasons why the Remuneration Committee should give their consent. You should make it clear that the issues are fairly straightforward and won't require a presentation or the attendance of the CEO at the meeting.

How to communicate it?

In terms of the tone of your response, a lot will depend here on the history of your relationship with the others and the performance of the business. You may or may not want to disclose your own view initially. So perhaps, '*Let's discuss it at the Remuneration Committee*' should be the response to the Execs.

The next piece of communication relates to how you introduce the issue to the Remuneration Committee. Do you normally leave your view on a matter unclear until it has been debated, or do you state your position, overtly or otherwise, in your introduction?

If the decision is to support the Exec's proposals, then the communication of it sounds easy. However, they will need to prepare for media or analysts' questions when it becomes clear.

If the decision is not to support the Exec, then the important thing is to communicate it decisively and not get into another debate.

What did the Chair of the Remuneration Committee do?

The situation was that the Execs were all reasonably new to the business. The CEO had been brought in two years ago to turn the company around. At that time, the business was capitalised at only £120 million, under half the current market capitalisation. He was paid a relatively low salary of £200,000, but stood to make approximately £3 million from his options at a pre-bid price. The view of the board was that the turnaround had been highly effective and the company was now poised for major growth, something that was not fully reflected in the share price.

The Chair's view was that the Execs had done a tremendous job and should be rewarded handsomely for their efforts. However, he felt that the way to do this was through the options that they had. He felt the guaranteed bonus was unacceptable.

He recommended that the proposal be put to the Remuneration Committee with a paper from the CEO. He suggested that as the issues were straightforward, there was no need for a presentation from the CEO. The Remuneration Committee declined the proposal. He then asked that the Execs' salaries be reviewed by the company's remuneration advisers to ensure they were at the appropriate level.

How did the CEO feel about it? It wasn't actually too difficult to deal with. He was given a *"That's life, Jim"* message. His reaction was basically, *"Ah well, it was worth a try."*

The remuneration consultants recommended a modest increase in base salaries.

Money 2

Zippo is a £400 million capitalised company listed on the London Stock Exchange. Due to a fall in the share price, 50 per cent of executive share options are hopelessly under water. The share price would have to double before they became worth anything. A new Director is about to be appointed with two times his salary in options at today's depressed striking price.

Existing Directors are delighted for their new colleague. However, they feel passionately that the option scheme needs reviewing. They have a proposal that they would like approved by the Board immediately so that it is in place before the new Director starts.

The proposal is that the current Directors sacrifice their existing options, which would be cancelled, and receive a new allocation on the same terms as the new Board member.

How should the Remuneration Committee, of which you are Chair, respond? What are the issues?

Why has the share price performed so badly? Is it management, sector blight, stock market fluctuations, or something else? How has it performed relative to that of other companies in the sector? Whatever the reason, if the options were intended to tie in management, they won't now. This may be fine if you don't rate them, but what if you do and they have performed relatively well? If you want to keep them, how mobile are they? What will they do if you don't give in? Would they leave? How demotivated will they really be? If you give in to them, what will they ask for next?

The option scheme is part of the overall remuneration for Directors, so the issue needs to be considered in that context. What is the overall remuneration scheme like? Are there any targets to be met before the options become exercisable? It is unlikely that if there are these will have been met, as most schemes with targets involve relative or absolute share performance. What about the rest of the employees? If there are other employee share schemes, are these working or do they need considering as well?

If you choose to agree with the Execs, could you do what they want, legally? What shareholder approvals would be required and how are shareholders likely to react to such a proposal? Is this an issue that is likely to be picked up by the press? If so, should this have any bearings on the deliberations of the Board? What knock-on consequences are there?

How will the relationship between the existing Directors and their new colleague be affected by the decision you take? If you agree and the shares continue to underperform and someone else joins, will he expect the same opportunity to renegotiate his options?

Fundamentally, you have to decide two things: first, is this something you wish to put to the Remuneration Committee or reject out of hand?; secondly, if you do decide to put it to the Remuneration Committee, you need to consider your own views on the matter as well as how to manage the discussion properly. There may also be a personal issue if you have equity or options.

The issue over how quickly something needs doing also needs resolving. If you support the Directors' proposal, does it really need doing straightaway?

How and what to decide?

Putting it to the Remuneration Committee, or not, is the first decision to take. As with the 'Money 1' case, even if you are strongly opposed to the proposal yourself, you may feel that if the Execs are serious then the Committee ought to consider it. Some might offer to sound out the other members of management so that they know whether it is worth doing the work to put up a properly prepared paper.

If the Remuneration Committee does consider management's pro- posal seriously, what should it take into account? Most of the issues above will need to be thought through. The members should also be clear about their purpose as a Remuneration Committee and seek to balance the potentially conflicting interests of motivating management and protecting shareholder value.

When it comes to what to decide, the alternatives appear straightforward. You could reject the idea out of hand and refuse to allow it to be discussed at the Remuneration Committee. Another suggestion might be to tell the Exec that while you don't agree with their proposal, you would be happy to discuss it at the Remuneration Committee.

Perhaps you could give a non-committal response and tell them that you will discuss it at the Remuneration Committee if the Execs could prepare a detailed paper arguing the case for and against their proposal. Some might indicate their support for the proposal, but tell them that the performance targets will need renegotiating alongside.

You might tell them that while personally you think it is a great idea, you are not sure whether the rest of the Remuneration Committee will think likewise. You could helpfully suggest that you would be delighted to sound them out and see whether it is worthwhile pursuing.

Finally, you could make their day by telling them that you think the proposal is a wonderful idea and that you will have no problems getting it through the Committee.

Before taking any of these alternatives, you may want to consider talking to the company's advisers to see how other companies have dealt with this issue. Your lawyers or remuneration advisers will no doubt know. This is not an uncommon issue, particularly for smaller UK quoted companies. Of course, the remuneration consultants may see this as another opportunity to introduce a new scheme and earn some more fees.

How to communicate it?

This is one of those subjects where people tend to have strong convictions either way. It is also a highly emotive issue for the management. So, if the decision is taken to reject management's proposal, it is the Exec who will need communicating with carefully. Even if you feel very strongly that the proposal is outrageous and that they need a very clear message to that effect, you will not want to alienate them.

If you feel supportive of their proposal, then the communications with management are obviously easier, but the issue then is how to communicate with shareholders and the press. On the face of it, this looks like a tricky job. The upside for shareholders, other than having a happier management team, is hard to see. The process for gaining shareholder approval needs considering carefully. Is this a company that is watched or has a history of press comment over remuneration?

How should the Remuneration Committee respond?

This is very similar to the previous dilemma. While you may have sympathy with them, the principle of cancelling options and issuing new ones when the price goes down is something most of us feel uncomfortable with. The Company's other shareholders don't have the option to go back and pay a lower price. The Directors are hardly likely to come to the Remuneration Committee and offer to pay a higher price if history suggests their options were cheap.

Many businesses fall into the trap of releasing all of the options available for granting as soon as they possibly can. It is much better, unless someone new is being appointed, to drip them out over time. In this way the pricing tends to be fairer and the above situation is less likely to arise.

This may be a good opportunity to carry out a company-wide remuneration review, in terms of both the structure of the schemes and their levels.

What did the Remuneration Committee do?

The background to this situation was that although they had worked hard and profits relative to their UK competition were good, on an international basis they were below average. Overall remuneration for the Directors was comparatively good, both domestically and interna- tionally. The Chair of the Remuneration Committee personally thought that the proposal that the Directors had made was outrageous and felt they needed to know this. However, he did not want to ruin his relationship with them, so they were given no indication of his own position at the outset. It was agreed with them that this was a very important matter for the Remuneration Committee and that it should be reviewed immediately. He had decided that the distractive potential of this issue was quite considerable, so the sooner it was resolved the better. The CEO was asked to prepare a paper for the meeting. The company's remuneration consultants were also asked to prepare a short paper on the proposal.

The Remuneration Committee met a week later and unanimously decided to reject the proposal. They did so on the basis that it was not in the interests of shareholders. The CEO decided to force things and made it a resigning issue. This was despite advice from the Chair that he shouldn't. He told the Chair that all of the Execs would resign if the Non-execs didn't agree with their proposal. The Non-execs called their bluff. They didn't resign. The new Director joined and was made aware of the issue. Twelve months later, the CEO, who had unfortunately let the issue affect his performance, was fired and the new Exec took over.

Money 3

Hipco is a small, progressive two-year-old technology business. It designs websites and web community platforms for major corporates. Hipco has a tremendous reputation but due to the rapid increase in staff required to match the growth in contracts, it is still loss-making and consuming cash. All staff are paid partly in cash and partly in shares.

In order to build a stronger Board in readiness for a potential flotation in two years' time, Hipco has been searching for an independent Chair, a new chief operations officer (COO) and an independent director. Luckily, they have found what appears to be a Chair with the perfect profile, Al Dink. Al has started up a company, grown it successfully and then sold it for $100 million. He has a lot of experience in the United States (US) and in fundraising. Securing an equity stake in Hipco is the way he wants to be motivated.

Initial discussions with the proposed new Chair have gone well, that is until this morning when Al shocked Hipco's Managing Director, Simon Hip, by saying:

> *"Well, Simon, you have a fantastic opportunity and I'd be delighted to be a part of it. The only issue now is how much equity I'll be getting for lending my name and giving my time."*
>
> *"Great news," said Simon. "How much would you like to buy?"*
>
> *"Buy, buy? I assume you're joking, Simon. I'll be adding at least a $million of value to your company. I'm not buying anything. What I have in mind is you issuing me options which, if the float happens in two years' time at the values we talked about, will realise $5 million for me post-tax."*

How should Simon respond? What are the issues?

Here are two big issues raised by this situation. Is the Chair the right person for the job and, if he is, how should he be rewarded?

Al's manner appears somewhat high-handed and arrogant. Simon needs to consider carefully the characteristics he is looking for and match against them. For example, while Al has had one very big success, which he can fairly be proud of, he hasn't got public company experience. This could be very useful given Hipco's plans for a listing. More importantly, Simon needs to feel he can trust and relate well to the Chair and that there is a feeling of mutual respect.

One thing that isn't clear from the description of the situation is, who is helping Simon find candidates? Is he using a search firm, a potential venture capital investor, or someone else? If he is, then it would be normal for the basis on which the Chair is to be appointed and the rewards on offer to be discussed before the search gets under way. Outline terms, particularly whether there was equity on offer or not, would also be made clear to candidates when they are approached.

Assume for the moment that Al is the right candidate. Is what he has proposed fair? There is no doubt that the right Chair could add enormous value to the business. But $5 million? Well, in a business that is poised for explosive growth, yes, potentially they might. Coaching Simon through the challenges of growth, helping to organise funding and helping with making the right senior appointments could be well worth it. However, should Al buy his shares or get options? My experience is that views differ markedly on this. In the US, a 'name', usually someone who has led a successful NASDAQ issue, could easily command such a sum and options would be typical. Yet successful though he is, Al doesn't have this market profile. In the UK, it would be more normal for the shares to be purchased.

There is an assumption that equity will align interests between Simon, the rest of the staff and the new joiners. It is obviously more likely to than not. However, to make the assumption that it automatically does would be wrong. One common problem for young high-technology companies is that equity gets spread around too quickly and not always to the appropriate people. Problems then emerge when new equity needs to be issued or Board changes are required. Early on, when the value of equity is low, the cost of dilution is deemed to be negligible. Later on, the real cost becomes apparent.

Management by committee can take over. This may already be an issue for Simon. He will need the support of other shareholders. If Hipco is also about to enter successive rounds of fund-raising, the dilution for the new Chair and new investors will inevitably reduce Simon's stake. Fundamentally, he has to decide whether a smaller piece of a much bigger pie is what he really wants.

Another issue is to do with what happens if Al doesn't work out and he proves to be an inappropriate choice of Chair. How is his equity dealt with? If he has options, will they automatically lapse on cessation of his appointment as Chair? Perhaps there should be a probation period before the equity is purchased or options granted.

At the end of the day, these things are always open to negotiation, so Simon has to decide how much of a difference a new Chair could make and how much he wants to reward him for that difference.

Al has to decide how big an opportunity this is and how much he wants rewarding for what he will do for Hipco.

How to decide?

The first decision really relates to whether the potential Chair is the right candidate. Then, and only then, is it worth considering whether the terms are reasonable or worth paying.

It sounds as though Simon may need some professional advice from an investor or search consultant, or both. We don't know whether Hipco will be self-funding until float or whether it will need additional capital. Perhaps raising external funding now will give the company the opportunity for more choice of Chair and then the venture capitalists can negotiate with the potential Chair. It is always better to pick from a choice of more than one.

If Simon and the team do decide that they think Al is the right Chair, then rigorous referencing will be vital. It may be that this is the going rate for this Chair and it really isn't negotiable. It does seem to signify an inflexible approach, though, so this aspect of his character in particular should be researched.

What to decide?

There are a number of obvious alternatives:

- Simon may think Al is the right person for the job, but try to negotiate the cost down.
- He could simply tell Al that he is one of a number of suitable candidates but that he is too expensive, and see what happens.
- Simon may decide that he can't work with someone so apparently inflexible and just end the discussion amicably.
- He could use the excuse of having other shareholders' views to take into account before making a decision, to buy himself some time.
- Rolling over and saying yes is an alternative, one that sets the tone of the relationship and may not engender respect from his new Chair. It's also one that may turn out to be at a significantly higher cost than other alternatives.

What did Simon do?

One of Simon's mentors was a friend who owned a company that was moderately successful without having an independent Chair. He told Simon not to bother getting a Chair now and certainly not at the price suggested. Simon put off the decision until Al got fed up waiting and got himself busy elsewhere.

Six months later, funding became very tight. Hipco was over-trading in almost all respects. Simon was finding that his life was a logistical nightmare. However, the future potential of the business looked better than ever. Deciding to combine raising money with recruiting a new Chair, Simon approached a leading venture capitalist in his area and asked it for help. It introduced him to six potential Chairs, all of whom could have done the job. Simon picked the one he felt he could get on with best. The new Chair then focused on the fund-raising exercise, leaving Simon to focus on building the business.

Simon had told the new Chair the first time they met about his earlier experience with Al and how it had unsettled him. "Tell you what," the new Chair said, "let's not rush the equity. Why not work together on the fund-raising for three months; that should give you a good idea of what I might be able to do to help you succeed." Somewhat ironically, he ended up with a stake that was worth considerably in excess of $3 million when Hipco floated and was subsequently taken over.

Money 4

MAVCO's US business has been having a difficult time and is losing money. However, the recently installed US CEO, Chuck Wabb, appears to be doing all that's possible to turn it around. After many years' frustration and three changes of US CEO, there finally appears to be some light at the end of the tunnel. Chuck looks as if he might turn out to be a hero. He is, however, paid handsomely for his efforts. Indeed, he gets paid significantly more than the highest-paid European Director, yet runs a business only two-thirds the size of the German subsidiary.

This morning he has come to you, the English Group CEO, and said he wants a significant salary rise. In his usual friendly but slightly menacing way, he has told you that if he doesn't get what he wants he will leave.

Chuck took a long time to find and you think he has high potential, even to the extent that he could be a candidate for your job when you retire in three years' time. However, there is already friction in the ranks of the Divisional Managing Directors and you are fearful of their reaction if Chuck is given a big increase.

PS. One small detail that hasn't escaped your attention is that Chuck's proposals implies he would be earning more than you.

How should this situation be resolved? What are the issues?

Chuck's ability, potential and style are obviously issues. How good is he really? How sustainable is his turnaround? Is he capable of growing the business once it is restored to health, or are his skills restricted to sorting things out? Is he claiming all the glory? What about the contribution made by the rest of his team; are they by implication to be rewarded better as well? How effective would he be in the role of Group CEO? Does he command the respect of the other Divisional CEOs, even though they resent his salary? How loyal is he? Is he winding up the others deliberately? How serious is his threat? What's your fall-back position? Who else have you got to run the US business if he leaves? If you give in to Chuck, how soon will he be back for more? Do you need to assert your authority with him? You may well end up setting a dangerous precedent if you don't.

The remuneration issues relate to Chuck and to the company as a whole. With regard to Chuck, was his salary benchmarked at the outset? Is it the market rate locally and within the industry? What is the real cost of switching? Apart from search fees, what would be the risk of losing the turnaround momentum and would you have to pay more to get someone then?

From a Group perspective, you don't want to demotivate the others, but they must accept that world pay is not homogeneous. On the other hand, if you give in to Chuck, what will be the effect on others? Is there a clear remuneration policy? Does the company have an effective Remuneration Committee? Is it getting the right level of professional advice? Is the US CEO's package a matter for the Remuneration Committee if he isn't on the main Board? Is the balance between base salary, performance bonuses, capital incentives and other benefits appropriate? Are incentives structured to match objectives? Are there issues elsewhere in the business and at other levels? What about the impact of your own package? How do you feel about him earning more than you? If you are opposed to the idea, is this on principle or is it just an objection to Chuck earning more than you?

A final issue you will have to deal with is how you might feel yourself. Only the seriously weird enjoy being blackmailed. Anger and determination not to give in to someone doing this to you may well consume you. You may need to remember John Kennedy's wise words, *"Don't get mad, get even"*. This is one of the reasons that in these situations it is often extremely useful to talk to someone else before you say anything to the Chuck in your life. Your Chair could be ideal; maybe it's another mentor or CEO friend. A little informed objectivity can go a long way

What options do you have?

The obvious options appear to be:

- Pay him more, but no-one else.
- Give all the Divisional CEOs a rise.
- Call Chuck's bluff.
- Duck the issue and say that it is a matter for the Remuneration Committee.

There are also variations on these core options, eg you could agree to pay Chuck or any of the others more, but raise the performance targets for them to achieve new levels of remuneration.

What to decide?

This sounds like a situation where you will need to think things through carefully before deciding. An immediate, inspirational response may work, but there is an element of risk in giving one, especially since you don't need to.

Possibly the worst think is to fudge the issue and try to give everyone a little more. The obvious danger in doing this is that it won't make any difference motivationally and will still undermine your authority.

Thinking about who you will consult will be important. Even if you have a very clear idea about what you will do, and your Chair may not want to be involved in the process, it would be wise to inform him of what has happened and how you plan to deal with it.

Fundamentally, you have to make a judgement about how good Chuck is, decide whether you want to keep him and then, if you do want to keep him, how to satisfy him without causing either significant disruption or cost.

How to communicate it?

In the "*Pay him more but no-one else*" option, the key communication is obviously with the other Divisional CEOs. You could try this:

> "*Yes, I know it's unfair, but he's paid the market rate. None of you wanted the job, you could have applied. The contribution he is making to the Group is beyond the simple matter of the scale of his business. If we can be seen to be successful in the US, especially after all the criticism we have had, then the impact on our share price could be tremendous. I can appreciate how you feel, but there it is.*"

Or the more conciliatory and defusing:

> "*I can appreciate how you feel and I'll conduct an independent review of your packages. I'm not promising to increase them, but if it helps you feel that you are being paid fairly, then it's well worth the cost. If it shows that you are underpaid in relation to your performance, then naturally we'll consider what we can do to rectify it.*"

For the "*Give all the Divisional CEOs a rise*" alternative, assuming it is sufficiently large and that others in the company will know, then the communication issue is with others. Apart from the staff, stock market analysts and the press may well take an interest in the subject when the next results come out.

If it's "*Call his bluff*" that you go for, then how you communicate with Chuck is clearly crucial. What do you say to minimise the risk of him leaving or causing disruption? A "*Tough luck, buster*" response has the benefit of clarity and ends the debate, but has an element of risk about it. "*We'll see what we can do at the next pay review*" potentially takes the heat out of the situation. However, if he doesn't believe anything will happen or the review is a long way off, he may see this as calling his bluff. A more effective route might be to say:

"Chuck, you look to be doing a great job and the business appears at long last to be coming round. But given our history, I'm sure you'll appreciate we don't want to assume too much too soon. If the turnaround is sustained, then it will be much easier to argue the case for a bigger package. As I've said before, you are one of the few who has the potential to run the whole Group and the rewards for that are clearly a lot greater than for running a subsidiary, particularly with the potential of our Asian businesses. I can appreciate how you feel, but it would be a shame to blow your chances by being a little impatient."

Although he still may see this as *"Tough luck, buster,"* it does have the benefit of being honest, dangling a bit of a carrot and reasserting
your authority.

What did the Group CEO do?

The background was that the US business had never been a success since it was acquired. It has been a career-killer for several high- potential managers. Finally, there was someone who looked as though he had sorted it out. Although the Group CEO felt he couldn't trust Chuck, and he certainly didn't like him, he was loath to jeopardise the US business. The business until this point had been unsellable and all of MAVCO's European competitors had lost money in the US. Maybe, just maybe, he thought, if they could get it into a healthy enough state then they could sell it. He didn't dare tell Chuck this for fear of him either leaving or driving the value down to buy it himself.

His solution to his dilemma was to agree that the compensation should be reviewed for all Divisional CEOs. The result of this review was a small increase across the Board and the suggestion of a new, industry-comparable long-term incentive plan for the US linked to the growth in value of the US business unit. This scheme provided the US manager with the opportunity to make several million dollars if he hit his aggressive targets. The bottom line was that if he got the value up to $100 million in three years, he received $3 million.

The solution worked for the most part. Chuck got the value of the US business to $50 million in three years and received $1 million when it was merged into another business that was acquired. This business had a much more appropriate CEO who became CEO of the combined US business. The part of the solution that didn't work out so well was that the company's German leader left in disgust and the German business has significantly underperformed ever since.

Money 5

From the City's point of view, the Group CEO of Temco has had a splendid second year. Profits are up 30 per cent and this is despite flat sales. Temco's market capitalisation has trebled to £200 million since he took over. The balance sheet is in much better shape. A difficult capital expenditure project has been completed on time and within budget. The expenditure will reduce operating costs significantly. It has also reduced employment in the company by 1,500 people. Significant progress has therefore been made on a number of fronts.

Temco's CEO, Jim Hind, is expecting a very big bonus as well as a major grant of options as a reward for his efforts and as an incentive to develop the business further. Wages elsewhere in the company have been constrained as part of cost-cutting and although Jim is a superb motivator, morale has still not completely recovered.

Jim joined on a relatively low salary of £200,000 a year. He did not get too many options and, being relatively young, he couldn't afford to buy many shares at the time of his appointment. So keen was Jim to get his first job as a plc CEO that he wasn't concerned about the short-term rewards. His current profit on options if he exercised all of them today would be £500,000 pre-tax, an amount he considers derisory when compared with his contribution to shareholder value. Jim has grown considerably in confidence and his expectations now are very high.

As well as being Chair of Temco, your friend is also Chair of Zyball, another public company. Unfortunately, Zyball has had a rough time with the City and with the press of late. The reason for this is a profits collapse occurring after what looked like a fairly glittering five years. This coincided with the pay-out of some large bonuses related to the previous five years' performance. To make matters worse, the CEO exercised and sold a major part of his options just before the last share-dealing window closed. There have been calls for your friend's resignation. He is furious and highly embarrassed about the Zyball situation. He has lost faith in Zyball's CEO, whom you had always considered a little bit of a wide boy. At last, he is about to follow your advice to fire him and recruit a new CEO.

Naturally, the situation at Zyball looms large in your friend's thoughts. Although he thinks Jim has done a fantastic job at Temco and feels sympathetic to the argument that he should receive a significant rise and bonus, he is very worried about the reaction from the press and the City.

What advice would you give to your friend? What are the issues?

Let's consider Jim first. It appears that he is clearly underpaid for what he has achieved. He is therefore quite reasonably expecting a significant increase in salary, a decent bonus and better capital incentives. This assumes, of course, that the results are valid, that the much-improved performance is sustainable and that Jim is the right man for the next phase of development. I wonder if we would have added the previous sentence if the Chair hadn't been involved with Zyball. If the Chair were to be more concerned about potential embarrassment than Jim, he might end up losing him. Jim is bound to be highly marketable. How easy would he be to replace? In fact, it probably wouldn't be that difficult to find a quality CEO for a company that had had most of its problems sorted out and the benefits of a big capital expenditure programme starting to come through. Yet the impact on morale within the company if a highly regarded leader leaves because he hasn't been fairly rewarded could be quite considerable.

There are likely to be other people at Temco who are underpaid. So, another issue may be the overall remuneration within the company. What would a full review show? How does Temco's pay compare with its industry and the local job market? If it was significantly under the industry norms, what impact would be normalising it have on profitability?

For the Chair there are a number of other issues. Should the situation at Zyball influence what happens at Temco? Will the analysts and press make the connection? What if they do; how are they likely to react? Can he ensure that Jim and his staff are rewarded fairly and avoid attack? He may also be asking himself, particularly if he was Chair at the time, why Jim got such a poor deal on joining. Moreover, why wasn't anything done about it last year? Additionally, the reason Jim has so few options is probably that his salary is so low. Most option schemes link the amount that can be vested to a multiple of salary.

What about his own remuneration at Temco? If he is relatively well paid compared with Jim, then the problem might be worse. If his remuneration is in line with Jim's, then there may be the opportunity to raise Jim's significantly and his own modestly. It is always easier to defend in these situations if you are below the market yourself.

There may be some additional process issues, eg does the company have a properly composed and functional Remuneration Committee? Is there an annual pay review approach in the company? Is this linked to the year's results and so on?

What to decide?

Assuming this is someone you know well, then you may have the opportunity to influence the outcome of events at Temco. There is a degree of risk in most of the alternative courses of action.

Your friend could decide that what happens at Temco has nothing to do with Zyball. Then he might endorse a significant improvement in Jim's package and take the risk that either the press and City won't notice, that they notice and feel it is perfectly in order, or that they notice, there's a bit of a fuss, but it quickly dies down. If this is the route he wants to take then he might, if he has time, use some intelligent public relations to ensure that the Temco record is well understood and applauded. The wrong judgement about this could result in exactly the sort of hostile reaction he fears.

In this scenario, he still has to decide what to do about Jim's salary, how significant he wants to make the uplift and how it should be structured. He could take the balanced approach and give Jim more of everything so that all aspects of his remuneration are fair and in line with the market. The benefit of this approach is that it avoids an issue later on. If he decides to avoid the "*more of everything*" scenario, then which aspects of Jim's package should he focus on – salary, benefits, performance bonuses or capital incentives such as options?

He may fear the embarrassment so much that he decides to play safe and only countenance a modest rise for Jim. The embarrassment of losing a highly respected CEO later might be greater, of course.

He could resign from Zyball or even completely withdraw and resign from both companies – not the way most directors would choose to end their careers.

How to communicate it?

The most important people to communicate with are Jim, the other Directors, Temco's staff, advisers, institutional shareholders, analysts and press followers. He will also need to be mindful of communicating carefully with the Board, advisers, the institutional shareholder and followers of Zyball.

Whatever option he picks, he will need to prepare a thorough communications plan to ensure he has addressed his key audiences with appropriate messages. Due to the pressures of such moments, this is sometimes not done and regretted later when one very important group has been overlooked.

If he goes down the "*tough it out*" route, building support in as many influential places as possible will be important. Brokers' reports or press comment that is highly favourable about the company won't stop the critics, but will alleviate the pressure.

In order to prepare for taking the above alternatives, he will need to be armed with the details, so a full salary review and benchmarking exercise seem inevitable.

If he decides not to give Jim a significant uplift, it sounds as though inspirational communication and motivational skills will be required. Jim may feel very angry and let down. He may lose confidence and trust in his Chair, and what sounds like a healthy Board could become disunited. Some Chairs in this position would find a way to get Jim to share the problem and for him to come up with the solution. Perhaps this approach could be taken:

"Jim, the Board is proposing to give you a significant increase but we are very concerned about the PR implications of doing so, particu- larly given the background at Zyball. We would welcome your input on how to handle it."

But is this approach acceptable and does it undermine the Chair?

What happened?

The Chair was a genuine person who had done his best to control a difficult CEO at Zyball. When he fired him, he then discovered all sorts of other issues and Zyball was quickly in the position of issuing profit warnings. While the situation was chaotic, he remained convinced Zyball was a good business with high potential and was determined to restore its reputation. However, his own position as Chair was seriously challenged in the press

– *"He has presided over one of the biggest messes of the year."* and so on. Consequently, his lack of confidence and his unwillingness to risk more damaging profiles were just too great.

When he talked the situation through with you, you asked:

"Have you thought of resigning?"

"I'm not going to walk away from a mess. I've got a responsibility to sort it out. I'd regret it forever if I didn't at least have a damn good try."

"I don't mean Zyball. I mean have you thought of resigning from Temco? John [the Senior Independent Director] is perfectly capable of taking over. You could say you were resigning so that you could

focus more on restoring the health of Zyball."

The Chair thought that this was an excellent idea and the next day met John to discuss it. John tried to discourage him, saying that resigning from Temco was unnecessary and that he was overreacting:

"You've got 30 years of good reputation behind you. This is the first blot on the copybook. Why don't you put it into perspective? Sure,

there will be a fuss. Just tough it out."

He was, however, determined and then went on to talk to Jim. Jim did not want to lose his Chair, even to the extent of saying that he would tone down his expectations for this year. The Chair was touched by Jim's loyalty but was still determined to resign. He told Jim that just because he was resigning, this didn't mean that he wasn't interested and he would still be available for advice.

He did resign from Temco and spent the next two years almost full time at Zyball. Zyball's fortunes were restored and, more than that, it became a leader in its market. It has recently been sold to a US company in the same sector.

Temco has also flourished and through some good acquisitions has built a commanding position in its industry. Jim's shares are currently worth around £10 million. His former Chair sleeps very well at night.

Money 6

As Jim Pickle gently put down the phone to his HR Director after saying, *"Thanks Pam, very helpful,"* a giant thought-bubble began forming in his head. *"Aargh. Why today of all days? I'd better phone the garage."*

Jim had led the buyout of PickCo from a UK plc two years ago. The deal was well timed and, as the company was in some distress, was also attractively priced. The company was bought on a multiple of six and a half times Earnings Before Interest and Tax (EBIT).

The private equity backers are delighted with performance (revenue is up £10 million at £100 million and EBIT is now £13 million compared with £6 million). Jim's strategy of new product development

more aggressive marketing and cutting costs – is really paying off. With 30 per cent of the equity, finally after years of hard work for measly bonuses, the management team believe that at last these efforts will make them rich.

The remuneration culture in the company before the buyout was very paternal, with salaries at average levels for the industry, bonuses on the low side, but an excellent range of benefits. There was a non-contributory pension scheme and somewhat better company cars than average for those eligible. Staff turnover was low (5 per cent per annum). In fact, Jim's £10,000 bonus for doubling profits the year before the buyout was one of the triggers for the buyout. He felt that he and team were not being fairly rewarded and that they never would be under corporate ownership.

All that has changed since the buyout; Jim introduced what he described to the staff and unions as "a new spicier and spikier bonus scheme". Average annual salary increases have been held at around 2 per cent for middle management and the rest of the staff. The pension scheme is now contributory and benefits have been trimmed.

Individual bonuses linked to performance can now be as much as 25 per cent of salary for middle management and staff in general, out of a total bonus pool of 10 per cent of the total salary bill if company performance objectives are met. The top team's bonus was spikier still, with most getting 100 per cent this year and Jim earning 200 per cent. This was a result of the bonus pool for them being 10 per cent of excess of EBIT over budget (uncapped). The share of the pool was based upon the size of their equity stake.

While the mood in the company has been very positive and Jim is held in high regard, there has been a growing feel of 'us and them'. Some of the benefits changes were not as well communicated as they might have been. A result, much to Jim's irritation, was that his new nickname is 'Spicy Pickle'. Although the unions have been very collaborative to date, they are not happy about some new working practices they've heard Jim wants to introduce. These are scheduled to come into effect just a few weeks before the busiest period of the year.

The call from Pam was to let him know that Fred and Sam (the two key union representatives) wanted to meet him urgently this morning to discuss these changes.

"I've got an uneasy feeling about this, Jim. They've nodded everything else through so far, but I think this is one they're really prepared to go to war on. The last thing we want is a strike. Remember

I mentioned the idea of getting SoftTouch to do some benchmarking for us? Well, I really think that we should do this and this might be a way of assuaging Fred and Sam today. While they are at it, they could benchmark the board's packages as well so that we can demonstrate that you're not out of line."

"Definitely need to ring the garage." thought Jim. Today was the day they were due to deliver his new Mercedes SL. When he ordered it, he was basking in a sea of congratulations and employee goodwill. He had always been frugal on cars, his current seven-year-old 'C class' needed replacing and he had enjoyed driving his friends on a recent holiday. He had absolutely no doubts that he deserved it but even before today was wondering how it would go down in the company.

Before he could dial the number, the phone rang again. This time it was John, the Marketing Director.

"Hi Jim, sorry to interrupt but I've had a journo on the phone from the Star [the local paper]. He's doing an article on local fat cats and would like to interview you. He knows we're not a public company but someone has told him that we've made people redundant, cut benefits and kept salary rises at a low level so that the Directors could improve profits and get big bonuses from the buyout. His angle is that fat cats aren't just in big companies; most MDs are greedy. I think you should see him today if possible and persuade him that the staff have done just as well as the top team."

"Thanks, John, why don't you pop over in an hour or so and we'll chat it through."

After quickly calling the garage and telling them to deliver the car to his home, Jim had a scheduled interview with Jane Canadup, a very promising candidate for the new FD position. The current FD, who was solid but not a sparkler, was struggling a little with growth and had agreed to retire as long as he had a decent pay-off.

The meeting with Jane went well. Jim felt she had just the right kind of approach. She was bright, disciplined, a good listener and challenged him very smoothly on the strategic soft spots. His only concern was how expensive she might be. She wanted 50 per cent more than the previous FD and also four times her salary in options.

He wasn't sure how the private equity backers would feel about that, even though they had introduced her into the process. They had been delighted with performance to date even if they had joked about how soft they'd been on performance objectives.

As he always did before he decided what to do on a big thing, Jim decided to ring his Chair, Mary, to get her views.

You are the Chair and remuneration has been on your mind for a couple of months now. To date, there hasn't been a formal Remuneration Committee. Essentially, Jim, the lead investor, and you have decided remuneration in consultation with the HR Director and then the Board have rubber-stamped your proposals.

How should you guide Jim? What are the issues?

The obvious issues are the unions' attitudes to new working practices, the fairness and effectiveness of the company's bonus systems, the press interest in the company, the terms for the exiting and new FDs and what Jim should do about his new car. However, the central issue is how the Board can regain control of the remuneration agenda and avoid being rushed into a series of sub-optimal decisions.

As Chair, you have to take responsibility for Board remuneration. It sounds as if Jim is highly capable, hasn't been that greedy and will listen to good advice. This is a nice position to be in. However, it does sound as if he is unsure as to what to do and potentially inexperienced or out of practice at dealing with conflict, so you need to support him.

The car is an easy issue and a bit of a red herring. He has done the right thing in sending it home and taking it off his agenda for today. Yet, will it be any less embarrassing to him next week? He shouldn't be embarrassed at having a nice car if that is what he wants, given his success. The wise thing, though, is to have a modest car to take to work and use the nicer one for pleasure. We don't know from what has been said whether he has done this.

The press love remuneration stories and have become ever more sophisticated on the subject, so it would be a big mistake to underestimate or ignore them. As Chair, you will want to know why the Marketing Director hasn't dealt with this issue. He could have. Involving Jim directly puts him in the difficult position of defending his pay. The success of the company and growth in employment is a nice line but it is unlikely to cut much mustard with a sceptical journalist. If the Marketing Director isn't up to it, then should Jim or you deal with it?

Does PickCo need a more formal approach to remuneration issues and should it now have a formal Remuneration Committee? It does sound as though it might be helpful to establish a clear remuneration strategy, deal with some of the anomalies that have built up and put more effort into remuneration communications. Yet the Board mustn't overcomplicate things either.

If they are going to form a Remuneration Committee, how should it be composed? We don't know for sure who is on the PickCo Board. It is probably quite small, comprising the Chair, Jim as CEO, the FD, the lead investor and possibly another Non-exec. Hence, a remuneration committee, if formed is likely to be made up of you, as Chair, the private equity backer and the other Non-exec if there is one. Jim and his HR Director will inevitably provide support. The result, therefore, is effectively the same people taking part but with more planning and formality. The committee may also decide it does need regular benchmarking data and the advice of a remuneration consultant.

SoftTouch may be the right people to help, despite their awful name, but a proper pitch should be conducted to choose the most appropriate firm.

With respect to the retiring FD, the issue is: what is a decent pay-off? A year's money would be fairly typical. Is it all right for him to keep his equity? If he has a modest percentage, there seems little harm. It saves the company or the other shareholders using cash to buy him out. As long as the Board are comfortable that he won't become disruptive later, it may be better to use PickCo's cash to grow the business. However, if the new FD wanted to buy equity or someone else wanted to increase their stake, it may change this view.

What about Jane's demands? The key judgement here is about how good she is. She may be able to add 50 per cent more value than the incumbent. What alternative candidates are there? It should be easy to benchmark her demands against the rewards given to similar people in similar roles. You may want to know why she isn't putting up any money for equity. It might be that she hasn't got capital but it may say something about her view of potential value growth.

With respect to the options, we need to know details of the current scheme. Is there room to grant such an amount? Is four-times too much as a one-off? Do they all need to be granted in one go or can you grant a smaller multiple and agree a further grant if first-year objectives are met? If the private equity backers have introduced Jane, then this is a signal that they think she is suitable, but not a guarantee. They should be able to give a good view of her suitability for the role.

We then come on to what might be the root causes of current discontent within the company: the fairness of rewards overall, the new working practice proposals and, in particular, the bonus scheme. Is it a communication issue or is there a fundamental problem with structure and content?

Bonus systems should be clearly linked to performance to be effective, with performance being measured against a relevant set of objectives. These objectives in turn need to be specific, measurable and attainable. It is normal for the ratios of salary to rise with grade and for there to be tension over these differentials. However, it sounds as if in this case the top team might be confusing what they should get as a result of being a shareholder and what they should receive for doing their jobs by linking bonuses to equity percentages. It sounds as though the bonus system needs a review.

Introducing new working practices just ahead of your busiest spell is tempting because presumably the benefits will be greater. However, in practice, they are often rushed as a result, create too much pressure and force people into stand-off situations.

A good remuneration calendar can help enormously. Ensuring that the timings of objective-setting, performance reviews and financial results are synchronized makes the whole remuneration game much easier to play. Part of HR Director's job is to put this in place. On the subject of the HR Director, how good is she? It sounds as though she is making sensible suggestions, but does she command sufficient respect at Board level to enable her expertise to be acted upon? Her judgement is important and it isn't clear whether Jim respects it.

Finally, no real mention was made of pensions. This may be because PickCo has a scheme that has no deficit and is viewed as good by the staff. But it is always worth checking.

How should you decide what to do?

In this case, you have a clear mandate and also some clear responsibilities. Your CEO is asking for guidance and you should give it. You need to help him deal with the short-term issues of the press and the union discussions and then take responsibility for the bigger issue of determining how in future remuneration issues are to be dealt with in PickCo.

An experienced Chair will need little help here and should be able to go through the issues one by one with Jim and provide some wise advice. He also needs to take a little pressure off Jim and so maybe he should deal with some of the issues himself.

What to do and how to communicate it?

The Chair went through the issues one by one. He endorsed Jim's decision to send his new car home. Jim was very nervous about talking to the journalist and even more nervous about his Marketing Director doing it. The marketing man was first class at marketing and dealing with the press on product issues and general promotion but remunera- tion was new and tough territory for him. The Chair offered to deal with the journalist. Jim was reluctant to 'whimp out'. Is it whimping out? Should the Chair insist?

His advice with regard to the exiting FD was straightforward and that was that a proposal ought to be made to the private equity backers. He should make it clear that the man had performed well to date and was therefore a 'good leaver' and that he was doing the company a favour by retiring early. A year's money, allowing him to keep his equity and car and agreeing to commute part of his payment into pension, seemed like a reasonable deal if he was prepared to help a new FD with the transition.

His advice with regard to Jane's terms was simple also, but he had a few questions to ask before giving it.

"How good do you think she is? How well do you think that you will work together? What's her market rate? What are the packages for other jobs that she could get? What else is she being offered at the moment?"

His view was that very good FDs are hard to find, very good FDs you think you'll be able to work with are in even shorter supply so they should pay up and get on with it if she met these requirements. However, he didn't like the idea of such a big option grant upfront so advised that Jim negotiate a gradual grant in line with achieving objectives.

What happened?

Jim followed the Chair's guidance and took up the offer of his direct involvement with the press. They recruited Jane but at a 40 per cent, rather than 50 per cent, higher salary than her predecessor's. She was granted options to the value of three times her salary, but an agreement was made to enable her to have an additional grant of once salary after a year as long as she achieved performance objectives.

A Remuneration Committee, with a few simple objectives, was formed and comprised the Chair, Jim, the lead private equity backer and a Non-exec. Remuneration consultants were appointed but not SoftTouch. They were initially taken on but made a bit of a mess of the benchmarking so after a proper pitch process another firm was appointed.

The implementation of new working practices was delayed. It turned out that the union leaders had some good points and, as a package, the series of changes would have led to a fall in productivity and signifi- cantly lower bonuses for the workforce. The original proposals were a collection of individual changes and hadn't been thought of compre- hensively. Jim had delegated this to his Operations Director, who was a little high-handed and hadn't thought through all of the implications beforehand. This easily resolved in practice as soon as Jim became more involved. Unfortunately, though, this undermined his Operations Director, who left shortly afterwards.

Pam, the HR Director, was tremendously good throughout all of this and gained influence. Finally, Jim sold his new Mercedes. He found that he just felt too uncomfortable driving it around.

Dilemma 8:

RemCoCoCo

Landing back into Heathrow on time from Chicago Sarah was in a buoyant mood. The board went really well, yesterday and chairing a US board is working out to be a lot more fun than she anticipated, albeit after a challenging start. Finally, she also has what she describes as her first BWF (Board Work Free) weekend for a long time. Her daughter Jessica is bringing her new boyfriend around for lunch on Sunday and her youngest son Henry is taking her to Wimbledon this afternoon to say thanks for helping him to get his First at Oxford. It's now five years since her other son Sam died and it's been far from easy but this last year has just started to feel a whole lot better.

While waiting at the baggage carousel she decided to check her messages and saw one from Jamie. She has always rated Jamie. He was by far and away the best divisional chief executive officer (CEO) when she was the Group CEO of Zakando plc. His naturally sunny disposition combined with his analytical prowess always stood out. On top of that she could never forget the incredible support he gave her when she lost Sam.

In preparation for his retirement next year Sarah had encouraged Jamie to take on a non-exec role. *"Don't wait until you retire to start looking."* she had said. *"It takes time to find one that is a good fit and the headhunters will always prefer serving CEOs."* Within months Jamie had secured his first non-exec role at Bamco PLC. The company was, as he described it, an almost perfect match.

"Refreshingly entrepreneurial. Given the pace of growth over the last five years and the listing two years ago, they could really benefit from my large corporate organisational and process skills. Looks like there is loads that I can add and at the same time I reckon that I will learn a lot from finally being on the top Board and from being in a much faster moving sector than ours."

Jamie was excited about the prospect of getting well established at Bamco before he retired and using it as a base to build a nice portfolio.

Normally calm and in control, Jamie's rather breathy voicemail surprised her. Sarah had never had a call like this from him before and he sounded genuinely worried.

"Hi Sarah, hope all's well and that you had a great trip to Chicago. Need to have an urgent coffee with you. Sunday morning if possible. I can come to you to make it easier for you. It's to do with Bamco plc. As you know I have just joined the Board and the Remuneration Committee ("RemCo"). Attended my first RemCo meeting today and was stunned by what I heard. Frankly just don't know what to do next. May even resign. Could really do with some of your wise counsel before Monday."

Sarah decides to give Jamie a call from the car on the way home hoping that she can avoid having to meet up tomorrow. As much as she admires Jamie and would love to help him she was really hoping for what she has called over the years an FFD ("Full Family Day").

She discovers quickly that Jamie is right to be anxious and that it is indeed a tricky situation. He joined the Bamco Board just two months ago and agreed to serve on the RemCo which is chaired by a long-standing friend of Hilary's who was a sales and marketing director for a previous business they both worked in. Friday's meeting was his first and, from the agenda and papers, he was expecting it to be fairly straightforward.

As Bamco's Founder and Chair, Hilary Bango still holds 60 per cent of the equity. Her remuneration is fairly modest as Chair, simply the going rate for a public company of Bamco's size. Given that, and the fact that there was a thorough review of remuneration including benchmarking last year, Jamie thought that it ought to be an uncontentious meeting. He was therefore somewhat stunned when Hilary started the meeting rather than the RemCo Chair, Jane, and made a proposal which wasn't in the papers.

Bamco, surpassed analysts' forecasts in its first year following Initial Public Offering (IPO) by 20 per cent. Yet sadly this year, due to regulatory changes and the impact of Brexit uncertainty on one of its main markets, it has underperformed by c10 per cent and the share price has taken a bit of a hammering, falling back pretty much to the IPO price. Last year in the warm glow of post-IPO out-performance, the shareholders had approved a 60 per cent rise in the CEO's pay as a result of a somewhat flaky peer group analysis, growth in the size of the company and the overperformance. The pay of the other Execs was also increased by 20 per cent to 40 per cent each.

A new long-term performance bonus share plan was also put in place which as a result of this year's performance won't be issuing any shares.

Bamco's CEO, Harry Bane, was brought in from outside as a safe pair of hands from a global corporate to succeed Hilary a year before IPO when she moved up to Chair. He is in awe of Hilary's entrepreneurial flair and after 25 years in a very conservatively run group has found his time at Bamco both exhilarating and scary in equal measure. He rarely looks forward to RemCos as Hilary insists he attends every one even though he is not a member.

The second highest paid at Bamco, Mark Bork has a combined Chief Financial Officer (CFO) and Chief Operating Office (COO) role. He is highly competent and viewed as a successor to Harry when he retires in two years' time. It has to be said though, that he hasn't been as comfortable in the plc environment as before and occasionally wonders whether being CEO of a plc is all it is cracked up to be. Mark's natural ability and the fact that he feels he is the anointed one can make him a little cocky and high-handed at times both inside and outside the company. The last analysts' conference call, for example, became a little tetchy when a junior analyst probed a little too deeply for Mark's liking and Harry had to more or less contradict him to get out of the hole he had dug for himself.

As a consequence one or two of the analysts and governance officers of the leading institutional shareholders have been suggesting to Hilary that Mark focuses on one role or the other and that Bamco appoints a Head of Investor Relations or a Communications Director or both. Jamie has been a bit disappointed with himself and with Hilary that this issue only recently became obvious. Although when he thinks back Hilary's remark that *"Mark is brilliant with the analysts, he wins every argument."* might have been some sort of signal.

Jamie's description of the meeting started with Hilary's introduction which in essence was that:

"As this is Jamie's first meeting we ought to make it clear how this committee works. It is a very important committee and that's why Jane Chairs it. Jane is very independently minded and understands that although, of course, we have to do the right thing by all shareholders, as majority shareholder nothing can be approved without my full endorsement. That in part is why I attend all RemCo meetings and start them off by letting you know what the parameters are for the debate. In this way we save a lot of

time and have a position we know will get approval from shareholders.

Now today we have a delicate matter to discuss and I thought I should set the scene before handing over to Jane to chair the formal meeting. For clarity Jamie, what I am about to say will be not be minuted as the official RemCo meeting hasn't started yet.

As you all know last year everyone, well apart from the regulator, but they're genetically modified to like nothing, was delighted with us and it seemed we could do no wrong. But this year there's a degree of grumpiness being shown by the institutional shareholders that we probably need to address. Most of this I think is simply down to the share price and some aspects of performance but some of the govern- ance officers have even been questioning last year's benchmarking exercise. At the same time, the plan that we put in for our Executives won't deliver anything for them this year and given our own forecasts it isn't likely to do so next year either. As Harry has said in the paper unfortunately, as a result, we now have a few of the execs down as serious flight risks. Isn't that right Harry?

So, to address all this, I think we should do the following:

- *Pay an exceptional bonus of 10 per cent of salary to the Executives, payable in 12 months in shares from the option pool. This will show them that despite the difficult year we understand Brexit isn't their fault. It will add a helpful retention element to our packages and I would have thought that the other shareholders should be happy as it involves no cash up front.*
- *Secondly to promote Mark to Group FD and Deputy CEO and raise his salary by 20 per cent. This will also send a strong signal that Mark is doing well and is now the clear successor to Harry. That should also please them as although they don't always appreciate his intelligence they respect it.*
- *We'll also promote Lucy Sparkle, that terrifically bright and charming young thing in Mark's team, to be Head of Investor Relations. I've already spoken to Mark, haven't I Mark? and he would be very happy to do this for us and as Deputy CEO he can keep most of his Operations Director responsibilities but delegate a few bits and pieces to other people.*
- *To keep the institutional shareholders happy, we will also raise the dividend by a little bit as well but that's for another meeting.*

- *This I think should keep everybody happy and hard to see anyone objecting.*

I am sorry this wasn't in the papers but to be honest it was getting the papers that got me thinking about the problem. So, what I would propose now is that Jane starts the RemCo proper, that we take the papers as read and that the solution I have proposed emerges from our discussion. Jane over to you."

Sarah's heart sank she could see this wasn't going to be a quick reassuring call at all. Jamie continued:

"I couldn't believe what I was hearing and I couldn't believe that this was how it is supposed to be." said Jamie to Sarah. "The other Non-exec said nothing and the CEO and CFO who I wasn't sure should be there anyway for a discussion like that were really keen to get things wrapped up and get back to other matters. I kicked myself for not speaking to the other Non-exec before the meeting to get a sense of how it normally goes. I felt absolutely useless, used and was angry but felt powerless to stop them. I did raise the obvious points as diplomatically as I could but was swept aside and told I would get the hang of it in time.

I have seriously thought of resigning but feel a duty to the other shareholders and that I should stay on and help get this sorted. There's also the issue that if I resign, how good will that look for me after just a few months on the Board."

What are the issues and how should Sarah advise Jamie as to the options he has?

The issues

There are a wide range of issues including Hilary's role and behaviour, her lack of recognition of her conflict of interest, the way that the RemCo is operating, as well as those to do with various members of the Exec, the challenges relating to the current remuneration and how it is governed and that's before we get to the specific issues raised by her proposal.

The challenges with RemCo and remuneration appear to be simply an outcome of a more fundamental issue and that is the fact that although the company has become a public company, Hilary's mindset remains one of a complete owner of a private business. In summary, a perfect example of the

"*Majority of One*" issue that was described on page 65. She wouldn't be the first to suffer this affliction. It can be an incredibly hard transition to go through even if you get it intellectually. Even harder if, as all the symptoms suggest here, when you have a weak Board and an Executive Group who also haven't adjusted to life as a public company.

A broker friend of mine with extensive experience of helping companies IPO says that one of the first things he does is to sit down with a Board and ensure that they understand "*The rules of the RemCo game in PLC Land.*" He does this by taking them through the "*Remuneration*" section of the Financial Reporting Council's "*Guidance on Board Effectiveness*", regaling them with horror stories of the consequences of getting it wrong, connecting them to others who are a few years further advanced in the process and advising them on who are known to be very good RemCo Chairs. Sadly, in Bamco's case, Hilary's broker either didn't do this or she didn't listen (it turned out to be the latter).

If she had she would have remembered that the first paragraph on the topic in the FRC guide says "*The remuneration committee has delegated responsibility for designing and determining remuneration for the Chair, executive directors and the next level of senior management. It is vital that the remuneration committee recognises and manages potential conflicts of interest in this process.*"

From the little we know, Jane's background and character combined with her subservient relationship with Hilary are all issues which could be preventing her from fulfilling the role properly as RemCo Chair. As with the Chair or member of any sub-committee, relevant knowledge is barely half of what matters. Character and the ability to exercise independent judgement and influence are even more important. One clear signal that Jane is compromised is the fact that she has allowed Hilary to behave in such a way since IPO. The reinforcing effect of this can be deeply corrosive.

Other issues are the silence of the other non-exec member and the implication that Harry and Mark appear to attend RemCo meetings and are present even when their own remuneration is being discussed. There seems no natural ally for Jamie to work with. It is important in any RemCo that there are at least two strong non-execs and at least one that has a significant RemCo track record.

An obvious question is whether what happens at Bamco RemCos bears any relation to its terms of reference. Added to that, does Hilary's behaviour imply that the RemCo is going to be making more than a recommendation to the Board and is actually taking the decision. The issue of the "informal" start to the meeting also needs addressing and may lead Jamie to wonder how other sub-committees are run and whether Hilary attends them as well. For example, shouldn't the Nominations Committee be the one to consider the appropriateness of Mark's promotion and its implications for the appointment process for Harry's successor. Sub-committees are covered on page 172. In addition, it is always worth looking at the relevant code for your type of company and country.

It seems that whatever was in the RemCo papers has been disregarded and considered irrelevant by Hilary. So another issue is to know what was in there and whether there are other matters which need consideration.

There is no mention of the HR Director or remuneration consultants who in these situations will often attend for parts of RemCo as a valuable source of information. Another role the HR Director should play in these sessions is to help the Board consider other internal implications of whatever is proposed. For example, differential treatment for execs compared to the broader leadership group or the staff more widely presents an obvious morale issue. Jamie may have formed a view already on how strong the HR Director is and be interested in their views on what Hilary proposes to do. It is always worth meeting with the HR Director before you accept a RemCo position. Even if they turn out to be neither very human nor resourceful you will at least know what you are getting into.

Ironically, RemCo is one of the most asymmetrical jobs to do in termsof risk and reward so it pays to overdo your due diligence. The journalists will tend, understandably, to place responsibility for remu- neration issues with the Chair and members of the Remuneration Committee as well as the Chair. It is why it is also common for advice to be sought from the company's financial PR advisers as well as brokers before proposals are put to shareholders.

In considering the specific remuneration issues raised by Hilary's proposals, after refreshing himself on the FRC Guidelines, Jamie will probably be concerned about the following:

- On "*paying an exceptional bonus of 10 per cent of salary to the Execs*". This can't be justified by performance and when such a bonus is paid and how it is paid are secondary to this. It would

clearly fall outside the existing bonus arrangements and institutions generally don't buy paying a bonus for retention when in their eyes people have underperformed.
- With regard to Mark's promotion, this should fundamentally be an issue for the Nominations Committee and then the Board rather than RemCo. RemCo may have a role, perhaps in a consultative way with regard to the remuneration implications, if relevant but the decision to promote Mark is not within a RemCo remit. More generally, promoting people simply to give them extra cash is not usually a recipe for success. Paying Mark more is likely to be a less effective signal than improved performance. Moreover, the market reaction to the news that he is now the anointed one may not be as Hilary hopes. Finally, on Mark it is probably worth coaching him that competitive behaviour with analysts rarely pays off.
- On the issue of creating a Head of Investor Relations, again this is not a RemCo issue unless she is joining the Exec Group and RemCo is considering her package and its consistency with, and impact upon, the total executive remuneration. This is really one for the Nominations Committee.
- Happily Hilary realises that the issue of the dividend is for another meeting.

Jamie has a considerable advantage being relatively new and therefore not responsible for earlier decisions and with the power of fresh perspective and intact credibility. Yet what power does he really have as a member of RemCo and being a non-executive? He has little formal power other than that of refusing to recommend the proposal to the Board and refusing to sign the remuneration report.

Options

It may instinctively feel to Jamie that this is a *"fight or flight"* situation but as with most conflict situations other alternatives may be available. Reflecting on the five basic responses to a conflict situation that we set out on page 143 might be helpful: *"Accommodate"*, *"Compete"*, *"Avoid"*, *"Collaborate"* or *"Compromise"*.

"*Accommodate*" - In this situation the response might be to hide under the cover of being new, give them a polite warning about the dangers of what they are doing and then let them get on with it.

"*Compete*"- In its extreme version this response could be a blunt opening to a conversation with Hilary along the lines of: "*I was appalled by what happened at RemCo. I think this is a completely inappropriate way of dealing with the situation and I'm going to resign if you insist on pushing this through*". A less extreme version would be to Figure out another way of getting what you think should had happen even if Hilary doesn't want it.

"*Avoid*" - In its extreme version this response is to resign. A lesser version might be to accommodate as above but to ensure that his reservations are clearly noted and take any other action to reduce his risk.

"*Avoid plus*" – This response, which borders on "*Compete*", is to take the second avoid option as above, so to acquiesce but not to resign and then prepare to use the ensuing mess to emerge as Chair of RemCo and sort it out.

"*Collaborate*" - This is probably a two-step process firstly to enlist support from others. Perhaps from Harry or Mark or other non-execs after helping them realise that they will all suffer collateral damage if Hilary goes ahead with the proposal. The company's advisers may also be helpful to involve in a situation like this. They may provide a more objective view of the risks Hilary is taking. If this can be done without alienating Hilary, then Jamie will need to collaborate with her and Jane and others to find a better solution.

"*Compromise*"- This could simply be to do a deal with Hilary to water down her proposals, eg perhaps accepting the exceptional bonus but not Mark's promotion and insisting on revisions to RemCo composition and operation.

Whichever Jamie chooses, given his experience and the situation he is in, he will probably need to enlist the support of others to navigate through to a more comfortable position than he is now in. So, before he decides it is well worth him reflecting on the other Board members and how helpful they might be. He should also consider the role of Harry and Mark in this. They are reputationally quite vulnerable here and may or might not realise it.

What happened?

Happily, Sarah had come across similar characters to Hilary before. She had also chaired a RemCo before and was up to date in terms of what institutional investors considered best practice. She was known for being gutsy as well as a natural optimist but even though Jamie knew this her first words were a bit of a surprise:

"Well thank God they've got you in there and lucky you, here's a chance to make your mark."

Experienced in coaching people, Sarah didn't just give Jamie the playbook for such situations but through some brilliant questions expertly got him to think about the most important issues, understand what choices he really had as well as to recognise that he had slightly more power than he realised. Especially if he could enlist a few other people to help.

After asking a range of clarifying questions to ensure that she really understood the situation and also understand better who Hilary respected on the Board or amongst her advisers, it became clear that the main person Jamie thought that she totally trusted and listened to was her lawyer Geoffrey Silk from Magic Circle and Astute. Jamie also felt that in the aftermath of the share price fall she had come to rely on the lead broker from JP Stanley.

"*Great stuff!*" said Sarah "*and what do you think they might think of what you have just experienced and the idea that you may resign?*". Although Jamie had only met them once he thought that they may counsel against pursuing the course of action Hilary proposed.

Sarah then followed up with: "*And what do you think Hilary thinks of you?*".

"Well I may be a bit jaundiced by Friday's experience but I would say at best a necessary expense that looks good on the website but little else." replied Jamie.

She knew Jamie naturally responded well to a challenge, made a judgement and then took a calculated risk.

"*Well here's a chance to step up, show her that you can make a massive contribution and also win your RemCo spurs in the process. Alternatively you could just roll over, avoid all the hassle and walk away but then who is in control of the PR around your departure and how are you going to avoid looking like yet another divisional CEO who couldn't hack it as a non-exec. You also need to think about how you resigning so quickly will look for her.*

With their confidence in the company a little fragile, many institutions might think you've discovered something far more sinister."

"So you think I should stay and fight" said Jamie.

"Well that has to be your call Jamie but you're a high integrity guy and if you are determined about making a career as a Non-exec, you should think about it seriously. However if you do decide to stay I wouldn't exactly describe it as stay and fight. You can be a bit more cunning than that."

"*In what way?*" responded Jamie.

"*Well focus on the outcome you want. You said earlier that what Hilary proposed would rile investors, was appalling in governance terms and wouldn't actually solve the issues the company is facing for all but a very short period. I feel sure the broker and the lawyer will see it that way too. You also said that if you stayed that you'd want to find a way of hitting pause on her plan, getting a proper process around deciding what to do and finding a way of pressing Hilary's reset button before she blows herself up.*"

"*Exactly.*" thought Jamie. As did the thought that he should email Hilary and Jane tonight saying that he had been reflecting on Friday's meeting and wanted an urgent face to face chat with her and Jane on Monday afternoon. He felt it wise to not give too much away in the email and was conscious that the main board papers were going out on Friday so there wasn't much time if he was going to achieve the desired outcome. His sense of the relationship between Jane and Hilary led him to think that they might speak before he met but he wasn't concerned by this. Hilary, as ever glued to her phone, saw Jamie's email immediately, agreed to meet and told Jane she needed to be there as well. "*I'm so sorry Jane but he's new and we don't want him doing anything silly. So, best to head him off at the pass don't you think.*"

Jamie also got on the phone, first with Bamco's broker, Charles Borgon, on Monday morning. He was cautious on this call and contained it to introducing himself and saying that as he had just joined Bamco's RemCo he was interested in where the broker thought the company was on remuneration and to find out what feedback, if any, he had picked up from shareholders. Jamie couldn't believe his luck when Charles said: "*To be honest mate no-one bothered about it at IPO or at end of first year as they'd all had such a big uplift and a number of them bailed out at that point. Those in now are a mix of those at the IPO who are hacked off and thinking of selling if Hilary and Harry bodge the next results presentation or do anything silly, as well as the event-driven hedgies who want that to happen. So, hope you're not going to do anything racy."*

He then spoke to the Company's lawyer Geoffrey Silk who he had only met once before and had made the offer of having coffee to get to know each other. As Jamie told Sarah later: *"What a great return on a Latte!"* In another stroke of luck they were able to meet up late Monday morning and Geoffrey started the conversation with:

"I'm so pleased to see you joining the Board Jamie, Hilary is wonderful but she desperately needs a proper non-exec with a bit of steel and an eye for good process. I think it is going to be a choppy year ahead and she needs someone other than me and Charles (the broker) to tell her what she needs to hear."

It was easy for Jamie to build on this dream opening, share his challenge and enlist Geoffrey's support. They agreed that Jamie would suggest a call with Hilary, Jane, Charles and Geoffrey as well as the Company's PR adviser, Jessica, for Tuesday morning. The purpose being to advise RemCo on the likely reactions of Hilary's proposal from the market (Charles & Jessica) and, as her most trusted adviser and someone who knew Harry and Mark, for Geoffrey to provide some basic commercial rather than legal input. *"I wouldn't expect too much from Jessica (the PR adviser), she will sit on the fence until she senses which way the wind is blowing."* said Geoffrey, *"but Hilary is bound to call Charles and me beforehand to try and get us onside. So, I will call Charles and ensure that we speak with one voice."*

Jamie's conversation with Hilary and Jane was a somewhat testy affair as soon as Hilary realised Jamie had his own mind and it was not completely in tune with hers. However, she agreed to have the call with the advisers and, after all this was over, to review how the RemCo operated thinking that was a battle for another day and an easy gift.

Unsurprisingly, Charles rattled Hilary with his blunt assessment of the likely response to Hilary's proposal from the market. *"Given the market's a little skittish on the stock anyway I'm afraid we'll be talking of a 15 per cent fall driven by some of the remaining 'long-onlys' losing patience and the hedgies calling for your head. Realistically I can't see Mark moving, can you? So, I'm not sure I see the need to poke the bear and I'm sure Jessica will tell us that it'll be an easy gift for the City press who will sadly pounce on it."* Geoffrey then followed up with: *"As you know it's not my job to call the market but I have to say having been in a fair few of these situations and looking at it from a purely commercial perspective I would strongly agree. I also don't think it is fair to set Jane and Mark up in this way and it would leave you very exposed, Hilary."*

As Sarah's son Henry would say *"Game, set and match!"*. Jamie then proposed that the Company turn the negative into a positive and leave remuneration arrangements unchanged for this year as acknowledgement of underperformance against expectations. His suggestion for dealing with flight risks was to quietly target those as agreed with RemCo below the Exec Group using a budget agreed by RemCo to reduce departures. With support from Jane, Hilary put up a bit of a fight against this initially but in the end recognised reality and caved in, albeit somewhat ungraciously.

RemCo's subsequent recommendations were approved by the Board and a few months later, as a result of an independent Board review suggested by the broker, terms of reference of the sub-committees were refreshed and Jamie was appointed Chair of RemCo. Two years later, after a little improvement in performance, the business was bought for a small premium to the value it IPO'd on. Hilary, deeply disenchanted with what she described as *"life in the goldfish bowl"* used her capital to buy out a friend's majority stake in a private business and is much happier.

Dilemma 9:

Journalistic licence

Paul, the Chief Executive Officer (CEO) of NIMBO plc, is in a foul mood. He has just complained to you, his Chair, for the fifth time in three days about *"that bloody hatchet job in the* Financial Times *last week."*

It seems that everyone he meets has seen it and wants to discuss it. Naturally, you can understand why he feels uncomfortable discussing an article in which he was described as *"The charisma-free and deeply suspicious CEO of NIMBO"* and which went on to say, *"Although not liked by his industry peers and staff, he is envied for the way he has driven down cost."*

The article also made a number of other specific criticisms relating to the Group's inability to make an acquisition following several abortive attempts. In addition, it suggested that labour relations had soured because of a restructuring programme. On the other hand, it did point out that NIMBO was the best performer in the industry and, although it was not liked, it was a feared competitor and innovator.

Your own view of the CEO is that he is highly capable if not highly personable. He has made a number of shrewd judgements, not least over people. He is not as bad as he is made out to be and lets himself down in the way he handles public relations (PR). Previous attempts to coach him in this area have failed. You are also a little embarrassed over the fact that he is now on to his third PR agency in as many years. He is normally good in front of a crowd and one-to-one, but has lost faith and confidence in dealing with the press. They make him uncharacteristically nervous.

In a rather unfortunate moment this morning he has, in his anger, fired off an email to the Chair of Nikkei to complain about the '*inaccurate and libellous reporting in the* Financial Times.' He has threatened legal action and wants the particular journalist to be removed from the Paper. He called the journalist the day the article came out and said that he would never give another interview to the Paper and that he would withdraw advertising immediately.

You think the matter is getting a little out of hand and feel the need to do something. But what? What are the issues?

The obvious issue is that the CEO has handled the Press badly, whether the criticisms are fair or not. His lack of skill in this area is undermining his judgement, his ability to do his job and the Company's reputation. You may wonder, though, why if he is so good in other areas, he appears to have such a blind spot over PR. Is he really as good in other areas? Is there any basis for the criticism over labour relations, for example? Could he be under too much pressure? Is it a lack of confidence? Should he be CEO of a public company if he can't handle the media part of the job?

As Chair, you have ultimate responsibility for the company's reputation. You also have responsibility for the performance of the CEO. So, you need to do something, otherwise you are abdicating responsibility. Any further progress down the current path is bound to undermine the Company. Your own ability to handle the Press may be important. If you aren't strong in this area, then the risk is even greater.

You have apparently been very supportive of him. Is the way you have been trying to influence him appropriate? Does he need firmer guidance? What exactly has been done to coach him before? How much training has he had? Was it at the appropriate level? Have you tried joint interviews so that you can actually observe what it is that goes wrong? Does the business have a clear set of messages, which it is trying to deliver to a defined group of target audiences or does the PR strategy need forming/developing? Are the current PR advisers appropriate?

A good relationship with the *Financial Times* is important for any UK listed company. It has an excellent reputation for even-handedness and the quality of its journalists. To have a poor relationship is clearly unhelpful to developing the Company's reputation. What can be done to get the relationship back onto a healthy footing? What also should be done about the letter to the Nikkei Chair? What is likely to be the response? Is the problem confined to one newspaper and one journalist in particular, or is it much broader? It would be surprising if it were so confined.

What do the key institutional shareholders feel? Are investor relations good? Poor handling of the press is bound to be picked up by them, so they will need some background.

How to decide?

In order to decide anything, you need to understand exactly what it is that is going wrong. Having done so, you then need to determine whether the CEO is capable of fixing it.

Dealing with the press can be one of the most stressful and least enjoyable aspects of a public company CEO's role. Is there anything you as Chair could do to reduce the pressure for the CEO to enable him to perform better? Would the CEO be better moving to a less stressful environment?

A lot depends here on how well you know the CEO, how much respect there is between you and therefore how easily you can influence him. This is a dilemma where your judgement as to whether the CEO can deal with the situation is key.

What to decide?

It would appear that you definitely need to do something. If you don't, the share price and reputation of the company are in danger of being undermined. You have two problem areas: what to do about the Nikkei letter, and what to do to sort out the CEO.

You could ignore the Nikkei issue on the assumption that there will be a polite letter back saying something to the effect that they are:

"Sorry that the CEO feels disappointed by the article. As I am sure you will appreciate, editorial freedom resides with the Financial Times and is not influenced by Nikkei in any way. I have passed on your letter to the editor of the paper and I am sure he will talk to the journalist and respond to you directly."

There will then be another polite letter from the editor thanking you for your letter and saying that he has reviewed the article with the journalist and that while the language may have been a little harsh, the Paper stands by its view.

With regard to the more important matter of the CEO's general approach, the first thing you may decide to do is to make sure that this is the only problem he has and that it isn't a symptom of other deeper problems.

Could a *"low profile, no interviews for a period"* approach work? You can certainly try this, but if you are a public company you have to report your results regularly. If you are a consumer company, the general Press as well as the financial Press will be interested. Once they think they have a fertile source of critical articles, it is hard to avoid it.

Can you use someone else as the company's spokesman without undermining the company? For the results, many public companies use the Finance Director (FD) as a key spokesperson. NIMBO could do this if the FD is good with the Press. It can work in other situations as well, but often only if that spokesman is the Group Communications Director. Occasionally, other Execs, particularly if they are heir apparent, can make it worse. What many businesses do is to have a number of different people in the company as spokesperson for different issues. In this way, dependence on one key Figure is reduced, the load is shared and the company appears to have more breadth of senior talent.

Should you just give the CEO the simple objective of resolving the situation? You might do this as a threat: *"Sort it out, improve your relations with the press, or we'll have no alternative but to make a change."* Before you issue a threat like this, you must be prepared to carry it out and have a contingency plan.

Alternatively, you could do it in other, more supportive ways through much more active coaching, more rigorous rehearsing and so on. If the CEO really has had all the training that is possible to have, then training isn't an option. If it is only the one journalist at the Financial Times, then you might decide it is a simple matter of letting things cool off and then getting the CEO, perhaps with yourself, to launch a charm offensive. If this is the situation, then you have to get the CEO to remove the personal angle. The CEO needs to build confidence in dealing with the issue. Maybe targeting other journalists who feel more positively to write some balancing pieces would help build confidence.

How to communicate it?

For the CEO, this is a highly personal and threatening situation. You therefore need to communicate in a way that is sensitive, firm and recognises the threat to the Company. Once you have decided which course of action to take, you will probably want to communicate it quickly to the CEO.

Depending on what you have decided to do, you will want to speak to the PR agency and other key advisers as well as the rest of the board. This will need doing in a way that doesn't further undermine the CEO.

What happened?

The Nikkei response was pretty much along the lines described above. Hence it wasn't an issue for long, although clearly it didn't improve the relationship between the journalist and the CEO.

As it turned out, dealing with the press wasn't the only part of the CEO's game that wasn't going well. There were some tensions among the Execs and a feeling that the business was starting to outgrow him. Paul had done an excellent job in focusing the company and squeezing as much profit out of it as he could, but he was struggling to come up with a growth strategy.

The Chair considered three main options:

- Fire him.
- Get someone else on the board who was more imaginative and more personable and who would be capable of being a successor in 12 months' time.
- Try to coach him strategically and on the PR front.

It was true that Paul wasn't the most imaginative of people, but it was also true that he was good at implementing the ideas of others. He was a very proud man and was aware of where things might be heading. Nothing filled him with horror more than the thought of being fired, especially after the press that he had had.

The Chair realised this and decided that the best thing to do was to be completely frank. After setting out what he saw as the situation, he painted pictures of the three alternatives above. He then asked the CEO which one he would prefer. The CEO went for getting someone else in who could be a successor in 12 months' time. Why? Because he certainly didn't want to be fired and he realised that he wasn't enjoying the job any more. Even with coaching, he felt that he would end up in a job he didn't like. Essentially, he and his Chair did a deal that saved face, recognised his contribution and avoided damaging the reputation of the business. The successor has worked out reasonably well. The company has a far better reputation and has made a number of good acquisitions. It isn't as tightly managed as before and is currently looking for a Chief Operating Officer. As for Paul he used his pay-off to buy into a private equity-backed private business that needed turning around and is thoroughly enjoying a lower profile life.

Dilemma 10:

The revolution

Wilnet had a spectacular year as one of the few UK internet site development companies of critical mass. It has taken full advantage of explosive market demand and its reputation for highly creative projects delivered on time to a premium price.

When you joined as Finance Director (FD), six months before the float, you knew nothing about the internet market. You were bored stiff by your previous job in one of the big five accountancy practices. Wilnet's charismatic Chief Executive Officer (CEO), Bill Fortis, and the effervescent culture he propagated were therefore of considerable appeal. The cut in salary was well worth the 10 per cent of the equity in options that you were offered. Problems with basic financial controls and pricing policy were things you felt well equipped to sort out. Hence, Wilnet looked like the opportunity you had always dreamed of and well worth the risk.

Any high expectations you may have had when you joined have been surpassed. Getting on top of control and other issues didn't take long. Wilnet's listing went extremely well and it has been tremendous fun to work with a winning team in such a high-growth area. Today, just two years since the float, your equity and options are worth £8 million.

At the time of the listing there was a lot of heated debate. This was not just over whether to float, but also which market to go onto. The Chair still goads the rest of the board by saying that if Wilnet had gone to NASDAQ, as he had advocated, the business would have 10 times the value. Although he is right, you sense that Bill, and for that matter yourself, would not have been that comfortable with life as a NASDAQ company.

Wilnet's board consists of six quite different personalities. Jeff Hupe, a lively New Yorker, is Chair. Jeff had previously floated a company on NASDAQ and has added an enormous amount in terms of experi- ence, credibility and contacts. He was superb at the time of the float. His only weaknesses are a low boredom threshold and a desire to get an instant response to everything. As a former mentor of Bill's, he was involved right from the outset. Jeff has 10 per cent of the equity.

Another founding Director was Alan Tosper. He owns 20 per cent and runs the media and publishing sector. Alan is a bit of a loner. He runs the most successful part of the business, yet is probably the least comfortable member of the team. Nobody would be surprised if he just up and left one day, cashing in his chips and starting all over again.

Dave Sorpet couldn't be more different, a real team player with a tremendous sense of humour. He covers the fast-moving consumer goods sector, which, although not as profitable, has developed some of the most leading-edge products. Dave is more modest than Alan and has also put more time into developing the Company's overall positioning.

Apart from being CEO, Bill is the technical brains behind Wilnet. In addition, he runs the business that supplies the technology sector itself. Bill is highly rated by analysts and he and Wilnet have been getting some tremendous publicity. His only regret is that he only had enough money to buy 5 per cent of Wilnet's equity.

Wilnet's final board member is John Forbes. John is a highly polished corporate financier by background. He joined Wilnet just before he retired in the run-up to the float. Jeff and he get on especially well but he enjoys a good relationship with all of the board. Wilnet's smooth rise has meant he hasn't had to do a great deal recently.

The major contribution you have made to Wilnet's success has been well recognised. Not being one of the founders meant that for a while you felt you were treated very much like an outsider. However, you now feel that the others are, at last, slowly accepting you into the fold.

This morning, just before a board meeting, the Chair and Alan asked if you would join them for a quick meeting. You are aware that there are tensions between the Chair and the CEO, but feel that Bill and Alan get along well. Indeed, Bill has often defended Alan's somewhat selfish behaviour. So, what they have to tell you is something of a shock.

Jeff opens the meeting by telling you that he and Alan believe the time has come to replace Bill. They believe that this is necessary on the grounds that the business has outgrown him; he's too inward-looking and not strategic enough. In their view, the best course of action is to replace Bill while the Company is strong. They have decided to confront the issue and to appoint Alan as CEO. Jeff and Alan want your support for this idea so that they can move forward and appoint lawyers. In that way, they can present it as a fait accompli to Bill and avoid a messy or protracted boardroom bust-up. They believe their views will come as a shock to Bill. *'Too right,'* you think. They've come as a big shock to you. *'How long have they been plotting this?'* you wonder.

Despite the fact that they do have a bit of a point about the business outgrowing Bill, you feel a deep loyalty to him. Instinct tells you Alan would wreck the business as CEO. Wilnet is a people business, after all. Shareholder confidence, once knocked, is probably unrecoverable. All sorts of thoughts are racing through your mind. You decide to play for time and say:

"While I've been aware of tensions, I had no idea you two felt as strongly as this. I think it is important that we consider all the issues involved here. I'm a bit disappointed that you have sprung it on me like this today just before a board meeting. Consequently, I'd like to reflect on what you have said and I'd like to meet with you tomorrow to discuss it further."

They reluctantly agree. The plan was to tell Bill today. They insist you don't speak to him to alert him. You agree not discuss it with him until tomorrow. The board meeting was an odd affair and somewhat tense. Bill sensed something wasn't quite right and asks you after the board meeting what's up with the other guys.

How do you respond and how do you deal with the various conversations that will ensue? What are the issues?

Not a particularly pleasant situation to be faced with, especially if you are convinced that if Alan and Jeff get their way, the business will suffer serious damage. If they don't, then they'll probably have to go. Either way, a boardroom battle will ensue and undermine the Company with investors. The damage to your own wealth will also be significant. Assuming the voting rights are equal, that Dave will vote with Bill and John with Jeff, then the reason they approached you is obvious: your vote will swing it. They don't seem dumb enough to seek a vote and lose.

Could they be right? Has the business really outgrown Bill? What's the evidence for this view? Even if it has, is this the way to deal with it? Why have they chosen to do things this way? What will be the effect on the share price of Bill going? How would Bill react? Are they right about Bill but wrong about Alan? If you support Bill's removal, can you avoid Alan being appointed his successor? What does this mean for Dave? Will he be next?

Depending on your confidence and ambition, it might also cross your mind that you could be a compromise candidate for CEO.

Is there a solution available that doesn't involve such a dramatic split? What should John's role be? Has he already been consulted? What would he think? Could he be the one to sort things out? What do the Company's brokers and other key advisers think of the Chair and Alan? How damaged would the business be if they went?

Should you speak to Bill before responding to the Chair? You have agreed not to. However, you may consider that the way in which they have treated you means you are free to do whatever you consider right. Does deciding to talk to Bill mean implicit support for him? Jeff and Alan will probably see it that way. Should John be consulted first? Perhaps the combination of you and him might persuade Jeff to drop the idea.

Whatever happens, life on the Wilnet board will never be the same again.

How to decide?

Unless you take the decision to involve Bill, Dave or John, it looks difficult to make any progress. More information is likely to have little bearing. However, this is new territory for you, so maybe chatting it through with someone you think might have experienced something similar may help. Jeff sounds as if he is someone used to winning fights. If you decide to join forces with Bill, you may need some support. Should you enlist that support before you speak to him, or involve him in gaining it?

What is best for the Company? Working this out may not be straightforward, but helpful nevertheless. Does supporting Bill mean that Jeff and Alan would end up going? If so, what would be the impact and how could you do it with minimum damage? What's the legal position? Do Jeff and Alan have the power to do this? Is there anything in Bill's service contract to stop them?

This is definitely a situation where instincts matter a great deal. A lot has to do with the trust between the various board members. So, what are your instincts telling you?

No doubt the impact of the different alternatives on your own position and wealth will be taken into account. Would jotting down the different possibilities help?

What will the key institutional shareholders think? Asking them at this point may not be a great idea. Confidence evaporates surprisingly quickly in technology stocks. What about the Company's professional advisers? Do you have a confidant at one of them whose counsel you could seek?

What to decide?

Balancing what is in the best commercial interests of the Company with a concern for proper corporate governance and a desire to do what is fair to Bill could be difficult. The decision turns on how strong you think Bill is and whether supporting him will do less damage to the business. Whether or not you should talk to Bill depends upon this. Clearly, if you come down on the side of the Chair and Alan it would probably be best not to.

Deciding who to talk to first is therefore important. Much will depend on your relationship with John. He looks like a possible honest broker and calming influence. Yet if the bond between him and Jeff is the strongest, this could be a big mistake.

How to communicate it?

'Carefully' is the word that springs to mind. Bill is bound to be highly charged. Jeff is impulsive and could leap to the wrong conclusion. Alan will clearly be tense. You are in a state of shock and high anxiety.

In a situation like this, there is a high probability that what you say is not what gets heard. Using as few calm words as possible and concentrating on the facts will reduce the likelihood of confusion. That said, conveying how you feel may well help turn the situation, particularly with John and Jeff.

If you decide to speak to Bill be brief and if you have decided to support him, make sure that he is in no doubt. He's no idiot, so he will realise the seriousness of the situation immediately. He is bound to be angry, so making sure he doesn't do anything rash is important.

At this stage, it is wise not to tell anybody else within the Company and try to ensure that no-one gets the impression that there's a bust-up on the board.

What did the FD do to?

This was a very tricky situation. Alan and Jeff had a point about the business outgrowing Bill. However, their approach incensed the FD. He also felt that

Alan would be a disastrous choice as CEO. He thought that he would do a better job himself, but he didn't feel he was ready to be a CEO yet and certainly not in this situation.

Alan and Jeff's behaviour made him even more convinced that their proposal would be bad for Wilnet. Talking to Bill seemed the only way to block them. The option of enlisting Dave's support and trying to head them off without Bill knowing was quickly discounted. The FD and Dave would be no match for a committed Jeff and Alan.

When he spoke to Bill, he told him that the Chair had asked him to support the appointment of Alan as the new CEO because, '*Jeff thinks that while you have been great for the phase we have been through, Alan is the right man for the next phase.*' He continued:

"*I have to say I was shocked, Bill. I don't think it's a good idea at all. While you are bound to have to hand on at some point, it isn't now. Alan would be the wrong successor, anyway. I'm very concerned at the way they are going about it. You have to take this threat seriously, Bill. We need to try and stop this idea.*"

Bill was outraged and was determined not to let them take what he sees as his Company away from him. He couldn't understand how the Chair could have betrayed him: '*Alan must have put him up it. Wonder what he's told Jeff. Thought he'd been a bit sheepish last week.*'

To his credit, Bill calmed down very quickly and suggested that he and the FD both meet later with Dave and come up with a plan of action. Dave was as shocked as the FD and added some helpful insight. He had overhead Alan and Jeff a few weeks ago and was surprised to hear Alan taking credit for some of Bill's ideas and rubbishing Bill's new plan for expansion in Germany. At the time he put it down to one of Alan's grumpy moods and thought nothing more of it.

The plan was based on the premise that Alan had been feeding Jeff misleading information and that once Jeff was aware of this, it would be Alan who would be leaving. But how could they make Jeff realise this? He was bound to be suspicious of the FD's motives if the latter told him on his own. Could the FD see Alan and get him to yield? It took him a while to decide how to go about achieving his aim.

He decided that they should discuss the situation with John and be open with him. If he wouldn't offer support, then they would speak to Jeff and, as a final resort, threaten to resign en masse.

John had had a glittering career and been involved in many difficult situations. Somehow, he had always emerged calm, smooth and with honour. When the FD saw John he was very much in listening mode and was non-committal. He told the FD that he thought the best course of action was for him to speak to Jeff and establish exactly what had happened. Although he didn't say much, he did give the FD the feeling that he could be trusted.

The FD never really found out what John said to Jeff. The next morning Jeff asked Bill, Dave and him to join him in his office. He said:

"Guys I'm afraid I've made one hell of an error of judgement but I'm happy to report that it has now been rectified. Alan has decided to leave the Company at the end of the month. He's made a great contribution to the business over the last few years and we will be kind to him in the PR. Although he should go, I still think there are some issues we need to address together. Now is not the time."

Alan's successor was recruited as someone who had the potential to take over as CEO when Bill retires, in two years' time. He is well on track to do that. Wilnet has gone from strength to strength and is as highly rated as ever. Alan now runs his own small business and has benefited from keeping his Wilnet shareholding.

Dilemma 11:

I wish we'd told them earlier

Azco, a small public company, has issued a profit warning this morning, the first since it became a quoted company four years ago. The statement was brief but honest:

> *"We regret to announce that the directors of Azco have reviewed the latest information available to them and come to the conclusion that results for the year to 31 March will be some 30 per cent below those indicated at the interim stage and those being forecast by most analysts.*
>
> *The directors remain confident of the long-term outlook for Azco. The shortfall is entirely due to the launch of the company's new MZ product range. While sales of MZ, launched four months ago, have fallen below anticipated levels, the directors remain convinced of the range's long-term success and are encouraged by the highly positive reaction MZ has had among early customers and in the trade press."*

Azco's Chief Executive Officer (CEO) and Finance Director (FD) have been on the phone all morning with analysts, key institutional shareholders and journalists. The share price has fallen over 30 per cent. Both are upset and feel that the City has overreacted. Azco has been a strong performer since flotation, always met forecasts and enjoyed good relations with investors. Indeed, the FD is speaking at an investor relations conference next week. They have never been in a situation like this before and the shock is considerable.

As well as being Chair of Azco, you are also Chair of GLOBCO, a FTSE 100 company. The only reason you weren't at Azco this morning was that you were chairing GLOBCO's Annual General Meeting (AGM). It has to be said you also underestimated the reaction to the profit warning. You had expected that Azco's CEO and FD would handle communications well and the City would put the hiccough in results into context. As soon as the AGM is over, you call Azco's CEO to see how things have gone. You can't get through to him or the FD. GLOBCO's FD picks up the Azco story when checking the financial news to see how the AGM was reported. He alerts you to the fall in Azco's share price. You decide, as Azco's offices are not too far away, to get your driver to take you there. On the way, you call your Assistant to reschedule this afternoon's meetings at GLOBCO. Finally, you get through to the CEO; he sounds very stressed. You tell him you'll be arriving in 10 minutes and that you will do everything you can to help.

The reason you are prepared to be so supportive is that you genuinely feel that Azco is well managed and that the MZ range has enormous potential. Financial control and information systems have never been a problem at Azco. You trust the management.

What will you do when you get there? What are the issues?

The key dilemma, assuming all is as it seems, is how to rebuild the confidence of Azco's CEO and FD and then restore the company's reputation in the City. However, there are some other issues to address.

How important is the MZ range to the future of the company? It must be put in perspective. Is the MZ range as good as hoped? If it is, is the market as promising as suggested? A weakness in either of these, if Azco is heavily dependent on MZ, has the potential to turn what looks like a setback along the way into a major disaster. As Chair, how much
do you really know about the MZ range and its true potential?

A profit warning is often the result of inadequate financial control and reporting. Sometimes it arises because the Board doesn't pick up the signals. Neither sounds to be the case here. It is well worth checking nevertheless. You will have to have absolute confidence that the revised profit projection is delivered. You will also have to ensure that any other statements Azco makes, particularly with regard to MZ, are realistic. This can be tough to achieve when you are trying to establish confidence and get others to believe in the future.

Investor relations are clearly now a priority. Has Azco been as good at managing communications with the City as has been said? Whether it has or it hasn't, it's likely to need a different approach from here on.

How vulnerable is Azco to a bid as a result of the profit warning?

This could be a perfect time for a competitor to strike. Azco's low share price, long-term potential, shell-shocked management and low support in the City may make it an ideal target for someone who has faith in MZ.

Does the shortfall in MZ revenue impact on the cash flow adversely? If so, how significantly and is this a stock timing issue or something more serious? How strong is Azco's balance sheet? MZ needs to be put into context again.

Morale across the company following a shock like this could be low. You will want to ensure that the spinning bottle of blame is left in the cupboard. The impact on the wealth of staff could be quite considerable if Azco has any share-based incentive schemes. Many of the staff in a company like Azco will hold shares.

Azco will inevitably consume more of your own time for the next few months. Have you got it? If not, can you clear sufficient space to make time? How can you use the other Non-executive directors (Non-execs) and advisers to help? They can do more than be aware. Whether you plan to use them or not, they are bound to be interested and may have some useful input.

For Azco's CEO and FD, the next few months will be very pressured. Does Azco have any spare resource to allow greater delegation of things that are now a lower priority for the top team? The more you can reduce pressure on them, the better things will be.

One very familiar technique in situations like this, which I am personally not a big fan of, is the offering up of a sacrificial lamb. In this case, maybe the MZ director, if there is one, or perhaps the FD could be the likely victims. Sometimes this is well deserved, but frequently it isn't. Moreover, it is often the wrong lamb that gets slaughtered.

Do small public companies ever really recover from situations like these? My own brief research suggests that very few do. An analyst I know says that: *"Once you've disappointed the market you are always disappointing to the market."* The market is unforgiving and it can only take one slip to obliterate a long track record of success.

How to decide?

"What's to decide?" you might think. Why don't they just keep their heads down and deliver the results? If they have absolute faith in what they are doing, then it should just be a matter of time before they get the results they hope for.

Of course, they should focus their efforts on delivering the results.

Obviously, they shouldn't be panicked into doing anything silly. However, a fall in share price of over 30 per cent is significant. The issues above need to be addressed.

Hopefully, the existing bid defence plan will have been well prepared. If so, it may be a straightforward matter of updating it and refreshing the memory of the Board as to its contents. Part of the update will include identification and assessment of the likely bidders.

Deciding what to do about MZ may be more difficult. Step one is to ensure that the Board members have an accurate picture of the real status of the product. They may also decide to prepare a contingency plan in the event that MZ completely fails.

The right time to develop a communications plan to restore confi- dence is when you have made a judgement on the likely progress with MZ and the rest of the business. A temporary setback plan will be quite different to a batten-down-the-hatches major disaster plan.

There may be some decisions required in relation to management at Board level and below. How well do you really know the team? There must have been a meeting of the Board prior to the issue of the profit warning. You will no doubt reflect on that meeting and what you were told.

What to decide?

They could, as has been mentioned, just keep quiet and focus on ensuring that they surpass the revised expectations.

Shock may result in a defensive and over-sensitive response. This would only make it worse. Clamming up and arguing with the press or analysts is never a sensible thing to do, no matter how hurt you feel. Clam up and you risk people assuming the situation is worse than reported. Before you argue, remember that journalists and analysts get to have the last word.

In every situation, the optimist will look for a way to turn such a difficulty into an opportunity. You'd have to be a raving optimist to do that here. However, if the Wilnet team can recover they will emerge all the stronger.

How to communicate it?

As Wilnet's Chair, you need to inject calm confidence while still recognising the seriousness of the situation. The main groups to communicate with are the key institutional shareholders, the analysts and journalists who follow Azco, the staff, customers and suppliers. This assumes of course that key advisers are fully appraised already.

There is always the danger of over-promising to make up for the current disappointment. The wise manage somehow to avoid this temptation or impulse. Another danger, especially for the over-stressed, is that of manic patterns of behaviour emerging.

In these situations, it can be powerful to use others to communicate on your behalf. When you are under pressure you don't always remember your fans. Azco may well be able to use those who regard it or MZ most highly to say so.

What happened?

The Chair was a large engaging man with a natural uncle's style. He exuded warmth and confidence. His presence that afternoon soon cheered up the CEO considerably. He told the CEO two things very quickly. The first was that he would be as supportive as he possibly could. The second was that he was concerned that Azco could become a takeover target. He felt that the bid defence plan initially drawn up just after the flotation four years ago would be out of date and asked for it to be reviewed with advisers urgently.

He made no attempt to probe any further on MZ or question the way the communications had been managed in the morning. This had the effect of the CEO feeling obliged to say that he hadn't handled things well. After a good start, he let one of Azco's more pompous institutional shareholders rattle him and became a little over-defensive. This made him nervous about the next conversation and that didn't go well either. Fortunately, he recovered well for the remaining conversations and regained his normal balanced style.

The Chair suggested that they hold a Board meeting as soon as possible to make sure all the directors had a good understanding of the MZ situation and to approve new bid defence and investor relations plans. You suggested they do this in about a week to give time for sufficient preparation.

When the directors met, the mood was supportive. The atmosphere grew a little more tense when the FD explained that it was really very difficult to be certain about the revised projection. The MZ situation was difficult to call. Overheads had been significantly increased in anticipation of strong sales. People just didn't seem to be buying. No-one knew why. All aspects of the launch had been reviewed, including pricing. The decision, given MZ's favourable customer response, was to premium-price. Early adopters had been delighted and sales in prospect were more than enough to meet the revised projection. It wasn't clear-cut that MZ was a disaster, but there was some concern over the timing of sales. The 30 per cent cut in forecast profit was a conservative guess.

It wasn't long before the Chair's concerns about a potential bid were realised. Three weeks later a US competitor made a bid for Azco. Its offer was at a price only 5 per cent below the pre-profit warning price. The effect of a bid at this price was to cause analysts to question whether they had overreacted and suspect the competitor knew something they didn't. As this was the competitor's first bid and it was seen as opportunistic, the analysts also believed the competitor would pay substantially more, so Azco's price rose a further 20 per cent in the week following the bid.

Through some brilliant presentations and some good press, Azco managed to fend off the US bid. The price fell back briefly but it was still above the pre-profit warning price. Six months later, when MZ was starting to produce some real results but was still below the revised projections, a German competitor made a bid at a 30 per cent premium. This was increased a little. The offer was recommended by the Azco Board on the basis that if offered very good value for shareholders.

The Azco team became a lot wiser and a lot more streetwise as a result of this experience. They are, however, not terribly happy with their new owners and are looking for a challenge elsewhere. As a result of the sale they have sufficient capital to buy into another company.

Dilemma 12:

Bone & Sons

Bone & Sons is a £70 million turnover family-owned business. It has a high reputation for its specialist engineering skills. Its products are known throughout the world, although market leadership now rests with a German competitor. The company has never made a loss throughout its history, but it has struggled in the last few years to make much more than £1 million profit.

The present Chief Executive Officer (CEO), Jim Bone, is the grandson of the founder. His brother Joe is sales director. Both of their wives are Non-Executive Directors (Non-execs). Each brother holds around 20 per cent of the equity. An institution holds 35 per cent, which it acquired in the late 1960s after the autocratic son of the founder died, leaving a massive estate duty problem. Various family members hold the balance of the equity. They are not involved in the business on a day-to-day basis.

The institution has historically taken a 'hands-off' approach to the business, but has become increasingly concerned about performance. Jim has always sought to keep it at arm's length and it holds only ordinary shares with no special rights. The current investment executive has, however, worked hard on his relationship with the business and persuaded the Executive Directors (Execs) that the company would benefit from the appointment of an independent Chair to help identify the way forward. The fact that Jim came under some pressure from family shareholders at the Annual General Meeting (AGM) has also been of some help. It is difficult to tell how serious the discontent was given the complicated voting rights of the different classes of shares and the heat and steam generated by a few with very little equity.

When the institution approached Simon, he was able to say that he knew the company and had dealt with it as a customer in his previous life. This helped to sell him to the Bone brothers and he has now been in the Chair for some six months.

What he found in the company was in line with his expectations. The

Bone brothers, a mixed-ability group aspiring to be average, had done little to develop the business or to identify where its profitable operations and markets lay. Instinctively, he feels that the company could be made much more profitable in the short term and that there is considerable scope for further development, given significant capital expenditure.

The company's Finance Director (FD) Sue, a fairly recent appointment with whom Simon is quite impressed, has decided to analyse the situation and prepare a report for the Bone brothers. She has put together a well-argued paper setting out a package of measures both to secure the short-term future and to go on to expand and develop the business – the latter at a cost of around £20 million. While the business has clear potential it has no cash, so any expansion will require a large element of additional equity funding.

The brothers accept that this must be the way forward and they appear persuaded that this will require a radical management shake-up. In his late 50s, Jim has already indicated that he'd like to take things easier and the proposal for (as yet unidentified) management change is also accepted. The paper has also been given to the institution, which is showing some enthusiasm for the principle. It has also got into the hands of a number of family shareholders.

How would Simon deal with the following?

1. Jim Bone introduces Simon to his 28-year-old son, an engineering graduate who, after working for five years at a large engineering group, has recently taken an MBA. To Jim, he is the answer to the management change. Simon happens to know his former employer quite well and he tells Simon that, while the son is not without ability, he is very naïve and has a lot to learn commercially. Jim believes passionately that the current change programme, which his son is leading, will round out his experience and demonstrate to others just how good he is. Jim has told Simon he has no doubt at all that his son is the right person to be his successor.
2. Joe's wife talks to Simon after a Board meeting. She tells him that Joe has never had the chance to show him his true worth, having always been in the shadow of Jim. Jim, she tells Simon, is only CEO because of a cruel accident of history – the fact that he was

born first. She hopes that Simon will now give him the opportunity to show what he can do as CEO. She also tells him that Great Aunt Mildred, who owns an 18 per cent stake in the business, would support his appointment (Joe was always her favourite). Simon admires her tremendous loyalty but it's rather a pity as he thinks Joe is hopeless.

3. Simon takes a phone call from Jeremy Bone, a cousin who has just under 2 per cent of the shares. He has just lost his seat as a Member of Parliament (MP) so he is looking for something to do to exercise his talents. He tells Simon he is very well connected in the City and has shown the paper to some of his contacts. He feels he can deliver the £20 million required for the development of the business provided, of course, that he himself becomes Chair.

4. A very insistent and not very pleasant director of Vulture Co, an investment bank Simon has never heard of, persuades Simon to meet him. The wife of one of his colleagues is a Bone shareholder and has shown him Simon's plans. He tells Simon that what he really has is a massive problem and that what all the family shareholders want is to get out now rather than be diluted and take additional risks. He tells Simon that Vulture Co would be prepared to buy it now and suggests that Simon, as Chair, is duty-bound to give shareholders the opportunity to consider this.

5. Sue, the FD, goes to see Simon. She has been talking to her old colleagues at one of the big five accountancy firms and they say that a management buyout (MBO) is the answer. She is therefore letting Simon know, as a matter of courtesy, that it is her intention to lead an MBO of the company. She has done so immediately after informing Jim likewise.

6. Some of the family members are so incensed by the FD's suggestions that they have written to the Chair and asked for the FD's immediate removal.

7. The investment executive of the institution rings up and asks Simon how things are going.

What should Simon do? What are the issues?

There are a large number of issues in this case. The really serious ones, such as the capability of the board, the position of the business and the disunited shareholder base, are being made much more difficult by the emotions involved and numerous minor issues. We have a situation that has got out of control in a major way. Snatching at a solution is likely to be a mistake. A great deal of thought is needed before any action is taken. The situation is, however, much easier for the Chair, Simon, than had he just been a Non-exec. So, what are the issues?

Well, Jim is obviously a problem. He's operating as though it's his company and not the family's as a whole. We know he only owns 20 per cent of the equity, but how much do his supporters have? How capable is he? He appears to be ready to hand over but hasn't prepared for succession. What's the relationship with his brother really like? How strong is his view that his son is the right successor?

Jim's son presents another issue. Is he really a capable successor? Even if he is, is this the right way for him to become the leader? The process may make it impossible for him to be successful. Does he want to anyway? It is so terribly hard to be objective about someone you love, so who is going to manage the succession process?

Joe is a problem as well. It sounds as though he shouldn't be in the job he has, never mind being CEO. We don't know whether he shares his wife's feelings towards Jim or her ambition. If not, then he may not be the problem he first appears. How easy will it be to deal with his wife?

The FD, Sue, may be the only really competent member of the Exec on the Board and seems understandably frustrated. What if she goes? But has she overplayed her hand? Is her position with the family recoverable? She says she wants to lead the buyout; is she capable of being CEO? How easy will it be for her to get funding? Which of the family members want her removed? Are they being reasonable? Even if they aren't, this needs responding to.

We then come to Jeremy: a real danger or a red herring? Much depends, obviously, on how much of the equity he and any of his supporters have and how the rest of the family and the institution see him. How good would he be as Chair? How real is the £20 million? Even if he has no real power, he could be a very disruptive influence and hamper a resolution of the company's problems.

The institution is clearly becoming frustrated. The Chair has a few communications issues to resolve with them. For example, what do they expect from him as an independent Chair, what should he tell them about what has just happened, and how involved in any resolution process should they get? What rights do they have with their 35 per cent stake? The fact that they introduced Simon suggests that they might have significant influence. What is their relationship with the FD? Would the institution be interested in funding the buyout?

Can the Chair now play the honest broker? How good is his relationship with Jim and Joe? Does he have the time that will now be required to sort things out? Does he want to? How is he motivated, given that he seems not to have any equity interest in the company? On what basis was he originally appointed? How much did he know when he took the assignment? Does he need to strengthen his powers? If so, which ones and how will he achieve it? Is there any common ground which he can build on? Would any of the proposals involve a continuing role for him?

Who actually owns the balancing 25 per cent not owned by the brothers and the institution? We don't have a clear picture of how this part equity is split. Who can make the decisions necessary? Can Simon get a sufficient block of shares together to support any plan? How well do the shareholders know what is going on? Is there a constitution for ownership? Is there a declared dividend policy?

Is there a general family confidant? Someone who has the respect of most of them and someone they will listen to? Perhaps the family lawyer? This leads us to wonder what the family's advisers have been doing. Have they been as aware of the situation as they should have been? Are the family all advised by the same people?

Then there is the business itself. What's the real performance? Has it got a strategy? If so, is it appropriate? Has it got the resources to achieve it? How vulnerable is it? Is it really invest or die? What damage is shareholder disunity doing? How capable are the management beneath the Board?

In summary, a wide range of issues and questions to address.

How to decide?

This certainly doesn't sound like one that can be ignored in the hope that the dilemma will go away. Sometimes you do need things to get a bit worse before you can act. In this case it's probably got there. However, Simon may make the process of coming up with a resolution easier if he can organise a cooling-down period to enable a more considered analysis of the issues to take place.

If I had to pick three things to focus on in terms of deciding, I think I would pick the Board, the Board and the Board. Lack of an effective Board has got those involved into this pickle. It is hard to see them getting out of the mess they are in other than through changing the Board or its process. Simon probably knew what he was getting into when he took the appointment as Chair, so we are assuming he is capable of making a board change.

Although a shareholder map will be needed to determine exactly who owns what and what powers they have, the brothers, with the institution, have control. So, if Simon can find a solution acceptable to them which Great Aunt Mildred supports, he will get there. No doubt he realises that where there is such disunity it is rare to find a solution that will keep everybody happy. He'll need to understand who will come out of it worse off and be well prepared with how to deal with it. What is fair may be tough to get at. What is in the best interests of the shareholders and the company will be driving his thinking.

Separating the facts from opinions, particularly in terms of the capabilities of the Bones, will be vital. Backing up his own judge- ments with supporting evidence as well as the views of others is essential. Whether Simon can now play the honest broker is not clear, nor is it clear what power he really has. These are key factors in how he decides to tackle the situation.

If he can establish what might be a sensible strategy for the owners first, then he is more likely to build support. As there appears to be no family constitution, this will have to be done by speaking to people, canvassing their views and their objectives for their shareholding. A careful inspection of the Memorandum and Articles of Association as well as the investment agreement with the institution will be done beforehand. Particular care will be needed in the matter of different rights for different classes of shares.

Simon will have to form an early view as to whether he can organise a resolution to the key problems himself or whether he needs to enlist help from an external catalyst as well. As Chair he should. He will probably already know the family lawyer; if he has a strong relationship with him, they may be able to decide a lot together. If not, or if the lawyer is linked to one side in particular, then he may need to consider a new independent adviser to advise the company.

The FD would normally be a key player in resolving a situation like this. The Chair now needs to decide whether to allow her to make a buyout bid, in which case she can't be involved in assessing other proposals. Can she continue to work at the company? Should she resign in order to make his bid? Whatever Simon decides, he needs to make it clear at the outset to the FD and those who are pressing for her removal. If he is going to support her in staying, this will need doing with strong conviction. It will, however, become even more complicated if Sue proposes that Simon is Chair of the buyout.

What to decide?

Simon's first decision is to be clear about who he feels he is working for and how involved he wants to get. Then, in order to be able to work through the Board, he needs to organise a Board meeting. He must also allow the Board to consider the various options proposed. Yet how can they consider them properly without a clear understanding of the owners' objectives? This is what will provide a convenient rationale for a cooling-off period in which to consult the shareholders individu- ally. He must buy time and move the decision making to a rational basis. In order to do this, he may have to use the simple mantra, '*Let's not destroy the good name of the family or the business*' as his unifying common purpose.

He will need to speak to Sue, the FD to gauge how serious she is about a buyout and how feasible it is. If it looks like a non-starter but Sue is as competent in her role as suggested, then Simon will need to find a way of defusing the pressure for her removal.

He could instruct the company's key adviser to undertake a formal review of shareholder objectives, the position of the business and the options proposed and possible outcomes. He will obviously need to decide who he is going to speak to directly. It sounds as if there aren't too many sharehold- ers. He may therefore decide to speak to them all himself. This might be not just for the purpose of hearing what they think first-hand, but so that they feel more involved and taken more seriously.

With Simon having bought time and analysed the situation, the solution should emerge, whether it is one of the current proposals or not. He then needs to decide which option to put his authority behind. Some of the solutions may involve him more intensely than others. Some, because he feels strongly that they are not in the best interests of the company, may make him consider resigning.

How to communicate it?

If the Chair is adopting the independent arbiter role, he will need to be extremely cautious and probably quite formal in his style and tone. Casual remarks can easily come back to haunt you in these situations. He will need to ensure that he appears to treat Jim and Joe with equal respect and does not appear too close to the institutional investor or the FD, and must also show Great Aunt Mildred considerable respect. The ordering of communications shouldn't be too difficult. The key players appear to be Jim, Joe, Great Aunt Mildred and the institution. He will need to take careful notes at each point.

What did Simon do?

The person who was Chair in this case was a man of considerable presence who was very well respected in the City where the company was based. He had sold out of his own company a few years earlier and had one other appointment locally, as well as being on the board of a small public company. Jim was somewhat in awe of him and had become more and more insecure as the Chair got to know the business. Joe enjoyed the increased pressure that Jim had been under but didn't welcome the same feeling himself. The institution regarded the Chair highly, having made a considerable sum through backing him before. It was happy to trust his judgement but wanted things to be done properly. It was more than fed up with Jim and Joe, but rated the FD highly and had been impressed by what she had achieved at the company. As for Simon himself, he relished a challenge and thought it would be great fun to sort out Bone & Sons.

The company's advisers were not that useful. The lawyer really acted for Jim and his side of the family and had not been particularly friendly to Joe, his wife or Jeremy. The accountants had shown no interest beyond doing the audit each year and the audit partner was not someone to express an opinion knowingly.

Sue, the FD, was determined about her buyout, and the Chair and the corporate finance advisers felt that she would gain financial support to do it. She had some interesting ideas to grow the company free from the constraints of the family, which included scenarios involving a lot less than £20 million.

Jeremy was generally despised but also feared. A personal litigation lawyer by background, he had no business experience to talk of, but always knew the right thing to say and was highly devious.

Given this situation, the Chair decided to exercise the authority of his position and the respect in which he was held. He had reviewed the formal documents carefully before taking his appointment in the beginning, so knew that all he had to do was to get the two brothers to agree and he had a solution. He took the view that Joe would be happy if he had sufficient funds to leave his wife and Jim would be happy to play golf. Neither Jeremy nor Vulture Co had any real substance behind them, but it would be important to give their approach very careful consideration before rejecting it.

So, what did he actually do? First, he convened a Board meeting with one item on the agenda: consideration of the various proposals that had been put to the company. At the meeting he explained that due to the composition of the Board, the nature of the specific proposals and the absence of a clear strategy for the business or its ownership, it would not be possible for them to vote on any of them. No-one disagreed. Prior to the meeting, he had agreed with the FD and the Bone brothers that if Sue wanted to pursue the possibility of a buyout, she should be allowed to do so. However, if he were to do so, he would have to resign from the Board. Sue was happy with this. She saw it as an all-or-nothing opportunity and was convinced it was the right thing for everyone.

The Chair then proposed that a formal review be undertaken by an independent corporate finance adviser who was acceptable to the brothers and the institution. The scope of their work would be to review shareholder aspirations, the position of the business in its market, the strategy, capital investment requirements and funding options, and then review the proposals that had been suggested, including the buyout. He made it clear that if one of their recommendations was a sale of the business, they would not get the mandate for advisory work relating to this sale. He did this to ensure an impartial approach. He then proposed three firms to do the work, which he felt the institution would be comfortable with. He proposed that each of them come in to make a presentation to the board. They agreed this as well and didn't propose any other firms.

He suggested that the board approve a budget for the work and a timescale of eight weeks. Costs should be met by the company. If the brothers agreed then he would seek the institution's consent before informing shareholders that the exercise was taking place and that they should expect a call. So, he got his eight-week cooling-off period.

The three firms pitched. All would have done a good job. Jim and Joe each had a strong but different preference, so the third was picked as a compromise. This is why Simon picked three to pitch and not two. A consultative process was agreed as well as commitment to the decision that the status quo was no longer tenable and that the Board would make one recommendation to shareholders following the review.

The firm chosen did an excellent job. All the shareholders were canvassed and they produced an insightful review of the company's position, its likely value and its outlook. They found that, of the family shareholders, only Great Aunt Mildred felt passionately about the business remaining in family hands. It was clear that neither Jim nor Joe had a strong desire for a fight or to develop the business. Life was all getting a bit complicated for them. However, all of the family, with the exception of Great Aunt Mildred again, were deeply concerned about how much the company was worth. Most of them would be quite happy to realise their shareholdings if they received a sufficiently big sum. None of them had any appetite for putting any more money in or increasing the risk profile. The institution saw considerable potential in the business but only with a much stronger management team. It didn't want to sell out yet as it felt it would realise much more if the company could be developed.

So, the advisers reviewed the various options for giving those shareholders who would be happy to sell the chance to do so. They felt that the two best options were a management buyout or an outright sale. Great Aunt Mildred then became pivotal for a few weeks. At first, she had been seriously opposed to the idea of a buyout and deeply suspicious of Sue. However, when Joe told her that he didn't really want to be the CEO, her thoughts turned to the family's reputation. She was torn between feeling that a sale was a failure for the family and the risk that the FD, Sue, would get the company on the cheap. In the end it was Joe who persuaded her that by letting Sue bid against a trade buyer she would have to pay a full price.

At this point, the institution became the key player. It was keener on the management buyout, even to the extent of organising an institutional purchase of the business and syndicating a part of its shareholding. This made the family worry that the institution, which had introduced Simon, might be taking advantage of them. This was only softened by the fact that it offered 5 per cent more than the trade buyer and allowed Great Aunt Mildred to keep a 5 per cent stake. She thought it was bound to sell the business within 10 years and wanted a share in the upside.

The buyout took place and Simon was re-appointed Chair. Great Aunt Mildred ended up being delighted. Her 5 per cent became worth considerably more than her original 18 per cent. The Bone brothers are happily playing golf, though not with each other. Joe has left his wife and she now runs a successful small business which she bought with the proceeds of the settlement.

Dilemma 13:

Falling in the Strid

Peter was appointed Chair of Trekkers Ltd a year ago, some six months after a management buyout. Trekkers is led by the rampantly-entrepre- neurial Alex Strid. He and his management team own 40 per cent of the equity.

The glowing picture that the lead venture capitalist painted of Strid and his team before Peter's appointment has been confirmed. Trekkers is about to exceed its current year budgeted profit of £7.5 million on sales of £50 million.

The only blot on the landscape is the performance of the South African distribution business, which is well below budget. Strid has assured Peter that he is going to take personal responsibility for this and plans to go out there again next week. He has also told Peter that he wants to be able to free up more of his time to look at new opportunities. In order to do so he proposes appointing John Vicker, the operations director, to the role of UK Managing Director (MD).

Peter supports this proposal at a meeting with the lead venture capitalist who sits on the Board. He too is happy despite some reservations about the appointment of Vicker. Peter was able to reassure him. As he leaves the meeting, Peter jocularly confirms that Strid's wife will not be joining him on the South African trip this time – an issue he had queried when agreeing Strid's last expenses!

On the eve of Strid's departure, Vicker calls and asks to see Peter urgently. He agrees to meet him at a local hotel. It's a bit of a surprise when Peter finds all the Executive Directors (Execs) apart from Strid are also there.

It proves to be a long and very difficult meeting, the summary of which is that:

- The executives think that Strid has 'lost the plot' and is no longer contributing to the business. He is not putting in the hours and, on the rare occasions when he attends meetings, he makes no

contribution other than to rubbish the efforts of others.
- South Africa is a disaster and everyone except Strid wants to shut it down. Nothing is achieved by his frequent trips, where he is normally accompanied by Mrs Strid. They always fly first class.
- Strid's brother has just been appointed distribution manager for the UK at an inflated salary and without going through the company's appointment process. Peter also learns that the company employs his daughter and son-in-law. The daughter is paid nearly twice as much as her supervisor and drives a company BMW Z3.
- Strid, a rugby fan, has committed the company to a £30,000 sponsorship deal with the local club where his son is a player and whose Chair is MD of a major customer. The Board has not approved this. There is talk of Strid joining the club Board.
- The company electrician carried out the installation of electric gates at Strid's new house. No payment has been received.

Peter's first reaction is to ask why this has not been raised before. He is reminded by the Finance Director (FD) that the company has just passed the 18-month period since the buyout. This is significant because before this date, any director leaving the company would have had to sell his shares back at par and, *"We knew that the venture capitalists would always side with Alex."*

Peter thanks the directors for bringing this issue to his attention and says he wants to give it some thought before giving them his considered view. As he leaves a somewhat embarrassed Vicker takes him aside and says he ought to be aware that his daughter too worked in the business on similar terms to Strid's girl. Vicker became uncomfortable with this and she has now moved to another job.

What are the issues?

There is a lot going on here. The reality is hard to get at from what we know so far. So, the main issue must be to find out what is actually going on and then prioritise. Most of the issues are likely to revolve around Strid.

For instance, has he "lost the plot"? Has success gone to his head? Has he lost contact with reality? Is he defrauding the company? If he is, how seriously? Is it a matter of degree or should any misappropriation of funds be treated in the same way? He appears, if the allegations are true, to be confusing what is his money and what is the company's. How much of Trekkers' success is really down to him? His lifestyle indicates boredom, insecurity and that he may be a bully. Is this right? Will he change? Can he be influenced by any of the current Board members?

There are also issues relating to Vicker, which make a quick judgement very risky to make. Can Peter trust what he says? Would he be capable of taking over? Does he really have the respect of the rest of the Exec? He has gone out on a limb. If Vicker is telling the truth and Peter doesn't do anything, what will his reaction be?

The way the Board is working also presents some problem. Trekkers' Board is far from united and not effective. Strid appears to be 'a majority of one'. The Chair seems not to be fulfilling the role and to have no influence over him. Is this simply because he has let him get on with it, or is it that he won't be able to? He doesn't appear to have spotted these problems or the breakdown in relationships on his Board.

Then there is the subject of the shareholders. What should be said to the venture capitalists and when? The potential loss in shareholder value is considerable.

As for the business, that also faces some challenges, despite its tremendous profitability. Is the South African business really under control or is it a potential black hole? Is there malpractice through the company? The atmosphere at the top can't have gone unnoticed and must be affecting morale generally.

If Strid has to go, how will Peter deal with the matter of his equity?

There is also a logistical issue, no matter what perspective Peter comes from. Should he speak to Alex before he departs for South Africa or should he let him go and speak to him when he gets back?

How to decide?

In this case, the decision as to whether Peter wants to resolve the various dilemmas involved looks easy, assuming he is highly competent. Perhaps he didn't have his eye on the ball because of the excellent financial performance. Not to grab hold of the situation and sort things out would be to abdicate his responsibilities as Chair. His credibility with Trekkers' backers would be destroyed. Ironically, a Chair who isn't very competent might not realise it, but still try to resolve the situation anyway.

Determining whether or not Vicker's allegations are true is vital before any decision can be made. The Chair is unlikely to do so with the rigour required before Strid's departure for South Africa. If he is to conduct a formal investigation what should its focus be? Is it into whether Strid has "lost the plot", or into the financial irregularities and abuse of his position, or both? Should he also ask the auditors to confirm the latest financial position just in case the bad news is even worse?

He needs to find out what his alternatives are. Even if he lets Strid go before saying anything, time is short.

He may want to get a better feel for Vicker and his colleagues.

It is hard to see any decisions being reached without the involvement of the company's lawyer. He may also need to consult an employment specialist if any of the directors will need to be removed.

What to decide?

Any decision should be dependent upon the emerging facts.

If Strid is innocent of the allegations made, then the Chair may decide to fire all or some of the rest of the team. Replacing an entire team will be difficult. However, it is obviously a high-performing business. This means Peter has time to do it properly and Trekkers will probably be attractive to candidates.

What if Strid is guilty of the financial irregularities but certainly hasn't lost the plot? He could be just plain greedy. He may be thinking he's the one who makes all the money and that no-one would sack him for what to him seem relatively minor amounts. Should he be sacked? Should he be asked to put back the money involved and sort out the other issues?

A scenario where Strid has lost the plot in terms of running the business but where the allegations over the money aren't true is the most difficult. In this case, Strid would have to go and the rest of his colleagues would be in doubt as well. Keeping control of that situation would be tricky.

The Chair's decisions will no doubt be based on what is ethically right, what is best for the business and what is acceptable to the shareholders.

How to communicate it?

Communications in this case need to be very serious and probably quite formal. Careful notes will be required and the Chair will not want to have any of the important meetings on a one-to-one basis. His most important meeting at the beginning of the process is with his key shareholder. If they either panic or don't support him in continuing as Chair, then he will have no role. In order for them to have confidence in him, he needs to appear calm and to be crystal clear about what he intends to do. This needs to be carefully considered, fair and highly professional.

So, who needs communicating with and in what order? I suppose Peter needs to tell his partner at home that he's going to be pretty busy for the next few weeks. He needs to speak to the venture capitalist, the company's lawyers and the auditors. Having informed them, he may decide to convene a meeting of these people with Vicker and the FD for the allegations to be repeated and for a plan of action to be approved.

Vicker will be highly stressed by the circumstances, whether he is trustworthy or not. So he needs to be spoken to regularly throughout.

As to what to communicate to Strid when he returns: if he emerges with honour from the investigation, then it is straightforward. If not, and it is decided he should go, he should be dealt with swiftly and professionally.

What did the Chair do?

He decided not to speak to Strid before his departure because the 10 days that Strid was away would give him the time to investigate the accusations being made. He kicked himself for not having got as involved in Trekkers as he should have. It all seemed to be going so well. Strid was so persuasive and the others hadn't given him any clues to how they were feeling. The Chair was actually a very high-calibre man. Peter cleared his diary of everything so that he could spend the entire time dealing with Trekkers while Strid was away.

Vicker and the other directors were told that the allegations they were making were very serious and that if they proved unfounded, they would be dismissed. The auditors were then instructed to undertake a formal investigation as discreetly as they could. They confirmed the following:

- That there was no authorisation for the rugby club sponsorship. Business with the club's Chair had also increased by 30 per cent to a rate of over £1 million per annum.
- The electrician did carry out work at Strid's home. The electrician's time sheet showed that he had spent a total of seven hours on the work.
- Strid has been to South Africa five times, always with Mrs Strid and always travelling first class.
- The terms on which members of his family were appointed were unclear, but certainly appear to have been outside company procedures. The auditors point out that the company's systems are not really adequate for a business this size and helpfully offer to undertake a separate review.

While the investigation was going on, Peter spent a lot of time with Vicker and the other directors. The main purpose of this was to form a view of them and, in particular, Vicker's capability to be MD. His time was well spent and he discovered a great deal else that was not right in the company. The most useful was revealed by looking at Strid's diary for the previous 12 months. This showed that Strid had spent very little time on company business other than playing golf with customers and suppliers.

The Chair became impressed by Vicker, his grasp of the business, the respect felt for him by the rest of the team and the way he was conducting himself in this difficult situation. He was less impressed by the FD, who had been bullied by Strid and hadn't the personality to stand up to him or to ensure that others, who could, knew what was going on.

At the beginning of Strid's trip, Peter contacted the lead venture capitalist, the company lawyer and the auditor. All were as amazed as he was, as well as being equally embarrassed. The lawyer helpfully produced a review of Strid's contract. The venture capitalist cleared his diary for the two days between the completion of the auditor's investigation and Strid's arrival home. He did this so that if the consequence was Strid's removal, any necessary approvals, particularly in regard to Strid's equity, could be obtained.

Vicker had impressed the Chair so much that he decided that his plan of action would be to remove Strid immediately upon his return and appoint Vicker as CEO. Although he wasn't told at this point, the Chair also felt the FD would have to go as well.

The chairman was at the company the morning Strid arrived with the lead venture capitalist. Meeting off-site was considered and this was actually felt to be the better idea, but they all thought that Strid was bound to go into the business first, whatever time they fixed a meeting. They asked to see him immediately. Strid was in a very relaxed mood and had no idea what was coming.

"Alex, I'm afraid we have some rather serious and very bad news for you. You have lost the confidence of the investors and you are being dismissed both as a director and as an employee of the company. This is not a debate. We have the full support of the Board and all of the shareholders, that is apart from yourself. The reasons for this are as follows. We have been made aware of some serious financial irregu- larities in the company. These have been investigated by the company's auditors and confirmed to be true. We have also been reviewing your contribution to the company and believe that you have not been undertaking the obligations of your contract.

However, we do recognise the contribution you have made to the business in the past and although we are under no obligation to do so given the circumstances, we are proposing to make the following offer by way of settlement. A copy of this, the auditor's report and papers relating to your termination will be given to you in a moment. We have made provision in the settlement for you to receive proper legal advice. The company's lawyers have confirmed that what is being done is perfectly reasonable and feel sure that if you seek either their advice or the advice of another competent lawyer, they will recommend you accept.

We will offer to pay out the full terms of your two-year employment contract, including the value of all benefits. If you decide you would like to keep your car, then it will be valued and this amount will be deducted from the settlement. With regard to your shareholding in the company, we are proposing that the company purchases it under the provisions in the investment agreement with the venture capitalists. An auditor's valuation will be obtained as quickly as possible.

In summary, Alex, the investors and I have lost confidence in your ability to manage the business and there is no alternative. We would like you to leave the premises immediately and hand over your keys to the offices."

Strid was stunned. He listened incredulously before erupting when the Chair had stopped speaking. He then became highly emotional and had to be physically restrained by the lawyer.

Wisely, Strid picked another good lawyer to advise him. His advice was that there was little he could do, as the offer in respect of his contract was so generous. Subsequently, the lawyer advised challenging the valuation that the auditors came up with. Strid refused to sell his equity back to the company at the price they suggested. Trekkers' investors and the rest of the management decided that the best tactic was to let him keep his equity for the time being. Realising quite what a high spender Strid was, the Chair felt he was bound to be back before too long to negotiate. This proved very shrewd.

The Board recovered from the trauma. Vicker turned out to be an excellent leader, even to the extent of remotivating the FD enough for him to stay. Strid subsequently started another business in direct competition which, although small, is highly profitable and keeps him and his family in the style that he considers appropriate.

Appendix 1

Bibliography

30-Second Brain: The 50 most mind-blowing ideas in neuroscience, each explained in half a minute. Anil Seth. 2012. Icon Books Ltd. ISBN 978-1-84831-647-8.

48 Laws of Power. Robert Greene. 2000. Penguin. ISBN 0-14-028019-7. Against Empathy: The Case for Rational Compassion. Paul Bloom.2018. Vintage ISBN 978-0-099-59782-7.

A Guide to Game Theory. Fiona Carmichael. 2004. FT Prentice Hall, ISBN 0 273 68496 5.

All In: The Future of Business Leadership. David Grayson, Chris Coulter & Mark Lee. 2018. Greenleaf Publishing. ISBN 978-1-138- 54922-7.

Behave: The Biology of Humans at Our Best and Worst. Robert M. Sapolsky. 2018. Vintage..ISBN 978-0-09-957506-1.

Black Box Thinking. Matthew Syed. 2016. John Murray Publishing. ISBN 978-1-47361-380-5.

Corporate Financial Strategy. Ruth Bender & Keith Ward. 2008. Butterworth Heinemann ISBN 0-7506-8665-0

Corporate Governance and Chairmanship. Sir Adrian Cadbury. 2002. Oxford University Press. ISBN 978-0-19-925200-8.

Dark Data: David J Hand, Princeton University Press ISBN 978-0-691-18237-7

Decision Making. Peter Ferdinand Drucker, Harvard Business Review, John Hammond, Ralph Keeney, Alden M. Hayashi, Howard Raiffa. 2001. Harvard Business Review. Harvard Business School Press. ISBN 1-57851-557-2.

Directors' Dilemmas. Patrick Dunne. 2005. Kogan Page. ISBN 0-7494- 4345-6.

Effective School Boards: Strategies for Improving Board Performance. Eugene Smoley. Jr. 2008. John Wiley & Sons. ISBN-13: 978-0-7879-4692-0.

Emotional Intelligence: Why It Can Matter More Than IQ. Daniel Goleman. Random House. ISBN 978-0-553-38371-3.

Emotional Intelligence 2.0. Travis Bradberry. 2009. TalentSmart®. ISBN 13 978-0-9743206-2-5.

Factfulness. Hans Rosling. 2018. Sceptre. ISBN 978-1-47363-746-7.

Games and Decisions: Introduction and Critical Survey. R.Duncan Luce & Howard Raiffa. Reprint of 1957e. Dover Publications Inc. ISBN 0-486-65943-7.

Games People Play: The Psychology of Human Relationships. Eric Berne. 2010. Penguin. ISBN 0-14-104027-1.

How Emotions are Made: The Secret Life of the Brain. Lisa Feldman Barrett. 2018. Pan Macmillan. ISBN 978-1-5098-3752-6.

Influence: The Psychology of Persuasion. Robert B. Cialdini. 2006. Harper Business ISBN 0-06-124189-X

Inside The Nudge Unit. David Halpern. 2016. WH Allen. ISBN 978-0-7535-5655-9.

Introducing Logic – A Graphic Guide. Dan Cryan, Sharron Shatil & Bill Mayblin. ICON Books ISBN 978-1-8483-1012-4.

Judgement: How Winning Leaders Make Great Calls. Noel M. Tichy & Warren Bennis. 2009. Penguin. ISBN 978-1-59184-293-4.

Keeping Better Company. Jonathan Charkham. 2008. Oxford Univer- sity Press. ISBN 978-0-19-924319-8.

Logic Made Easy: How to Know When Language Deceives You. Deborah J. Bennett. Norton. ISBN 0-393-32692-5.

Managing Uncertainty. Patrick Viguerie, Hugh Courtney, Claton M. Christensen, Hugh Courntney, Jane Kirkland, C.K. Prahalad, Jane Kirkland, Gary Hamel, Clayton M. Christensen. 1999. Harvard Business Review. Harvard Business School University Press. ISBN 978-0-87584-908-9.

Non-Executive Director's Handbook. Patrick Dunne & Glynnis Morris. 2008. CIMA Publishing. ISBN 978-0-7506-8419-4.

Nudge: Improving Decisions About Health, Wealth, and Happiness. Richard H.Thaler & Cass R. Sunstein. 2008. Yale University Press. ISBN 978-0-300-12223-7.

Predictably Irrational. Dan Ariely. Harper Collins. ISBN 978-0-00-725653-2.

Prisoner's Dilemma. William Poundstone. 1993. Anchor Books. ISBN 0-385-41580-X.

Quiet: Power of introverts in a world that can't stop talking. Susan Cain. 2013. Penguin. ISBN 978-0-14-102919-1

Rebel Ideas: Mathew Syed, John Murray (Publishers) ISBN 978-1-473-61391-1

Risk: The Science of Politics and Fear. Dan Gardner. 2009. Virgin Books. ISBN 978-0-7535-1553-2.

Running Board meetings. 3rd edition. Patrick Dunne. 2007. Kogan Page. ISBN 978-0-7494-4974-2.

Six Thinking Hats. Edward De Bono. 2016. Penguin. ISBN 0-14-013784-X.

Superforecasting: The Art and Science of Prediction. Philip Tetlock & Dan Gardner. 2016. Random House. ISBN 978-1-84794-715-4.

The Art of Statistics: David Spiegelhalter ISBN 978-0-241-25876-7

The Art of Thinking Clearly. Rolf Dobelli. 2014. Sceptre. ISBN 978-1-444-75954-9.

The Cambridge Book of Thinking and Reasoning. Holyoak & Morrison. 2005. Cambridge University Press ISBN 978-0-521-53101-6.

The Company Chairman. Sir Adrian Cadbury. 1995. Prentice Hall. ISBN 978-0-13-434150-7

The Culture Map. Erin Meyer. Public Affairs ™. ISBN 978-1-61039-250-1.

The Enigma of Reason: A New Theory of Human Understanding. Hugo Mercier & Dan Sperber. 2018. Penguin. ISBN 978-0-241-95785-1.

The Influential Mind. Tali Sharot. 2017. Little, Brown Book Group. ISBN 978-1-408-70608-4.

The Little Book of Big Management Theories. James McGrath & Bob Bates. 2017. Pearson Education. ISBN 978-1-292-20062-0.

The Little Book of Rhetoric. Brian O'C. Leggett. 2012. EUNSA IESE Business School. ISBN 978-84-313-2892-4.

The Neurotic Organization. Manfred Kets De Vries & Danny Miller, Jossey Bass. 1984. John Wiley & Sons. ISBN 0-87589-606-5.

The Paranoid Corporation and 8 other ways your company can be crazy: advice from an organizational shrink. William & Nurit Cohen. 1993. American Management Association. ISBN 0-8144-5129-2.

The Wisdom of Crowds. James Surowiecki. 2005. Random House. ISBN 9978-0-349-11605-1

Thinking, Fast and Slow. Daniel Kahneman. 2012. Penguin. ISBN 978-9-141-03357-0.

Wharton on Making Decisions. Stephen J. Hoch & Howard C. Kunreuther. 2004. John Wiley & Sons. ISBN 978-0-471-68938-6.

Why we Sleep. Matthew Walker. 2018. Penguin. ISBN 978-0-141-98376-9.

Winning Decisions. J. Edward Russo & Paul J.H. Schoemaker. Doubleday/Currency. ISBN 0-385-50225-2.

Appendix 2

Useful Links

Codes, principles and legislation

Copies of all the current corporate governance Codes world-wide are available on the European Corporate Governance Institute's web- site at https://ecgi.global

Artificial Intelligence in the Boardroom
https://www.fca.org.uk/insight/artificial-intelligence-boardroom
Audit and risk committee terms of reference. December 2018. Charity Commission.
    https://www.gov.uk/government/publications/charity-commission-governance-framework/appendix-5-audit-and-risk-committee- terms-of-reference
Companies Act 2006.
    https://www.legislation.gov.uk/ukpga/2006/46/contents
Corporate governance in central government departments: code of good practice. April 2017. HM Treasury.
    https://www.gov.uk/government/publications/corporate- governance-code-for-central-government-departments-2017
Directors' Remuneration: Report of a Study Group chaired by Sir Richard Greenbury. Greenbury Report. 1995. Gee Publishing. 978-1-86089-012-3.
Equality Act 2010. http://www.legislation.gov.uk/ukpga/2010/15/contents
Higher Education Code of Governance. 2014. Committee of University Chairs (CUC). https://www.universitychairs.ac.uk/wp-content/uploads/2015/02/Code-Final.pdf
Higher Education Senior Staff Remuneration Code. Committee of University Chairs. 2018. https://www.universitychairs.ac.uk/wp-content/uploads/2018/06/HE-Remuneration-Code.pdf

NHS Foundation Trust Code of Governance. July 2014. Monitor, NHS Improvement. https://www.gov.uk/government/publications/nhs-foundation-trusts- code-of-governance

Quoted Companies Alliance Corporate Governance Code https://www.theqca.com/shop/guides/208266/corporate-governance-code-2018-downloadable-pdf.thtml

Review of the role and effectiveness of non-executive directors. Sir Derek Higgs. 2003. The Stationery Office. https://webarchive.nationalarchives.gov.uk/20121106105616/http://www.bis.gov.uk/files/file23012.pdf

Report of the Committee on the Financial Aspects of Corporate Governance (Cadbury Report). Sir Adrian Cadbury. 1992. Gee Publishing. 978-0-85258-915-1.

Wates Corporate Governance Principles for Large Private Companies. June 2018. UK Financial Reporting Council. https://www.frc.org.uk/getattachment/48653f86-92c3-4cd6-8465-da4b7cac0034/;.aspx

UK Corporate Governance Code. 2018. Financial Reporting Council. https://www.frc.org.uk/getattachment/88bd8c45-50ea-4841-95b0-d2f4f48069a2/2018-UK-Corporate-Governance-Code-FINAL.PDF

Guidance, reports, articles and other sources

2019 themes for Remuneration Committees of listed companies. Nicholas Stretch. 2019. Ashurst. https://www.ashurst.com/en/news-and-insights/legal-updates/2019- themes-for-remuneration-committees-of-listed-companies/

90% of top performers have it. Do you? Dr Travis Bradberry. 2017. World Economic Forum. https://www.weforum.org/agenda/2017/03/15-signs- you-have-emotional- intelligence/?utm_content= bufferfd 840&utm_medium=social&utm_source=twitter.com&utm_campaign= buffer

AI in the Boardroom: The Next Realm of Corporate Governance. Barry Libert, Megan Beck, and Mark Bonchek. 2017. MIT Sloan Management Review. https://sloanreview.mit.edu/article/ai-in-the-boardroom-the- next-realm-of-corporate-governance/

USEFUL LINKS

BoardEffect. Board portal software. https://www.boardeffect.com Board Intelligence. Products and services that unlock the potential of boards and executive committees. https://www.boardintelligence.com/

Catastophe theory. E.C. Zeeman. 1976. Scientific American, Inc. https://www.math.hmc.edu/~thompson/F13/zeeman.pdf

Corporate Culture and Role of Boards. July 2016. UK Financial Reporting Council. https://www.frc.org.uk/getattachment/3851b9c5-92d3-4695-aeb2- 87c9052dc8c1/Corporate-Culture-and-the-Role-of-Boards-Report- of-Observations.pdf

Corporate Governance Guidelines. October 2018. BlackRock. http://ir.blackrock.com/interactive/newlookandfeel/4048287/CorporateGovernanceGuidelines.pdf

Culture Amp: the people and culture platform. https://www.cultureamp.com/

Culturescope. iPsychTec. https://ipsychtec.com/culturescope/

Delivering Through Diversity. https://www.mckinsey.com/~/media/mckinsey/business%20functions/organization/our%20insights/delivering%20through%20diversity/delivering-through-diversity_full-report.ashx

Diligent. Modern governance software. https://diligent.com/en-gb/ Does Money Really Affect Motivation? A Review of the

Research. Tomas Chamorro-Premuzic. 2013. Harvard Business Review. https://hbr.org/2013/04/does-money-really-affect-motive

Emotional intelligence and board governance: leadership lessons from the public sector. Margaret Hopkins, Deborah O'Neill and Helen Watkins. 2007. Journal of Managerial Psychology.

Executive Remuneration - Discussion Paper. Department for Business Innovation & Skills. 2011. https://assets.publishing.service.gov.uk/government/uploads/system/uploads/attachment_data/file/31660/11-1287-executive- remuneration-discussion-paper.pdf

Eye contact: Don't make these mistakes. Jodi Schulz. 2012. Michi- gan State University Extension. https://www.canr.msu.edu/news/eye_contact_dont_make_these_mistakes

Fair Process: Managing in the Knowledge Economy. W. Chan Kim and Renee Mauborgne. 2003. Harvard Business Review. https://hbr.org/2003/01/fair-process-managing-in-the-knowledge-economy

Four faces of the CFO Framework. 2016. Deloitte Development LLC. https://www2.deloitte.com/us/en/pages/finance/articles/gx-cfo-role-responsibilities-organization-steward-operator-catalyst-strategist.html

Glassdoor. Site with jobs, salary information, company reviews, and interview questions – all posted anonymously by employees and job seekers. https://www.glassdoor.co.uk

Global Family Business Index. 2019. EY and the Center of Family Business of the University of St. Gallen, Switzerland. http://familybusinessindex.com/

Governance Overview. BlackRock. http://ir.blackrock.com/governance-overview

Guidance on Board Effectiveness. July 2018. UK Financial Reporting Council. https://www.frc.org.uk/getattachment/61232f60-a338-471b-ba5a- bfed25219147/2018-Guidance-on-Board-Effectiveness-FINAL.PDF

Guide to cognitive biases. https://en.wikipedia.org/wiki/List_of_cognitive_biases

High income improves evaluation of life but not emotional well-being. Daniel Kahneman. 2010. PNAS. https://www.pnas.org/content/early/2010/08/27/1011492107.abstract

How companies are winning on culture during Covid-19 https://sloanreview .mit. edu/article/how-companies-are-winning-on-culture-during-covid-19/

How emotions affect logical reasoning: evidence from experiments with mood-manipulated participants, spider phobics, and people with exam anxiety. Nadine Jung, Christina Wranke, Kai Ham- burger and Markus Knauff. 2014. Frontiers in Pyschology. https://www.frontiersin.org/articles/10.3389/fpsyg.2014.00570/full

How leaders can get honest productive feedback. Jennifer Porter. 2019. Harvard Business Review. https://hbr.org/2019/01/how- leaders-can-get-honest-productive-feedback

ICSA: The Governance Institute. https://www.icsa.org.uk/

USEFUL LINKS

Inclusion & Diversity. Apple. https://www.apple.com/diversity/ Is there an optimal board size? Corporate Board: role, duties and composition, 5(1), 5-14. Wang, Y., Young, A., & Chaplin, S. 2009. International Scientific Journal. http://doi.org/10.22495/cbv5i1art1

Nasdaq Market Place Rules https://listingcenter.nasdaq.com/rulebook/nasdaq/rules/Nasdaq%205600%20Series

NCVO Charity Ethical Principles https://www.ncvo.org.uk/images/documents/policy_and_research/ethics/Charity-Ethical-Principles.pdf

Paying For Advice: The Role of the Remuneration Consultant in UK Listed Companies. Ruth Bender. 2008. Cranfield School of Management. https://core.ac.uk/download/pdf/140320.pdf

Power Dynamics in Organizations. Professor Linda Hill. 1994. Harvard Business Review. https://hbr.org/product/power-dynamics-in-organizations/494083-PDF-ENG

RAPID®: Bain's tool to clarify decision accountability. 2011. Bain & Co. http://www.bain.com/publications/articles/RAPID-tool-to-clarify-decision-accountability.aspx

Remuneration Committee: Terms of Reference. NHS England. 2013. https://www.england.nhs.uk/wp-content/uploads/2017/05/item6-5.pdf

Remuneration Committees: The New Challenges. Criticaleye. https://www.criticaleye.com/archive.cfm?id=304

A Report into the Ethnic Diversity of UK Boards. Sir John Parker, The Parker Review Committee. 2017. https://www.ey.com/uk/en/newsroom/news-releases/17-10-12-final-recommendations-of-the-parker-review-published

The annual Review of the Effectiveness of the Code of Conduct. Remuneration Consultants Group. 2018. http://www.remunerationconsultantsgroup.com/assets/Docs/2018%20The%20annual%20Review%20of%20the%20Effectiveness%20of%20the%20Code%20FINAL.pdf

Review of the effectiveness of independent board evaluation in the UK listed sector: Governance Institute https://www.icsa.org.uk/assets/files/pdfs/Publications/board-evaluation_full-report.pdf

Spencer Stuart 2020 Board index trends report https://www.spencerstuart.com/research-and-insight/uk-board-index/trends

Stakeholder Engagement: A Roadmap to Meaningful Engagement https://www.fundacionseres.org/lists/informes/attachments/1118/stakeholder%20engagement.pdf

The essential trustee: what you need to know, what you need to do. May 2018. Charity Commission. https://www.gov.uk/government/publications/the-essential-trustee-what-you-need-to-know-cc3/the-essential-trustee-what-you-need-to-know-what-you-need-to-do

The Family Constitution Guide. 2014. Taylor Wessing LLP. https://united-kingdom.taylorwessing.com/documents/get/88/the-family-constitution-guide.pdf/show_on_screen

The role of the Senior Independent Director. January 2017. Legal & General. https://www.lgim.com/files/_document-library/capabilities/the-role-of-the-senior-independent-director.pdf

We're Not Very Self-Aware, Especially at Work. Erich C. Dierdorff and Robert S. Rubin. 2015. Harvard Business Review. https://hbr.org/2015/03/research-were-not-very-self-aware-especially-at-work

Index

Action bias 237
Advisors 29,48
Advisory Groups or Boards 19-22
Agendas 202-206
Alignment 12-14,117-120,167
Anchoring bias 237-238
Angel investors 56
Angelou, Maya 86
Annual General Meeting (AGM) 69
Any Other Business 212
Apple inc 132
Articles of Association 75
Artificial intelligence (AI) 175,263-264
Audit and Risk Committee 15-16,175-178
Autonomy 122
Asymmetric sensitivity 67,87,102
Auditors 177
Authority bias 239
Awaydays 199-202

Bain & Company RAPID® 228,229
Bar-Eli, Michael 237-238
Bayes, Thomas 249
Beethoven 112
Beneficiary Board members (in Charity context) 58
Bennis Warren 104,121
Biases 236-254
Big Data 262-265
Black box thinking 92,242,256
Black Lives Matter 109
Board role of 6-10
Boardelta xvi,149,160,217
Board Intelligence (the company and the app) 149,212,262
Boardpacks (the app) 262

Board reviews 156
Body language 123- 128
Boeing (the company) 256
Boulton, Sarah viii
Boyatzis, Richard 96
BP plc 181
Bradberry, Dr Travis 95-96
Brand 164,170
Brexit xviii,66
Bridges Social Entrepreneurs Fund 28
Bridges Fund Management 61
Budgeting 168
Business context 49-58

Cadbury, Sir Adrian 7,24,77,78
Cain, Susan 112
Capita plc 130
Care Quality Commission 65,81
Carmichael, Helen 112
Carillion plc 161
Casciani, Cindy 114
Catastrophe theory 143-146, 231-232
Centrality 122
Chair 22-31,117,124,156,157-164,177,187,188,190,191,201-212,214-215,259
Chamorro-Premuzic, Tomas 184-185
Characteristics of successful directors 110
Charities 2, 58-62,206
Charity Commission (UKCC) 17,79
Charkham, Jonathan 8, 22
Charles De Gaulle 244
Chartered Governance Institute (formerly ICSA) 17,163,174
Chartered Management Institute 89

417

Chief Executive Officer (CEO) 11,39-41,116,117,124,177,187,190,191,201-212,259
Chief Financial Officer (CFO) 11, 41-44,114-117,177,233-234
Chief Legal Officer see Company Secretary,117, 207,202-212
Chief operating Officer (COO) 11
Cialdini Dr Robert 248
Clapham set 5
Clifford Chance 63
Codes of best practice 76-82
Cohen, Sir Ronald 61
Collective intelligence 131
Combined Code- Corporate Governance code 2018 35,77
Committee of University Chairs (CUC) 183
Common law and fiduciary duties 74
Communications (Board) 259-262
Communications director 11, 46-48,117
Company's Act 2006 71
Company's constitutional documents 75
Company secretary 11, 44-46,117
Composition and board building 106-116,192-197
Composition sub-committees 18
Confirmation basis
Conflicts of interest 72-73
Conflict 137- 146
Constructive challenge 126-128
Context of board 2-4, 48-68
Convening meetings 213
Cook, Tim 132
Covid-19 see Pandemic
Cranfield University 149,172
Cryan, Dan and Shatil, Sharron and Mayblin, Bill 253
Cuckney, Lord 209-210
Cultural diversity 134-137 and see diversity and inclusion, 164-173
Culture xvii,xvii,4,7,9,10,13,25,28,29,40,41, 50,52,77,80,85,104,106-108,118,126,134,135,137,153,160,164,165,167,169-171,173,179,192-194,197,198,213,217,242,257-261
CultureAmp 170
Culturescope 170
Cummins, Janet 112
Cybercrime 175

Dark Data 264
Data phase 251
Dawson, Stephen OBE 61
Deaton, Angus 184
De Bono, Sir Edward 242
Decisions 219- 254
Decisions Review 256
De-Facto Director 70
Deloitte 42-43
Dierdorff, Erich and Rubin, Robert 86
Dilemmas 226-228,269-406
Diligent 262 (the app)
Directors Duties 69- 76
Directors Dilemmas Book xv
Directors and Officers Liability insurance 37
Diversity and inclusion (D&I) 4, 109,131-137,190, 197-198,244-245
Dixon Paul 70
Drinkwater, Rosie 116
Dunning Kruger bias 240
Dynamic budgeting 168

Early, Mid Late approach 204,207, 230-231
Edison 112
Effectiveness and pressure curve 94,167 231 -232
Einstein, Albert 251,271
Einstein's riddle 251
Emotional contagion 100,103
Emotional intelligence 93-97
Endowment bias 245
Equality Act 132
Erasmus programme 66
ESSA- Education Sub Saharan Africa 38,134

418

INDEX

Ethnic diversity see Diversity and Inclusion
European Corporate Governance Institute 76
Executive 10-12
Extroverts 111-112
EY 63,198
Eye contact 124-125
EY Foundation 38,59,61,134,198

Facial expression 124
Facts and Interpretation 235-236
Fair Process 156-157,169
Family company 56-57, 119
Feedback 97
Feelings 100-101
Fermi, Enrico 253
Fermi Labs 253
FIDO (Facts Interpretation, Decision, Outcome) 142-143
Fiduciary duties and common law 74
Financial implications (of decisions) 232-234
Financial Reporting Council (FRC) 9,17,24,32,34,40,76,158,163,175,178,188-190
Finger switch 124
Fisher Geoff viii
Floyd, George xviii
Financial Conduct Authority 263
Financial Times 134
Financial Times Board Director Programme viii, xvi,70,126,149
Fonda, Henry 119-120
Freeman R Edward 171
Frequency (of meetings) 205-206

Gender diversity see diversity and inclusion 4, 131-137
Gill, Ali viii,126
Glassdoor 68,170-171
Goldwyn, Sam 99
Goleman, Daniel 93
Governance 7
Governance advisory services 68-69
Government Boards 3

Greenbury, Sir Richard 78
Greene Robert 128
Green Park 133
Grenfell Tower 161
Grierson, Nigel 122
Groupthink 14,130,131,137,240
Gucci 134

Hampton Alexander report 2021 4
Harvard Business School 86, 121,184
Heavy hitter boards 129-130
Higgs, Sir Derek and Review 4,33-36,79,89,159,188
Higher education (HE) code of Governance 81
Hill, Linda 121
Hill of Influence 123
Hogg, Sir Chris 8
Human Resources Director 11,191
Hyperbolic Discounting bias 243

Impetus PEF 61
Inclusion see diversity and inclusion
Incompetence Opera 240
Indemnities for Directors 73
Independence 31
Independence regulations (for professional service firms) 75
Independent director (ID) 31-33,122
Inertia bias 243-244
Influence and power 120-128
Inner conflict 138
INSEAD 134
Instant gratification bias 243
Institute of Directors 149
Internal Revenue Service (US) 58
Introverts 111-112
Invest Europe 149
Investors 2
Isms bias 244-245

Jackson, Katharine viii
Janis, Irving 241
Jeffrey, Neil and Neeley Prof Andrew 172
Judgement 101,110-111

419

Jung, Wranke, Hamburger, Knauff 100

Kahneman, Daniel 31,184,219
Kahneman, Daniel and Lavallo, Dan 248
Kahneman, Daniel and Tversky, Amos 245-247

Larcombe, Brian 258
Law of approach and avoidance 101
Lawson, Pete 112
Leap Confronting Conflict 38,59-61,112-114,134,142,260
Legal and General Investment Management 34,36
Length of meetings 208
Lewin, Kurt 101,138
Lindstrom Zea viii
Listing rules 75
Loss aversion bias 245

Management Board 70
Management Buy in 257
Marsh, Dame Mary 9
Maslow's Hierarchy of needs 37,109-110,114
Mauborgne Renee and Kim W Chan 156-157,169
McKinsey 131
Media and social media 66-68
Meetings, managing 213
Me Too 109
Meyer, Erin 134
Michigan State University 124
Miller, Neal and Dollard, John 138
Minutes (Board) 217- 219
Mirroring bias 247
Mission 164,167
MIT Sloan 170-171
Monitor (re NHS Trusts) 65
Muzio, Edward 122-123

NASDAQ 32
National Council for Voluntary Organisations (NCVO) 9,25,79
National Health Development Agency 65
National Health Service Foundation Trusts 65, 76,80
Neuroses 130-131
New Independent Director syndrome 105
New York Stock Exchange 32
NextGen Boards 130,134
NGO Co-ordination Board Kenya 58
Nominations Committee 188-198
Non-Executive Directors Handbook xv
Not Invented Here (NIH) bias 247
Nudge Theory 254

Oliver and Young 33
Outside Director 31-33

Pandemic, impact of xvii,13,23,63,66,107,136,142,149, 170-171,181,194,216,262
Papers 209
Parker 133
Patrons 38
Patt, Anthony and Zeckhauser, Richard 237
Pell, Rothermich, Liu, Paulmann, Sethi and Rigoulot 101
People section 85-149
Peter Olawaye 60
Physical meetings 216
Pinsent Masons 70
Porter, Jennifer 98-100
Personal power 121
Planning fallacy bias 247
Positional power 121
Post purchase rationalisation bias 248
Power and influence 120-128
Power Dynamic 29
Power Sources of
Premium Listing 76
Principle of commitment 248
Private Equity (PE) 27-28,118,181-182
Process section 153-265
Procrastination 138

INDEX

Professional service firms 3, 62-63
Psychological projection 103
Pyschoses 130-131
Public Bodies 3, 63-65,80,182
Purpose 1-76 (section), 164

Quoted Companies Alliance 9

Recency bias 249
Regulators 177
Removing Directors 146-148
Remuneration committee 16,178-188
Remuneration Consultants 185-187
Remuneration Consultants Group (RCG) 187
Respect 104-106
Responsibility by pass xvi
Resources 7
Restricted Reserves 60
Risk Committee see Audit and Risk Committee
Roles of see title eg Board
Rosling, Hans 236
Running Board Meetings book xv
Ruth Bender viii

Sadan, Sacha 34
Sapolsky, Robert 270
Schoenewolf, Gerald 103
Schulz, Jodie 124
Scott Fitzgerald, F 31
Selection bias 249
Self-Awareness 86,90-91
Senior independent director (SID) 4, 33,117,118,159,163,188
Senior Manager's regime 75
Shadow Director 70
Shakespeare, William 248
Size of Board 108
Slaughter and May 70
Social diversity see diversity and inclusion
Social media see media and social media
Social Mobility Foundation 133
Socrates 219

Spencer Stuart 5
Stakeholders 28-29,164,171-173
Statistics 263-265
Statutory Duties and Obligations 70
Steele, Murray viii,126
Stephenson, Lesley viii, xvi
Strategy 7,164,167,168
Sub-committees 5, 15-18,173
Succession 110,191-193
Supervisory Board 70
Suroweiecki, James 228
Sutton Trust 133
Syed, Matthew 92,131,242,256

Taylor Wessing 56
Technology 213,262-265
Tenure 190
Terms of reference (TOR) 173
Tetlock, Philip and Gardner, Dan 264
Thaler, Richard and Sunstein, Cass 254
The Office for Students 183
Thom, Rene 143
Thomas, Kenneth and Kilmann, Ralph 139-142
Thorp, David 258
Tipping points 143-146
TKI test 139-142
Training and Development 148-149
Travers Smith 70
Trustee 36-38
Twelve Angry men 119-120
Two-Tier system 70

UKCC see Charity Commission
University boards 4, 65-66,182-183
University of Warwick 4,65,116
Unrestricted reserves 60

Vacillation 138-139
Values xiii,xvii,xviii,4,9,29,52,82,98,104,114,118,126,164,165,167,170,171,179, 228,228,245,248
Van Gogh 112
Venn diagram 5, 27,165

Venn, John 5
Venture Philanthropy 60
Virtual meetings 216
Vision 164
Voice 126
Volunteers 37

Wald, Abraham 249-251
Wales, Jimmy 166
Wang, Young and Chaplin 108
Warwick in Africa 90
Wates Principles 9,79
Wates, Sir James 9
Webster, Martin 70
Wheeler, McArthur 240
Wikipedia 166
Wilkinson, David 86
William and Nurit 130
Witney, Simon 70

USAF 250

Yale University 241
Young board members 61

Zebra puzzle 251
Zeeman, Professor Sir Christopher 143-146
Zell, Ethan and Kirzan, Krizan 91
Zone of comfortable debate 126
Zone of uncomfortable debate 126
Zygos 34,36

3i Group plc
   xvi,27,47,114,146,147,257,260,271
5 Cs in decision making 235